Contents

Acknowledgments vii

Introduction: Theory of Mind, Development, and Foundational Human Cognition 1

1. Developing a Theory of Mind: Initial Overview 15
2. Preschool Theory of Mind, Part 1: Universal Belief-Desire Understanding 33
3. Real-World Consequences: Social Action 57
4. Preschool Theory of Mind, Part 2: Desires, Emotions, Perceptions 71
5. Extended Progressions in Theory-of-Mind Understanding 93
6. Theory Theory: Reconstructing Constructivism 117
7. Alternatives and Extensions 145
8. Infants, Actions, and Mental States 169
9. Origins and Development 195
10. Evolution, Chimps, and Dogs 209
11. The Social Brain: Neural Regions Developed for Theory of Mind 227
12. Searching, Learning, and Listening: Exploration, Pedagogy, and Testimony 249
13. Further Developments: Minds and Brains, Gods and Souls 265
14. The Landscape of Mind 287

REFERENCES 299
AUTHOR INDEX 341
SUBJECT INDEX 351

Acknowledgments

NO BOOK LIKE this can be written without an informed point of view. My own research and "insider" appraisals color my thinking and this book. I value, and have striven for, conclusions and interpretations that are firmly data driven (while admittedly theory laden too), but many examples developed in most detail come from my own work. I believe that I make abundantly clear the efforts and research of a great many others; I hope so, and I ask these other researchers to forgive my personalistic mode of presentation. In fact, "theory of mind" has advanced as it has not just because of the ideas and the findings it has produced but because of the efforts of a number of unusually apt and insightful scholars who, although often at odds, are also extremely collegial and open to argument, data, and other points of view. I'm blessed to count a number of them as friends and many others as colleagues. Theory of mind has been fortunate in the extreme to have captured the interests and efforts of such a fertile, intelligent crew.

Even my own thoughts in this book have been aided, advanced, inspired, and informed by many others. Of special note here are Alison Gopnik, Candi Peterson, Susan Gelman, Carl Johnson, Paul Harris, Janet Astington, Josef Perner, Alan Leslie, and Liz Spelke. Even the research I claim as my own is collaborative, often with some of the persons I just mentioned, and still more clearly with a great number of exceptional students whom I have been fortunate to work with: David Estes, Karen Bartsch, Jacqui Woolley, Mita Banerjee, Anne Hickling, Carolyn Schult, Margaret Evans, Ann Phillips, Kristin Lagatutta, Mark Sabbagh, Jennifer Amsterlaw, David Liu, Sarah Dunphy-Lelii, Jenny

LaBounty, Tamar Kushnir, Marjorie Rhodes, Cristine Legare, Amanda Brandone, Jon Lane, and Lindsay Bowman among others.

More specifically, Chapter 5, "Extended Progressions in Theory-of-Mind Understanding," represents collaborative work with Candi Peterson and David Liu. The portion of Chapter 5 where I talk about universality borrows heavily from Wellman (2013), which appeared in a volume edited by M. Banaji and S. Gelman. Chapter 6, "Theory Theory: Reconstructing Constructivism," would have been impossible save for the thinking, friendship, and collaboration of Alison Gopnik (and that chapter borrows portions from a fuller treatment of some of these ideas that can be found in Gopnik & Wellman, 2012). Chapter 11, "The Social Brain: Neural Regions Developed for Theory of Mind," owes its debt, both empirically and conceptually, to David Liu, Mark Sabbagh, and especially Lindsay Bowman (because in part, Chapter 11 borrows portions from Bowman & Wellman, 2014). Chapter 13, "Further Developments: Minds and Brains, God and Souls," stems from long, fruitful collaborations with Carl Johnson as well as research undertaken with Jon Lane and Margaret Evans.

More generally, my ideas have been shaped by my reading of others. Philosophers, clinicians, psychologists, and anthropologists have influenced my thinking, to the extent that it is impossible for me to appropriately acknowledge them.

For more than 20 years Sheba Shakir has assisted me remarkably in administering my grants, publications, and university business; and working on this book.

Not only persons but organizations have contributed. My research has been consistently and generously funded by the Eunice Shriver National Institute of Child Health and Human Development of the National Institutes of Health. I have received crucial funding from the National Science Foundation and the McDonnell Foundation as well. I was able to begin writing in earnest because of a special Bellagio residency from the Rockefeller Foundation. I benefitted greatly from several delightful stints as a visiting professor at the University of Queensland. Finally, my home institution, the University of Michigan, has been an immense source of support to me for more than 30 years. It is one of the world's great institutions of higher education and has certainly aided my continuing education by being an unfailing source of ideas, colleagues, and great students.

Last but not least, I thank my family: Karen, Ned, and Daniel, plus more recently Chelsea and Chase.

MAKING MINDS

Introduction

THEORY OF MIND, DEVELOPMENT, AND FOUNDATIONAL

HUMAN COGNITION

IN 2010, A group of Chilean miners were trapped in a collapsed mine below more than a mile of rock and dirt. Upon being discovered alive underground, via an electronic probe, here is the first message one man sent to his wife:

> We *thought* we were going to starve to death down here. You can't *imagine* how much my soul hurt at being underground and not being able to tell you I was alive....What I *want* now is to see you as I emerge from the belly of the earth. [emphasis added] (Tresniowski & McNeil, 2010)

This man's text radiates one of the most fundamental aspects of human life: thinking of one another in terms of thoughts, wants, hopes, imagining, and knowing.

Literature does this too. Consider this passage from Romeo and Juliet. At an early point, when Romeo has become smitten with Juliet but realizes she is a Capulet (whereas he is a Montague), he confides his feelings to his friend and clansman, Benvolio. Then

> BENVOLIO: Be ruled by me, *forget* to *think* of her.
> ROMEO: Oh, teach me how I should forget to think.
> BENVOLIO: By giving liberty unto thine eyes; *examine* other beauties.
> ROMEO: He that is strucken blind cannot forget the precious treasure of his eyesight lost. [emphasis added] (Shakespeare, 1597/1961, p. 398)

Great literature presents us human lives. Narratives, tragedies, comedies, romances all tell our stories. At a certain level of analysis (amid wonderful differences and particularity), literature tells one story, a story focused on the understanding of human thoughts, emotions, desires, and actions. This everyday understanding of persons as thinking, forgetful, wanting, remembering beings is known among scientists as a "theory of mind."

We humans live socially—raised by parents, in familial communities constantly interacting with, caring about, and working with other people. We not only live socially, we think socially—developing and depending on extensive knowledge about social life, social entities (persons, friends, rivals, clans, families), as well as social actions and interactions (loving, aggressing, advising). Conceivably, the vast array of social cognition that humans acquire could be a loosely connected, even disconnected, array of separate facts, ideas, and conventional truisms. But the claim behind the phrase theory of mind is that human social cognition is founded on an understanding of ourselves and others in terms of our inner, mental, psychological states. Shakespeare, the miners in Chile, all of us construe people in terms of wants, thoughts, likes and dislikes, intentions, and memories, revealing an everyday theory of mind. Children do too, as is clear in transcripts of everyday conversation:

CHILD (3 YEARS, 9 MONTHS): Can you eat snails?
MOTHER: Some people eat snails, yes.
CHILD: Why?
MOTHER: Because they like them.
CHILD: Mommy, do you want to eat snails?
MOTHER: No, I don't think I'd like to eat snails.
CHILD: I don't like to eat snails.... People eat snails.
(Bartsch & Wellman, 1995, p. 85)

In contrast, we do not, very often or deeply, see ourselves in terms of mere external appearances or overt observable behaviors. Alison Gopnik and her colleagues (Gopnik, Meltzoff, & Kuhl, 2001) captured this with a compelling example. Consider a family sitting around the dinner table. We "see" the entire unfolding scenario in terms of persons and actions: spouses and children, speakers and listeners engaged in conversing and teasing, passing the potatoes, preferring the dessert over the vegetables. If we attended instead to the overt and apparent, unfiltered through our theory of mind, we might see the following:

Bags of skin stuffed into pieces of cloth and draped over chairs...that move in unpredictable ways,... with small restless black spots that move at the top of the bags and a hole underneath that irregularly makes noises.... This is, of course, a madman's view of other people, a nightmare." (Gopnik, Meltzoff, et al., 2001, pp. 4–5)

Twenty-five years ago, theory of mind was almost unheard of; today it is widely discussed. When I Googled the phrase "theory of mind" recently, I got more than 1.5 million hits. One key reason for this widespread interest has been rich, provocative data provided by developmental psychologists showing that even young children insistently attribute such states as desires, beliefs, and emotions to self and other. Such findings have intrigued various scholars: Primatologists have considered the extent to which "mentalizing" is uniquely human. Evolutionary scientists have considered how theory of mind evolved and whether it was the breeding ground for advances in human intelligence more generally. Anthropologists have debated whether a mentalistic understanding of personhood is or is not universal and indeed, whether childhood theory of mind is crucial for all cultural learning to take place. Clinicians have considered the extent to which deficits in theory of mind account for various social impairments, especially in the case of individuals with autism. Neuroscientists have asked whether mentalizing is specially supported in the human brain and the extent to which it is modularized and specific. Religious scholars have suggested that an everyday theory of mind provides the foundation for a universal human interest in god and the supernatural.

In this book, I provide deeper examination of how theory of mind develops, thereby providing a sequel to *The Child's Theory of Mind* (Wellman, 1990). Conceivably, in the years since 1990, not only the importance of the topic (1,500,000 hits) but the nature of theory of mind itself has become widely and well understood. However, the accumulating findings include gaps and contradictions. Further, the literature on theory of mind encompasses deep-seated disputes. These disputes in turn reflect current divides about how to best characterize foundational human cognition—as massively domain specific or domain general; as manifesting naïve theories, conceptual modules, or networks of learned connections. Yet I believe data and theories are more telling and commensurate than we had any right to expect initially, include much more signal than noise, yield a number of clear conclusions, and indeed have achieved some uncelebrated consensus amid the disputes and unknowns. In this book, I try to articulate that story.

My title deserves a note. This is not a book about making neurons to construct brains that make minds. It is not a book about cognitive development writ large—making minds in the broadest sense. It is about making minds in the specific sense of developing our theories of mind. It is about how we, and our children, develop our everyday understanding of our own and others' mental lives. No one can step inside someone else's mind and know it. So every mind we sense, interact with, and attribute to others is, by necessity, a mind we make.

FOUNDATIONAL HUMAN COGNITION

Several emphases help organize my perspective. One concerns an emphasis on the importance of an everyday theory of mind to our human cognition. Much of the interest in and research on theory of mind over the last 25 years—the now thousands of papers from scholars around the world—results from the hypothesis that theory of mind might be something like a foundational human cognition. The following quotes illustrate this:

> The mind contains a number of innately channeled conceptual modules, designed to process conceptual information concerning particular domains...[such as] a naïve physics system, a naïve psychology or "mind-reading" system, a folk-biology system, an intuitive number system, [and] a geometrical system for re-orienting and navigating in unusual environments. (Carruthers, 2002, p. 663)

> The cognitive capacities of any animal depend on early developing, domain-specific systems of knowledge. Just as infant animals have specialized perceptual systems for detecting particular kinds of sensory information and specialized motor systems guiding particular kinds of actions, infant animals have specialized, task-specific cognitive systems: systems for representing material objects, navigating through the spatial layout, recognizing and interacting with other animals, and the like. These specialized systems provide the core of all mature cognitive abilities. (Spelke, 2003, p. 278)

The first quote comes from a scholar advocating "massive modularity"—the mind rests on a set of innate mental modules, and naïve psychology is one. The second is from a scholar advocating "core knowledge," a related but somewhat different perspective. For now, I simply want to emphasize the general underlying claim that human cognition is composed of deep and distinctive cognitive systems that elaborate and process specific information in certain characteristic ways. This claim is consistent with a range of theoretical perspectives on the nature and origins of such knowledge. But to begin, just assume there are such systems; then knowing what they are would be crucially revealing and important. Knowing the nature of such systems would help specify cognitions that humans find easy versus difficult to make or to acquire. That is, foundational human cognitions would provide a framework for thinking about intuitive and counterintuitive human understandings, a perspective on "natural concepts" versus exotic ones. Having a road map of such foundational human cognition could further help identify basic cognitive perspectives common to all humans, amid the numerous cognitive differences we develop over our lives in our different societies and local environments. Indeed, given a set of distinctive, separable systems, those would chart the cognitive architecture of the human mind: Foundational human cognitions would provide the building blocks—the foundation—for the analysis and refinement of other more complex or derived human cognitions.

A frequent exemplar for such a basic cognitive system, obvious in the previous quotes from Peter Carruthers and Elizabeth Spelke, is naïve psychology or theory of mind. The proposal of foundational human cognitions is an empirical one, and I think the empirical data are clear that theory of mind constitutes such a foundational cognitive domain. These data also help address the question of just what foundational human cognition might look like. Indeed, the data for theory of mind suggest that "core" human cognitive systems are different from some of the claims made for them.

How might we know foundational human cognition when we see it? Perhaps cognitive neuroscience can be relied on to detect it (see Chapter 11). Maybe so, but I prefer a more cognitive analysis. At this level of analysis, a simple picture one might draw about foundational human cognitions would be that they are evident early in human life, represent systems so basic that we share them with our animal kin, and once in place are set for life. In this picture, a core cognitive system would be relatively unrevisable by individual experiences in development. Indeed, those who talk of core knowledge do claim it is set or fixed by evolution and unchanging from infancy to adulthood (e.g., Scholl & Leslie, 2001; Spelke, 1994, 2003) and often claim core cognitive systems are indeed those we share with all other primates or even all mammals (Spelke, 2003; Spelke & Kinzler, 2007). But I believe such claims are problematic, or seriously incomplete, at least for theory of mind. Theory of mind requires a more complex and more *developmental* picture. In this more complex picture, foundational human cognitions are developmentally basic in the sense of being rapidly apparent but also in developing themselves in ways that influence considerable additional developments built on them. In this development, foundational cognitions—concepts, processes, systems—themselves undergo substantial change, change that then fundamentally influences other cognitions. Some foundational cognitions also constitute foundational human cognition in being only minimally apparent in nonhuman species, even other (nonhuman) primates. Theory of mind, in particular, stands as a distinctively human capacity at least in its more developed childhood form (if not its earliest infant beginnings), and it is a foundational cognitive system that is developmentally dynamic, not static.

DEVELOPMENT

Consider again the basic claim behind theory of mind—human social cognition centers on a construal of self and others in terms of mental states. Given a developmental story, that claim focuses on a cognitive achievement. Adults in Anglo-European societies (to limit things for now) attribute, predict, and explain people via their mental states; and moreover, their children progressively come to do this.

Philosophers (e.g., Stich, 1983), psychologists (e.g., Wellman, 1990), and anthropologists (e.g., D'Andrade, 1987) now agree that our everyday mentalistic understanding is organized around three large categories of mind and behavior: beliefs, desires, and actions. Basically, in our everyday thinking we construe people as engaging in *acts* they *think* will get them what they *want*. The Chilean miner assured his wife he was alive because he believed she would think him dead and he wanted to ease her mind. Because Romeo and Juliet wanted to be together, but believed their families would violently disapprove, they saw each other in secret.

According to anything like this consensus analysis, an understanding of beliefs is a core feature of our everyday theory of mind. People engage in acts they think will get them what they want. Of course they can be wrong—in which case they think and act mistakenly, often thwarting their own desires. Mistakes, errors, ignorance, and wrong ideas are the very stuff of our everyday psychology and thus the very stuff of our everyday lives. At the end of Shakespeare's play, Romeo comes to the church crypt and finds Juliet (apparently) dead. Bereft, he kills himself. But Juliet (deeply drugged to feign death) awakes, and on awakening finds Romeo dead by her side. Seeing him dead, she kills herself. Both deaths are tragic, but Romeo's act is a tragic mistake, based on a tragically false belief.

Theory-of-mind reasoning goes beyond this, of course; it is an organized system (a theory) of interconnected constructs and implications that includes perception, emotion, urges, ignorance, and so on overlapping with beliefs, desires, and actions. Thus, theory-of-mind research encompasses a variety of conceptions, competences, and tasks, which I outline in Chapters 2, 4, 5, and 8. But for decades, much research has focused on understanding of belief as assessed in false-belief tasks. To illustrate, a classic type of false-belief task used with children of different ages (as well as adults, apes, and individuals with autism) is presented as a natural-seeming dramatic skit (admittedly more "Punch and Judy" than Shakespeare). The child sees a character, Judy, place an object (candy) in a drawer (which is then closed). But when Judy goes away (and thus cannot observe), the candy is moved to a cupboard (by Punch perhaps) and the cupboard is then closed. Judy returns wanting her candy. Where will Judy look for the candy? Correct responses on this changed-locations task predict that Judy will mistakenly look for the candy in the drawer, and think (mistakenly) that that is where it is (not the cupboard). Theory-of-mind understanding requires realizing that mental states distinctively contrast with reality and with overt behavior, yet nonetheless shape behavior. Understanding false belief provides a nifty demonstration of this understanding.

As I outline in Chapters 1 and 2, numerous findings show that young preschoolers fail such false belief tasks, whereas older preschoolers routinely pass them. To be clear, however, even when failing standard false believe tasks still younger children understand something about the mind (Chapter 4) and even infants evidence initial understanding of people as intentional actors whose actions are guided by goals, perceptions, and subjective awareness (Chapters 8 and 9). Because of findings such as these, all viable perspectives on theory of mind acknowledge that theory-of-mind performances change with age—the cognitive achievement that constitutes theory of mind has some sort of developmental story. Indeed, even without false-belief tasks or specialized infant research, any casual observer of childhood would note the sizable changes that occur with development: The young infant attends to people; older infants interact with people; and toddlers and preschoolers talk with and talk about people including talk about their wants, thoughts, hopes, and imaginings. Different accounts tell different stories of what changes and how, but development and developmental data provide a crucial perspective for understanding and evaluating the alternatives.

To see why, briefly consider two alternative proposals. According to the first, theory of mind is based on an innate, mental module that reads actions in terms of underlying mental states, a module that becomes available early in life (on a consistent, mostly maturational timetable) and that can be specially damaged in certain individuals, leading to the social-communicative impairments seen in autism. Nativist, modular positions somewhat like this are frequent in the literature on theory of mind; recall the earlier quote from Peter Carruthers (2002; and more specifically, Alan Leslie has described such a theory-of-mind module in Leslie, 1994, and Scholl & Leslie, 2001). Such accounts envision (and would receive support from) several sorts of data: potentially, findings showing that (a) typically developing children robustly evidence theory-of-mind understandings (even false belief) and do so early in life, even in infancy; (b) normal children do so across all cultures on a consistent, maturational timetable, despite wide differences in languages and social experiences; (c) individuals with autism are specifically impaired in theory-of-mind understandings, notably false belief (in comparison to other individuals, including other impaired individuals); and (d) theory-of-mind reasoning is localized in certain specific brain circuits, and it is those circuits that are impaired in autism.

Thus, even this sort of position makes certain developmental predictions (b in the preceding) that differ for normal and autistic individuals (c). Now, consider a contrasting, distinctively different proposal according to which theory of mind arises from the sheer accumulation of social information from others. Adults tell and show children how to think about (and talk about and interact with) people as mental beings, and children go from being ignorant about all this to absorbing the ideas of those around them. According to such a position, human infants show an early attention to communicative interaction, and, crucially, these interactions provide social knowledge about others. Exposed to this knowledge, children pick up increasingly complex, mentalistic understandings of persons, lives, and minds. Social-experiential accounts akin to this sketch also abound in the literature (e.g., Carpendale & Lewis, 2004; Garfield, Peterson, & Perry, 2001). Such accounts require (and would receive support from) several converging sorts of findings: potentially, data showing that (a) theory-of-mind understandings unfold via numerous incremental steps as children learn more and more; (b) theory-of-mind achievements are attained on different timetables and trajectories by children with different social-communicative experiences, most dramatically perhaps children with autism or with deafness; (c) indeed the nature of theory of mind (the nature of folk psychology) will be different for children growing up in different cultural communities, as they learn the ideas of their folk; and (d) specialized brain circuitry dedicated to adult theory-of-mind reasoning is the outcome of experience-driven development.

Although they approach the facts in different ways, these modular and experiential-learning alternatives agree that theory of mind "develops." In very real senses, therefore, understanding of theory of mind has been, and must be, constrained by data as to how development actually progresses—which initial states lead to which intermediate and asymptotic states, influenced by which mechanisms. Rich developmental data are now increasingly available. They form the focus of this volume, the lens through which I synthesize and organize current understanding. The results of such a synthesis of current understanding might take several forms; but regardless, a developmental perspective is required to best understand our human theory of mind and to advance understanding beyond current impasses. My title, *Making Minds*, reflects this focus on theory of mind as a developmental achievement. As is clear in the preceding discussion, the needed informative data should also encompass a variety of sources— it should come from normally developing and atypically developing individuals, across contrasting countries and cultures, and include behavioral and brain findings.

A CONSTRUCTIVIST PERSPECTIVE: THEORY THEORY

Any developmental treatment of theory of mind requires two overlapping foci: Descriptively, what do children understand about the mind, and when? Theoretically, what sorts of alternative explanations account for this developing understanding (and what are their successes and failures)? I concentrate more on the descriptive data first (Chapters 1 through 5) and then move on to theory (Chapter 6) and theoretical alternatives (Chapter 7). However, to be meaningful at all, data require some organization and interpretation, a framework to help organize and present even the initial data. My background framework remains the theory theory (Gopnik & Wellman, 1994; Gopnik & Wellman, 2012; Wellman, 1990)—the theory that our everyday psychology really is a theory, an intuitive theory, an everyday mentalistic theory of human actions and lives; in short, a theory of mind. A theory-theory perspective is by no means universally accepted, but a wide variety of scholars admit that theory of mind is theory like in some profound fashions: "Human infants are endowed with several distinct core systems of knowledge which are theory-like in some, but not all, important ways" (Carey & Spelke, 1996, p. 515). How so?

The study of theory of mind evidences a classic tension, one reflected in the study of cognitive development more broadly (Gopnik & Wellman, 2012). On the surface, children both seem to have abstract structures of thought (theories) *and* to learn them. But how could such highly structured abstractions be learned? Nativist accounts, embodied in modularity and core knowledge theories (Scholl & Leslie, 2001; Spelke & Kinzler, 2007), embrace the structure, coherence, and abstractness of basic childhood knowledge.

This is a key sense in which they agree that the knowledge in question is theory like (as in the previous quote from Carey & Spelke, 1996). But these approaches assume that such abstract knowledge structures are innate, are not themselves revisable on the basis of experience-dependent data, and in fact could not be learned. Empiricist accounts, embodied in connectionist and dynamic system accounts (Elman et al., 1996; Thelen & Smith, 1994), embrace the learning but insist the resulting knowledge constitutes a distributed collection of associations and functions. Structure with no (or impoverished) learning confronts learning with no (or impoverished) structure. This tension is manifest in the two alternatives I considered earlier: modular versus experiential-learning proposals about theory-of-mind development. Jean Piaget (e.g., 1983) classically called for a constructivist resolution to this tension—abstract representations were constructed based on children's interactions with the world. In this sense, theory theory is an heir to Piaget, a constructivist proposal about theory of mind where everyday theories provide the structure and are learned.

Of key relevance to this perspective is that theories—scientific and everyday theories—encompass a very intriguing interplay between (at least) two levels of analysis: theory versus data, or observations versus the underlying theoretical constructs and propositions recruited to account for the observations. And this is a dynamic interplay: Scientists form and revise scientific theories based on data; children construct and revise intuitive theories of the world as a result of experience, that is, data and evidence.

Theories must live in the world of data and must account for data, but they contrast with data in being bodies of knowledge that go beyond a collection of observable facts. David Premack and Guy Woodruff (1978) acknowledged this in their original article on theory of mind: "An individual has a theory of mind if he imputes mental states to himself and others. A system of inferences of this kind is properly viewed as a theory because such states are not directly observable, and the system can be used to make predictions of others' actions" (p. 515). So, theories recruit unobservable theoretical constructs to make sense of, to explain, the data and to allow prediction of new as-yet-unobserved phenomena, findings, and regularities. The key feature is not that theoretical constructs are necessarily, literally unobservable but that they function at a different level than the data they explain.

This essential and distinctive interplay between theory and data helps shape and reveal three characteristic aspects of theories: their structure, function, and dynamic character. These are equally three distinctive features of the sorts of everyday knowledge I want to examine, and in particular, of everyday theory of mind.

Structure and Hierarchy

Theories may be specific—describing how delimited phenomena operate—or more general and abstract. Ever since Thomas Kuhn wrote about scientific revolutions, it has been recognized that scientific theories are hierarchically structured. Data relate to specific theories; specific theories are framed by paradigms (Kuhn, 1962) and research traditions (Lakatos, 1970; Laudan, 1977). Celestial mechanics, for example, frames an understanding of the heavens in terms of space, matter, and physical energy (rather than spirits, gods, and personified constellations); it provides a research tradition within which more specific theories of astronomical phenomena are generated. Cognitive developmentalists have used the term *framework theories* (Carey, 2009; Wellman, 1990; Wellman & Gelman, 1998) to capture everyday higher order generalizations about causal specifics. Belief-desire psychology is at this general level of consideration; theory of mind is a framework theory that frames more specific everyday theories. As an idiosyncratic example, consider my everyday, specific theory of my exotic Aunt Lib. To understand her I appeal to beliefs and desires in general; but generic, abstract beliefs and desires won't suffice. I must, more specifically, home in on her exotic and flamboyant likes and desires coupled with her at-times bizarre, iconoclastic beliefs to account for her often downright peculiar actions and conversations. Of course, there can be more than just three levels—data, specific theory, framework theory—but in general theoretical principles or commitments of more abstract or general nature at "higher" levels frame more specific/concrete models at "lower" levels that make more direct contact with data at the "bottom."

Explanations, Predictions, and Interventions

A theory organizes the entities and forces that it privileges into causal-explanatory frameworks to account for, make understandable, and make predictable phenomena in its domain. A theory influences interpretation of the evidence, allows wide-ranging predictions about what will happen in the future, provides explanations of the data, and benefits from and helps direct interventions on the world to try to change it.

It is worth re-emphasizing that these features are important for everyday thought, not just scientific thought. In particular, our everyday psychology—our theory of mind—provides a framework theory of human action and states. Within this everyday framework theory, people and their actions and experiences are the data focal to our everyday psychologizing; beliefs, desires, and the like are the theoretical constructs we use to understand, predict, and explain the data. More specific theories and accounts—my Aunt Lib theory—are constrained by the more abstract frameworks that help generate them. I gain considerable satisfaction (and affection for her) in being able to explain Aunt Lib to myself, even when I fail at predicting what she'll do or say next.

Construing theoretical knowledge in layers such as these helps unpack how theories can function not only to organize, make sense of, and explain the data, but also, developmentally, to help define and generate the data in the first place. That theories both develop from data and are used to define and generate data might seem intractably circular except for theories' hierarchical character. Framework theoretical ideas parse and organize the data, allowing development of more specific models that account for the data and that guide research that generates more data as well as revised models that can, at times, lead to revision of the very frameworks themselves. By virtue of their structure and function, theoretical frameworks outline domains; specific theories advance more detailed explanations of phenomena within these globally defined domains and consonant with the larger explanatory framework. Moreover, a framework theory not only outlines a domain, it outlines a domain for further *development*, for further data-driven learning and exploration.

Data-Driven Development

Cognitive structures, à la Piaget (1970), were claimed to be constructed out of action experiences and revised in the face of more such experiences. Similarly, a theory-theory account claims theoretical constructs, assembled into theory structures, not only generate and organize data; they change in the face of the data. Of course, Piagetian constructivism can be considered to have failed, in part, because of its inability to capture in any convincing detail just how learning and structuralism could actually go hand in hand. How could such deep structures and frameworks be constructed on the basis of action experiences? Theory theory has been subject to some of its severest critiques on just this same point.

The past few years, however, have seen the advent of new computational ideas that credibly demonstrate that (and how) causal structure of notably abstract, hierarchical character is, in principle, learnable from the data. These computational learning methods have two key features: probabilistic Bayesian inference and hierarchical structure. In Chapter 6, I outline in more detail how hierarchical Bayesian models (HBMs) demonstrate that observational data-driven experience, if processed via appropriately "stacked-up" hierarchical theories, can result in abstract as well as specific learning and development.

As a brief foretaste here, probabilistic Bayesian models, and hierarchical Bayesian learning, begin with Bayes's rule, a rule for inductive inference first formulated by Rev. Thomas Bayes in the 18th century. Dependence on Bayesian inference has an appropriate appeal because Bayes's rule itself provides a very general way to capture an interplay between theory and data: Bayes's rule considers both hypotheses (H) and data or evidence (E), and focuses on the probability of a focal H given the observed data E. Furthermore, Bayes's rule is about inferential learning, in the sense of revising one's hypothesis in the face of new data. So, an initial probability is considered for the possible H, $p(H)$, and on encountering E, that prior probability is updated to become the posterior probability—the probability of the H given the E. So, $p(H) \rightarrow p(H/E)$. Under the right circumstances, the updated, posterior probability can be calculated via Bayes's rule.

This crucial juggling of hypotheses and evidence is not confined to scientific thinking; it takes place in everyday practice. Is my backache due to bad posture or a herniated disc? Evidence (from trying yoga and/or getting an X-ray) help me learn which is most likely or help me consider a different hypothesis altogether. This sort of integration of prior knowledge and new evidence captures just the sort of thing Piaget meant when he talked about assimilation and accommodation, and part of what I mean by saying theory theory encompasses data-driven development of everyday theories.

Bayes's rule has been around a long time; the recent advances in Bayesian computational learning rely critically on probabilistic learning that considers multiple hypotheses. Typically there are many hypotheses that can account for some set of data. If we view the learner's task as definite and deterministic—finding *the* hypothesis that definitively accounts for the data—the problem becomes very, very difficult, even impossible, to solve. This is part of the "riddle of induction" (Goodman, 1955) and also of arguments about the "poverty of the stimulus" (Chomsky, 2006)—how can the learner induce the correct answer when so many alternative hypotheses fit the small amounts of noisy data observed in everyday experience? It turns out that more thoroughly integrating probability into the learning mechanisms provides key purchase on the learning problem. Although many hypotheses may be compatible with the evidence, some hypotheses can be judged more probable and others less.

The second key feature of recent hierarchical Bayesian modeling goes still further in this direction by thinking about the multiple, various hypotheses as ordered in a hierarchy (e.g., Tenenbaum, Griffiths, & Niyogi, 2007)—there is a stack of hypotheses, or theories, such that some hypotheses at Level 1 are constrained (and generated) by others at Level 2, and those at Level 2 may be further constrained and generated by still others at Level 3, further up the stack. Theories at the higher levels represent more abstract or more general knowledge; those at lower levels are more specific or concrete and closer to data. And, in principle, the probabilities of theories at Level 2 (or 3) can be updated and revised on the basis of changes to those at Level 1, in much the same Bayesian way that hypotheses at Level 1 are updated and revised on the basis of the data (E).

It is not just theoretically possible to infer complex hierarchical hypotheses from probabilistic patterns of data; it can actually be done. Computational scientists, using these hierarchical probabilistic Bayesian ideas, have produced hierarchical Bayesian inference and hypothesis revision in several intriguing demonstrations (see Chapter 6). These computational examples of hierarchical Bayesian learning—ways in which data-driven learning can yield local changes to specific hypotheses but also more profound changes of more abstract hypotheses (theory creation and theory change) as products of encountered experiences with the data—provide constructivist demonstrations to underwrite theory theory as at least a provisioned framework for thinking about theory-of-mind development.

Intriguingly, according to probabilistic hierarchical Bayesian models, and according to theory theory, theory change often, distinctively, yields many intermediate steps. Evidence progressively leads scientists, and children, to revise their initial hypotheses, resulting in characteristic series of conceptions. Progressive developments—and progressions responsive to the data of experience—are features I emphasize in what follows because these are increasingly obvious and insistent features of the rich data now available about theory-of-mind development in childhood.

CONCLUSION

Sherlock Holmes famously said, "It is a capital mistake to theorize before you have all the evidence" (Partington, 1996, p. 256). Thus, we need evidence—data—on the table, a lot of data, before fully engaging in refined theory-testing, theory-building tasks. That is the job of many of the chapters that follow, beginning with Chapters 1, 2, 3, 4, and 5. Of course, Holmes is a fictional character and his statement mischaracterizes the scientific process: Inevitably, in important areas of study, the data are complex and it is not useful (or interesting) to simply list and compile them as empirical laundry lists. The data must be assembled, organized, and understood as we go; and as just noted, it is scientific frameworks that usefully illuminate data patterns and help coax the fullness and implications of the data to come clear. Any consideration of data is partly theory laden; there is no theory-less way to do it. For an initial framework, I use theory theory; hence my developmental, constructivist title—children are in the business of making theories of mind.

I

Developing a Theory of Mind

INITIAL OVERVIEW

ON MARCH 5TH of 2007, NBCNews.com posted an article headlined "Mindreading Scientists Predict Behavior" ("Scientists try to predict intentions," 2007). It began with "At a laboratory in Germany, volunteers slide into a donut-shaped MRI machine and perform simple tasks, such as deciding whether to add or subtract two numbers." Scientists in the next room were trying to read these volunteers' minds; they were trying to judge what the person intended, in their thoughts before they acted, by examining their brain scans from magnetic resonance imaging (MRI). The researchers, led by a Dr. Haynes in Berlin, were reasonably successful—they were better than chance at identifying the subjects' decisions about what they would do later, in this case, adding versus subtracting.

In essence, participants were told to decide on their own whether they would add or subtract two numbers a few seconds before any numbers were actually flashed on a screen. During those few seconds, the scanner provided computer-enhanced images of the participants' brain activations and the researchers used those images to predict the subject's decision—with one brain pattern suggesting addition and another subtraction. As the story admits, "The research, which began in July 2005, has been of limited scope: only 21 people have been tested so far. And the 71 percent accuracy rate is only about 20 percent more successful than random selection."

Still the article cited various enthusiastic reactions:

"The fact that we can determine what intention a person is holding in their mind pushes the level of our understanding of subjective thought to a whole new level," said Dr. Paul Wolpe, a professor of psychiatry at the University of Pennsylvania. (para. 9)

Tanja Steinbach, an adult participant, said "It's really weird. But since I know they're only able to do this if they have certain machines, I'm not worried that everybody else on the street can read my mind" (para. 6).

The article ends by noting that in fact some commentators are alarmed by the implications of such mindreading. "Scientists are making enough progress to make ethicists nervous" (para. 19).

Mind-reading is indeed amazing. Yet, even 2- and 3-year-olds do this sort of thing everyday—even infants can succeed at figuring out someone's intentions. They succeed not with fancy machines but with their fancy 2-year-old brains and their ordinary, still-developing theory of mind. We all read minds in this ordinary (mundane but fully amazing) way. And we're better than these scientists—not infallible (but probably at least 70% correct, for simple things like inferring intentions in constrained situations and then using them to predict choice behavior) but also able to do so in less constrained everyday situations. How we do this is the story of theory of mind (and a great deal of research). That we do it every day does not deny the power and the wizardry of it. Mind-reading it is, yet it is ordinary, commonplace, and indeed ever present and necessary to our everyday lives.

In fact, acquisition of this everyday theory of mind is one of the most impressive intellectual accomplishments of human development. Much like human language, theory of mind is notably abstract but accomplished in basic forms by young children everywhere. And, again like language, both intriguing early competences and striking developments are readily apparent: Infants closely attend to other humans; 2-year-olds talk about peoples' wants and feelings and comfort others in distress; 3- and 4-year-olds talk about thoughts and begin to engage in lies and trickery; and nuanced theories of mind—in "folk psychologies"—are apparent in (and dramatically differ across) cultural communities worldwide. Indeed, revealing developmental data showing near-universal attribution by young children of mental states to self and others have helped fuel rampant contemporary interest in theory of mind. Lay adults and children are embedded in theory of mind; scientists, scholars, and the news-reading public are likewise now immersed in it.

In this chapter, I provide a brief overview of the course of childhood theory of mind to set the stage for more in-depth treatment of key topics and issues in later chapters. As a preface, it is important to note that sometimes theory of mind is described as a preschool achievement, equated with children's performance on false belief tasks. I advocate a much broader (and more interesting) construal, both conceptually and developmentally. Theory of mind describes our wide-ranging human understanding of agents' mental states such as intentions, desires, and thoughts and how action is shaped by such states. It refers to our everyday psychology, appropriately emphasizing the "mindreading" that so strongly characterizes our everyday, "commonsense" psychological understandings.

THE PROGRESSIVE COURSE OF THEORY OF MIND
DEVELOPMENT: INFANT BEGINNINGS

Developing an understanding of people begins at birth. Infants who are only a few days old prefer to look at people and faces, imitate people but not inanimate devices, listen to human voices, and so on. No data convincingly demonstrate that such young infants penetrate to a deeper, psychological, "mental" sense of persons beyond apparent, surface features. But it has now become clear that older infants do so.

Infant Understanding of Intentional Actions

The earliest examples of psychological construals of persons appear in intention understandings; by the end of the 1st year, children begin to treat themselves and others as intentional agents and experiencers. Box 1.1 (on the next page) provides one example of a method used to demonstrate intention understanding in infants (from Brandone & Wellman, 2009; Phillips & Wellman, 2005). In the initial demonstrations using a variant of this paradigm, infants saw an animated circle "jumping" over a barrier to reach its goal-object. Just as they do for intentional human acts like reaching, 9- and 12-month-olds look longer at the animated indirect test events over the direct ones, showing an abstract, generalized understanding of intentional agency (Gergely, Nádasdy, Csibra, & Bíró, 1995; Csibra, Gergely, Bíró, Koós, & Brockbank, 1999).

Other similar tasks provide converging results. In a classic one developed by Amanda Woodward (1998), infants were habituated to the sight of a hand reaching to and grasping one of two toys. Then infants saw two test events in which the locations of the toys were switched. In the *new goal/old movement* event, the hand reached to the old location and thus now grasped a different toy. In the *old goal/new movement* event, the hand grasped the same toy as in habituation, but it was now of course in the other location. If the infants encoded the habituation behavior simply in terms of the spatial movement of the hand, then the old goal/new movement event would be novel (because the hand executed a different trajectory than during habituation). However, if the infants encoded the habituation behavior in terms of the hand grasping a particular goal object, then the new goal/old movement event would be novel and noteworthy. Five- and 9-month-old infants looked longer at the new goal/old movement, indicating they saw the original action in terms of its goal.

As the stimuli depicted in Box 1.1 show, intentional actions potentially manifest an actor's psychological states, goals, desires, and intentions. Yet they are amenable to research with nonverbal infants because they are easily observable by infants. Results such as those in Box 1.1 and those of Amanda Woodward provide evidence of infant understandings that go beyond attention to surface behaviors—infants process actions in ways that correspond to an intentional, goal-directed construal of the actor rather than to a mere surface reading of his or her behaviors.

BOX I.I

INFANT UNDERSTANDING OF INTENTIONAL ACTION

  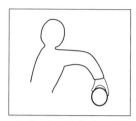

  Habituation event   Direct reach test event   Indirect reach test event

Much research on infants' understanding of persons relies on close examination of infants looking at agents and actions. Habituation-test (or familiarization-test) paradigms track a decrease in infants' looking when the same stimulus-event is presented repeatedly, followed by increased looking when a different stimulus-event is then presented. In this way, habituation-test paradigms set the infant up so that he or she will then look longer at novel, unexpected test events.

In the reaching paradigm (see top of box), infants view multiple trials of the barrier-reaching event in habituation. Then, the barrier is *removed* and the test events contrast two different construals of the person's actions: one in terms of intentions and one in terms of physical motions of the body. Suppose during habituation, the infant construes the agent's action in terms of its physical movement (the arm and hand up and then down in an arc); then, the indirect reach test event should be expected (as it repeats the same movement), whereas the direct reach will stand out as novel and so specially attention worthy. In contrast, if the infant initially construes the action as goal directed, then when the barrier is removed the direct reach is the expected action because in that case the agent continues to directly seek the goal. Under this second construal, the indirect reach would be more attention worthy because (although the agent's arm movement remains the same as during habituation) the agent no longer seems straightforwardly directed to the goal: 8-, 9-, 10-, and 12-month-olds consistently look longer at the *indirect* reach test event.

Infants look equally to both test events in control conditions where they are first habituated to a display with no barrier, *or* first habituated to the exact same over-the-barrier arm movements but where there is no goal-object.

Moreover, infant understandings of intentional action appear not only in (passive) looking-time research, but also in more active-interactive paradigms. For example, Tanya Behne and her colleagues (2005) engaged infants in a game where a woman gave them toys across a table. Interspersed were trials where she held up a toy but did not give it over, sometimes because she was unwilling to do so and sometimes because she was unable (e.g., she could not extract the toy from a transparent container). Nine- to 18-month-olds (but not 6-month-olds) behaved more impatiently (e.g., reaching, turning away) when the woman willfully kept the toy than when she was making good-faith efforts to pass it along. Infants thus appreciated something of the intentional differences between *unable* and *unwilling* scenarios, although the surface behaviors and outcomes were equivalent.

Relatedly, intentional action is not only directed toward specific goals: It is nonaccidental. Thus, Malinda Carpenter and her colleagues (1998) had 14- and 18-month-old infants watch an adult model several two-action sequences on complex objects (e.g., pushing a button and then moving a lever), thereby producing an interesting event (e.g., delivering a marble down a chute). One action was marked vocally by the adult as intentional ("There!"), and one as accidental ("Whoops!"). Infants imitated almost twice as many intentional as accidental actions and only very rarely imitated the entire two-action sequences (see also Gardiner, Greif, & Bjorklund, 2011; Olineck & Poulin-Dubois, 2005).

When viewing actions such as those in Box 1.1, or such as pushing buttons and moving levers, infants might conceivably identify only the spatial directedness and objective efficiency of the overt behavior toward its overt target—a behavioral or "teleological" rather than intentional understanding of goal directedness (Gergely & Csibra, 2003). Note, for example, in Box 1.1 the hand actually gets/grasps the object; in pushing levers, hands actually grasp them and make them move. Behaviorally "grasping," "moving," and "obtaining" things might be more or less all the infant knows about goals; for babies, goals might be overt action-results rather than intended action-aims. Inferring a goal when it is unfulfilled, and thus nonovert in the actor's movements or outcomes, however, could demonstrate an understanding that intentions exist beyond the surface actions performed. So, in a seminal study (Meltzoff, 1995), 18-month-olds witnessed an adult try *but fail* to fulfill several novel, object-directed goals (e.g., trying to hang a ring on a hook). Although infants never saw the actions successfully modeled, when given a chance to act on the objects themselves, they "imitated" the successful action much more than the failed (actually witnessed) actions. Fifteen-month-olds, but not 12-month-olds also display this pattern (Carpenter et al., 1998).

Of course, motoric productions of the sort required for action imitation arguably require a demanding response from the infant, more so than attentive looking of the sort required for tasks such as those in Box 1.1. So, consider a version of the displays in Box 1.1 where now in habituation the actor reaches over the barrier for the ball but falls short of ever successfully grasping that target object. If habituated to such unsuccessful actions, 10- and 12-month-olds, but *not* 8-month-olds, interpret the actions in terms of the (never actually seen) intentional goal of grasping the object (Brandone & Wellman, 2009). When the barrier is removed, in the test events, 10- and 12-month-olds expect the previously unsuccessful actor to directly grasp the object and so look longer if she or he does not. Eight-month-olds habituated to *successful* reaches appreciate them as intentional (directed to the goal of getting the ball) but not the failed reaches that fall short of their goal. But, 10-month-olds can and do read through the direct behavioral features of the act itself (the hand never grasps the ball) to infer the actor's intention (she or he wants to grasp the ball) nonetheless. These data, and others like them (e.g., Hamlin,

Hallinan, & Woodward, 2008), demonstrate progressive understandings in infancy—in this case an intention understanding that proceeds from seeing actions in terms of external targets to seeing them in terms of less obvious internal plans and goals.

In the research I have discussed thus far, the actions presented to infants were pre-packaged and carefully segmented in various ways—for example, infants were habituated to a single reaching behavior shown for multiple trials. In everyday behavior, however, such action segments merge more seamlessly in ongoing streams (e.g., a mother goes to the closet, gets a mop, mops the floor, rinses the mop, etc.). Dare Baldwin and her colleagues (Baldwin, Baird, Saylor, & Clark, 2001) created videos of such everyday streams of action and then asked adults to identify portions that were "meaningful in terms of understanding the actor's intentions." Adults showed high levels of agreement in how they conceptually parsed the physically continuous videos. Ten- to 11-month-old infants were then shown such videos. In familiarization trials, infants saw a video several times. Then they saw the same video once again in two different test formats. In *intention-completing* test videos, a pause was inserted in the video at a point that adults had identified as the endpoint of an intentional-action segment. In *intention-disrupting* test videos, a similar pause was inserted but this time in the middle of, instead of at the end of, an intentional-action segment. Infants looked longer at the intention-disrupting test videos. In this way, infants were parsing ongoing behavior along the same sorts of intentionally meaningful boundaries that adults identified.

Infant Understanding of Intentional Experiences

In common parlance, "intentional" means goal directed and applies to action; but in the wider scientific and philosophic sense, "intentionality" indicates a distinctive kind of subjective orientation of agents to the world. For example, seeing my computer keyboard and being aware of its presence counts as an intentional experience. Seeing, that is visual awareness, has its experienced-objects (like action has its goal-objects) and this is true whether the eye movements that landed my sight on the keyboard were themselves deliberate or not. Intentional experiences do not necessarily require intentional actions (just as intentional actions do not necessarily require success). So, the infant intention understandings that need to be addressed encompass understanding of action *and* experience: Persons not only engage in intentional action, they subjectively experience the world. Seeing provides one example of that; and seeing is a useful research example, amenable to research with infants, because acts of seeing can be presented to and observed by infants. For example, an infant can observe someone shift their gaze to look at some object, like at a computer keyboard.

Potentially, infant gaze following, where infants follow an agent's line of sight (or head orientation) toward an object, would be produced by an understanding that the agent sees something—the person has a visual experience of some sort and that's what I'll see if I look over there. Intriguingly, infants gaze follow, in some ways, by 8 and

9 months of age (and even earlier). When watching an adult shift his gaze to look at some salient toy, infants of this age shift their gaze, too, to follow the adult's gaze to that toy. But, alternatively, infant gaze following could possibly be merely behavioral: Tracking others' head-eye orientations might simply yield for the infant interesting sights to see, and so someone's gaze is worth following even *without* a recognition of the agent's visual experience (Baldwin & Moses, 1996). By 12 to 14 months, however, infants also follow an adult's gaze around a barrier—even if this requires leaning or moving behind the barrier on their own—coupled with visual checking back and forth, apparently to verify that they and the agent are seeing the same thing (Dunphy-Lelii & Wellman, 2004; Moll & Tomasello, 2004). Indeed, by 20 to 24 months children orient an object away from themselves (depriving themselves of the interesting sight) to insure others will see it (Lempers, Flavell, & Flavell, 1977).

Still, it is possible that even in appropriately gazing around barriers, infants could be responding to the agent's eye-ball (or head-nose) orientation, coupled with some tracking of overt obstacles, without a deeper sense of the agent's intentional experience (Moore & Corkum, 1994). Indeed, at 12 months, infants often "gaze follow" the head turns of adults who wear blindfolds.

But recent data confirm a deeper understanding of visual experience. Andrew Meltzoff and Rechelle Brooks (2008) gave 12-month-olds advance experience with blindfolds occluding their own vision. After such experiences, they were significantly less likely to "gaze follow" a blindfolded adult, suggesting that their sense of what the adult can see—visually experience—guided infants' actions. At the same time, 18-month-olds do not often gaze follow a blindfolded adult—probably because they have come to understand that blindfolds occlude visual experience. But in this same study 18-month-olds were given experience with a special blindfold that looked opaque yet was easily seen through when worn. After experience with *that* blindfold, 18-month-olds did gaze follow the head turn of a blindfolded adult. Thus, by 12 to 18 months, it is infants' sense of the person's visual experience (not just overt eye or head directedness) that often controls their gaze following.

In both their understandings of intentional action and their understandings of intentional experience, infants (at least older infants by about a year of life) show us they have progressed beyond just acquiring behavioral rules to codify human action—for example, they know more than that "goals" are those things an agent obtains or that "sights" are just interesting things that are there when an agent gazes or orients. One additional way to emphasize their progress is to say that infants understand persons' knowledge-like states. Thus, for the infant, persons not only can have intentional experiences about some here and now event; their experiences can accumulate and update (or fail to update) over time. Michael Tomasello and Katharina Haberl (2003) examined this with 12- and 18-month-old infants who interacted with three objects. Critically, a target adult joined in these interactions for two of the objects but was absent for the third. After these interactions, the target adult came back, saw all three objects displayed on a tray, and said to the infant, "Wow! That's cool! Can you give it to me?" while gesturing ambiguously in the direction of all the objects. Three objects were now familiar for the infant, but one (unnamed and unspecified in gesture) was new (and so "cool") to the target adult. Infants gave the target adult the object that was new for the adult. Thus, they tracked the adult's experiences sufficiently to know that (a) her experience was not updated when theirs was (a recognition of the "subjectivity" or person specificity of experience) and so (b) she was previously unaware of the third object. This sort of tracking someone's previous awareness and unawareness of some object or event encompasses a rudimentary understanding of knowledge-like states: A person who has become aware of X knows some things about it; one unaware of X is ignorant of it. (In Chapter 8, I describe how infants' appreciation of knowledge-like awareness is limited relative to older children's understanding of knowing, but it is knowledge like.)

In short, initial infant insights about intention culminate in their understanding that intentional agents behave according to their goals (desires and emotions) constrained by their experiential awareness (and unawareness). This desire-awareness understanding of persons constitutes an impressive albeit initial understanding of mental states—intentional mental states. This desire-awareness understanding also encompasses a rudimentary but impressive sense of agents' awareness or unawareness (knowledge or ignorance) of events, a recognition that if persons' experiences of situations are not updated as events change, then they can be ignorant of key circumstances.

FALSE BELIEF WITHIN BELIEF-DESIRE REASONING

Infants' capacities, as impressive as they are, fall far short of the understandings of preschoolers. The desire-awareness sensibilities of infants' appreciation of intentional actions is not the belief-desire, causal-explanatory reasoning of preschoolers.

To begin, consider the depiction in Box 1.2. As depicted there, an agent might have a false belief about (for example) where an object is—think it is in the drawer—beyond just being ignorant of its location. Beliefs thus more definitively focus on a person's mental "contents." Remember Romeo and Juliet. Theirs is a story about desires, emotions, perceptions, *and more*. Romeo not only desires Juliet and sees her there inert beside him in crypt, he does not know what has happened to her. However, this is a story about more than just ignorance. Romeo not only does not know what has happened to Juliet, *he believes she is dead*. Understanding the possibility of an internal realm of mental contents (ideas, thoughts, images) is the hallmark of a "representational" theory of mind. Understanding false beliefs, when contents of the world (Juliet is alive) contradict contents of thought ("Juliet is dead"), provides a powerful, yet everyday, illustration of such representational understanding. Equally, but more mundanely, for Judy (in Box 1.2) candy in the cupboard contradicts her thoughts ("candy in the drawer").

BOX 1.2
FALSE-BELIEF UNDERSTANDINGS

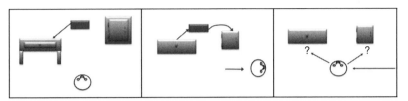

False-belief tasks have children reason about an agent whose actions should be controlled by a false belief. Such tasks have many forms, but a common task employs a change in locations, as depicted at the top of the box. The child (not shown) sees the character, Judy, put her candy in one of two locations. The character leaves and while she cannot see, the candy gets moved. The character returns, wants her candy, and the child is asked "Where will Judy look for her candy?" or "Where does Judy think her candy is?" Older preschool children answer correctly, like adults. Younger children answer incorrectly. They are not just random; they consistently say Judy will search in the cupboard (where it really is). Note that the task taps more than just attribution of ignorance (Judy doesn't know); rather, it assesses attribution of false belief (Judy thinks—falsely—her candy is in the drawer).

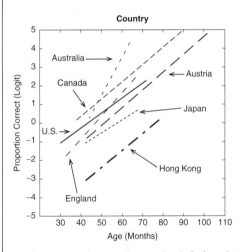

A frequently used alternative task uses surprising contents (rather than a change of location). For example, children see a crayon box, say they think it holds crayons, and then on opening see it holds candles. They are asked what someone else who has never looked inside will think the box holds—crayons or candles.

Several task factors make such tasks harder or easier; but nonetheless, children go from below-chance to above-chance performance, typically in the preschool years. Moreover, as shown in the graph on the left (combining results from Wellman, Cross, & Watson, 2001, and Liu, Wellman, Tardiff, & Sabbagh, 2008), children in different cultural-linguistic communities can achieve false-belief understanding more quickly or more slowly; yet in all locales, they evidence the same trajectory—from below chance (below zero in this graph) to above-chance performance in early to later childhood. This is true even for children growing up in non-Western cultural communities speaking non-Indo-European languages. And is true even for children in traditional, nonliterate societies.

The slippage between beliefs and reality is one reason there has been so much research on children's understanding of false belief (hundreds of studies in meta-analyses by Liu, Wellman, Tardiff, & Sabbagh, 2008; Milligan, Astington, & Dack, 2007; Wellman, Cross, & Watson, 2001). Another reason for this voluminous research is that when researchers were first becoming interested in theory of mind, several easy-to-use, "standard," false-belief tasks were developed (Box 1.2), and these have proved nicely revealing. For one, they consistently show an important developmental transition. Indeed, as shown in Box 1.2, because they have been used worldwide, false-belief tasks reveal a universal childhood theory-of-mind developmental achievement. Equally intriguing, the timing of coming to understand false beliefs differs across countries.

There is more to say about false belief, and the empirical usefulness of false-belief tasks; but regardless, a focus on a single task or achievement is limited and misleading. So, it is important that by 3 to 4 years, children not only expect people to act in accord with their beliefs, even when those are mistaken or false, but also explain persons' actions by citing their mental states including their beliefs (Schult & Wellman, 1997); come to understand about lies and deception (Siegal & Peterson, 1998); appearances versus reality (Flavell, Green, & Flavell, 1986); that someone's external expressions need not display their internal emotions (Harris et al., 1986); and more. As a single intriguing example, 3- and 4-year-old children explicitly judge that a person's ideas, thoughts, and dreams are "internal," immaterial, not-real experiences. Among other things, they can easily judge that whereas a real dog can be petted, and seen with the eyes, and seen by many people, a thought-about dog cannot (Richert & Harris, 2006; Watson, Gelman, & Wellman, 1998; Wellman & Estes, 1986).

Even standard false-belief tasks themselves encompass reasoning about more than just beliefs. Judy *wants* her candy; she did not *see* it move; and when she looks for it in the drawer, she will be *disappointed*. To reiterate a point from my introductory chapter, philosophers and psychologists often characterize our everyday system of reasoning about mind, world, and behavior as a belief-desire psychology (D'Andrade, 1987; Fodor, 1987; Wellman, 1990). Such an everyday psychology provides explanations and predictions of action by appeal to what the person thinks, knows, and expects coupled with what he or she wants, intends, and hopes for. Why did Judy go to the drawer? She *wanted* her candy and *thought* it was in the drawer. Everyday psychological reasoning also includes reasoning about the origins of mental states (Judy wants candy because she is *hungry*; Judy thinks it is in the drawer where she last *saw* it). That is, "belief-desire" psychology incorporates a variety of related constructs such as drives and preferences that ground one's desires and perceptual-historical experiences that ground one's beliefs. It also includes emotional reactions that result from these desires, beliefs, preferences, and perceptions: happiness at fulfilled desires, frustration at unfulfilled desires, surprise when events contradict one's firmly held beliefs. Children's performance on standard false-belief tasks stands as a marker of important developments in this network of belief-desire reasoning about self and others.

Children's development of this network of belief-desire reasoning is influenced by the experiences in their lives, and it dramatically impacts their social actions and interactions with others. One way to appreciate this is to note that amid the consistent trajectories shown in Box 1.2, from below-chance incorrect judgment to above-chance correct judgments in the years from 2 to 6 or 7, there is also obvious variation in the timetable across countries. There is considerable variation across individuals too. Although almost all normally developing children eventually master false belief, some children (in any cultural-language community) come to this understanding earlier and some later. For example, the age when U.S. children can first solve false-belief tasks (Wellman et al., 2001) or start to talk about persons in terms of beliefs as well as desires (Bartsch & Wellman, 1995) can vary from 2 to 5 years or more. Whereas some children can reason about the internal-mental causes of emotions and actions at 2 years of age, others have difficulty explaining why people act and feel the way they do at 4 and 5 years. This variation has been important for identifying factors that impact the achievement of theory-of-mind understandings and the outcomes that are influenced by theory-of-mind insights.

Consider briefly factors that impact theory-of-mind achievement. Living in social networks, such as having siblings or larger social kin groups, enhances preschool theory of mind. Josef Perner and his colleagues (1994) were the first to report that preschool children with one or more siblings pass false-belief tests before children with no siblings. Further studies have pointed to play experiences with older versus younger siblings (Cassidy, Fineberg, Brown, & Perkins, 2005; Peterson, 2000; Ruffman, Perner, Naito, Parkin, & Clements, 1998), and to interactions with older people in general (Lewis, Freeman, Kyriakidou, Maridaki-Kassotaki, & Berridge, 1996), as promoting children's early understandings of belief and mental representation.

Family and social experiences of these sorts may be influential in part because of their connection to pretend play. For preschoolers, more partners equals more opportunities to pretend (Perner et al., 1994). Consistent with this, Marjorie Taylor and Stephanie Carlson (1997) found that 3- and 4-year-olds with extensive fantasy experiences (e.g., imaginary playmates, frequent pretend play, multiple pretend figurines and toys) were more likely to pass false-belief tasks than children with less involvement in fantasy play. This is sensible because children who engage in frequent pretense more often discuss roles, negotiate scenes, transform objects, and use mental-state language in their play (Howe, Petrakos, & Rinaldi, 1998). Indeed, the use of shared negotiations and role assignments during pretense (Astington & Jenkins, 1995) as well as pretend role enactments with siblings (Youngblade & Dunn, 1995) predict children's false-belief understanding.

Relatedly, individual differences in children's knowledge about mental states have been linked to early social conversations. Although mental-state talk typically occurs in all households, these conversations vary from family to family in terms of which states are discussed, the tendency to provide causal explanations, and in parental encouragement for child participation (Lagattuta & Wellman, 2002; Ruffman, Slade, & Crowe, 2002). These parent-child conversations about mental states, about emotions, and about the causes of action influence how quickly children come to theory-of-mind milestones (e.g., false belief; Bartsch & Wellman, 1995; Dunn & Brown, 1993; Ruffman, et al., 2002). Language competence more generally also impacts theory-of-mind achievement (Astington & Baird, 2005). And, more specifically, several studies have reported that parent-child conversation about the causes and consequences of actions and emotions are particularly important in facilitating childhood theory-of-mind insights (Dunn & Brown, 1993; Lagattuta & Wellman, 2002; Peterson & Slaughter, 2003).

How about outcomes? The claim is that theory of mind profoundly shapes and impacts our lives. Changes in belief-desire understandings, of the sort marked by changes in understanding false beliefs, therefore should, in principle, impact children's lives. Indeed, differences in false-belief understanding as measured in the preschool years do predict several key childhood competences, such as how and how much children talk about people in everyday conversation, their social interactional skills, and consequently their interactions and popularity with peers (e.g., Astington & Jenkins, 1995; Lalonde & Chandler, 1995; Watson, Nixon, Wilson, & Capage, 1999). Achievement of theory-of-mind insights influences children's use of deception, their strategies for arguing with and persuading others, and their actions in games like hide-and-seek (e.g., Bartsch, London, & Campbell, 2007; Peskin & Ardino, 2003). These findings are important and revealing for confirming theory of mind's real-life relevance, and I review them more fully in Chapter 3.

All these findings affirm that something definite and important is happening in children's theory-of-mind understandings in the preschool years. But what? Recent research claims that infants—at 12 to 15 months—already recognize that actors act on the basis of their beliefs and false beliefs (Onishi & Baillargeon, 2005; Scott & Baillargeon, 2009; Surian, Caldi, & Sperber, 2007). If true, such findings would argue that coming to an awareness of false belief (and relatedly, a representational theory of mind) is not as central a part of the preschool transition as it once seemed. This is a topic of considerable importance, as well as ongoing debate, and I discuss the data, their significance, and implications in depth in Chapter 8.

To foreshadow that discussion, I believe the infant studies, at a minimum, help confirm that infants understand actors as goal directed; that infants track the changing experiences of other persons that yield for them awareness or unawareness of key events (at least in simplified scenarios); and that infants expect aware and unaware agents to act differently. Thus these findings help underwrite the description previously that infants achieve a desire-awareness sensibility of intentional action that encompasses an initial sense of knowledge-like (and ignorance-like) states.

At the same time, the child's theory of mind demonstrably changes in power and character beyond infancy. Theory of mind understandings begin in infancy but also progress; earliest understandings of intentional action give way to later richer belief-desire systems of understanding. Within such a crude progression are several more precise ones.

PRESCHOOL PROGRESSIONS IN THEORY-OF-MIND UNDERSTANDINGS

The best-established progression concerns comparisons between children's understanding of desires and intentions versus beliefs. When tested in closely comparable tasks whose formats are similar to preschool false-belief tasks (as in Box 1.2), toddlers evidence an understanding that people can have differing desires for the exact same object or event but not that they may have differing beliefs (Wellman & Liu, 2004, provide a meta-analysis of numerous studies). Comparisons on closely comparable tasks also show understandings of knowledge and ignorance in the face of failing to understand false belief (Wellman & Liu, 2004)

These sorts of developmental changes are intriguing. Indeed, as I noted in my introductory chapter, in very real senses all credible accounts now predict patterns of change and stability over a number of years as theory of mind unfolds. A comprehensive understanding of theory of mind, therefore, increasingly requires data as to how development actually progresses—which initial states lead to which intermediate and asymptotic states, influenced by which mechanisms. That sort of data is emerging—more detailed, extended progressions of understandings that characterize theory of mind. A clear example is encompassed by an established Theory-Of-Mind Scale (Wellman & Liu, 2004) that encompasses carefully constructed tasks assessing childhood understanding of the following:

1. Diverse Desires (DD; people can have different desires for the same thing)
2. Diverse Beliefs (DB; people can have different beliefs about the same situation)
3. Knowledge Access (KA; something can be true, but someone may not know that)
4. False Belief (FB; something can be true, but someone might believe something different)
5. Hidden Emotion (HE; someone can feel one way but display a different emotion)

The tasks are similar in procedures, language, and format, yet U.S. preschoolers evidence a clear order of difficulty, just as listed, with understanding diverse desires being easiest and understanding false belief and then hidden emotion being hardest. In shorthand, DD>DB>KA>FB>HE. The same five-step progression also characterizes Australian (Peterson, Wellman, & Liu, 2005) and German (Kristen, Thoermer, Hofer, Aschersleben, & Sodian, 2006) preschoolers, and a very similar progression characterizes Chinese children (Wellman, Fang, Liu, Zhu, & Liu, 2006) and those from Iran (Shahaeian, Peterson, Slaughter, & Wellman, 2011). The extended series of developmental achievements in infants', young children's, and older children's mental-state understanding fits a theory construction perspective that expects children to achieve a progression of intermediate understandings as initial conceptions fail to adequately explain behavior and thus get progressively revised in the face of increasing evidence. But regardless, such progressions provide crucial developmental data that help clarify several theoretical alternatives. I review them more fully in Chapter 5.

AUTISM AND CHILDHOOD DEAFNESS

Given claims for the importance of theory of mind in ordinary human social life and interaction, what would life be like for someone seriously deficient or different in theory of mind? The "theory-of-mind hypothesis for autism" argues that an individual with autism is a real-life example of such a someone. Many studies now show impairment in reasoning about mental states—for example, failures on false-belief tasks—in high-functioning individuals with autism (see Baron-Cohen, 1995). These sorts of deficits in psychological reasoning are not apparent in control groups of subjects with Down's syndrome, general intellectual impairment, or specific language delays. A theory-of-mind hypothesis about autism is probably not fully correct in any clear or comprehensive sense as an account of autism, but it has proven revealing and important. The hypothesis that individuals with autism are distinctively deficient in theory-of-mind understanding—indeed that such deficiencies are central to autistics' core difficulties in social relatedness—has not only shed important light on autism; but also, theory-of-mind research with individuals with autism has shed important light on theory of mind.

In particular, this research has helped address the question of whether theory of mind is domain specific, carving out a domain of specialized human social understanding, or rather the result of domain-general cognitions applied to the task of understanding persons. Conceivably, domain-general processes such as general competence at memory, attention, and language comprehension could fully account for theory-of-mind reasoning and development. Such factors are undoubtedly important; however, most scholars now believe that understanding of persons is advantaged or prepared by more specialized domain-specific processing as well.

In this regard, high-functioning autistics' performance on false photographs versus false beliefs has proved revealing (as has research on autistic's understanding of false drawings and false signs). False-belief tasks are outlined in Box 1.2; false-photograph tasks are comparable in format but target not mental representational devices but rather physical representational devices. For example, parallel to the task diagrammed at the top of Box 1.2, suppose the child sees a camera take a picture of the candy lying in the drawer, not in the cupboard. (The picture-taking process is shown to the child, but the picture itself is turned face down and never looked at.) The candy is then transferred to the cupboard, and the drawer and cupboard are closed. Then the child is asked, "In the picture, where is the candy?"; plus, "Really, where is the candy?"

High-functioning autistics consistently fail false-belief tasks yet consistently pass parallel false-photo tasks (Leekam & Perner, 1991; Leslie & Thaiss, 1992). Because these individuals' memory, attention, learning, and language comprehension are sufficient to understand false photos, such domain-general processing factors fail to account for their parallel difficulties with false beliefs. Data such as these lend support to more domain-specific accounts of psychological understandings.

Sometimes such data are taken to support claims for an innate theory-of-mind module (ToMM) and the related claim that autism represents a specific neurological impairment in just such a module. And indeed, to its credit, that sort of modular position first inspired research on theory of mind and autism (e.g., Baron-Cohen, Leslie, & Frith, 1985). To be clear, however, none of the research discussed so far requires that theory-of-mind reasoning reflects the working of an innate ToMM. Indeed, one implication of positing theory-of-mind modules is that individuals who are not impaired in the relevant modules—for example, are not autistic—should achieve mental-state understandings on a roughly standard maturational timetable. Yet, in many studies, deaf preschool children raised by hearing parents show delays and deficiencies on theory-of-mind tasks comparable to those of children with autism (Gale, deVilliers, deVilliers, & Pyers, 1996; Peterson & Siegal, 1995, 1999; see Peterson, 2009, for a review). These deaf children have not suffered the same sort of neurological damage that autistics have, whatever that might be, as evident by the fact that deaf children raised by deaf parents do not show theory-of-mind delays. Instead, the delays of deaf children raised in hearing families reflect impoverished language and communicative experiences in their early childhood.

Findings such as these, among others, challenge accounts of theory-of-mind development relying solely on modular-maturational mechanisms. Thus, although theory-of-mind investigations with individuals with autism undoubtedly inform us about some things, they potentially lead to confusions too. Autism is plagued not only by theory-of-mind impairments but by other cognitive impairments as well, including executive function and IQ deficits (Happé, 1995; South, Ozonoff, & McMahon, 2007). Thus, for individuals with autism, it is difficult to pinpoint differences due to theory-of-mind delays, tangled as they are with myriad other delays. Deaf individuals, to my mind, offer a better-matched comparison to typically developing children for considering theory-of-mind development amid delay. I focus on deaf children considerably more than individuals with autism in the rest of this book.

LATER DEVELOPMENTS

Children's understanding of mind and of persons continues to develop in important respects beyond the age of 5 or 6 years. Still older children develop increasingly reflective ideas about mental life, minds, brains, and more.

Children's understanding of thinking, for example, shows considerable development. As briefly noted earlier, even 3- and 4-year-olds know that persons experience internal, not-real, immaterial ideas and thoughts. Such young children know that thinking is an internal mental event that is different from seeing, talking, or touching an object and that the contents of one's thoughts (e.g., a thought about a dog) are not physical or tangible (e.g., Richert & Harris, 2006; Wellman & Estes, 1986). Relatedly, from 3 to 5 years of age, young children grasp something of the subjectivity, and thus diversity, of thoughts. In the diverse-desire item of the Theory-Of-Mind Scale described before (Wellman & Liu, 2004), 3-year-olds are able to state that whereas they themselves think Bill's dog is in the garage, Bill thinks it's in the yard.

However, such young children seem to have little or no understanding of the constant flow of ideas and thoughts experienced in everyday life and involved in actively, consciously thinking. For example, 7-year-olds and adults assert that a person sitting quietly with a blank expression is still experiencing "some thoughts and ideas" and that it is nearly impossible to have a mind completely "empty of thoughts and ideas"; but children 5 and younger do not share these intuitions (Flavell, Green, & Flavell, 1993, 1995, 1998). Preschool children have similar difficulties in reporting their *own* thoughts (Bauer, 2002; Flavell et al., 1995), and young children are surprisingly unaware that thoughts sometimes take the form of ongoing "inner speech" (Flavell, Green, Flavell, & Grossman, 1997).

John Flavell summarizes such findings by concluding that young children conceive of thoughts as essentially isolated mental happenings, rather than embedded in Jamesian streams of consciousness (James, 1890/1981). Only by 6 and 7 years do children become aware of "the chain-reaction-like flashings of whole sequences of thoughts, each cognitively cueing its successor" (Flavell et al., 1995, p. 85).

Relatedly, it is only beyond the preschool years that children develop a deepening appreciation of the mind itself versus the brain. To illustrate, researchers have asked children in preschool through high school whether they could perform various kinds of functions without a brain, and separately without a mind (Johnson & Wellman, 1982; Richert & Harris, 2006), functions such as mental acts (think, remember), perception (see, hear), feelings (feel interested, feel happy), and voluntary action (walk, talk). The youngest children respond identically when asked about the brain and the mind, and they conceive of the mind/brain as exclusively needed for purely mental acts. Thus, these younger children explain that they need the brain (and likewise the mind) to think or remember but argue they need only eyes (and not a brain/mind) to see, need only ears to hear, and need only legs to walk. Only later, by fifth grade or so, do children become generally aware that the brain is different from the mind; the brain is necessary for all functions, whereas the mind is more distinctly and exclusively necessary for mental acts; and brain and mind not only differ functionally they differ materially—although the mind is immaterial, the brain is material and solid.

One of the most intriguing sets of later developments, built on a preschool theory of mind but transcending it, concerns children's increasing willingness to entertain ideas of extraordinary minds and capacities. Arguably, increased appreciation of the mind as more mental versus the brain as more bodily is instrumental for forming and acquiring transcendental ideas, such as the possibility of mentality or spirit extending beyond bodily death or the possibility of supernatural agency in which mentality is freed from its ordinary constraints. One quick example illustrates some of these developments.

In an influential study, Justin Barrett and his colleagues (Barrett, Richert, & Driesenga, 2001) began to consider the development of children's ideas about the "otherness" of God. They demonstrated that as children come to appreciate the constraints of ordinary human knowledge and belief—for example, that people can have false beliefs—they recognized that God could have more extraordinary powers. For example, a standard measure of children's understanding of false belief was used, a surprising contents task (see Box 1.2), and children made inferences about God versus Mom. When preschool children recognized the limits of human knowledge (Mom would be mistaken), they often allowed a more "special" power to God, who would know the contents.

This finding, demonstrating children's belief in God's special mental power, has been extended and clarified in several ways (see Chapter 13). One interpretation I draw from these and other data about later progressions in children's theories of mind is that early preschool understandings provide the foundation for children's construction of later ideas, including their ponderings about mind and life. Early achievements support children's spontaneous questioning and ideas, but crucially also support children's receptivity to and assimilation of sociocultural teachings, doctrines, and ideas about God, superheroes, Santa, and more.

CONCLUSIONS

Theory of mind (a) is rapidly acquired in the normal case, (b) is acquired in an extended series of developmental accomplishments, (c) encompasses several basic insights that are acquired worldwide on a similar trajectory (but not timetable), (d) requires considerable learning and development based on an infant set of specialized abilities to attend to and represent persons, and (e) is severely delayed in both autism and in deaf children of hearing parents. Not all researchers would agree with all these points, but nonetheless this list represents an important consensus regarding theory of mind based on considerable empirical knowledge garnered from 25 years of research effort by developmental scientists across a range of disciplines and countries.

Several topics touched on in this overview are particularly rich in data or debate. They reveal more precisely how theory of mind develops. In the next chapters, I flesh out these rich data and the fascinating picture they provide regarding the development of a foundational human cognitive system. These data also set the stage for addressing deeper accounts about the nature of theory of mind and how it is acquired.

2

Preschool Theory of Mind, Part 1

UNIVERSAL BELIEF-DESIRE UNDERSTANDING

"MOVIES SHOULD HAVE a beginning, middle, and an end," French filmmaker Jean-Luc Godard was told, to which he famously replied, "Certainly; but not necessarily in that order" (Corliss, 1981). A story or chronology that starts in the middle can clarify, up front, some critical way station that serves both as the destination for earlier events and as the departure point for later ones. For theory of mind, preschool belief-desire understanding provides that point, both a capstone for earlier developments and the foundation for still further, later developing, conceptual insights; hard-won achievements that are also launch pads.

BELIEF-DESIRE PSYCHOLOGY

Child (age 3 years-7 months) tastes some glue.
CHILD: I don't like it.
ADULT: Why would you put that in your mouth?
CHILD: I thought that was good.
(Bartsch & Wellman, 1995, p. 112)

To reiterate, central to our everyday theory of mind is a construal of persons in terms of beliefs and desires yielding the key idea that people do things that they think will get them what they want—"I thought that was good." Naïve psychology is, of course, more comprehensive and complex than that. In a bit more detail, theory-of-mind reasoning, for preschoolers, encompasses at least the constructs and connections shown in Figure 2.1. Basic emotions and physiological states fuel one's desires; perceptual and evidential experiences ground one's beliefs and knowledge; actions not only occur, they result in outcomes to which the actor has additional reactions. Because Romeo *loves* Juliet he *wants* to be with her. Because he's *seen* his clan's conflict with the Capulets, he *knows* his family will violently object. So he proceeds in secret. When he is successful and can be with her, he is *happy* (indeed "lovestruck" and ecstatic). When unsuccessful and they are apart, he is *sad* (indeed starkly disappointed and crestfallen).

This everyday belief-desire psychology of action is a complex web of constructs and inferences, with a variety of interwoven interpretive, predictive, and explanatory resources. This is true even for preschoolers. Nonetheless it makes sense to begin by emphasizing children's understanding of beliefs and desires. Beliefs along with desires are central to understanding actions and minds; and one reason for this centrality is that beliefs and desires, in particular, are different from the world (they're *mental* states) yet at the same time connect our action to the world. In contrast, mental states, like fanciful imaginings and dreams, are more ethereal, standing apart from the world. Although the hallmark of beliefs (their job description) is that they aim to describe the world accurately, they can be wrong and fail at their job. Pure imagination cannot be wrong in this sense. It can be fanciful or mundane, bizarre or familiar, but not right or wrong because imaginings, unlike beliefs, are fictional not worldly.

So, among various mental states, ones like beliefs are particularly useful for reasoning about action, because, although mental, they are nonetheless distinctly directed at

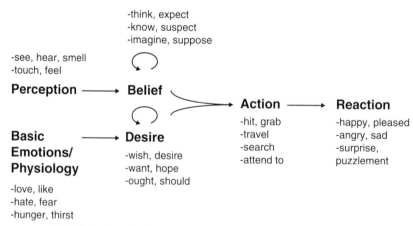

FIGURE 2.1 Simplified scheme for depicting belief-desire reasoning. Centrally, we see people as engaging in *acts* that they *believe* will get them what they *desire*. But also, basic emotions and physiological states fuel one's desires; perceptual and evidential experiences ground one's beliefs and knowledge; actions not only occur, they result in outcomes to which the actor has reactions. (From Wellman, 1990)

the world as well. Yet young children could certainly be ignorant of or confused about these useful states. Because they are both of the mind but about the world, are they to be understood in terms of the mind or in terms of the world, or (somehow) in terms of both?

BELIEFS AND FALSE BELIEFS

Belief-desire psychology is often claimed to reflect a representational theory of mind. The crude depiction of someone's belief (that that is an apple), sketched at the left of Figure 2.2, shows why. In our everyday adult conception, beliefs provide the believer with something like a representation of the world. Fanciful imaginings, like beliefs, can be representational in one sense—imagining a unicorn provides a representation of such a thing—but, critically, the representation is not meant to be a representation *of the world*. When we believe that X is so, that is what frames our acts to get what we want—we really believe it, not just engage in it as a fantasy. Shown on the right side of Figure 2.2 is a depiction of mental misrepresentation—he thinks the apple is a banana. Because of beliefs' connection to the world, in cases like this—false beliefs—we not only think wrongly, we act mistakenly, often thwarting our own desires. Romeo kills himself, mourning for Juliet, while in reality she is right there beside him, alive.

Because beliefs are nicely instructive in these ways, and because they are (along with desires) central to our everyday psychology, there is now an immense amount of research on beliefs, and especially false beliefs, to help us understand children's ideas.

Recall an example preschool false-belief task, a changed-locations task (Box 1.2 in Chapter 1): Judy puts her candy in the drawer and while she can't see, the candy gets switched to the cupboard. Judy comes back and wants her candy. "Where will Judy look for her candy, the cupboard or the drawer?" Typically the child is also asked various control questions such as, "Did Judy see the candy moved?" (correct answer: no); "Where is the candy really?" (correct answer: in the cupboard). Correct answers—saying that Judy will look in the drawer—require reasoning about desires but also, critically, beliefs: Judy *wants* her candy, and she *thinks* it is in the drawer. Correct answers

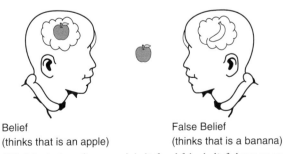

Belief
(thinks that is an apple)

False Belief
(thinks that is a banana)

FIGURE 2.2 Simplified depiction of someone's belief and false belief about an apple.

also show an understanding of the connection from mind to world; because Judy has a mistaken belief, she engages in mistaken actions. Indeed, such false-belief tasks probe a causal-explanatory framework, a framework that connects mind and world in *two* directions: from mind to world (e.g., via intentional actions) and from world to mind (e.g., via perception).

Beliefs, and false beliefs, come in many forms. So do "standard" false-belief tasks used in research with children. For now, I'll call these tasks explicit false belief tasks (to distinguish them from the possibly implicit understanding that may be being tapped by infant "false-belief" tasks, of the sort I discuss more fully in Chapter 8). This may not be the best way to make the infant–preschool distinction, but it is a useful shorthand. At the least, tasks such as the one in Box 1.2 require aware, thoughtful judgments to yield consistently correct answers. On a variety of such tasks, children of about 4½ years and older often succeed at explicit false belief judgments, whereas children younger than 3½ or so often fail, as graphed in Box 1.2. In failing, young children do not just answer randomly: They make a consistent false-belief error. They say Judy will look in the drawer, where it really is—even though she never saw the candy moved.

Despite the great many false-belief studies, findings, and task variations (including studies with contradictory interpretations and even at times contradictory findings), there is a consistent story that emerges clearly in meta-analyses that statistically sum up data and findings from numerous individual studies. The data in Box 1.2 come in part from an initial meta-analysis (Wellman et al., 2001) that included almost 200 studies encompassing almost 600 false-belief conditions and task variations and more than 5,000 children. (Conditions are groups within a study. If a study gave the same task to a group of 3-year-olds, a group of 4-year-olds, and a group of 5-year-olds, that would be three conditions.) The explicit false-belief tasks used across these studies were indeed quite varied: Some were about changed locations, some about surprising contents, some about still other things; some were verbal and some nonverbal; they asked children to judge behavior (Where will Judy look?) or thoughts (What does Judy think?), to judge real live humans, videotaped humans, toy figurines, or story characters.

The key findings from that initial meta-analysis are shown in Box 1.2, which shows a plot of proportions correct from all conditions arrayed against mean age of the children in a condition. The data present the percentage of children in a group (a condition) that answer correctly, with chance performance of 50% correct (because almost all studies use two potential locations or two potential identities) yielding a score of 0 in the data for Box 1.2. Notice the data are essentially orderly; early childhood competence becomes clear by about 4 and 5 years when children are largely correct, that is, they are above chance on a vast array of false-belief tasks and situations. Going backward in age from there, children become incorrect; and going backward to 2 and 3 years, there is clear below-chance performance, with consistent false-belief errors.

Of course there are differences across individuals (not shown) and across groups (partly shown) and across tasks (not shown). This variation is informative. To begin with, it addresses an ever-present concern: perhaps the specifics of these tasks (their language, the props, the "stories" involved) confuse or misdirect young children (children who actually know very well and robustly about false beliefs—but because of task peculiarities perform erroneously instead). Any experimental task must use specific materials, language, and questions, thereby instituting particular task demands. Perhaps different materials and methods yield a very different picture.

Part of the point of the initial meta-analysis was to address this crucial issue, the influence of various task modifications and simplifications on standard false-belief performance. For example, variations on a changed-location task can be more or less verbal or language laden. To reduce verbal demands, researchers can just depict the events and dramatically show, without words, that the protagonist does not see the crucial change of location. Then children can simply be asked about behavior (Where will Judy look?) without any use of terms like *think* or *know*. And the child can make his or her judgment by pointing—to the cupboard or to the drawer.

In meta-analyses, most of the many task variations investigators have tried make no reliable difference to performance (e.g., Wellman et al., 2001; but also Liu et al., 2008, and Milligan et al., 2007). They may have appeared as significant in one study or another, but rigorously aggregated across studies, a great variety of task variations have no consistent effect. For example, it makes no overall difference whether the main character is a real person, a picture of a person, a puppet, or a doll; whether the false-belief question asks about behavior ("Where will Judy look?"), thoughts ("Where will Judy think her X is?"), or speech ("Where will Judy say her X is?"); or whether children are tested verbally or less verbally. Just as in Box 1.2, performance on all these variations goes from below chance to systematically above chance over time in the preschool years.

Here is one intriguing and important example: What if the child is asked about her or his *own* false beliefs? For example, consider a surprising-contents task of the sort briefly described in Box 1.2: A child sees a typical crayon box, states it has crayons inside, but sees (when it is opened) that there are candles inside instead. Note, in this sort of task the child first experiences the false belief. Then the child is told of someone else who has never looked inside the box: "We'll show Punch this box all closed up; what will Punch think is in there, crayons or candles?" This version of the task asks about someone else's belief, Punch's. So, now consider a parallel task where we ask about the beliefs of the child instead. Again, the child first experiences a false belief—when shown the closed up box says, "I think it has crayons," and then finds, "Hey, there's candles in here." Then the child is asked not about Punch but about herself or himself: "Before you looked inside what did you think was in here, crayons or candles?"

Asking about self or other yields virtually identical results. Young children are equally below chance for themselves as for others, and increases in correctness over the preschool years go hand in hand for both self and other (Wellman et al., 2001). This is, of course, not only methodologically interesting—a strong example where changing the task demands fails to reveal some hypothetical "early competence" otherwise masked in other false-belief tasks. It is also substantively intriguing—children (and adults) can often be strikingly unable to understand their own beliefs (and false beliefs). To see this in action is sometimes remarkable.

ADULT: What do you think is in here?

CHILD: Smarties! (Candies)

ADULT: Let's open it up and look inside.

CHILD: Oh...holy moly...pencils!

ADULT: When you first saw the box, before we opened it, what did you think was inside it?

CHILD: Pencils.

(Astington & Gopnik, 1988b, p. 195)

Some task variables do affect performance; these variations do make performance on standard, preschool, false-belief tasks easier. But crucially, the results look like the stacked-up, parallel lines shown in Box 1.2. That is, on some explicit tasks children can answer correctly at a somewhat earlier age than they do on a different false-belief task, but in each case the essential developmental trajectory remains unchanged: Children go from worse to better in parallel fashions *and* performance of the very youngest children remains at or below chance. That is, although the task variables affect performance, they do so without interacting with age.

In short, children's conceptions of beliefs change importantly in the preschool years. Young children go from consistent error to consistently correct across all task variations. Even the simplest, most child-friendly tasks that require some sort of explicit answer on the part of the child (even a nonverbal point) show this basic developmental trajectory. Even totally nonverbal tasks do so (Call & Tomasello, 1999; Krachun, Carpenter, Call, & Tomasello, 2009); even reporting on one's own beliefs does so.

Countries and Cultures

A focus on false-belief research in preschoolers allows initial consideration of whether and how basic theory-of-mind acquisitions are universal or culture specific because such false-belief studies have been conducted in a great many different countries. As shown in Box 1.2, explicitly coming to understand beliefs and false beliefs looks like something young children achieve everywhere. In every country studied there is an informative (similar) developmental trajectory in which children become significantly correct after an initial phase of early consistent failures where they say Judy will look where the target object really is and think that is where it is.

However, the original meta-analysis (Wellman et al., 2001) was decidedly skewed toward children growing up in western-European style communities—the United States, England, Austria, Australia—and speaking an Indo-European language

(English, German, Spanish). Of the almost 200 studies in that meta-analysis, only one article came from China, only two from Japan, and only one from Africa.

Further examination of children from Chinese communities and languages has proved particularly revealing. Chinese children, of course, grow up in non-Western families, and Chinese languages are certainly not Indo-European. More than half of the world's children live in East Asia, with the largest number of those being Chinese. If we want to know about the nature of theory of mind, including Chinese children seems essential. Fortunately, in the years after that initial meta-analysis, researchers conducted numerous studies in China and many of these included one or more false-belief tasks. Headed by David Liu, therefore, we conducted an additional meta-analysis (Liu et al., 2008), one concentrated on Chinese children and encompassing 196 false-belief conditions from Hong Kong and mainland China.

Figure 2.3 shows the Chinese data along with that from the United States and Canada. It is clear in Figure 2.3, just as in the original meta-analysis, that country, or sociolinguistic community, does influence children's performance. In some locales, children (on average) come to false-belief understanding earlier or later in comparison to their peers in other locales. Yet again, the basic developmental trajectory is the same everywhere: In all locales, children go from below-chance performance (consistently judging the character will look where it really is) to above-chance performance (consistently judging the character will look, and think, mistakenly).

The exact pattern of results in Figure 2.3 is also intriguing, and perplexing. Children growing up in Hong Kong and in Canada are very likely to be bilingual in comparison to those in the United States and Beijing. On average, being bilingual helps children to advance more quickly in theory-of-mind insight, including false-belief understanding (e.g., Goetz, 2003). But that is not, in any simple or direct way, what is accounting for these results. Hong Kong children, who in these data are most likely to be fluently bilingual, are certainly not acquiring false-belief understanding most quickly. Children in the United States and Canada grow up in western-European cultures where autonomous, independent, individualized persons and selves are "authorized" and emphasized; Chinese children grow up in cultures where interdependent, socially embedded, communal persons and selves are authorized and emphasized (Nisbett, 2003). This surely impacts what they come to understand about persons and actions (as I show in Chapter 5). Similarly, Chinese languages (Mandarin and Cantonese) differ from English in several intriguing ways (as I address further in Chapter 7). But these factors do not, simply or clearly, account for our results: U.S. and Beijing children are on almost equal trajectories for understanding false belief; Chinese Beijing children differ from those in Hong Kong.

Amid differences in timing of the sort that are clear in Figure 2.3 and Box 1.2, an underlying picture clearly emerges: Everywhere, typically developing young children achieve a key theory-of-mind milestone, namely, the sort of belief-desire understanding assessed in a wide range of false-belief tasks. Of course, the message from these data is

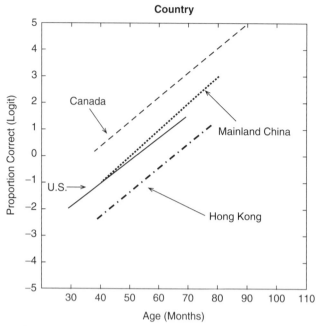

FIGURE 2.3 Developmental trajectories for performing correctly on explicit false-belief tasks.
Zero is at chance in this scoring; negative numbers are significantly below chance; positive numbers
are significantly correct. (From Liu, Wellman, Tardiff, & Sabbagh, 2008)

not that culture and language fail to shape children's ideas about mind—that somehow
basic preschool theory of mind is a culture-free product of "spontaneous" human cognition. This is clearly incorrect, as will become increasingly clear. Yet these data clarify that
culturally transmitted and culturally received information about persons and minds,
indeed cultural learning itself, honors, in early development, some foundational understanding of persons and minds framed by a deeply mentalistic construal of persons, lives,
and actions. Theory-of-mind findings, at their best, reveal some of this universal foundational human cognition at work as it dynamically develops. They reveal some of the bedrock on which the shifting sands of culture-specific developments rest. Such conclusions
are clearest in the preschool years because that is where the data are so international;
research with infants or children with autism, say, is much more constrained to one or
two cultural settings.

True Beliefs, Consistency, and Variability

When young children are consistently incorrect on explicit false-belief judgments, they
are often nonetheless correct on true-belief tasks. True-belief tasks, for example, have
Judy put her candy in the drawer (not the cupboard) and go away. While she is away
and can't see, someone takes her candy out of the drawer but *puts it back* in the exact

same drawer. Children correctly answer Judy will look in the drawer and Judy will think her candy is in the drawer, not the cupboard. In some other research by David Liu and colleagues (Liu, Sabbagh, Gehring, & Wellman, 2009), children were given 20 to 30 false-belief tasks and children who were consistently incorrect at false belief (less than 25% correct) were nonetheless consistently correct at true belief (greater than 90%). In research by Jennifer Amsterlaw and me (Amsterlaw & Wellman, 2006), children who were consistently incorrect at false-belief judgments (over a series of tasks, two per day or four per week, for 6 weeks) were nonetheless correct on 93% of their true-belief tasks over the same period.

These true-belief data are reassuring in showing that, at the least, on the parallel false-belief task children are not just being led to change their answers because of any old manipulation of the props and contents. Of course, it is also possible to make true-belief tasks complicated, with transformations that can fool children into failing as well (see Friedman, Griffin, Brownell, & Winner, 2003; Ruffman, 1996). And even correct true-belief responses may convey only that children are thinking about and reporting reality—where Judy's candy really is—not commenting on her thinking.

A crucial but nonobvious feature of the false-belief data is that individual children are typically both consistent and at the same time variable in their responses to false-belief tasks. In one study that gave 72 4-year-olds six false-belief tasks (each with varied contents, characters, and props), 31% were correct on five or six of the tasks; 56% were *incorrect* on five or six; and only 9 children (13%) were in the middle showing a more mixed pattern (Watson, 1999). In the still more intensive study mentioned earlier by David Liu, Mark Sabbagh, and colleagues (2009), 44 older preschoolers were given from 20 to 30 false-belief tasks (in a computer administered format). Of these children, 64% were consistently correct (got greater than 75% correct) on false-belief judgments; 30% were consistently incorrect (got less than 25% correct); and only 3 children (7% of the sample) were in the middle. This sort of consistent responding argues against the suspicion that asking multiple questions simply tires or confuses young children or prompts them to think they should change their prior response (thereby hovering confusedly around chance responding—about 50%) and further confirms that children are evidencing systematic, wrong conceptions in standard false-belief tasks.

That said, these very same data evidence important variability in any one child's responding. In both the studies just described almost *all* children evidenced some mix of two differing responses: realism responses (Judy will search where it really is) and false-belief responses (Judy will mistakenly search where it used to be).

Variability in children's answers is orderly, organized around some central tendencies, just as individual children's trajectories vary around the central trajectories depicted in Box 1.2 and Figure 2.3. The orderly central tendencies are important. But (orderly) intrachild variability is also important. This sort of variability turns out to be useful for understanding children's learning and development, as I return to in Chapter 6.

EXPLANATIONS

Although an initial focus on standard false-belief tasks is informative, it fails to reveal the nature, breadth, and coherence of preschoolers' emerging belief-desire psychology. A good place to begin to take up a fuller view is to consider children's explanations. By some accounts (e.g., theory theory, the theory that everyday belief-desire psychology constitutes a causal-explanatory theory), explaining persons' actions, lives, and minds is one of the central tasks of naïve psychology. That is, one of the prime functions of everyday belief-desire psychology is to make sense of human actions and minds, to fill in the "becauses" of human life, to answer the everyday "why" questions about what we are doing (Apperly & Butterfill, 2009; Davidson, 1980; Wellman, 1990). Why did Romeo kill himself? Because he thought Juliet was dead (because he saw her inert, unbreathing beside him) and—believing her dead—life had no more joy for him, so he desired to die himself. Such explanations give the reasons for our actions and states. Such explanations can appear simple—"he thought Juliet was dead"—but invoke complex causal structure: Perceptions influence beliefs, which together with desires lead to intentions that shape actions (as schematized in Figure 2.1; see also Malle, Knobe, & Nelson, 2007).

Empirical Importance and Frequency of Explanations in Childhood

Young children prove to be quite interested in explanation. They frequently seek and provide explanations, especially psychological explanations of the sort implied by theory of mind.

For example, Maureen Callanan and Lisa Oakes (1992) had mothers of preschoolers keep diary records of children's causal questions (e.g., "Why?"; "How come?") during everyday activities, such as mealtime. Children asked numerous causal questions about a variety of events including mechanical phenomena ("How does that wheelchair work?") and natural phenomena ("Why do stars twinkle?"). However, by far the largest number of children's questions focused on the causes of human activity—requesting explanations for people's motivations and behaviors (e.g., "Why did he do that?").

Of course, diary records can be more a reflection of parents' concerns than their children's. So, Anne Hickling and I (Hickling & Wellman, 2001) examined extended transcripts of everyday conversations for children's naturally occurring causal questions and explanations using explicit causal terms such as *why, because, how,* and *so.* These analyses began with more than 120,000 child utterances from the CHILDES database (MacWhinney & Snow, 1985, 1990) recorded for children in everyday parent–child conversation, week by week or month by month, as the individual children grew from 2 to 5 years of age. On average, causal questions appeared as early as there were recorded transcripts, with *why*-questions being some of the earliest causal utterances that children produced. Indeed, causal questions appeared earlier than causal statements (mean age at earliest appearance = 2;5 [years;months] vs. 2;8), and thus were produced more frequently than causal statements at age 2½ years (65% questions vs. 35% statements). These conversational data provide systematic, empirical support for the commonplace, anecdotal observation that there is an early period during which young children engage in intense explanation seeking, especially through use of *why*-questions.

Consistent with the findings of Callanan and Oakes (1992), the children in our study (Hickling & Wellman, 2001) requested explanations of human activities—why a person did something—in approximately 70% of their causal questions as 2-, 3-, and 4-year-olds. Explanations for physical-object events (20%), for events focusing on animals (5%), or for a variety of other entities such as plants or natural phenomenon like clouds (5%) were also requested, although less frequently. Young children thus actively seek explanations, and central to this early explanatory fascination is a curiosity about how to explain the activities of human beings (see also Hood & Bloom, 1979).

But do such data convincingly reveal young children to be active explanation seekers? Perhaps not: parents and teachers often suspect that all those *whys* might just be produced to get attention, gambits to keep the conversation going, to put off bedtime. Alternatively, perhaps children are asking questions, including *why*-questions, just as part of some process of language acquisition. Much research on young children's questions (e.g., Rowland, Pine, Lieven, & Theakston, 2003; Tyack & Ingram, 1977) tackles the language and language learning of children's questions in these early years; that may be what children are tackling as well—acquiring and practicing how to make grammatically well-formed questions.

Question–answer exchanges include (a) asking a question (e.g., why?); (b) getting a response (e.g., explanation); and (c) evaluating, processing, and potentially learning from the answer. The way in which children evaluate, process, and react to the responses they receive sheds key light on the nature of their questions to begin with. Assume even young children want (on average) an explanation when they ask *why*-questions. If so, getting an explanation in response to their questions should be more satisfying than getting nonexplanatory responses and answers. More specifically, if children get a nonexplanatory response (vs. an explanation), their relative dissatisfaction could be revealed in disagreeing, re-asking the original question, or providing their own explanation instead. If children get an explanatory response, their satisfaction could be revealed in agreeing or following up with a comment or question that incorporates that answer. Indeed, in further careful analyses of everyday conversations with their parents, 2-, 3-, and 4-year-olds reacted in just these fashions (Frazier, Gelman, & Wellman, 2009), evidencing relative satisfaction with explanatory responses to their *why*- and *how*-questions and dissatisfaction if parents attempted to foist off nonexplanations instead.

In these everyday conversations, however, parents' explanatory responses proved somewhat longer than their nonexplanations, so maybe children just prefer extended conversation rather than explanation after all. Fortunately, these processes can be brought into the lab for more experimental control. In an experimental setup, Brandy Frazier, Susan Gelman, and I (2009) had preschool children interact with an adult around a variety of items—toys, pictures, books, videos—some of which were designed to be "odd," that is, to provoke *why*-questions. For example, the child would see someone turn a light switch off with her foot; the child would be provided with paper and crayons for drawing and on opening the crayon box find all orange crayons. These items successfully elicited many *why*-questions (e.g., "Why are they all orange?"), and in response the adult provided carefully scripted responses (all equally long), half providing explanations ("It was a mistake at the crayon factory") and half nonexplanations ("You are right, all of them are orange"). Again, young preschoolers were typically satisfied with explanatory responses to their questions and in stark contrast dissatisfied with nonexplanations (often asking their questions again, frowning, and offering their own explanations instead).

Explaining Actions

Young children not only seek explanations, they provide them. When children provide explanations, they, like adults, include two parts: the topic or entity to be explained and the explanation itself. With regard to topic, in the Hickling and Wellman (2001) research, 81% of children's explanations in their everyday conversations explained the actions, movements, and states of themselves and others. So, just as in their requests for explanation, the focal entities for children's own explanations were largely people. This explanatory emphasis on persons has been confirmed in other research as well (Dunn & Brown, 1993; Hood & Bloom, 1979). For example, Judy Dunn and Jane Brown (1993) recorded 2-hour samples of conversations from 50 3-year-olds and their parents and found that explanations for human action and states constituted the vast majority of children's explanations. This is another way in which preschoolers' belief-desire understanding is explicit.

Conversational data such as these are complemented by experimental studies designed to elicit children's explanations (e.g., Inagaki & Hatano, 1993, 2002; Lagattuta, Wellman, & Flavell, 1997; Schult & Wellman, 1997). As one example, Carolyn Schult and I (Schult & Wellman, 1997) solicited explanations from 3- and 4-year-olds for a variety of human actions and movements: *intended actions* (a person wants to do something and does what they want), *mistaken actions* (a person wants to do something but mistakenly does something else), *physically caused actions* (a person's movement is caused by the wind, gravity, or some other physical force), and *biologically caused actions* (a person's movement is caused by a biological mechanism, such as fever, fatigue). To illustrate, for one mistaken action, children saw pictures of Alice who wanted chocolate syrup on her ice cream, reached into the fridge, pulled out a squeeze bottle and squeezed ketchup on her ice cream. Then they were asked, "Why did she do that?" For one physically caused action, they saw pictures of Billy who was standing on a stool and wanted to step off and stay suspended in air "floating above the ground." Billy stepped off and came right down to the ground. Then they were asked, "Why did he do that?" Children's responses were coded for psychological explanations (e.g., "She didn't know," "He wanted to try something different") as well as for physical ("He's too heavy," "Not a balloon") and biological explanations.

Consider just psychological versus physical phenomena and explanations. Nearly 100% of children's explanations for intended actions were psychological ("He wanted to"), even for 3-year-olds. Moreover 88% of 3-year-olds' explanations (and 93% of 4-year-olds' explanations) for mistaken actions were also psychological explanations (e.g., "She didn't know"). In contrast, preschoolers provided physical explanations almost exclusively for physically caused human movements. Note that both for mistakes and for physically caused acts, the target character wanted to do something, but in fact did something else instead (put ketchup on her ice cream, came down to the ground). Yet children's explanations differentiated between those two occurrences. For mistakes, their explanations referred to psychological constructs such as beliefs, desires, and so on. For physically caused actions, their explanations referred to physical constructs such as contact, solidity, gravity, and so forth. Kayoko Inagaki and Giyoo Hatano (1993, 2002) have also shown that preschool children provide psychological explanations for voluntary, but not involuntary, behavior (as Malle et al., 2007, show is true for adults as well).

Explaining Mental States

It is easy to think of belief-desire psychology as focused on the prediction—and explanation—of action. Recall David Premack and Guy Woodruff's (1978) early description: "The system [of mental states] can be used to make predictions of others' actions" (p. 515). But a focus on action alone is misleading, as the phenomena to be explained by folk psychology are considerably broader than that. As outlined in Figure 2.1, we explain people's beliefs (e.g., by appeal to their perceptions or inferences), we explain their desires (e.g., by appeal to their deep-seated fears and preferences), and we appeal to beliefs and desires to explain a person's other mental states, such as their emotions. To illustrate, "Why is Romeo so *sad*?" "Because he *wanted* to meet with Juliet but couldn't." So, psychological explanations go beyond actions to explain a person's mental states and, further, to provide explanations for a person's individuated life experiences. Explanations of emotions provide one particularly revealing window onto these facets of young children's belief-desire psychology.

In initial studies, researchers asked preschoolers, as well as older children and adults, to explain actors' emotional reactions (happy, sad, surprised, curious) in a variety of situations. For example, in early research by Mita Banerjee and me (Wellman & Banerjee, 1991), preschoolers heard "Jane was at preschool and got apple juice for snack. She was very happy. Why was Jane so happy?" Or, "Jeff visited his grandma and when he got to her house he saw that it was purple. He was very surprised. Why was Jeff so surprised?" Because scenarios such as these feature an obvious, external eliciting situation (the juice for snack, the purple house), not surprisingly some (about one third) of 3- and 4-year-olds' responses explained characters' emotions as resulting from an objective feature of the situation (e.g., "She's happy because they have juice"; "He's surprised because it's purple"). More frequently, however, preschoolers, like adults, explained emotions by referring to the person's other mental states—his or her relevant desires or beliefs (e.g., "She's happy because she wanted apple juice"). These psychological explanations were appropriately discriminate. That is, preschoolers typically explained happiness and sadness in relation to the person's desires, but they more frequently explained surprise and curiosity in terms of a person's beliefs (e.g., "He's surprised because he didn't think it would be purple"). (See also Hadwin & Perner, 1991; Ruffman & Keenan, 1996).

At their best, explanations not only attempt to identify the proximal cause of some event that has occurred; they attempt to make that occurrence sensible by reference to a larger framework. And indeed, at their best, young children's explanations of persons' emotional states provide revealing evidence for their larger framework of connected, coherent understanding of minds and lives. This sort of evidence helps underwrite referring to their knowledge as theory like, as manifesting a larger coherent web of terms, constructs, and connections. Kristin Lagattuta and I (Lagattuta & Wellman, 2001) provided data of this sort by having children explain scenarios such as the following:

> One day Anne goes to the circus with her favorite baby doll. When Anne is talking to Bozo the clown, Bozo accidentally steps on the doll and breaks it. Anne feels sad. Well, many days later Anne is at her friend, Jane's, birthday party. It is time for the party show. Anne sees Bozo the clown dance into the room. She starts to feel sad. *Why does Anne start to feel sad right now?"*

Across multiple studies, young children revealed impressive competence in explaining such emotions in relation to historical (past experience) and mental (thinking) causes. Nearly all 4- through 6-year-olds explained the person's emotions as caused by *thinking about the past* at least at times—"Anne's sad because she's thinking about her doll breaking." Between 3 and 6 years, preschoolers became increasingly consistent in producing such historical-mental explanations. Often older children provided still more precise explanations that we called *cognitive cuing explanations* (e.g., "Anne's sad because the clown *makes her think* about her broken doll"). Note that these explanations not only refer to thinking about the past but further explain that the thoughts about the past were caused by a reminder in the present scene. By 5 and 6 years, the large majority of explanations were cognitive cuing ones.

In several crucial ways these explanations reveal that in reasoning backward from effects to causes, young children's explanations also appeal to larger coherent systems of constructs and causes. First, young children connected together several different kinds of mental states and experiences into a single explanation (e.g., *thoughts* about a *past experience* triggered a *current experience* of feeling *sad*). Moreover, these explanations revealed a crucial understanding that a person's mental states and experiences cohere in an individual-specific, life-historical way. That is, young children summed together episodes and mental states, over the focal person's experiences, to create an explanation for *that* individual's reactions. In contrast, children consistently predicted that Anne's friend Jane, who had not had the prior negative experience, would feel happy instead of sad at the birthday party. (See also Lagattuta, 2007, 2008.)

MENTAL ENTITIES

Other topics, intriguing in their own right, further reveal the nature, coherence, and the everyday impact of preschoolers' emerging theory of mind. Children's conceptions of mental entities provide an important case in point. Mental states, like beliefs and desires, provide causes and reasons for action. Yet the mental world includes not only mental causes and reasons but also mental entities—mental "things." What do children know about mental entities, and in particular, how mental entities differ from physical entities? Jean Piaget made clear just what an interesting question this is.

Historically, research interest in children's understanding of mind goes back (at least) as far as Piaget's early writings (Piaget, 1929/1967). Piaget focused on both of the aspects of an understanding of mind just outlined: the use of psychological reasoning to explain human actions (e.g., how intentions and desires cause and explain human acts) and an understanding of the nature of mental entities (e.g., thoughts, dreams). However, he focused most on mental entities.

Piaget cogently argued that mental entities, because they are insubstantial and nonobvious, immaterial things, quite unlike everyday physical things, were devilishly confusing for young children. In particular, Piaget claimed that young children, preschoolers, were "realists" who think of mental entities as tangible, physical ones—for example, they believe that dreams represent real, physical entities (or at the very least objective pictures in public view); they believe that thinking is literally overt speech (with thoughts akin to the voice and not just in terms of uttered words but also in the sense of puffs of air emitted from the mouth).

> Childhood realism is characterized by two confusions, quite distinct from each other though mutually contributory. First, there is the confusion between thought and the body; thought for the child is an activity of the organism—the voice—it is thus a thing among things and its essential characteristic is material action.... Secondly, there is confusion between the sign and the thing signified, the thought and the thing thought of. From this point of view the child cannot distinguish a real house, for example, from the concept or mental image or name of the house. (Piaget, 1929/1967, p. 55)

To read Piaget is to confront a coherent and seductive vision of development: Naïve, adult psychophysical dualism—understanding of the subjective, mental world as contrasting with the objective, physical world—only develops in middle childhood (beginning around 7 or 8 years) after an initial period of profound a-dualistic confusion. Because ideas, dreams, and mental images are complex, subjective, private, seemingly abstract entities and experiences, not surprisingly young children thoroughly misunderstand them.

Piaget came to his conclusions by analyzing children's responses to open-ended questions such as "What is thinking?" and "What are dreams?" Contemporary researchers have more carefully probed children's understanding by systematically examining their judgments and explanations of carefully contrasting alternatives. In doing so, it is now clear that no matter how persuasive Piaget's vision, it is deeply misleading. Focally, children's understandings of thoughts, as a key example, show us a very clear and different picture.

Remember from the Chapter 1 that if 3-, 4-, and 5-year-old children are told about one person who has a dog in contrast with another person who is thinking about a dog, and then asked to judge which "dog" can be seen with one's eyes, which can be touched, and which can be petted, even 3-year-olds correctly make these judgments (Harris, Brown, Marriott, Whittall, & Harmer, 1991; Harris, Pasquini, Duke, Asscher, & Pons, 2006; Taylor, Cartwright, & Carlson, 1993; Wellman & Estes, 1986; Wellman et al., 1996). Young children judge that standard physical objects (e.g., a dog) are material (can be touched), externally perceptible (can be seen with the eyes), and public (can be seen by someone else); whereas mental entities (e.g., a thought about a dog) are immaterial, not externally perceivable, and private. Ordinary physical entities have certain objective, behavioral-sensory properties that ordinary mental entities do not.

How far does this go? Consider children's response that a thought-of dog (or equally a dream dog) can*not* be seen, touched, or petted, whereas a dog can. Of course, a dog that has run away (and so is physically absent) also cannot be seen or touched, but nonetheless is physically real. And a person's gall bladder cannot be seen or touched (ordinarily), and furthermore it is internal and hence "private," but it too is nonetheless a physical thing, rather than a mental thing. Is it that young children just see ideas and thoughts as physical (yet "absent") in the way that an object gone away, or an object hidden inside a container, is physical yet imperceptible? Or, perhaps young children hold still other subtle realist misconceptions. For example, ideas and dreams might indeed be conceived of as physical things but as special, insubstantial types of physical things, perhaps like smoke, or shadows, or air. Piaget (1929/1967), in fact, quotes older preschoolers as saying that thoughts are smoke, air, shadows, lights, and external pictures seen with the eyes.

David Estes, Jacqui Woolley, and I (Estes, Wellman, & Woolley, 1989) initially examined these issues by having 3-, 4-, and 5-year-old children consider mental entities, corresponding physical objects, *absent* physical objects, and such real but intangible things as sounds, smoke, air, and shadows. Children made judgments of whether the various entities could be touched, or seen with the eyes, and so on; but further, critically, they were asked to explain their answers. Again explanations proved especially revealing. In their judgments, the children said (appropriately) that mental entities could not be seen or touched but also said (appropriately) that absent objects could not be seen or touched, that air could not be seen or touched, and so on. However, they explained these judgments very differently in the different cases. These young children explained that mental items cannot be touched in part because of their peculiar *reality status*; "It's not real"; "It's not really anything." In contrast, physical items, even insubstantial physical things, like smoke, were nonetheless explained as real. In addition and essentially, young children explained that mental entities cannot be touched because of their *mental identity*—"just a dream," "only pretend," "only in his mind." In contrast, absent, not-possessed real objects cannot be touched because they are gone away, they are not there. That is, they have a distinctive status in terms of *location-possession*, not in terms of mental identity.

Young children's understanding of the peculiarly mental status of mental entities has been confirmed and elaborated in other studies. For example, as in the preceding quotes, children often say mental entities cannot be touched, or are not real, and if asked to explain may comment that this is because they are "inside," only in a person's "head" or "mind." But consider the case of a real physical object that is absent because it is inside a person—such as a swallowed raisin now in the stomach. Could young children (à la Piaget) think that thoughts are in the head in a real physical sense, like raisins are in the stomach? In a set of studies, Julie Watson, Susan Gelman, and I (Watson et al., 1998) assessed children's judgments of such comparisons as a person (John) thinking of a raisin or a jellybean versus a person (Joe) who swallowed a raisin or a jellybean. Three-, 4-, and 5-year-old children appropriately distinguished these in their judgments and reasoning. About raisins and jellybeans, these young children answered "Yes," there is *really* a jellybean inside Joe; and "Yes," if a doctor looked inside Joe with a special (X-ray) machine, he would see a raisin inside. About thought-of raisins or jellybeans, however, young children answered "No" there is not *really* a jellybean inside of John (not even "really inside John's head"), and "No" if a doctor looked inside John with a special (X-ray) machine, he would *not* see a raisin.

Aptly enough, as discussed thus far, children's judgments for mental items can have a primarily negative conceptual thrust: Mental entities can *not* be touched, can *not* be seen (with the eyes), and are *not* real. Yet (for adults), mental experiences also possess positive or affirmative aspects when contrasted to objective reality. Crucially, they afford the possibility of imaginary thought. One can think of things that are nonexistent, impossible, or fantastical; that were not, or are not, and could not be real or objective. What of children's understanding of the possibility of such positive features of mentation?

Three-, 4-, and 5-year-olds affirm certain positive features of mental entities that also distinguish them from their physical counterparts. For example, 3-, 4-, and 5-year-olds can easily judge that "No," really there are no "ants that can ride a bicycle" (or "spoons that fly"); and indeed, "No," they have never seen one (Wellman, 1990). Similarly they judge that "flying pigs" are not "really in the world"; that they are "very sure" that other people would say there are no such things; and that they know this because they've "never seen one" and no one has (Harris et al., 2006). But such young children also judge that "Yes," they can "close their eyes and think about an ant that rides a bicycle" (or "think about a pig that flies"; Wellman, 1990) and that people can imagine or pretend about them (Harris et al., 2006). Moreover, preschool children judge that mental entities—say a mental image of a balloon—can be changed "just by thinking," whereas real objects—say a balloon—cannot (Estes, 1998). In these ways, preschool children further reveal their understanding of how the mental and the real differ.

IMAGINATION

Fantastical ideas and entities—thoughts about ants that ride bicycles, made-up mental images, and dreams that portray fictional events—stem from mental states like imagining, not believing. At the beginning of this chapter, I noted that mental states of both imagination and belief are similar in being "representational" in one baseline sense. The contents of imaginary thoughts and beliefs represent a situation as something: If X imagines that an empty cup is full, her thoughts represent it as full. So too for beliefs: If X believes that an empty cup is full, her thoughts represent it as full. In this regard, understanding of imagination can require theory-of-mind understandings similar to those for understanding belief. Not surprisingly, then, during the preschool years children also develop understandings of such fictional mental states and their resultant mental entities.

Yet conceptually, fanciful imagination and belief also clearly differ. Beliefs are "supposed" to be accurate. They are representational in a still further sense (Perner, 1991). If we refer to someone's "belief that X," we refer not just to any old representation of X but to their representation of X as factually real. Although beliefs can be false, in general, they are meant to be true. In contrast, in imagination, truth is less an issue. Indeed, the whole point of imagining is to create an imaginary representational situation that is fictional and *not* meant to accurately portray the world.

Because beliefs, and false beliefs, are simultaneously mental but meant to portray the world as it is, it might be expected that this hybrid character could make understanding beliefs, on average, somewhat more difficult than understanding imaginings. In line with this analysis, multiple well-controlled studies confirm that this is true. Understanding imaginings and understanding beliefs develop hand in hand during the preschool years; but careful comparisons demonstrate that understanding counter-to-reality, imaginal representations is easier, by several months on average, than understanding counter-to-reality false beliefs (Custer, 1996; Gopnik & Slaughter, 1991; Woolley, 1995; see Woolley, 1997, for review). Here is a single example, based on a discrepant-pretense task.

Discrepant Pretense

This discrepant-pretense task assesses understanding of the subjectively different mental states of different persons within a shared pretense episode (i.e., those with or without exposure to a socially shared pretense stipulation; Hickling, Wellman, & Gottfried, 1997; Peterson & Wellman, 2009). The task deliberately uses a procedure parallel to standard false belief, tasks, which themselves, of course, manipulate shared versus discrepant belief.

Thus for discrepant pretense, the adult tester enlisted the child in pretense, while another adult, Gail, was there too. "See this glass. What do you think is in here? That's right it's really empty. But right now let's do some pretending. Let's pretend we pour chocolate milk in the glass. Here you do it." Then Gail leaves, and while she is away, the tester and the child go on to further pretend that the chocolate milk is all drunk up (so the empty glass is pretend empty as well as really empty). Gail returns and the critical test question is, "What does Gail think is in the glass, chocolate milk or nothing?"

In multiple different studies, 3- and 4-year-olds were better at discrepant-pretense tasks than the parallel false belief tasks (Hickling et al., 1997; Peterson & Wellman, 2009). Relatedly, Wendy Custer (1996) showed the same pattern of results with tasks that used thought bubbles to depict both beliefs and pretend imaginings.

THOUGHT BUBBLES

Figure 2.2 uses a thought bubble to pictorially depict thoughts and something of their mental-representational (and misrepresentational) qualities. So does Figure 2.4. Thought bubbles provide a particular way to refer to and characterize a person's mental representations. They thus provide an interesting avenue for testing children's conceptions. Note, for example, that in Figure 2.4 it seems easy to refer to the character's thought versus real objects and actions themselves. Or, in the case of the false belief in Figure 2.2, a thought bubble can clearly distinguish the person's thought that X is a banana from the reality that X is an apple.

Of course, although thought bubbles seem helpful and clear to adults, they may not be useful, or even comprehensible, for children. In fact, it is distinctly possible that thought bubbles might be difficult to understand because they employ special pictorial conventions. Research testing children's understanding of other pictorial conventions— for example, action-lines behind a figure's body to depict movement in static pictures or marks emanating from figures' mouths to depict sounds—suggests that children do not understand such conventions until 6 to 9 years of age (e.g., Gross et al., 1991; Stevenson & Friedman, 1986). Furthermore, thought bubbles depict thoughts in visible, tangible terms—pictorial marks on a material piece of paper. Such concrete depictions might well confuse young children because thoughts themselves are immaterial, invisible entities, and even 3- and 4-year-olds know this, as just discussed.

FIGURE 2.4 Thought-bubble depiction of a boy with a thought about a wagon. (From Wellman, Hollander, & Schult, 1996)

On the other hand, something about thought bubbles seems transparent and straight-forward. Thought bubbles depict thoughts as representations (as "pictures" having their own representational content)—they straightforwardly use a pictorial representation to depict a mental representation. If, or when, children develop a representational under-standing of mind, such a representational device might prove a sensible and easy-to-understand way to describe thoughts. Thus, exploring children's understanding of thought bubbles can help clarify their understanding of thoughts themselves, and men-tal representations.

Thought bubbles were used in several early studies on theory of mind as part of sto-ries about persons' actions, emotions, and thoughts (Hadwin & Perner, 1991; Miller, Kessel, & Flavell, 1970; Yuill, 1984). However, those studies did not test children's under-standing of thought bubbles; the researchers simply used thought bubbles along with parallel verbal descriptions to present their materials to children. Picture books for pre-school children also employ thought bubbles at times. But, intriguingly, this is actually rare (in contrast to speech bubbles in the comic books read by older children); in a survey of almost 200 such picture books for preschool children from English (Dyer, Shatz, &

Wellman, 2000) and Japanese (Dyer-Seymour, Shatz, Wellman, & Saito, 2004) sources, less than 3% of the pictures in such books ever had a thought bubble or even a speech bubble. Of course, even when present, young children may or may not appropriately comprehend these pictorial devices. So, in an initial series of studies Michelle Hollander, Carolyn Schult, and I (Wellman, Hollander, & Schult, 1996) directly asked, what do young children make of thought bubbles? Do they spontaneously infer, or can they even understand, that thought bubbles depict a mental realm of thoughts instead of the world of overt actions, objects, and events?

Even young 3-year-olds could quickly understand certain key aspects of thought bubbles. If shown a picture like Figure 2.4 and simply asked, "What is this?" as an adult pointed to the thought bubble, only 5% of 3-year-olds and less than 25% of the 4-year-olds spontaneously mentioned anything like thoughts, or dreams, or even speech. However, more important, young children could easily and quickly catch on. If simply told that "this shows what he is thinking," children could then easily and accurately go on to answer questions such as "What is he thinking about?" (saying "wagon" not "dog," even though the boy is equally "connected" to both). Better than 85% of 3-year-olds could do this for the initial and subsequent pictures (see also Parsons & Mitchell, 1999).

So, young children can quickly come to "read off" thought bubbles: If asked what a character is thinking, they (appropriately) report the contents of the character's thought bubble. But do they evidence a more revealing understanding? For example, do they understand that thought bubbles depict subjective experiences? Well, yes they do. Consider a task in which two cardboard paper dolls, a boy and a girl, looked in a dark box, and then the boy was turned over to reveal he had a thought bubble of a doll and the girl was turned over to show she had a thought bubble of a teddy bear. In this situation, children could easily answer "What does the boy think is in the box?" (doll), and "What does the girl think is in the box?" (teddy bear). And they could answer that "yes" the boy and the girl had different thoughts. Even 3-year-olds were 90% correct solving such thought-bubble tasks (Wellman et al., 1996).

Children could also pass other related tasks. Most intriguingly, 3- and 4-year-olds firmly distinguished pictures as something a character could see and touch versus thoughts as something a character could not see and touch, *even* when the character's thoughts were depicted in a thought bubble—a pictorial representation as visible and tangible to the child as the parallel real pictures (Wellman et al., 1996). Even deaf children easily come to understand that thought bubbles portray what someone is thinking (Wellman & Peterson, 2013).

In short, children, like adults, find a (potentially curious) representational device—a thought bubble—an easy and natural way to depict thoughts. In doing so, they reveal a burgeoning preschool representational understanding of thoughts and beliefs. To be clear, neither adults nor preschoolers think that thoughts are literally pictures in the head—remember even 3-year-olds don't treat thought bubbles as literal pictures like photographs or even literal pictures hidden from sight (say in a box or in the cranium). But as *mental* representations, thoughts are sensibly depicted as representational—just as in Figure 2.4—and this is sensible even to 3-, 4-, and 5-year-olds.

CONCLUSIONS

Children's ideas about thought bubbles help confirm more generally that their belief-desire psychology, like that of lay adults (nonphilosophers, nonscientists, non-theologians), evidences a naïve dualism. This sort of dualism affirms the commonsense notion of a world of real objects and events "out there," distinct from a mental world of thoughts and ideas "in here." It is a psychophysical dualism and one that affirms a number of subjective–objective distinctions:

1. Mental attitudes are individual and subjective. I can think rainy days are gloomy; you can think they are appealing and refreshing. The boy can think the box contains a doll when the girl thinks the exact same box has a teddy bear.

2. Thoughts are different from things. A thought about a tree is mental and imma-terial; a tree is physical and concrete. Relatedly, beliefs are different from actual-ity and imagination is unconstrained by reality. Judy can believe her toy is in the closet, although it is in the cupboard. There *are* no ants that ride bicycles and I've never seen one, but I can think of one.

3. Mental acts are not bodily behaviors. (My body may be chained, but my thoughts can be free.) Thus mental acts and events are private; your thoughts, desires, and feelings can be hidden and at odds with your objective reports, expressions, and acts. Joe can be thinking of wagons while instead walking his dog (Figure 2.4). Equally, one's body functions (physically, involuntarily) quite apart from one's thoughts, desires, and intentions. Billy can want to stay floating, suspended in air, but he drops down to the ground nonetheless.

4. However, importantly, some mental states and representations connect to the world and shape action. Beliefs, mental images, desires, preferences, and the like can arise due to objects and events in the world; beliefs, desires, and preferences are "about" those real-world states and things. In the other direction, beliefs and desires, in particular, cause, shape, and provide the reasons for our overt actions—actions that are very much objective, consequential, and concrete. When we think mistakenly, we act mistakenly.

In sum, young preschool children come to understand that mental kinds of things are both less and more than the real: They can't be touched or seen, are not material; yet they include the fantastical and the fictional—events and things not possible in the real world of physical objects and occurrences. The mental, unlike the real, can be false or imagi-nary, can be nonmanifest in action or expression, can be influenced "just by thinking."

And this is only half of their broad, coherent understanding because the mental world is not merely separate from the physical world of objects and actions—it niftily connects to it. Beliefs (and images) can arise from the world (e.g., via perceptual experience) and beliefs (and desires) direct action (even mistaken, erroneous action via, e.g., ignorance and false belief).

Preschool children can predict beliefs via knowing someone's perceptual experiences, can predict actions via knowing someone's beliefs, can explain actions by appealing to someone's beliefs and desires, can explain beliefs by appealing to someone's perceptual experiences (including not having or not updating certain perceptual experiences), and can explain emotions by appealing to one's desires and beliefs. The richness, coherence, and systematicity of the preschool theory of mind (captured roughly in Figure 2.1) is not to be underestimated simply because it emanates from diminutive 4-year-old heads.

3

Real-Word Consequences

SOCIAL ACTION

IT IS COMMONPLACE to picture (even caricature) some scientist or philosopher in his armchair working away on his theory, a hypothetical idea about something (e.g., dark matter) far removed from everyday life or practicality. Preschool theory of mind is *not* like that, it is not merely hypothetical ideas trotted out to answer peculiar questions posed by odd child psychologists in armchair situations. Preschool theory of mind is not only coherent, intriguing, and broad; it demonstrably influences children's lives. Preschool theory of mind helps direct the child's social actions and interactions.

Beyond practical importance, the influence of theory-of-mind development on social action is of theoretical importance because it further reveals the breadth and nature of preschool theory of mind. It is of theoretical importance too, because the breadth and practical impact of preschool theory of mind help answer the key question of what is different between preschool theory of mind and earlier infant understanding. That is, regardless of the proper interpretation of the intriguing and important infant research (see Chapters 8 and 9), preschool theory-of-mind insights and transitions—exactly those discussed in the last chapter—are powerful and transformative. The evidence for this claim concerns, in part, how preschool theory-of-mind understandings predict and influence several key childhood competences.

Given the nature of the available research, understanding the influence of theory of mind in preschoolers' actions, interactions, and social competence requires looking, once again, at false beliefs. Although understanding false beliefs provides at best a limited marker of complex developments, nonetheless, it is informative. Because researchers early on developed easy-to-administer, false-belief tasks, they have been often employed in other research. In particular, individual variation in understanding false beliefs has been used both (a) as an outcome measure to address what sort of factors influence theory-of-mind development and (b) as an antecedent measure to investigate the impact of theory-of-mind developments on other things. Here my focus is this second set of relations: whether and how theory-of-mind differences lead to other differences in children's lives. The common assumption, often unanalyzed, has been that, of course, theory-of-mind advancement is consequential for children's actions and not just their conceptions. Thus, a recent *New York Times* article on children's transition to school included a paragraph on what was termed "the all important theory of mind." But is this assumption warranted? Is theory of mind important in this sense, let alone all important? The short answer is yes: As children acquire an explicit preschool belief-desire psychology, their social actions and interactions are changed. The expanded answer is more interesting and more convincing.

As a preface to the expanded answer, it is important to recall that, over the course of the preschool years, most typically developing children come to robust understandings of how action is shaped by mental states and experiences, not only in straightforward situations but also when mind and action are at odds because of ignorance, false belief, and mistaken ideas. But, some children come to these understandings developmentally earlier than other children as indexed in their responses to standard false-belief tasks. So the data, properly understood, do *not* concern whether there are important consequences of coming to theory-of-mind understanding or not. Rather, they concern whether coming earlier or later to theory-of-mind insights, as indexed by a milestone like false-belief understanding, impacts children's lives.

SOCIAL SKILLS AND COMPETENCES

Consider, to begin with, some important relations between theory-of-mind understanding and global, aggregate measures of children's social skills and actions. In particular, several studies have consistently indicated that coming early or later to false-belief understandings relate to global measures of peer acceptance and popularity—preschool children with enhanced false-belief understanding are more popular and accepted. This is true of 3- to 5-year-olds in Israel (Diesendruck & Ben-Eliyahu, 2006), 4- to 6-year-olds in Australia (Slaughter, Dennis, & Pritchard, 2002), 3- to 6-year-olds in the United States (Cassidy, Werner, Rourke, Zubernis, & Balaraman, 2003; LaBounty, 2008; Watson et al., 1999), and 3- and 4-year-olds in Canada (Astington, 2003; Astington & Jenkins, 1995; Moore, Barresi, & Thompson, 1998). These studies have measured peer acceptance via teacher ratings of peer popularity (LaBounty, 2008; Watson, et al. 1999), but they have also measured peer status via peer sociometric ratings (Cassidy et al., 2003; Diesendruck & Ben-Eliyahu, 2006) and peer nomination of "children I like to play with" (Astington, 2003; Slaughter et al., 2002). In most of these studies the link between theory of mind and popularity or acceptance remains significant when covariates such as the child's age or language competence are partialled out. Similar positive links are found between false-belief understanding and teachers' aggregated or global ratings of children's social skills (Diesendruck & Ben-Eliyahu, 2006; Lalonde & Chandler, 1995; Razza & Blair, 2009).

Beyond aggregate or global measures, a few studies have examined the link between children's false-belief understanding and social skills in finer detail. An initial study by Chris Lalonde and Michael Chandler (1995) has served as a prototype. They examined the connection between theory of mind and a large number (40) of different positive social behaviors assessed by teacher ratings and they looked for appropriately differentiated relationships by including two categories of child behavior hypothesized to differ in their relation to theory of mind. Their *intentional* category was meant to refer to those behaviors that "require some measure of insight into the mental lives of others" (Lalonde & Chandler, 1995, p. 167) and included things such as "Converses with others on topics of mutual interest," and "Able to comment on differences between his/her own wishes and those of others." In contrast, their *social conventions* category was meant to include routinized prosocial behaviors that would require only a rudimentary understanding of social situations and included things such as "Says 'please' when asking for something," and "Follows time limits set by caregiver." The intentional behaviors were in fact often significantly correlated with false-belief understanding (with correlations as high as .40 or more), whereas several social-conventional behaviors were not.

Lalonde and Chandler's (1995) intentional and social-conventional categories were not precisely defined and included some arguable items that do not seem to fit neatly into their assigned category (e.g., "Tries to explain his/her misbehavior" was coded as social conventional, and "Plays simple board games" was coded as intentional). This led Janet Astington and her colleagues, among others, to question the validity of Lalonde and Chandler's category selections. However, using much the same methods, revised in some thoughtful ways, Astington mostly replicated Lalonde and Chandler, finding theory of mind to be related to the "intentional" items. This was true even when controlling for language ability (Astington, 2003), which had not been assessed in Lalonde and Chandler.

Jennifer LaBounty (2008) took this one step further and created specially constructed subscales composed of items from parent and teacher questionnaires (such as the Kochanska "My Child Scale"; Kochanska, DeVet, Goldman, Murray, & Putnam, 1994). She created several clusters of *cognitively loaded* prosocial behaviors such as empathy (composed of items such as "Will try to comfort or reassure another in distress") or social-cooperative behavior (e.g., "May draw parents' attention to mishaps or damage she or he caused."). She also created a cluster of *formulaic* behaviors argued to be social but not highly social cognitive such as, "Comments when a parent changes his/her appearance" or "Follows household rules." Children's false-belief understanding, measured with a battery of eight false-belief tasks, indeed predicted cognitively loaded prosocial behaviors but was unrelated to formulaic behaviors in 3½-year-old children. This pattern of convergent and discriminant relations remained when children's IQ and executive functioning were measured and partialled out as well.

A broad perspective characterizes many of these studies (Cassidy et al., 2003; Dunn, 1995; LaBounty, 2008) where "theory of mind may be thought of as comprising two different kinds of understandings—understanding of mind (cognitive states like beliefs and desires) and understanding of emotions (emotional sensitivity to others)" (Cassidy et al., 2003, p. 198). Generally, both aspects of psychological understanding predict pre-schoolers' social skills and prosocial competence (see, e.g., Cassidy et al., 2003; Cutting & Dunn, 1999; Eisenberg, Zhou, Liew, Champion, & Pidada, 2006; Knafo, Steinberg, & Goldner, 2011), but at the same time the patterns for "mind" and "emotion" understanding often differentiate.

The relationships reviewed thus far have been concurrent ones in which children were administered false-belief tasks (and/or emotion-understanding tasks) and parent/child/teacher ratings or observations were collected at more or less the same time. With such data, enhanced theory of mind could be leading to enhanced social skills, or vice versa. Very likely the relation between these is bidirectional, but even so it is important to know whether indeed part of the story is that theory-of-mind insights do influence social behaviors. Direction of influence is better tested via longitudinal data. Longitudinal associations between earlier social cognition and later social action are less well studied. But the data available are nonetheless supportive. Judy Dunn and her colleagues (2002) found that social-cognitive reasoning (false-belief understanding but also emotional perspective taking) in preschool children predicted positive peer relationships for those children both at the same time point and later when the children were making the transition to school. That is, an aggregate social-cognitive score (separate belief and emotion perspective measures weren't reported) provided significant longitudinal predictions. Longitudinal predictions of social competence at 6 and 7 years from earlier false-belief scores at 4 and 5 years were also apparent in the longitudinal data of Janet Astington and her colleagues reported in Astington (2003).

Jennifer Jenkins and Janet Astington (2000) further investigated the effects of theory of mind on social outcomes over time but with a specific focus on children's engagement in play, including especially social pretend play, an everyday form of frequent social interaction for preschool children. With that focus, they found a longitudinal relationship between theory of mind (false-belief understanding) and social play behaviors: Earlier theory of mind predicted the later positive (cooperative) behaviors that are revealed within social pretense episodes but not vice versa. Natalie Eggum, Nancy Eisenberg and their colleagues (Eggum et al., 2011) followed a sample of almost 200 children from 3½ to 4½ and then 6 years of age. Emotion understanding at 3½ predicted prosocial orientation in parent ratings (e.g., "tries to make you feel better when you are upset," "feels sorry for other kids who are being teased") at 4½ and 6. Mind understanding (tested only at

4½ with false-belief tasks) predicted prosocial orientation at 6 years. In further research, theory-of-mind understanding at age 5 predicted teacher report of prosocial behavior 1 year later (Caputi, Lecce, Pagnin, & Banerjee, 2012) and theory of mind in preschool predicted teacher report of social skills in kindergarten (Lecce, Caputi, & Hughes, 2011; Razza & Blair, 2009).

Interim Summary

These various findings are important for confirming theory of mind's real-life relevance. But the links are neither as strong—the correlations typically run about .30— nor as direct as some have assumed. Janet Astington (2003) put this nicely by saying that theory of mind is "sometimes necessary, never sufficient" (p. 13) to guide children's social-communicative interactions. This makes sense if we recognize that a child could understand someone else's beliefs or desires but insist on their own anyway, at least at times. A child could understand that others have internal feelings that can differ from his own but ignore them in one situation or another. As these examples suggest, in fact, basic theory-of-mind understandings are not the sorts of insights that simply, directly, and inevitably translate into appropriate social behaviors.

Moreover, enhanced theory of mind by no means would be expected to always translate into *prosocial* behavior. Some data suggest that enhanced theory of mind can translate into manipulative, gain-seeking behavior as well, for example, in effective bullying (Sutton, Smith, & Swettenham, 1999). Some findings suggest it could be associated with oversensitive behavior later in life, for example, in the transition to peer relations at primary school (Dunn, 1995). From this perspective, of course, the expected relation between adult theory of mind and adult social skills and interaction would have the same features; "mature" theory-of-mind understanding is only "sometimes necessary, never sufficient" to guide social-communicative interactions, both prosocial and anti-social interactions.

Importantly, children's performance on false-belief tasks (as a marker of an emerging belief-desire psychology) is also associated with other kinds of real-world behaviors such as lying and persuading, as I describe shortly. Before that, however, it's helpful to consider the relation between theory of mind and preschool children's development of executive functions because this provides needed background and perspective.

DISTINGUISHING THEORY OF MIND AND EXECUTIVE FUNCTIONING

At the same time that sizable developments are occurring in preschool children's mentalistic understanding of persons, executive function abilities are dramatically improving. "Executive functioning" encompasses several constructs and abilities including planning, inhibitory control, working memory, and cognitive flexibility that are themselves heterogeneous (Garon, Bryson, & Smith, 2008; Zelazo & Müller, 2011). Not surprisingly, then, there are several possibilities for how theory-of-mind developments might be explained by more general developments in executive functioning. For my purposes, these several possibilities can be loosely grouped into *executive function expression* accounts and *executive function emergence* accounts (Moses, 2001).

To illustrate, consider an analysis of how advances in inhibitory control might account for advances in false-belief understanding (e.g., Carlson & Moses, 2001). Task performances often require the ability to inhibit an initial or prepotent response (e.g., not to shout out a correct response but to raise your hand) or to inhibit salient thoughts (e.g., not to think about your birthday presents so as to wait more patiently for the time to open them). Ability to inhibit salient experiences and inhibit typical or prepotent responses is one of those executive-function competencies that develops markedly in the preschool years. And, performance on theory-of-mind tasks arguably requires this sort of inhibitory control—for example, the real nature of events and situations is of obvious importance to young children; but in false-belief tasks, to be correct the child must inhibit a prepotent tendency to say or point to where the item really is (e.g., in the cupboard—see Box 1.2) and attend instead to the character's belief about where it is (in the drawer). By hypothesis, in an executive function expression account, young preschoolers explicitly understand false beliefs, but their expression of that understanding is masked by the executive function demands of standard preschool false-belief tasks. On the strongest claims, that would make the preschool theory-of-mind developments, more or less, nothing but executive-function development.

In contrast, in an executive function emergence account, young preschoolers do not yet explicitly understand false belief and must develop that notion. Executive functions such as inhibition, attention shifting, and flexibility are, in this account, instrumental (perhaps even necessary) to achieve this conceptual development. As one illustration, begin (again) with the assumption that for young children, attention to and focus on reality is very salient—it grabs young children's attention. This attention-grabbing nature of reality itself problematizes any attention to or consideration of ephemeral, nonobvious things like mental states for younger children. To increasingly consider the possibility of mental states (as distinct from reality), children must inhibit immediate, exclusive attention to reality and shift attention to consider the (less obvious, less salient) mental states also potentially at play. Executive functions allow children to inhibit immediate, exclusive attention to reality and thus foster emergence of, attentional shifts to, and understandings of mental states.

I favor executive function emergence accounts, as will become clear throughout this book. But, executive function expression accounts have gained increased consideration and favor recently in light of data potentially showing infants may understand false belief (see Chapter 8). The balance of research, however, supports executive function emergence over executive function expression accounts. For example, research shows that, whereas theory of mind and executive function intercorrelate in the preschool years, they do not overlap completely. When Stephanie Carlson and Lou Moses (2001) first conducted a thorough individual differences analysis of performance on theory-of-mind tasks (including, focally, several false-belief tasks) and executive-functioning tasks (including, focally, inhibitory control tasks), inhibitory control tasks correlated highly with theory-of-mind tasks (approximately .60) and a significant (but reduced) correlation remained even after age, verbal intelligence, and several other control measures were partialled out. This sort of result has now been replicated often. At the same time, however, a "theory-of-mind factor" emerged in Carlson and Moses's principal components analysis, alongside of executive-functioning factors. And, regression analyses indicated significant *independent* contributions of theory-of-mind and executive functioning to false-belief performance. Consider as well that executive function competences not only correlate substantially with theory-of-mind performance among 3-year-olds and 4-year-olds, executive-function competences at age 3 and 4 longitudinally predict increased theory of mind at age 5 and 6, and executive function competence at age 3 longitudinally predicts increased theory of mind at age 4 (e.g., Hughes, 1998; Hughes, Ensor, & Marks, 2011). In these ways, executive-function abilities seem to contribute more to the emergence of developing theory-of-mind abilities rather than merely their expression.

Further, to return to the topic of this chapter, false-belief understandings significantly predict aspects of children's social interactional skills and popularity with peers, even in studies where executive functioning is controlled and factored out, both concurrently (e.g., LaBounty, 2008) *and* longitudinally (e.g., Hughes et al., 2011). Rachel Razza and Clancy Blair (2009) provided an important recent example. They looked at false-belief understanding and social competence (measured by comprehensive teacher ratings) longitudinally, but included executive-function skills as well. False-belief performance in preschool was positively associated with social competence in kindergarten after controlling for executive-function skills. This research is notable as well in that Razza and Blair studied a low-income Head Start sample that complements the findings from other research that mostly has studied middle-class children.

Moreover, theory-of-mind advances impact aspects of children's lives and actions beyond the interactional skills and social acceptance covered so far.

LIES AND DECEPTION

Full-fledged deception involves doing something to intentionally instill ignorance or false belief in someone else—hiding an object or act so others won't know where or what it is, changing an object's (or action's) appearance so that it looks like something it is not, describing something as X when it is Y. Lying—describing something as X when it is Y—provides a good example: Lying involves someone making a *false statement* with the *intention* to *deceive* (where deception itself involves the intention to produce a false belief). Given this definition, the connection between theory of mind and lying or deception seems as if it ought to be particularly revealing and straight-forward; lying and deceiving are important everyday behaviors of a sort that could more directly require and reveal a representational theory of mind. A fair number of studies now exist on preschoolers' deception and still more exist on children's lying, originating with the seminal work of Jean Piaget (1932). I focus on lying as my pri-mary example.

To begin with, the preschool years, when demonstrable changes in children's theo-ries of mind (e.g., understanding of false belief) unfold, are when childhood lying (and deception) emerge and dramatically increase. For example, although parents' opinions about the age at which their children deliberately lie to them vary, a majority of par-ents place the age at 4 years (Stouthamer-Loebel, 1991) or a bit earlier at 3½ (Newton, Reddy, & Bull, 2000). Such everyday lies involve false denials ("I didn't do it"), false blame ("He did it"), false claims ("Dad said it's OK"), false boasts ("I can do that, too"), and false ignorance ("I don't know who messed it up").

This preschool emergence of lying (and deceiving) roughly parallels preschool developments in the understanding of knowledge or belief and specifically false belief. But, looked at in this general way, the link is not very tight or convincing. For one thing, whereas parents do report large increases in lying and deception over the preschool years, with 3½ and 4 marking a notable transition, they often report at least some false denials, claims, boasts, and so on for their 2-year-olds (e.g., Newton et al., 2000), children who are presumably too young to have achieved key explicit false-belief insights.

Experimental studies confirm parental claims. Experimental studies of young chil-dren's lying have typically employed a "temptation" paradigm. Prototypically, a hidden toy is placed by an adult in a container on a table "for later," and the adult leaves the room explicitly telling the child not to peek. As recorded on video or via a one-way mirror, most young children peek at the toy while the adult is away. On returning, the adult asks the child, "Did you peek?" Young children who peeked often say that they did not—they "lie." In a study with old 2-year-olds and young 3-year-olds by Michael Lewis and his col-leagues (Lewis, Stanger, & Sullivan, 1989), children as young as 2 years, 9 months (the youngest tested) lied in this fashion.

In this study by Lewis et al. (1989), 88% of the children peeked. When asked if they peeked, about a quarter of the peekers said nothing at all. Of those that said something (about 75% of the peekers), about half admitted they peeked, but half asserted they had not. In total, then, 36% of these young 2- and 3-year-old children "lied." It is also true that, corroborating parental reports, experimental studies have found that between 3 and 5 years, lying substantially increases (e.g., Polak & Harris, 1999; Talwar & Lee, 2002). Alan Polak and Paul Harris (1999) found that 84% of 5-year-olds "lied" in one of their two studies using a temptation paradigm.

Pulling these various findings together, one problem for any link between lying and understanding false beliefs is that "lying" begins quite early. Another problem is that in many of these studies, if children are tested on their false-belief understanding, there is often little or no direct association between that conceptual insight and children's lying behavior—for example, nonsignificant correlations in Newton et al. (2000) and in Experiment 1 of Polak and Harris (1999). But, in still other studies, preschool advances in lying or deception have been significantly linked to preschool achievement of false-belief understanding. Thus, Polak and Harris (1999) found a clear association in their Experiment 2 (which they argued was appropriately improved over their Experiment 1 that found no association).

Two considerations help clarify this initially contradictory pattern of results. First, conceptually, a child can say something that effectively deceives someone else but without truly lying, that is, without an intention to deceive. The child could be making an innocent mistake (e.g., forgot he peeked), but more focally could be engaged in something genuinely nefarious yet without an intention to deceive or to inculcate mistaken ideas. In particular, children could be attempting to control someone else's *behavior* as opposed to manipulating someone else's *belief.* If mom points to a broken vase and says "Did you do that?" (or an experimenter asks, "Did you peek?"), children could say "I did not" when in fact they did because such a false claim simply and effectively avoids any negative consequences (e.g., punishment). They may or may not use that statement because it avoids such consequences *by way of creating a false belief.* Young children, and especially very young children, could instead recognize that, in such situations, the causal agent gets the punishment; and so to avoid the punishment, simply deny being that agent. Thus, they could easily "lie" without lying; utter a falsity without attempting to manipulate mom's (or the experimenter's) belief, merely manipulate her behavior. For this reason I frequently used scare quotes previously in saying that even quite young children "lie."

Equally, consider a competitive situation—if you get the prize, I do not. I can greatly increase my chances of getting the prize by having you fail. And I can have you fail by sabotaging you (tying your hands, erecting a barrier between you and the prize, etc.) just as well as by deceiving you (manipulating your knowledge so that you are ignorant of where the prize is or falsely think it is elsewhere). Children can sabotage others' plans and efforts without attempting to specifically sabotage their *ideas.*

One way to tackle these interpretive issues is to adjust the tasks and circumstances so as to clarify the sort of behaviors involved. Thus, Beate Sodian (1994) argued that if sabotage is distinguished from deception, her research shows that children's deception is linked to their false-belief understanding. Continuing with a primary focus on lying, a related approach would be to adjust the situation so as to minimize any punishment for the "transgression," thereby minimizing behaviors simply designed to avoid punishment. In recent research, Victoria Talwar and Kang Lee (2008) took this approach to study children's lying. By studying childhood denial of a behavior that had no serious associated punishment, then such acts might show a tighter association with an understanding of false belief.

Talwar and Lee (2008) used a temptation method in which they induced children to commit a very minor transgression, peeking in a low-key guessing game with a no-peeking rule. For example, a purple Barney-doll toy was placed behind a child who was told not to peek when the adult left the room for moment. After videoing whether the child actually peeked, the adult interviewed the children to assess whether they would admit the peeking or whether they would lie and deny peeking. Children's performance on a battery of false-belief tasks was indeed an independent, positive predictor of lying to conceal their peeking in this less-serious, nonpunishment situation.

As in a few other studies (e.g., Polak & Harris, 1999), Talwar and Lee (2008) also included a second part to their study. Children were interviewed to determine whether they could keep up their lie by concealing the knowledge they had gained during their transgression. So children were asked some follow-up questions about what they guessed (i.e., what they were supposed to have guessed but what was actually, accurately informed by their peeking). For example, "How did you know the toy was Barney?" In these conversations, some children were better at maintaining their lies, whereas others directly or indirectly leaked that they had seen the (hidden) object in question. For example, lie leakers said things such as "It was purple"; "It looked like Barney." Here again, children's performance on false-belief tasks predicted individual differences, in this case differences in maintaining rather than giving away their lies.

These findings argue that the ability to reason about false beliefs is a critical predictor of important real-world social behaviors, arguably exactly the sort of real-world social behavior that theory-of-mind reasoning ought to shape and produce. However, consider executive-function capacities again. One might suspect that lying (and maintaining a lie) may only be associated with false-belief reasoning because of a common association with executive-functioning abilities—the child's developing ability to control and plan some behavior rather than another. Lying almost certainly requires some minimal level of executive control to overcome one's prepotent tendency to simply say what is so, to fixate on and blurt out what really occurred. Therefore, to address this alternative interpretation, in both of their two studies, Talwar and Lee (2008) assessed executive-functioning abilities (i.e., performance on a battery of preschool executive control tasks). In both studies, false-belief reasoning was a unique, independent predictor of children's lying performance even when controlling for executive-function abilities. These findings strongly support the claim that it is the conceptual advances in understanding false belief, and not simply other task demands, that are associated with lying.

Parenthetically, not all lying is antisocial. White lies are not only condoned, they are encouraged for some situations. Thus if a child receives an unliked present from grandma, they are encouraged to say not only thank you but how nice it is. Fen Xu and colleagues (Xu, Bao, Fu, Talwar, & Lee, 2010) reported on the development of this sort of lying in Chinese and North American children.

HIDING AND SECRETS

Lying to deny a minor (or major) transgression is an attempt to hide something. What about children's performances in an everyday, straightforward hiding activity, such as hide-and-seek? Hide-and-seek is a frequently played game and one that children not only enjoy but often instigate themselves (Peskin & Ardino, 2003). Thus children's abilities to participate successfully in games such as hide-and-seek could reveal realistic links to false-belief reasoning. Indeed, in Chris Lalonde and Michael Chandler's (1995) study, teacher ratings of "follows rules in simple games without being reminded" was highly correlated with false-belief performance. Arguably, hide-and-seek, in particular, represents the sort of game playing that should require children to recognize cases in which others should be kept ignorant of things that they themselves know. Better yet, hiding oneself in hide-and-seek involves absolutely no need to avoid transgression.

I remember playing hide-and-seek often when my sons were young, and when being the seeker, after counting to 10, asking rhetorically out loud, "OK here I come, I wonder where [child's name] is?" At this point the child himself would say, with a laugh, "under the bed." This is one of many anecdotes about how bad young children can be at hide-and-seek. Surprisingly, however, there are few studies of hide-and-seek. Joan Peskin and Vittoria Ardino (2003) undertook such a study. They had 3-, 4-, and 5-year-olds individually play hide-and-seek with a familiar adult. The quasi-naturalistic task took place in a familiar room in the child's preschool, a room that had several distinct hiding locations—under a table covered with a floor length table cloth, two large empty cupboards, and so forth. Each child played as seeker and also as hider, and the children's behaviors were coded as successful or unsuccessful. Successful behaviors kept the seeker ignorant of the hider. Unsuccessful hiding actions in contrast included the child telling the adult where he was going to hide; the child not hiding from, but remaining in plain sight, while the adult hid her eyes; the child calling out to the adult during her seeking; and so forth. When being the seeker, unsuccessful actions included telling the adult where she should hide, counting to 10 but keeping one's eyes wide open while doing so, and so forth. Of 3-year-olds, 83% were unsuccessful as hider and seeker; however, 78% of the 4-year-olds and 94% of the 5-year-olds played appropriately. Importantly, children were also given a small battery of theory-of-mind tasks—false-belief tasks. Hide-and-seek success was highly correlated with theory of mind (correlations of .60 and better).

Being a hider in hide-and-seek involves keeping a secret—keeping your whereabouts secret from the seeker. Secret keeping is a ubiquitous adult activity, beyond the confines of hide-and-seek, and secret keeping is a larger, real-world task for children as well—keeping the contents of a birthday present secret until the opener opens it, not telling someone ahead of time about a surprise, and the like. Again, anecdotes abound about young children as poor secret keepers. A classic situation in real life, in Sunday comics, and in TV sitcoms, is where Mom and child wrap a secret present for Dad (or for Sally at school or for grandma) and, as the wrapped present is handed over, the young child announces, "it's a tie" or "it's a baby doll." Again, surprisingly little formal research has explored children's explicit conceptions of secrets, but Peskin and Ardino (2003) not only studied young children's hide-and-seek: They also studied their secret keeping.

In the secret-keeping task, 3-, 4-, and 5-year-olds were in their preschool kitchen area. They were first engaged in hiding a birthday cake from a specific adult teacher and told repeatedly, "It's a secret. Don't tell." Then that teacher appeared and under a simple pretext the child was left alone with the teacher in the kitchen with the hidden cake. As soon as they were alone, the teacher said, "I'm hungry; I wonder if there is anything to eat here?" If the child initially made no mention of the cake the teacher repeated her statement, "I'm hungry." Unsuccessful secret keeping straightforwardly involved telling the teacher about the cake or pointing at and into the bag where it was hidden.

Only 33% of the 3-year-olds kept the secret, whereas 67% of the 4-year-olds and 89% of the 5-year-olds did so. There was a high correlation between children's performance on a battery of false-belief tasks and keeping a secret—a correlation of .62. That is, children who were better at false belief were also better at concealing knowledge from—keeping a secret from—a relevant third person.

In both these studies—one of hide-and-seek and one of secret keeping—Peskin and Ardino (2003) administered a small battery of executive-function tasks as well. Executive control was also correlated with hide-and-seek success and with successfully keeping a secret. But clear associations between false-belief performance and successfully hiding, seeking, and secret keeping remained after executive-control abilities were accounted for. In short, as children became competent at false-belief reasoning, they were more likely to participate in these games correctly. For hide-and-seek, children who were better at false belief were better able to hide from a seeker without giving away their location; and when playing the seeker, they allowed the hider to hide without peeking. For secret keeping, children who were better at false belief were better at concealing a realistic surprise. The fact that false-belief reasoning was associated with appropriate action in these real-world situations demonstrates both that (a) children's conceptualizations of mind are progressively maturing over the preschool period and (b) this has predictable consequences for their social actions and lives.

PERSUADING OTHERS

Proper lies and deceptions (including white lies) have a persuasive element—they're designed to persuade someone to believe something untrue. Of course, much persuasion is not based on untruth, but a substantial amount *is* based on belief management. At the same time, at their most general, persuasion attempts can be nothing but simple pleas ("please, please, please") and emotional appeals (tears). So, once again, young children's first attempts at persuasion might be more behavioral and rote and as such not arguably related to theory of mind. Karen Bartsch and her colleagues (e.g.,

Bartsch & London, 2000; Bartsch et al., 2007) have tried to focus more specifically on acts that seem to persuade via information provision and management. To illustrate, in their studies children might see a replica of a puppy who was "very gentle and really quiet." A puppet, Tricia, came along and was told, "Tricia, puppy wants you to pet him." Tricia says, "Oh no, because I think puppies bite." At this point the child was asked what to say to Tricia to get Tricia to pet the puppy: "Should we tell Tricia the puppy is gentle or the puppy is quiet?" A second puppet, Chris, was also used, who didn't want to pet the puppy because "I think puppies bark too loud." Again the child was asked what to tell Chris.

The idea here was to see if the child would attempt to persuade Tricia and Chris with different arguments, appropriately based on their differing beliefs. Doing so would indicate a clear use of and sensitivity to, belief-based persuasion. Note that the probability of being correct on this task—telling Tricia the puppet is gentle and also telling Chris the puppy is quiet—on the basis of chance alone was 25% (choosing one of two alternatives correctly for two choices in a row). In a variety of studies, 3-year-olds were essentially at chance and older children got better, typically with even 4-year-olds better than chance and 5-year-olds better still (Bartsch & London, 2000; Bartsch et al., 2007).

Bartsch, Wade, and Estes (2011) found very similar patterns with a series of manipulations designed to increase the ease and everyday feel of their persuasion tasks. In one study, for example, children were just asked, "What should we tell Chris to get him to pet the puppy" (thereby eliminating the potentially awkward/complex part of the question, "Should we tell him the puppy is gentle or the puppy is quiet?"). In another study, children were to persuade live persons instead of puppets. Essentially, across all these variations, 3-year-olds were at chance, whereas 4- and 5-year-olds were above chance (and belief-based responding increased as well from 3 to 4 or 5 years of age). Bartsch and her colleagues (2007) then showed that this sort of interactive persuasion behavior correlated positively with false-belief understanding (correlations of .52 and .69 for 3-year-olds and 4- and 5-year-olds, respectively). Moreover, there was a consistent developmental pattern whereby transitional children would pass false belief and fail persuasion but not the reverse. Such a pattern provides good evidence that false-belief understanding was not only associated with belief-based persuasion but provided a prerequisite for it.

Virginia Slaughter and her colleagues (Slaughter, Peterson, & Moore, 2013) showed something very similar but with still more (real-life) impact. In their study, 3- to 8-year-olds had to persuade a puppet to eat raw broccoli or to brush his teeth in an interactive situation in which the puppet responded and resisted. Eating your vegetables and brushing your teeth are two things that preschool children clearly receive persuasive messages about. The number and quality of persuasive arguments that children advanced was significantly correlated with a battery of theory-of-mind tests and remained significant after controlling for age and verbal ability.

CONCLUSIONS

These sections and topics, along with Chapter 2, increasingly reveal the breadth, coherence, and power of what preschool children come to know. That 4- and 5-year-old children understand false beliefs, true beliefs, mental entities, dreams, imaginings, and thought bubbles as revealed in judgments but also as employed in their explanations, evidences an impressively coherent, connected set of mental understandings. Moreover, these cogent and connected insights influence children's social actions, including their interactions with adults and peers. They influence preschoolers' engagement in the lies, deceptions, secrets, and persuasive arguments that also strongly characterize adult everyday interactions worldwide. They additionally influence children's game playing; indeed, game-playing skills that emerge in preschool, and especially those that depend on assessing others' knowledge and beliefs, initiate a set of game-playing skills that continue to develop through adulthood. Hide-and-seek leads to "Battleship," to poker, to prisoner's dilemma, and more.

4

Preschool Theory of Mind, Part 2

DESIRES, EMOTIONS, PERCEPTIONS

CHILD (age 2;11): I don't like ... I don't want to babysit Andy.
ADULT: How come?
CHILD: Because he cries when everybody hits him.
ADULT: Gosh, I would cry too, if someone hit me.
CHILD: I will not cry when someone hit me...
ADULT: I see. You think it hurts when people hit Andy?
CHILD: Yeah.
(Bartsch & Wellman, 1995, p. 127)

BELIEFS CAN SEEM colorless and distant in contrast to much of the mental world we confront—more vivid and immediate are our heartfelt desires, fondest hopes, and heated emotions. Freud was a master at reminding us that wants and feelings propel us to act and react. These are the motivations and experiences that color our lives and direct, even bias, our thinking. This is as true in naïve psychology as it is in Freudian psychodynamics. In Freud's colorful metaphor, beliefs and reason (the ego) were the riders on the horse of the desires and urges (the id) that "supplies the locomotive energy" (1933).

The plethora of research on false beliefs and representational mental entities, along with the demonstrable relations between false-belief reasoning and preschoolers' lives, should not create a false impression that to have a theory of mind is to understand false belief, or to understand false belief is to have a theory of mind. Beliefs (thoughts, ideas) function alongside other mental states even within full-fledged, belief-desire reasoning.

Moreover, younger children could conceivably understand some of these other states with no good understanding of representational mental states and devices—such as beliefs, images, and thought bubbles—at all. At some young age children may focus on the horse and ignore the rider.

Indeed, very young children understand much about desires—a bedrock of belief-desire reasoning—and basic emotions as well. This is neatly apparent, to begin with, in children's conversations.

TALKING ABOUT DESIRES AND EMOTIONS

With the emergence of language, children begin to explicitly talk about people. Recall that in their everyday conversations, the vast majority of children's why-questions—"why/how did that happen?"—are about people, and likewise the vast majority of children's own explanations, "that happened because of Y," are explanations of why people did things (Hickling & Wellman, 2001). In this talk, children not only refer to people: They refer to people's mental states. For example, Daniela O'Neil and her colleagues (O'Neill, Main, & Ziemski, 2009) videoed 3- and 4-year-olds as they ate snacks together at their preschool. In an intensive study, 25 children were taped twice a week, every week, for 21 consecutive weeks. How did these young children initiate conversation with each other as they assembled around their food? In this situation (full of food, implements, cups, etc.) and for this age and context (where children spent hours interacting over toys, books, blocks, sand, paint), it would be easy for children to begin by essentially commenting on and asking about objects. But instead almost 80% of children's conversational openings referred to people—they began conversations by asking about their listener (41%) or commenting on themselves (39%). Moreover, almost 30% of their conversational initiations mentioned someone's mental states—a child's desires, preferences, and emotions in particular, with occasional mention of someone's beliefs and knowledge.

For young children's everyday conversations, when children mention someone's mental states, they typically do so by using desire terms such as *want, wish*, and *like* as well as emotion terms such as *happy* and *sad*. Such words appear in about 5–10% of children's utterances even as 2-year-olds (Bartsch & Wellman, 1995; Wellman, Harris, Banerjee, & Sinclair, 1995; Ruffman et al., 2002) and occur increasingly after that. A key question, however, is whether very young children are really talking about someone's mental-intentional states. Conceivably, such very young children could more simplistically be (mis)using desire or emotion words to refer to external aspects of a person's actions, appearances, and situations instead and be generally ignorant of or confused about internal states.

Consider early talk about desires. Early comments that someone *wants* something could plausibly just be talk about the behavioral attractiveness of objects. "He wants cake" might mean (simply) cake is the sort of thing people go for. "I want cake," might mean simply, "Give me some." Call this a situationist understanding, one that might reflect a misunderstanding of desire terms, or more deeply of desire itself. Equally, a young child's (mis)understanding of and initial talk about emotions—"He's happy"—could be confined to the notion that certain situations simply elicit corresponding overt emotional reactions (e.g., birthdays make one "happy," where "happy" translates into smiling and laughing). In contrast to such a situationist understanding, a mentalistic understanding of desires would acknowledge that they cannot be equated with situations—some curmudgeon may very well find cake undesirable. And, similarly, emotional reactions do not follow directly from eliciting situations but are subjective (if you like birthdays, having one makes you happy; because I dislike them, the same occurrence is sad or depressing to me).

Desires and emotions as mental states also relate to and produce actions. If I want cake, I'm likely to reach for it. Initial conceptions of "desire," and initial understanding of terms such as *want* and *like*, could thus also be simply references to actions such as seeking, finding, obtaining, and the like. Similarly, emotional states are often associated with typical action dispositions. If I fear snakes, I'm likely to avoid them; if I am sad, I'm likely to cry. For young children, a term such as *afraid* could refer only to a person's avoidance; *sad* could refer only to a person's tears or woebegone demeanor.

So, we need to consider two possibilities. One is that young children's comments (and understandings) evidence limited references to situation-action scripts. Such a child might seem to talk about "desire" or "emotion" appropriately—by using terms such as *happy, sad*, and *want* as shorthand expressions for how certain situations or stimuli lead regularly to certain actions (of instrumental or expressive sorts)—without any deeper understanding of the subjective-experiential states that mediate such situation-action regularities. (Within philosophy, there are arguments that emotional term meanings may actually decompose into no more than this; Ryle, 1949.) The other possibility is that young children's early talk about desires and emotions in fact demonstrates an appropriately explicit awareness of the distinctly subjective-experiential states of desire and emotion. Young children might recognize that such states exist separate from, or even in contrast to, external situations and overt actions.

Intensive study of young children's everyday conversation provides evidence supporting the second of these alternatives. The clearest evidence comes when children say things such as the following:

ADAM: Want some? [to adult]
ADULT: No. I don't want some.
ADAM: OK. But I want some.

In this conversation the child, Adam, contrasts two different desires about the same physical reality—you want some, but I don't. Aptly, these types of utterances are called *contrastives*. In comprehensive analyses of hundreds of thousands of everyday conversations, children as young as 2 years regularly (albeit not frequently) produce such informative contrastives (Bartsch & Wellman, 1995; Ruffman et al., 2002; Wellman et al., 1995). The following conversational contrastives are examples from *2-year-old* children (Bartsch & Wellman, 1995; Wellman et al., 1995):

PETER: I wanna come out. But I can't come out.

ABE: I like Michael. I like Michael, Mommy.
MOTHER: Do you want to go outside and play with Michael?
ABE: No. Not right now.

ABE: No... You like it?
ADULT: Yes, I do.
ABE: But I don't like it.

FATHER: Marky's mad at your Daddy. (Mark is Ross' brother)
ROSS: But I'm happy at my Daddy!

CHILD: I was sad. But I didn't cry.

The first two of these contrastive conversations are about desires; the last two are about emotions. More intriguingly, in these contrastive conversations children make several subjective distinctions. Two of the preceding excerpts contrast one person's subjective experience with that of another—about the exact same physical object (e.g., Daddy), one person is mad but another is happy. The other examples contrast desire or emotion with overt action: "I wanna come out, but I can't come out"; "I was sad, but I didn't cry."

Such examples demonstrate key aspects of a naïve, mentalistic understanding of persons. Early childhood talk about persons encompasses the understanding that people possess internal psychological states distinct from the physical world because such states are distinguished from the situational occurrences that may elicit them and distinguished from the behaviors and expressions that may result from such states. Moreover, different persons possess different such states, even in the same situation and about the same overt objects and events.

Slightly older children can at times be very expressive about this:

(Age 3;7) ROSS: This, what I got on my bread, was sour on my tongue... I don't like it. (Hands bread to his father)
FATHER: Why do I have to eat it?
ROSS: Because I don't like the sour part.
FATHER: What makes you think that Daddy's going to like it?
ROSS: Because you like sour stuff. So eat it.
(Bartsch & Wellman, 1995, p. 86)

Ordinary conversations importantly give a picture of children's everyday life and help certify the centrality, and preciseness, of children's early mentalistic understanding of folk—themselves and others. Such conversations may also give a specially sensitive look, as children's best understandings may be clearest when engaged with familiar others in situations of interest to them. However, conversational analyses can also be limited. In conversation, ideas and concepts must be expressed in words, and sometimes even adults can't do this, let alone 2-year-olds in the throes of learning language as well as dealing with potentially complex topics such as (internal-subjective construals of) desires, emotions, and minds. Parents contribute to these conversations too. Perhaps this aids children to best express themselves, but also perhaps (and at times, surely) the conversations reflect parental concepts and understandings more than those of their children. Moreover, collecting such voluminous conversational data is labor intensive, so such data are available (in sufficient depth and detail) for only small numbers of children—five or six children can be large samples for this sort of research. Nicely, a complementary package of natural and experimental evidence is available for early theory of mind.

Betty Repacholi and Alison Gopnik (1997) provided a now classic experimental demonstration of young children's appreciation of individuated, subjective emotional-desire experiences: the broccoli-crackers study. They had 18-month-olds taste two snacks to evoke negative and positive preference: broccoli (negative) and goldfish crackers (positive). Then an adult, facing the child, tasted each snack saying, "Yum" and smiling at one snack, but saying, "Eew" and frowning at the other. In a *Match* condition, the adult liked the crackers and disliked the broccoli, matching the child's preference. In a *Mismatch* condition, the adult liked the broccoli instead. Then the adult held her hand halfway between the two snacks and said, "I want some more, can you give me some more?," carefully avoiding actually referring to one item or the other. The 18-month-olds (but not 14-month-olds) overwhelmingly gave the adult more of what she, the adult, had liked, even in the Mismatch condition. And it was not the case that these toddlers simply gave the adult the snack they themselves did not like—keeping the best for themselves—because in the Match condition, infants gave the adult the crackers. Thus, children demonstrated an understanding of desires as subjective—realizing that the adult wanted broccoli, contrary to their own preference for crackers.

This broccoli-crackers method (see also Egyed, Király, & Gergely, 2013) represents an example of a *diverse-desires* task, assessing children's understanding of how desires can differ across individuals (even desires for the exact same objects). A broccoli-cracker sort of diverse-desire task can be called a "not-own desire" task—the child judges that someone else has a desire that does not match his own. Consider a different diverse-desires task in which the child is told and shown:

> Ann likes playing outside and really likes to swing. Joy likes playing inside and really likes toy pots and pans. Now it's time for free play and children can go to the playground or to the kitchen corner. Who goes where?

In this sort of task, the child must judge that two different people (neither himself) have two different desires leading to two divergent actions. Two- and 3-year-olds can judge correctly in these tasks as well (Wellman & Liu, 2004).

Cogent reasoning about desires and emotions encompasses more than just the notion that different people have different desires. In particular, it should encompass (as the Ann–Joy task begins to) reasoning about the connection between desires and actions, both behavioral acts and also emotional reactions (just as depicted in Figure 2.1). Consider an early study with 2-year-olds (Wellman & Woolley, 1990). In this study, young children made judgments about child characters, such as Joe and Bill, in three situations. In the *Finds-Wanted* situation, a character wants something that might be in one of two locations; the character searches in one location and gets the object. So (with accompanying pictures that help tell the story and help these young children keep track), "Joe's pet bunny has escaped and he wants to find it. Here are two places it might be (garage and shed), Joe looks first in the shed, and look what is there—his bunny."

The *Finds-Nothing* situation was nearly identical to Finds-Wanted except that on searching in the first location, the character found that nothing was there. The *Finds-Substitute* situation was also identical to Finds-Wanted, except that on searching in the first location, the character found an attractive object but not the one said to be wanted. Children were asked to judge whether the character would be happy or sad after searching the first location; 2-year-olds appropriately predicted happiness for the Finds-Wanted situation (100% of time) but sadness for both Finds-Nothing and Finds-Substitute characters (about 80%) of the time. Children were also asked what the character would do next, stop searching or search somewhere else; 2-year-olds appropriately predicted stopping search in Finds-Wanted situations (80% of time) but continued searching for both Finds-Nothing and Finds-Substitute characters (about 90% of the time).

These judgments show ways in which 2-year-olds appreciate desires and emotions as internal mental states separate from external objects or overt behaviors, just as is evident at times in their spontaneous conversations. Consider the carefully matched Finds-Wanted and Finds-Substitute situations. In Finds-Wanted, Joe wants a bunny and finds it. In Finds-Substitute, Bill wants a dog but finds something else—in fact he finds a bunny just like Joe found. If we consider persons at the level of overt movement and resulting objective outcome, Joe and Bill's acts are identical—the same exact behaviors yield the exact same object—look in the shed, find a bunny. But 2-year-olds distinguish this objective similarity from the subjective differences: Joe will be happy, Bill will be sad; Bill will look further, Joe will stop. They understand, at least at times, the outcome (getting a cute bunny) is not objectively happy making: It depends on the character's desires—desires that differ subjectively across different persons.

Other studies have confirmed these findings with slightly older children. Thus, 3-year-olds consistently use agents' desires to appropriately predict their behavior (Bartsch, 1996; Cassidy, 1998: Cassidy et al., 2005; Joseph & Tager-Flusberg, 1999; Rakoczy, Warneken, & Tomasello, 2007) and to predict their emotions (Hadwin & Perner, 1991; Rakoczy et al., 2007; Stein & Levine, 1989; Wellman & Banerjee, 1991). Angeline Lillard and John Flavell (1992) further confirmed that young children understand that desires need not match the current state of affairs (e.g., Jill *wants* juice for lunch even when milk is actually what's present for lunch); and Lou Moses and his colleagues (Moses, Coon, & Wusinich, 2000) showed that 3-year-olds understand that deprivation and satiation influence desires, and so desires change over time (e.g., I might want crackers now, but if I eat lots of them I'll no longer want any).

Intriguingly, the claim that these young 2- and 3-year-old children understand desires as internal and subjective has been challenged (Perner, Zauner, & Sprung, 2005; Rieffe, Meerum Terwogt, Koops, Stegge, & Oomen, 2001). The suspicion is that maybe young children are proficient at ascribing "desire-like" states to persons, but they do this with a notion of objective desirability of objects (or objects in a situation) rather than a notion of subjective desires. Take the scenario just described in which Joe wants a bunny and finds it, but Bill wants a dog and finds a bunny; and Joe and Bill are judged to be correspondingly happy versus sad, respectively. Perhaps young children see this as two very different situations—(a) Joe's situation and search versus (b) Bill's situation and search—and see one bunny as (objectively) good in (a) but see another bunny as (objectively) bad in (b). Note in the Wellman and Woolley (1990) scenarios just described it is not the case that Joe and Bill are in the exact same situation at the exact same time, and it is not explicitly clear whether they find the exact same bunny. So it is not completely clear that they have subjectively different desires and subjectively different emotions about the exact same situation-event.

However, Hannes Rakoczy and his colleagues (Rakoczy et al., 2007) addressed this concern in two studies comparing situations such as the original Joe–Bill case (in which desires and outcomes were different but might conceivably be compatible because the situation also objectively diverged) versus modified situations in which essentially Joe and Bill are together in the exact same situation, go together to the exact same location, which yields the exact same situation (e.g., finding that *one* bunny): 3-year-olds were equally, appropriately correct in both such desire tasks.

And, of course, even 2-year-olds appear to comment on feelings about the exact same situation in some of their everyday contrastives:

ABE: You like it?
ADULT: Yes I do.
ABE: But I don't like it.

Emotions and desires are core psychological phenomena; explicitly distinguishing the subjective-experiential nature of such states represents a major milestone in children's understanding of the psychological nature of persons. And based on these data from everyday conversations and simple experiments, this is a milestone children pass quite early. There is certainly more to say about children's understanding of desires and emotions, but one thing to note is that in these studies, children seem to evidence some cogent understanding of desires and emotions well in advance of a representational understanding of beliefs. This is confirmed in direct comparisons between their understanding of these states.

TALKING ABOUT DESIRES IN RELATION TO TALKING ABOUT THINKING

To best understand children's talk about persons' desires and emotions—using terms like *want, like, happy, afraid*—it is useful to compare that to their talk about beliefs and knowledge—using terms such as *think, know, remember, dream*. Sometimes children use any of these terms in ways that clearly or arguably do *not* refer to mental states. Just as "I want that" might mean simply "Give me that," "You know what?" can certainly just be something to say to get someone's attention (not really referring to their knowledge), and "Remember the keys" can just mean "Bring the keys." But it is reasonably easy to weed out these nonmental, conversational utterances and identify those in which children genuinely seem to be referring to someone's mental states. Karen Bartsch and I (Bartsch & Wellman, 1995) did this, examining approximately 12,000 childhood utterances (from 10 children studied longitudinally) using terms such as *want, like, think*, and *know* to identify genuine references to desires as well as genuine references to beliefs. A very clear pattern emerged, as shown in Figure 4.1.

It is easy to see in Figure 4.1 that genuine references to desires (and emotions) appear quite early, but genuine references to beliefs appear substantially later—only beginning to appear about age 3 years and progressively, consistently apparent from 3 to 4 years. Parenthetically, the data show that talking about knowledge (e.g., via *know*) precedes talking about beliefs (via *think*). Figure 4.1 collapses together talking about both thinking and knowing (under the general heading of belief) to make the point that talk about desire (via *want* and *like*) precedes both of those.

The graph in Figure 4.1 depicts the data summed across 10 children, but the same general pattern was apparent for every child examined separately—references to desires were apparent from almost as early as the child began to talk in 2-word utterances; references to belief appeared only 1 to 2 years later. The point at which substantial talk about belief emerged varied across children (earlier or later, just as in the data for understanding false belief in Chapter 2), but the pattern was consistent.

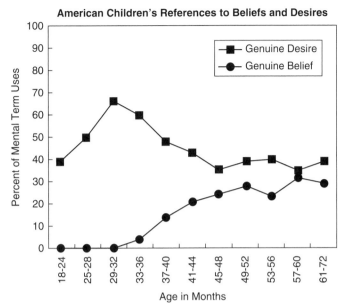

FIGURE 4.1 Children's genuine references to beliefs and desires in conversations with their parents. (From Bartsch & Wellman, 1995)

Other studies have confirmed this pattern. Using smaller samples of conversation from larger samples of English-speaking mother–child pairs, for example, Ted Ruffman and his colleagues (Ruffman et al., 2002) reported the exact same pattern. Moreover, children in China—both those growing up speaking Mandarin and those growing up speaking Cantonese—show this same general developmental sequence (Tardif & Wellman, 2000); indeed, so do children growing up speaking Spanish (Ferres, 2003) and deaf children growing up communicating in sign (Anderson & Reilly, 2002).

The sorts of *contrastive* utterances described earlier for references to desires and emotions also provide convincing data for references to thoughts and knowledge:

ADULT: Hey, it works. See?
ABE (3;4): I thoughted it was busted.

ROSS (4;8): Now she knows that I know. She used to think that I don't know when I really did.

ADULT: I thought you were downstairs.
ADAM (3;3): I thought me was upstairs.

ADULT: What are you making?
SARAH (4;9): Something good out of this paper. An' you don't know but I know.

ROSS (3;7): Do you think God is good?
ADULT: Yes.
ROSS: But we think God is mean.

ADULT: Why?
ROSS: Because he spanks me.
(Bartsch & Wellman, 1995)

Parallel to their conversations about desires and emotions, children make two different kinds of distinctions in these contrastives. In the first two preceding examples, the
child contrasts someone's thought or knowledge and what is actually so (distinguishing
mind and world, much as some desire contrastives distinguished outcomes from desires).
In the last three examples, the child contrasts one person's thoughts or knowledge with
that of someone else (distinguishing subjective differences between thoughts, much
as some desire contrastives distinguished subjective differences between two persons'
desires). When Karen Bartsch and I (Bartsch & Wellman, 1995) limited our focus to
just children's contrastive utterances (these clearer, arguably more precise references to
the mental world), an identical pattern emerged as that in Figure 4.1. Early contrastive
references to desires were frequent and appeared well before any contrastive reference to
beliefs.

In the preceding examples, very often the children are talking about themselves, about
their own mental states. Could young children's references to mental states (desires or
beliefs) be simply the awareness plus labeling of their *own* experiences? Or do children
also refer to the internal and hence unobservable states of others? If, at some young age,
children do nothing more than label their own states, they might be evidencing at best a
very limited understanding rather than using mental state concepts or constructs more
generally and insightfully (Smiley & Huttenlocher, 1995). However, the data show that,
at least by 1½ and 2 years of age, children do more than refer to their own states; they
comment on the internal states of others too. They do so first for desires and later for
beliefs. Children's genuine references to both desires and beliefs do tend to be mostly
about their own states but by no means always. Even at the youngest ages, they also refer
to others' internal states (Bartsch & Wellman, 1995; Ruffman et al., 2002). References
to others' states are, of course, further clear in some of children's contrastives. In many
of their contrastives, like the last three just quoted, young children go beyond commenting on their own states; they acknowledge differences between themselves and others,
attributing to others unique and independent states of desire and states of belief.

To me, these data show a genuine shift in children's explicit understanding from
construing persons in terms of their desires and emotions to only later recognizing the
ever-presence and importance of beliefs as well. But consider an alternative interpretation. Perhaps what looks like a developmental progression from an early mentalistic
reference to desire to a later belief-desire understanding is a simple reflection of how
adults talk to children. Specifically, perhaps adults do not talk to children about beliefs
until they are about 3 years old or so, and children follow parents' model as to what to
talk about: Talk about desires when mom does; only talk about beliefs later when mom
does. Karen Bartsch and I (Bartsch & Wellman, 1995) tested this possibility by coding

parents' talk to their children in the same transcripts as those used for the child data in Figure 4.1. In fact, parents frequently used terms referring to beliefs and thoughts in talking to their very young children—more than 25% of the mental term talk to 2-year-olds used belief and thought terms such as *think*. Moreover, in their use of such terms to talk to very young children, adults predominantly made genuine references to thoughts and beliefs (not empty, conversational use of such terms as in "Know what?" or "Remember the keys"). Thus, at a very young age, children hear people described in terms of beliefs as well as desires, yet such young children describe and refer to people in terms of desires, not beliefs. The shift in children's expressions and focus depicted in Figure 4.1 is all the more striking, therefore, because their parents (as good belief-desire psychologists) are talking to them about beliefs as well as desires from the beginning. Indeed, Elizabeth Meins and colleagues (Meins & Fernyhough, 1999; Meins et al., 2003) and Mele Taumoepeau and Ted Ruffman (2006) have reported how parents talk to their *infants* about beliefs as well as desires.

EXPERIMENTAL COMPARISONS

Experimental data complement the conversational data in also showing earlier understanding of simple desires and simple emotions than of beliefs. Recall diverse-desire tasks, such as the task where Ann likes playing outside and Joy likes staying in. Now consider a parallel *diverse-belief* task: Ann and Joy are at preschool and the teacher needs help finding the book for story time. Ann thinks the storybook is in the drawer, Joy thinks it's in the cupboard. Where does Ann go to search for the book? Where does Joy go?

Given parallel tasks such as these, which compare diverse desires versus diverse beliefs directly, young children are more correct at diverse desires than diverse beliefs. Moreover, they are first correct at diverse desires at ages when they are consistently incorrect for diverse beliefs. A meta-analysis (Wellman & Liu, 2004) confirmed this pattern of understanding desires before beliefs across multiple studies—indeed, in 13 of 13 studies, diverse-desire tasks (of various sorts) were easier for young children than parallel diverse-belief tasks. Kimberly Cassidy (1998) and Hannes Rakoczy and his colleagues (2007) have provided further demonstrations of 3-year-olds easily passing tasks that require desire reasoning but failing parallel belief-reasoning tasks (e.g., "Explicit Desire Conflict" tasks versus the "Explicit Belief Conflict" tasks in Cassidy, 1998).

One example from these various studies neatly captures this difference in early understanding of beliefs and desires while illustrating an additional aspect of an understanding of desires: Desires (as well as beliefs) can become old and outdated. As described in Chapter 2, in a self-belief version of a false-belief task (a surprising contents task in this case), the child might see a crayon box and open it to discover candles. The box is closed and the child is asked, "When you first saw this box, before we looked inside, what did you think was in here? Crayons or candles?" Alison Gopnik and Virginia Slaughter (1991) used exactly this task with young children, 3-year-olds, and typically enough almost all answered incorrectly: They said they thought there were candles, before they looked inside. In doing so, they fail to correctly understand or report their old, outdated belief.

Now consider a parallel self-desire task. In three different tasks, Alison Gopnik and Virginia Slaughter (1991) presented children with situations in which their desires became outdated and so changed. For example, initially the child desired one of two short books. That one was read to him and the child said (naturally enough) he now desired the other book. The test question for the past desires was just like the one for past beliefs: "When you first saw the books, before we read one, which one did you want? Book A or Book B?" In these tasks, the same 3-year-old children who failed the self-belief task were typically correct. Thus, they were considerably better at reporting past now-changed desires than past now-changed beliefs. Many children were consistently correct for desires and failed completely at beliefs. (See Gopnik, Slaughter, & Meltzoff, 1994, for similar data, and Lagattuta & Wellman, 2001, for data on young children's ability to deal appropriately with past emotions.)

Incidentally, note this means that young children's problems with self false beliefs cannot just be problems of poor memory, that is, just having a hard time remembering past mental states. If that was the problem, they would be poor at both their past desires and past beliefs. But they are poor on past, outdated beliefs even though easily able to report on past, outdated states more generally, namely, past, outdated desires.

CONCEPTUALIZING DESIRES AND EMOTIONS

How can we characterize the sort of understanding of mental states—in particular, a genuine subjective-internal understanding of desire and emotion—a child might have that nonetheless falls short of a representational understanding evident in understanding beliefs? Figure 4.2 captures one way to think of this difference in a simple graphical contrast between understanding beliefs (as used before in Chapter 2) versus a very basic understanding of desires and emotions. For desires, a young child could construe someone as having an internal urge (a yen) directed to the world. "He wants *that*." Or, John, on the left, "wants an apple" ("likes apples"); Jack, on the right, "doesn't want an apple" ("hates apples"). Note this depiction is of an internal state: John feels an internal longing for the apple, preferring it, desiring it. Note, also, this sort of understanding is appropriately subjective: John wants it, Jack does not; John likes it, Jacks hates it.

To repeat, this depiction is of a simplified construal of desires. Our adult construal of desires is complex and nuanced (as is our understanding of beliefs). And philosophers typically argue that even desires are best understood as representational. That is, *as understood by philosophers and adults*, desires are representational (in some ways),

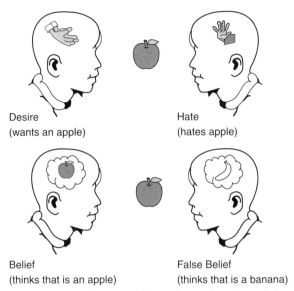

Desire
(wants an apple)

Hate
(hates apple)

Belief
(thinks that is an apple)

False Belief
(thinks that is a banana)

FIGURE 4.2 Graphical depiction of a young child's understanding of simple desires (top) and beliefs (bottom).

like beliefs (e.g., if I assert "John wants a unicorn," and I know that unicorns are imaginary, then I'm showing an understanding of desires that is, in part, representational). But a young child could have an initial simplified understanding. Desires, most simply understood, as in Figure 4.2, are internal, subjective, psychological states; but they are nonrepresentational states of "connection" with real-world objects and events. In contrast, beliefs in this depiction (and for 4- and 5-year-olds) are representational. For beliefs, there is mental content "in the head" that represents the world. Even 4-year-olds often understand beliefs in this way; remember the data in Chapter 2 on how easily they understand thoughts in terms of thought bubbles—the representational device used in Figure 4.2 for beliefs (but not desires).

We can distinguish, therefore, between one sort of understanding whereby certain mental states are construed as providing a subjective connection to the world, or a direct registration of the world, and another understanding whereby other states are construed as the person representing an external state of affairs. The hypothesis is that young children first understand mental states of the connections-registration sort and only later understand representational mental states as well (e.g., Apperly, 2011; Flavell, 1988; Wellman & Woolley, 1990). Such a conception accounts for their good performance on tasks of basic desires and emotions, before good performance on parallel tasks assessing understanding of beliefs.

We are talking for now about a very basic and simplified understanding of desires or emotions. Further understandings emerge and are required, for example, to understand such "complex" emotions as shame or pride and are required to understand more precise distinctions, for example, between desires and specific intentions. I have more to say about later emotion understandings in the next chapter.

PERCEPTION

Very young children are not limited to understanding desires and emotions. Among other things, they have early intriguing understandings of perception and perceptual awareness. I can outline the case for perception succinctly, thanks in large part to the efforts of John Flavell and his colleagues (e.g., Flavell, 1988; Flavell, Everett, Croft, & Flavell, 1981).

Children begin to use perception terms such as *look* and *see* from about 1½ years (Bretherton & Beeghly, 1982; Wellman, Phillips, & Rodriguez, 2000). Children refer to perception (via *look, see, show, hear, listen, touch, taste, smell*) as early as and just about as frequently as they refer to desires (Wellman et al., 2000). Moreover their understanding of perception progresses in an intriguing developmental fashion between 2, 3, and 4 years. John Flavell has called this a development from a Level-1 to a Level-2 understanding of perception (e.g., Flavell, 1988) or a shift from Level-1 to Level-2 perspective taking (e.g., Flavell, 1978). Let's talk about this in terms of visual perception, although the same story can be told for hearing, touch, and so forth.

A Level-1 understanding of perceptual awareness emphasizes children's ability to infer what *object* someone else sees. Level-1 understanding of perception therefore encompasses children's understanding that others may not see the same things they themselves see, and thus that two different people (e.g., self and other) may see different objects. Level-2 understanding of perception, in addition, involves inferring people's perspectives, or differing perceptual experiences, of objects, for example, what people see when they see the exact same object but view it in different ways (e.g., you see its front and I see its back). Level-2 understanding (and hence Level-2 perspective taking) usually is evident only in children older than 3 years of age.

Following from these descriptions, in a typical Level-1 task, the child sees one object or thing that another person cannot, and who instead sees a different object. For example, a large card with a picture of a dog on one side and a picture of a cat on the other side is held between the child and adult. The child is asked, "Do *you* see the dog or the cat?" and "Do *I* see the dog or the cat?" Two- and 3-year-olds are routinely correct on both questions (Flavell, Everett, Croft, & Flavell, 1981; Gopnik & Slaughter, 1991; Moll & Meltzoff, 2011). In a related task, a child and adult face each other across a table that holds a small object—say, a grapefruit-sized ball. On some trials a screen is placed on the table so the object is on the child's side of the screen, and on other trials the screen is placed so the object is on the adult's side hidden from the child's view. The child is asked, "Can *you* see the ball?" and "Can *I* see the ball?" Children as young as 2 years are largely correct on both questions (Masangkay et al., 1974; Wellman et al., 2000).

In a typical Level-2 task (paralleling the dog–cat Level-1 task), a child might see a turtle drawn on a sheet of paper placed face up between himself and an adult, with the turtle's feet toward the child and the turtle's shell toward the adult. The child is asked, "Do *you* see the turtle standing on its feet or lying on its shell?" and, "Do *I* see the turtle standing on its feet or lying on its shell?" Or, the child might see a grapefruit-sized plastic head of a witch (with ugly pointy nose in front and scraggly hair streaming behind). After the child plays with the figure for a while (and labels its face and its back), the witch is oriented on the table facing the child (or facing the adult). Then the child is asked, "Do *you* see the witch's face or her back?" and, "Do *I* see the witch's face or her back?" The 2- and 3-year-olds who perform quite well on the Level-1 tasks perform quite poorly on the parallel Level-2 tasks; and 4-year-olds perform well on both sets of tasks (Masangkay et al., 1974).

John Flavell (e.g., 1988) argued that for Level-1 tasks, the child need only understand persons as connected, via lines of sight, to objects in the world, much as desires are construed as connecting people to the world (i.e., connecting the person to the apple) in Figure 4.2. Level-2 perspective taking, however, requires the child to understand that persons' visual experiences represent the object as a certain way—upside down or right side up, its front or its back, as fuzzy and unclear or precise and sharp—much as beliefs are construed as representing the world in Figure 4.2. In Level 1, visual objects exist as entire objects and people are aware of them or not. In Level 2, visual objects exist as entire objects, but people may only see parts of them, facets of them, whatever is in their precise viewpoint. And people may miss-see them; they see a black bird but it's only a leaf's shadow. Hence in Level 2, people's visual representation of the object is distinguishable from the object itself.

To further support the claim that older preschoolers understand perception in terms of perceptual representations, Flavell and colleagues (e.g., Flavell, Green, & Flavell, 1986) went on to test children's understanding of appearances versus realities and developed a number of appearance-reality tasks. A sample, and classic, appearance-reality task uses a deceptive object, such as a sponge shaped and painted to look remarkably like a rock, or a plastic egg that looks remarkably like a real egg. Children are asked what they think it is ("a rock") then allowed to play with it where they discover that it's "a sponge!" Then children are asked a reality question: "Really and truly what is this? A rock or a sponge?" And they are asked an appearance question: "What does this look like to your eyes? A rock or a sponge?" (Of course, some children, or the same child on different items, are asked the reality question first and the looks-like question second and some the other way around.) Younger children typically fail these tasks, giving the exact same answer for the reality and the looks-like questions (Flavell et al., 1986). On some items, children fail by reporting reality: "It is a sponge and it looks like a sponge." On others, children fail by reporting appearance: "It looks like an egg and it is an egg." So it is not that once young children are acquainted with the item's real character they can't report anything else. It's that they don't distinguish appearance and reality properly.

On the whole, 3-year-olds fail appearance-reality tasks and 4- and 5-year-olds pass them. Moreover, progress on appearance reality typically correlates nicely with progress on false belief—as expected if both were indexing some similar representational understanding of mental states (Carlson & Moses, 2001; Gopnik & Astington, 1988). Of course, just as people have wondered if standard false-belief tasks might be misleadingly hard for young children, others (including John Flavell himself) have wondered if standard appearance-reality tasks might just be misleadingly hard for young children. Many variations on the tasks (including heroic efforts to simplify the tasks by Flavell) make little difference—young children fail nonetheless. This is much as was true for false belief; many variations of false-belief tasks all yield similar findings. But also, as in the case of false belief, it is indeed possible to construct some simpler, easier task variations that do reliably enhance young children's performance at appearance-reality judgments (e.g., Deák, Ray, & Brenneman, 2003; Hansen & Markman, 2005). Similarly, Henrike Moll and Andy Meltzoff (2011) argued that the Level-1 versus Level-2 distinction is not clear-cut and devised tasks that 36-month-olds did well on that nonetheless had some Level-2-like properties. But, again, just as was the case for false belief, essential trajectories remain the same—there is an early point when young children who pass Level-1 perception tasks fail (even simplified) appearance-reality tasks or Level-2 tasks.

With regard to a Level-1 understanding of perception, it is reasonable to ask just how much young children know about perception. This is parallel to the suspicion that perhaps early understanding of desire was behavioral and overt (not appropriately subjective and mental). A similar suspicion about Level-1 understanding of "perception" might be that young children don't understand visual perception as some sort of internal, subjective experience but rather as an externalized line of directedness from eyeballs to objects. Indeed, in his early work, Flavell (1978) essentially concluded that Level-1 perspective taking may represent merely the young child's geometric understanding of lines of sight—how sightlines can extend from eyeballs to objects—and not an understanding of visual experience (see also Butterworth & Jarrett, 1991). But in fact, Level-1 understanding of others' perception does include a real sense that others are having a subjective, internal experience. How so?

For one thing, we (Wellman et al., 2000) showed that children understand that seeing yields an inner experience because they know the action of seeing often produces inner, subjective experiences such as emotions and desires as well. For example, children know that looking at something pleasant (or unpleasant) yields an inner feeling of pleasure (or displeasure) for the viewer. This is evident in Level-1 perspective-taking tasks with a twist in which 2-year-old children are asked not only about what the viewer sees but what he or she feels.

Indeed, recall from Chapter 1 the study with 18-month-olds' understanding of blindfolds: 18-month-olds do *not* gaze follow blindfolded adults (whereas 12-month-olds do). Ordinary blindfolds block visual experience, and perhaps 18-month-olds know this.

But ordinary blindfolds also provide an overt cloth in front of one's eyes blocking the child's view of the adult's eyes. Perhaps all 18-month-olds appreciate is that such an overt cloth cuts the overt line of connection from eyeballs to object. But after appropriate experience with special blindfolds that allow for vision, 18-month-olds did appropriately gaze follow (Meltzoff & Brooks, 2008). That special blindfold allowed vision but nonetheless also provided an overt cloth in front of one's eyes, blocking the child's view of the adult's eyes *and* blocking the overt connection from adult's eyeballs to object. If, for 18-month-olds, "vision" is just eyeball directedness, then both blindfold conditions are the same. But if vision is about a "subjective awareness," visual experience, these two conditions differ enormously because one allows visual experience and one does not. Eighteen-month-olds appropriately treated these two conditions—regular blindfolds versus special blindfold—as vastly different. Perception is not just overt (eyes contact objects); perception yields subjective internal psychological experience, and young children know this.

Appealing to Figure 4.2 again, in essence young children come to an understanding of perceptual awareness, a Level-1 understanding, much like the depiction in Figure 4.2 for desires. For this Level-1 construal of perception, think of a depiction (not of hands inside the person reaching for, wanting the apple, but) of something like an internal flashlight shining on and detecting the apple. This perceptual directedness is an appropriately subjective, internal state because it is easy to also imagine a different person, whose flashlight is oriented elsewhere, or is turned off, not detecting, not seeing, the apple. Level-1 perceptual understanding is appropriately internal and experiential (just as is early simple understanding of desires and emotions); Level-2 understanding is representational (much like an understanding of beliefs).

DESIRE-AWARENESS REASONING

So, before explicitly understanding thoughts and beliefs, children understand various other mental states—internal, subjective states of desires, emotions, and perceptual experience. How does all this go together, if at all? That is, conceivably, such young children could be evidencing some initial, essentially separate understandings of desires, emotion, and perception; or they could be evidencing a more coherent naïve psychological understanding encompassing interconnections between some or even all of these states.

The first possibility, that toddlers' understandings of desires, perceptions, and emotions are essentially separate, is plausible because often, initial understandings are fragmented and only later become coordinated. Moreover, although philosophers and psychologists argue that adults' folk psychology rests on understanding the existence and interrelations among several mental states (e.g., Churchland, 1984; Davidson, 1980), on this claim about the "holism" of mental states, it is the interconnection of desires with beliefs that is critical.

> According to this widely accepted view, ... each of these concepts is situated in a network of related concepts such that their meanings are interdependent .... Concepts of desire without attendant concepts of belief, or beliefs denuded of associated desires, would be fundamentally nonsensical. (Moses & Chandler, 1992, p. 289)

Thus, a coordinated understanding of various mental states could be based on the interplay of beliefs and desires. If so, this understanding would await the time when children first begin to understand beliefs, at around 3 and 4 years and older, with earlier understandings of desires, perceptions, and emotions being partial, incomplete, and conceptually separate.

The alternative possibility, however, now seems more plausible. First, conceptually, even without a conception of belief, an understanding of desires, emotions, and awareness could together form an initial coordinated naïve psychology. On this extension of arguments about mental-state holism, a conception encompassing only a single mental-state concept would certainly be deficient, but a system encompassing several might be adequate, even powerful. Specifically, understanding of the intentional states of attending to, wanting, and emotionally reacting to objects encompasses several important features that could yield very young children a coherent system for understanding human behavior. In shorthand, I'll call this a coherent *desire-awareness* understanding. These states, for example, include both mind-to-world and world-to-mind directions of fit (Searle, 1983). That is, as adults, we tend to construe some internal states as directed toward changing the world, making world fit mind. Desires, for example, lead to (and thus underlie) acts such as reaching, searching, and asking for objects. If our desires are unsatisfied, we typically change our actions, trying to fit world to mind. Other states, such as belief but also perceptual awareness, instead accommodate themselves to objects, that is, mind fits world. If our initial perception (or belief) proves wrong, we typically change our minds, fitting mind to world. An initial connected understanding of perceptual experience along with desire could thus encompass a significant duality: understanding of both intentional action toward the world and intentional experience of it.

Of course, young children might have a less interesting, impoverished sort of "holism" if they simply failed to differentiate emotions, desires, and perceptions. But for young children, these states are both connected and distinct. One way to see this is that, conceptually, construing persons in terms of emotions, desires, and awareness offers a range of interconnected inferences and predictions; and, empirically, we now know that 2-year-olds make many of these inferences and predictions. For example, if someone wants something, then getting it makes them happy; if they definitely do not want something, then getting it anyway makes them unhappy (Repacholi & Gopnik, 1997;

Wellman & Liu, 2004; Wellman & Woolley, 1990). Additional inferences depend on the understanding that perception anchors one (and hence connects one's desires and emotions) to the external world: If someone likes something and sees it, then they are likely to be pleased; if they dislike something and see that, then they may be disgusted or displeased (Moses, Baldwin, Rosicky, & Tidball, 2001; Wellman et al., 2000). Betty Repacholi and her colleagues (Repacholi, Meltzoff, & Olsen, 2008) demonstrated that even 18-month-olds know "if she can't see me doing it, she won't get angry." These are simple but profound inferences or predictions, available even to toddlers. Such coherent inferences are also often evident in young children's talk. Young children, for example, often mention such connections as these (Wellman et al., 2000): *perception leads to emotion* ("Hear it popping? That scares me," or "He's happy 'cause he saw a cowboy"), *perception leads to desire* ("He saw cookies on TV and wants some"), and *desire for perception* ("I want to hear it," or "He doesn't want a look").

Note that such a desire-awareness reasoning system could easily encompass an initial, simple understanding of knowledge: If someone sees something, that establishes an internal, subjective awareness of, engagement with, and connection to that object. And such a connection can continue (just as a desire for the object could continue, or being scared of it could continue) even if the object is now hidden from the person's sight. Knowledge (in this simple Level-1 sense of an activated internal awareness of the object) does not disappear just because the object becomes occluded. Conversely, never seeing the object in the first place, because it is hidden from sight although in the very same room with you, yields a simple form of ignorance. This is because not seeing it fails to establish the critical internal, subjective connection ("If she can't see me doing it, she won't get angry"). It fails to establish the appropriate subjective awareness of or engagement with the object.

Such a coherent desire-awareness understanding of persons not only encompasses a simple "engagement" form of knowledge, it also encompasses a mental–physical dualism, namely, the distinction between overt behavior or overt situations versus internal, subjective feelings and experiences. Moreover, it encompasses a causal-explanatory framework for thinking about persons' actions and experiences, for example, in the inferences just outlined: Getting something you want makes you feel happy; seeing something that you like and that is available causes you to want it. Not only predictions but young children's early explanations also tap into and reveal this framework—"He's happy 'cause he saw a cowboy." Before children offer belief-desire psychological explanations of the sort emphasized in Chapter 2, they still offer psychological explanations. Recall, even 2- and 3-year-olds seek and provide such explanations. Naturally enough they do so by citing perceptions, emotions, and desires—"He's crying 'cause he's sad"; "He's not afraid, 'cause he doesn't see that snake." "She put ketchup on her ice cream because she wanted to." Appropriately, very young children's most frequent explanation of human action is that the actor did the act *because he wanted to* (see Bartsch & Wellman, 1995, and Hickling & Wellman, 2001, for 2- and 3-year-olds' everyday conversational explanations of action; and Schult & Wellman, 1997, for experimentally induced explanations of human action).

This sort of coherent naïve psychology, integrating together a subjective, internal sense of persons' desires, emotions, and perceptual engagement—in a way that encompasses an initial sense of a person's knowledge and ignorance—is impressive, and it is apparent in very young children: 2-year-olds. Indeed this sort of understanding, I believe, underpins the still earlier conceptions and competences in infants, as I address in Chapter 8.

REAL-WORLD CONSEQUENCES

Young children's understanding of persons as desiring, feeling, aware agents manifests itself in their everyday behavior and interactions, just as older children's belief-desire psychology impacts their social lives. Young children, even infants, get into conflicts with and oppose other people (see also Reddy, 2008). Young children, even infants, recognize agents who help versus hinder someone else's action (Kuhlmeier, Wynn, & Bloom, 2003) and react to persons who fail to give them something desirable (Behne et al., 2005). Such everyday reactions can at times be based on, and so can reveal the impact of, the child's understanding of internal states of intention and desire.

During the second and third years (12–36 months or so), for example, Judy Dunn (1988) documented increases in young children's knowingly teasing others as well as their conflicts with both their parents and with their siblings (see also Reddy, 2008). Indeed, as young children get more and more clear on the nature of desires and the differences between desires between persons, they manifest what mothers and pediatricians call "the terrible twos." Of course even younger children, infants, do things their parents don't like; but numerous authors have claimed that what sets the terrible twos apart is the insistence children often show in contrasting their desires with that of their parents, vigorously exercising and experimenting with the nature of divergent desires in the real-world case of "what I want" versus "what mom wants." At this age, children can often (annoyingly, terribly, in addition to teasingly) insist on being oppositional—in opposing their parents' desires—to such an extent that they thwart their own preferences in the endeavor to maintain/proclaim their independent desires. My wife once reported to me the following exchange with our then 2-year-old:

MOTHER: Here's a cookie.
CHILD: No!

At this age, the line between teasing and terrible is lost in the process of staking out differences.

One way to quantify some of this is to examine children's verbal conflicts more closely. Thus Karen Bartsch and I (1995) coded children's everyday conflicts as expressed in their talk, looking for conflicts of desire and also conflicts of belief. For example, *Desire*:

ADULT: We'll turn it on later.

CHILD (2;10): You turn it on later?

ADULT: Yep.

CHILD: No. I don't want it on later...I want it on now. You said you will turn the cowboys on!

ADULT: I said I'll turn them on later.

ADULT: Don't.

CHILD (2;10): I want...don't want...I don't want it on [a Band-Aid].

ADULT: Well you gotta have it on. Leave it on.

CHILD: No.

CHILD (2;9): I wanna watch TV, I wanna watch TV

ADULT: You can in a little while.

CHILD: I wanna watch something now.

ADULT: Nothing good is on until 11 o'clock. Why don't we practice tumbling for a while.

CHILD: I don't wanna tumble.

Belief:

ADAM (3;3): Does you think have sugar...some sugar in here?

ADULT: I don't have any sugar

ADAM: I think you have sugar.

CHILD (3;10): Leslie make me angry.

ADULT: Why?

CHILD: If she thinks something is silly. I don't think it's silly at all.

ADULT: Oh, you had a disagreement.

CHILD: Uh huh. She thought her necklace was silly.

ADULT: She thought it was silly?

CHILD: Yeah. But I didn't think it was.

(Abe and his father are watching a TV program about snakes with a female narrator.)

ABE (3;8): Is that a poisonous snake, dad?

ADULT: No.

ABE: I think if she tells about it...I think if she says it's a poisonous snake...you're gonna be wrong.

ADULT: You're right, I would be wrong. But it's not a poisonous snake, she just said it wasn't.

ABE: It looks like a poisonous snake.

ADULT: Yah. But it's not

Beyond a frequent focus on television, these young children are reasoning about people, but not only reasoning about them, they are arguing with them—in disputing different possessions, attempting to persuade someone to a different course of action, or taking sides in or trying to resolve various conflicts.

Some disputes revolve around people's physical aspects (e.g., who is bigger or stronger), some around aspects of social interchange (e.g., whose turn it is or who possesses certain objects); but others involve specifically psychological aspects, including whose desires will prevail or whose beliefs are correct. By implication, if children move from a conception of persons in terms of desires to a conception that includes beliefs, that transition should influence the nature of their disputes and conflicts as well. That is part of what Karen Bartsch and I (Bartsch & Wellman, 1995) analyzed. The upshot of this analysis was quite clear. Awareness of differences in desires, and conflicts over whose desires are to be satisfied, were indeed found to be common in the very early talk of children. But, disputes about thoughts and beliefs, about whose representations of reality are correct, appeared later.

Children's frequent engagement in psychological disputes—conflicts with others about desires and beliefs—suggests a larger hypothesis. Not only are their disputes shaped by their mental-state understandings, their mental state understandings may also be shaped by their disputes. Disputes may provide formative, and early, experiences for children, heightening their awareness that psychological states differ across persons and that psychological contents can certainly differ from the real-world state of affairs that they are about. Piaget (1932) advanced such a hypothesis, but he emphasized children's conflicts with peers in the school years. Contemporary conversational data underwrite the ubiquity of conflicts at much younger ages between children and siblings and also with parents, suggesting the possibility of a still larger role for such experiences in shaping children's social cognition.

CONCLUSIONS

Theory of mind, in some of its forms and insights, is achieved early. Early acquisitions are especially clear in very young children's understandings that go beyond agents' situations, behaviors, and overt expressions to penetrate to their subjective desires, emotions, and perceptual experiences. But early theory of mind is also dynamic: It develops. How does that unfold? Describing preschool theory-of-mind development as a shift from desires to beliefs (as in Figure 4.2) or from connections to representations (or even more comprehensively from desire-awareness psychology to belief-desire psychology) is too simplistic. Such descriptions provide an arbitrary, preliminary convenience that extracts certain compartmentalized moments from an extended progression of development. Figure 4.2 depicts two crude stair steps, but the terrain is more flowing and more interesting than that, as I detail next.

5

Extended Progressions in Theory-of-Mind Understanding

TENNESSEE WILLIAMS (IN *Camino Real*) said, "Humanity is just a work in progress" (Partington, 1996, p. 737). So too is theory of mind in the preschool years: It is a progression of insights and developments.

SCALING THEORY OF MIND

Although Figure 4.2 falsely suggests there might be just two steps for children as they come to understand mental states, that figure nevertheless utilizes a pictorial shorthand that can be helpful for thinking further about theory-of-mind understandings. So, consider Figure 5.1 on the next page, which extends this shorthand to depict a variety of understandings a child might achieve about various mental-state distinctions. Among other things, as shown in that figure a child might understand that people can have Diverse Desires (people can have different desires for the same thing), Diverse Beliefs (people can have different beliefs about the same situation), Knowledge-Access (something can be true, but someone without access to it would be ignorant of it), False Belief (something can be true, but someone might believe something different), and Hidden Emotion (someone can feel one way but display a different emotion). Figure 5.1 also suggests that tasks could be devised that would have very similar formats but nonetheless tap these differing insights about mental states.

David Liu and I (Wellman & Liu, 2004) used this sort of reasoning to begin to establish a Theory-of-Mind Scale (ToM Scale) to characterize and measure preschool

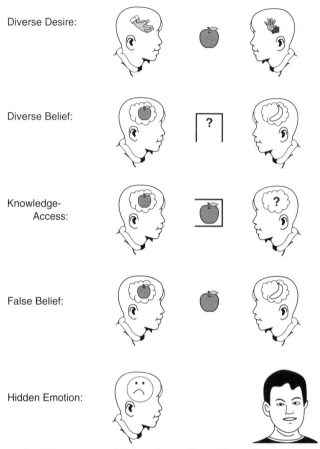

Diverse Desire:

Diverse Belief:

Knowledge-Access:

False Belief:

Hidden Emotion:

FIGURE 5.1 Graphical depiction of a child's understanding of five different mental-state contrasts

theory-of-mind progressions. Just as outlined in Figure 5.1, this particular scale is composed of five carefully chosen steps assessed through parallel tasks measuring childhood understanding. So, in brief, the scale captures childhood understanding of (a) Diverse Desires (DD), (b) Diverse Beliefs (DB), (c) Knowledge-Access (KA), (d) False Belief (FB), and (e) Hidden Emotion (HE). Table 5.1 describes the steps and illustrative tasks in more detail. Each task had features similar to the false-belief tasks described in Chapter 2 and very like the diverse-desire tasks described in Chapter 4. A simple two-part scenario about a character or characters was enacted with drawings or simple props (e.g., picture of a cupboard or closet, a small figurine of a boy), and a target question plus a warm-up question or control question were asked. In these ways the tasks were comparable in procedures, language, and format. Yet in several converging studies, U.S. preschoolers have evidenced a clear order of difficulty, listed in Table 5.1, with understanding diverse desires being easiest and understanding hidden emotion being hardest (Wellman et al., 2006; 2011; Wellman & Liu, 2004; Wellman, Lopez-Duran, LaBounty, & Hamilton, 2008). For shorthand, I refer to this sequence as, DD>DB>KA>FB>HE. The same five-step progression also characterizes Australian (Peterson & Wellman, 2009; Peterson et al., 2005) and German (Kristen et al., 2006) preschoolers tested with these tasks.

Conceivably, all these mental-state insights might have been equally hard for children: All concern subjective, internal states (desires, ignorance, beliefs, feelings) that are potentially at odds with overt behavior or external reality. All concern explicit aspects of theory of mind achieved by normally developing children within the

TABLE 5.1

Example Theory of Mind Scale items

Task	Brief Description
1. Diverse Desires	Child judges that two persons (the child vs. someone else) have different desires about the same object: Given two possible snacks (carrot, cookie), child states his preference but then must predict snack choice of other person (who has the opposite preference).
2. Diverse Beliefs	Child judges that two persons (the child vs. someone else) have different beliefs about the same object when the child does not know which belief is true or false: Child states her belief that object is in the garage, hears other person's belief that it is in the bushes; child never sees where item is but must predict whether other person will search in the garage or in the bushes.
3. Knowledge-Access	Child judges another person's ignorance about the contents of a container when child knows what is in the container: Child sees toy dog in nondescript drawer, drawer is closed, child judges if other person (who has never seen inside) knows what is in drawer.
4. Contents False Belief*	Child judges another person's false belief about what is in a distinctive container when child knows what is in the container: Child sees familiar band-aid box, discovers it has pencils inside, then must judge belief of someone else who has never seen inside.
5. Hidden Emotion	Child judges that a person can feel one thing but display a different emotion: Character is hurtfully teased but doesn't want his friends to know his feelings; child judges how character will feel (sad) and what he will show on his face (happy).

*Note: Other false-belief tasks can be used. For several reasons (see Wellman & Liu, 2004), Contents False Belief is the task included in the standard five-step scale.

toddler/preschool years. Even more conceivably, children would understand some states before others, but earlier-understood versus later-understood states would not be consistent from one child to the next. Because of inevitably different individual experiences and differing family foci of conversations (e.g., emotions vs. wants vs. ignorance), any group of children might very well evidence a scatter of different patterns. In contrast to either of these alternatives, the scaling data consistently confirm distinct regularities in children's developing understanding of mind—about 75–85% of children tested in the United States and Australia, for example, evidence the same pattern: DD>DB>KA>FB>HE. It is worth emphasizing how consistent children are; by chance alone, for example, less than 20% of children's responses would be consistent with this pattern.

The steps in this scale evidence an important developmental property: The scale forms a strict Guttman scale (1944, 1950) in which patterns of success and failure are such that if a young child knows one thing (passes a single task), it is almost always diverse desires; if he or she knows two things, it is almost always diverse desires and diverse beliefs; and so on. This means that if a child gets a total correct score of 4 versus 2, for instance (where total scores can range from 0–5 of the five tasks correct), this not only tells you the child who got 4 knows more things; it tells you to a very good approximation *what* the child with a 2 knows (DD and DB), what remaining things he fails to know, and what else beyond those two things the child with a 4 knows (KA and FB but not HE). Table 5.2 shows the stair step Guttman pattern.

A Guttman scale is very strict, requiring perfect adherence, so a child that is one off the pattern (say, gets DD, DB, and FB correct without getting KA correct) and a child that is four off (e.g., gets hidden emotion, HE, correct but fails everything else) both count as misses. Children's responses to this ToM Scale are significantly scalable, even in this strict sense. But, it is also possible to analyze the data more probabilistically (and by doing so to extract still more information from the total set of item successes and

TABLE 5.2

Guttman scalogram for the five core items						
Diverse Desires	−	+	+	+	+	+
Diverse Belief	−	−	+	+	+	+
Knowledge-Access	−	−	−	+	+	+
Contents False Belief	−	−	−	−	+	+
Hidden Emotion	−	−	−	−	−	+

80% of children evidence one of these six patterns

Other Patterns 20% of children evidence one of 26 other possible patterns failures). This can be done via more complex statistical modeling, such as Rasch modeling (Rasch, 1960). Rasch modeling with children's ToM Scale data also confirms a developmental progression across the five items that is highly significantly different from chance (Wellman et al., 2006; Wellman & Liu, 2004). Moreover, Rasch modeling also provides an estimated distance metric—an arbitrary continuum of numbers that can estimate not only, for example, that passing diverse belief is harder than passing diverse desire (DD>DB) but how much harder. For example, on an arbitrary scale ranging from 0 to 10, is diverse belief best thought of as 1 harder or as .5 harder or 2.2 harder than diverse desire? Rasch modeling shows that for English-speaking preschoolers, these five items are fairly widely and evenly spaced; on a scale ranging from 0 to 10, diverse desire places at about 1.5, diverse belief at about 3.0, and the next items at 3.9, at 5.0, and then 7.2. So the items are not precisely equidistant, but each has good separation from its neighbors. Using this same 0 to 10 metric, for example, two different false-belief tasks (one surprising contents and one changed locations) place at 5.0 and 5.1 (Wellman & Liu, 2004)—very close together indeed.

Empirically, a scale like this could be formed from any collection of items as long as children only first pass some items then successively pass some more (smiling then walking then being able to add 2 + 3). Theoretically, however, a scale progression is more valid and useful to the extent that it reflects an underlying conceptual progression or trajectory (Guttman, 1944, 1950). For this scale, the focal states to be understood, albeit different in many respects (e.g., feelings vs. knowledge), are conceptually similar in being subjective and thus contrasting across individuals and with objective events or behaviors. That is, two persons can have contrasting desires for the same object or situation; similarly, they can have contrasting beliefs, or one can be knowledgeable when the other is ignorant. Relatedly, a person's mental state can contrast with behavior or with reality, as when a person feels one thing but expresses something different, or believes something not really true. Thus, these items all reflect the fact that mental states can be said to be subjective rather than objective in varying ways, and the scale establishes increasing steps in understanding mental subjectivity. In this way, the scale establishes a progression of conceptual achievements that characterize theory-of-mind development *and* a method for measuring that progression. In fact, the ToM Scale has been translated into multiple languages (Italian, Spanish, Turkish, Korean, Japanese, French, Hebrew, Mandarin, Cantonese, and more); it can measure the accumulating theory-of-mind insights of children in a great many countries and communities worldwide.

Because it works in these fashions, the scale allows a more precise articulation of and attack on several important, largely unaddressed questions. For example, in what way and for which aspects might early theory-of-mind understanding be universal? Or, when children are delayed in theory-of-mind understanding (as are most individuals with autism or with deafness), are they demonstrating delay in a typical developmental trajectory, different trajectories altogether, or both?

Culture and Development, Sequences and Timetables

Sequences

To begin to address some of these issues, consider this question: What processes account for the consistency of sequence I've talked of so far, DD>DB>KA>FB>HE? Clearly, a consistent sequence could result from innately programmed maturations. Or similarly, it could result from maturationally unfolding gains in basic cognitive processes, say increases in executive function or in cognitive capacity. But alternatively, a consistent sequence might also result from processes of conceptual learning (processes of constructivist learning, for example, as proposed in theory theory) in which initial conceptions lead to later conceptions, shaped by a robust pattern of relevant information and experiences. If they are shaped by relevant information and experiences, however, then in principle sequences could be very different.

Assume that theory-of-mind understandings *are* the products of social and conceptual experiences that vary from one community to another, then Western and Chinese childhood experiences could be crucially different. Just as discussed in Chapter 2, Chinese children (in contrast to, say, U.S. and Australian children) grow up in non-Western cultures and participate in childhood experiences different from those of their Western, English-speaking peers. As one example, Chinese languages are non-Indo-European and differ from English in ways that could influence early adult–child conversations, which are known to influence theory-of-mind understandings in English-speaking children. Of special interest here, Chinese languages use a different collection of mental verbs than English does (Tardif & Wellman, 2000). In particular, the English terms *think* and *believe* refer equally, and ambiguously, to beliefs that may be true or false. But Cantonese and Mandarin have specific verbs for "think falsely," and these are used by preschoolers (Lee, Olson, & Torrance, 1999; Tardif, Wellman, & Cheung, 2004). Such diverging language experiences might contribute to important differences in young children's developing theories of mind.

Culturally, various authors have contrasted an emphasis on persons as sharing group commonalities and interdependence—evident in many individuals from East Asia—versus an emphasis on persons as distinctively individual and independent: evident in many individuals in the United States and Western Europe (e.g., Markus & Kitayama, 1991). These differences include a difference in stress on common knowledge and perspectives versus diversity of individual beliefs and perspectives. Moreover, Western and Chinese adults seem to manifest very different everyday epistemologies. Everyday Western epistemology is focused on subjectivity and belief; Confucian-Chinese epistemology focuses more on knowledge acquisition and the consensual knowledge that all right-minded persons should learn. In particular, Richard Nisbett (2003) and Jin Li (2002) have argued that Western epistemology is focused more on truth and falsity of belief and representation, whereas Chinese epistemology is focused more on pragmatic knowledge acquisition. Donald Munro (1969) provided a corroborative analysis in his historical examination of Chinese philosophical thought, *The Concept of Man in Early China*.

In consonance with some of these linguistic-philosophical analyses, developmentally there appear to be cultural differences in how Chinese versus U.S. preschoolers acquire words such as *think* and *know*. Both English- and Chinese-speaking preschoolers acquire a word for *know* as one of their earliest mental-state verbs, before a word for *think* (Tardif & Wellman, 2000). But Chinese children receive more emphasis on knowing relative to thinking. In conversation with young children, both Chinese and U.S. parents talk frequently about people and their mental states, but Chinese parents comment predominantly on knowing (Tardif & Wellman, 2000), whereas U.S. parents comment more on thinking (Bartsch & Wellman, 1995). In Chinese preschools and homes, there is great emphasis on acquiring practical knowledge, such as how to fold one's blanket properly after a nap, tie one's shoes, write Chinese characters, and recite both songs and poems precisely (Li, 2001; Tobin, Wu, & Davidson, 1989). English-speaking preschoolers must also master new knowledge, but the Chinese emphasis on knowledge acquisition at an early age is remarkable (Kessen & The American Delegation on Early Childhood Development in the People's Republic of China, 1975; Tobin et al., 1989).

These sorts of differences, and others, led us (Wellman et al., 2006) to assess theory-of-mind understanding in Chinese children (vs. U.S. and Australian children) using the ToM Scale methods. Before outlining relevant sociocultural differences still further, here's what the English–Chinese ToM Scale comparisons revealed: The scale sequences differ in a crucial respect—focally, understanding of belief and understanding knowledge systematically differ. For Western, English-speaking children, an early understanding of beliefs (revealed in understanding of diverse beliefs) precedes understanding of knowledge-access, which precedes understanding of false belief just as outlined previously (e.g., Wellman & Liu, 2004). For Chinese children, however, an early understanding of knowledge access preceded any understanding of belief (Wellman et al., 2006). So, relative to the DB before KA order observed for English speakers (DB>KA), the Beijing preschoolers reversed the DB and KA steps (KA>DB). The resulting scale sequence, although just as reliably consistent across children as the original U.S. one, placed expertise with knowledge (people who perceive an event know about it) reliably ahead of belief diversity (different people have different ideas and opinions about the same thing). Importantly, Chinese and U.S./Australian children passed the same total number of scale steps at equivalent ages (so it was not the case that one group or the other was more advanced overall), but the task ordering in China was clearly different.

These data thus support a general hypothesis that systematic cross-cultural variations in parenting philosophies, cultural conceptions, conversation, and socialization draw certain mental-state concepts to children's attention before other ones. To amplify a bit more, both the United States and Australia are often classed as individualistic, independent cultures where children are encouraged to think for themselves, to form and assert their opinions freely, and to listen to others' varied views without privileging the traditional wisdom of elders over the creative new ideas of the young (Greenfield, Keller, Fuligni, & Maynard, 2003). China, by contrast, is a collectivist, interdependent culture (Greenfield et al., 2003; Nisbett, 2003) where parents teach filial respect and encourage acquisition of culturally uniform traditions of knowledge and skill. Indeed, in individualist cultures such as the United States and Australia, there is an emphasis not only by parents, but throughout society, on personal rights and opinions ahead of collective responsibilities and shared values; whereas in China, the opposite emphases pertain (Li, 2002; Munro, 1977). Furthermore, empirical evidence shows that Australian and U.S. parents (e.g., Sigel, McGillicuddy-DeLisi, & Goodnow, 1992) encourage young children to assert their own opinions and acknowledge others' differing views; whereas Chinese parents discourage the voicing of discordant personal views while fostering knowledge of culturally agreed ideas and know-how (e.g., Johnston & Wong, 2002; Stevenson et al., 1990).

Naturally enough then, these differing styles of childrearing seem to lead U.S. and Australian children to form their initial conceptualizations of mind in terms of differences of opinion, thus explaining early mastery of the DB task. The Chinese approach to childrearing seems to redirect theory-of-mind development so that key concepts of mind are initially constructed around the insight that people can be knowledgeable versus ignorant.

The U.S./Australia-China ToM Scale findings arguably reflect these culturally variable socialization practices. However, other explanations are possible. Crucially, English-speaking preschoolers' relatively earlier mastery of opinion diversity could conceivably reflect the typical presence of siblings in their households. Having siblings (Perner et al., 1994) and sibling-directed pretend play, conversations, and disputes (Brown, Donelan-McCall, & Dunn, 1996; Randell & Peterson, 2009) are consistently associated with enhanced theory of mind in childhood. Arguably such interactions expose preschoolers saliently to belief diversity. Yet this stimulus to early mastery of diverse beliefs was unavailable to the Beijing preschoolers because of their nation's one-child family policy.

Ameneh Shahaeian, Candi Peterson, Virginia Slaughter, and I (Shahaeian, Peterson, Slaughter, & Wellman, 2011) identified Iran as another collectivist culture that shares China's overall elder-transmitted, knowledge-oriented parenting approach, but without other idiosyncratic features of a Beijing upbringing. In fact, like China, but distinct from both the United States and Australia, Iranian culture embraces interdependent and education-oriented Eastern cultural traditions that are widely uniform throughout society, firmly rooted in a long philosophical history, and relatively isolated from contemporary Western influences (e.g., Rudy & Grusec, 2006). Of course, Iran's Muslim tradition differs from the Chinese Confucian/communist belief systems in many respects; but when it comes to childrearing, both cultures share some similar parenting philosophies and practices that differ sharply from the modal Anglo-Western (U.S. or Australian) approaches. Comparative studies of Iranian versus U.S. parental beliefs and childrearing practices (e.g., Price, 2006; Rudy & Grusec, 2006; Sharifzadeh, 2004) have highlighted Iranian parents' consistent endorsement of collectivist family values emphasizing parental warmth and responsibility but in the context of filial duty and respect for elders. There is close monitoring of children's behavior and low tolerance for their assertions of independence or disagreement. Iranian parents disapprove of permissiveness and strongly promote learning, often sacrificing luxuries to further their children's acquisition of knowledge and traditional values.

In these key regards, Iranian parenting practices match those of Chinese parents (e.g., Chao, 1994; Chen, Dong, & Zhou, 1997). However, children in Iran, just as in the United States and Australia but unlike in China, typically are not single children—they have siblings, often multiple siblings.

In our research (Shahaeian et al., 2011), Ameneh Shahaeian tested numerous Iranian preschoolers using the theory-of-mind scale. Those Iranian children followed the alternative developmental sequence of theory-of-mind mastery observed before in China (Wellman et al., 2006)—in particular, they passed KA before DB. In contrast, an age-matched Australian control group passed DB ahead of KA, just as in the research cited before with U.S. and Australian (and German) children.

Timetables

I have been arguing, based on developmental sequences that differ across cultural contexts, that early experiences are critical for the development of theory-of-mind capacities. But of course, sequences are not the only issue—developmental timetables also matter. The false-belief data, for example, those outlined in Chapter 1 in Box 1.2, already show that timetables can vary; some children are quicker and some are slower to achieve false-belief understanding. But, in the bigger picture, this may not be all that much variation. As depicted in those graphs, pretty much everywhere children achieve a similar understanding of false belief in the preschool years. A similar suspicion might taint the sequence data as well. Sequence differences are intriguing, but look: Children proceed through more or less the same steps and at more or less the same time—in the preschool years. Tightly restricted—not identical, but restricted—timetables might well reflect development of theory-of-mind understandings as largely under maturational control. But if early progressive theory-of-mind understandings are built one on top of the next, shaped by relevant information and experience, that process should be able to produce very different timetables.

As previously discussed, false-belief understanding *is* seriously (not modestly) delayed in children with autism. Most adolescents and adults with autism perform poorly on false-belief tasks. But then autism is replete with neurological impairments, general across the board cognitive impairment and delays. Autism could certainly have its own delayed maturational timetable. A more telling test case of the role of experience concerns deaf children. Deaf children do not suffer from the same central neurological and intellectual impairments as individuals with autism; they have peripheral hearing loss instead. Thus these children more clearly reflect departures from the normal course of experience rather than departures from the normal course of brain functioning.

Important as well, there are two main groups of deaf children to consider. Deaf children of deaf parents grow up with ordinary conversational, language experiences—albeit in sign language—and so grow up with others who communicate and interact with them profusely. (These children are often called native signers.) But most deaf children—95% or so—are born to hearing parents. They grow up with very different early experiences. For example, despite valiant efforts to learn sign, hearing parents rarely achieve real proficiency. Especially when their child is young, hearing parents mostly communicate with their deaf child using simple signs or gestures to refer to here and now objects (Vaccari & Marschark, 1997; Moeller & Schick, 2006). Also, usually only one person in the family—often the mother—is the "designated" primary communicator and the person who mostly interacts with the child. The deaf child in a hearing family (often called late signers) begins with little discourse about persons' inner states, thoughts, and ideas; is likely to have restricted play with others; and generally has less access to the free-flowing, turn-taking, perspective-negotiating dance of social interactions.

Deaf children of hearing parents (but *not* deaf children of deaf parents) are substantially delayed in understanding false belief, often as delayed as high-functioning children with autism (Peterson, 2009; Peterson & Siegal, 1995). Again, however, a focus on false belief alone is limiting. For example, delay on that one task does not tell us whether children are delayed on a standard trajectory of achievement, develop on a very different trajectory, fail to develop altogether, and so forth. Comparisons on something like the ToM Scale could answer these (and other) questions.

Thus, it is notable that when deaf children (of hearing parents) receive the ToM Scale, they too evidence a consistent sequence of progression. For deaf children in Australia (Peterson et al., 2005) and the United States (Remmel & Peters, 2009), it is the same sequence—DD>DB>KA>FB>HE—that characterizes their hearing English-speaking counterparts *but* a sequence that is delayed at every step of the way. It takes deaf children 12 or more years to progressively achieve what hearing children (and deaf children of deaf parents) progressively achieve in 4 to 6 years (Peterson & Wellman 2009; Peterson et al., 2005).

To be clear, these deaf children's delays don't simply reflect difficulty understanding the questions. In these studies, deaf children are tested by people familiar to them in their everyday school activities using a mixture of signed and oral presentation that is also familiar and well-practiced within their school interactions. Moreover, they demonstrably understand the test situation and language, as is clear in their highly correct performance on the various warm-up and control questions that are also part of the ToM Scale tasks.

Longitudinal Sequences and Timetables

The data discussed so far are cross-sectional; they come from testing each child once on all five tasks and tallying the patterns of successes and failures. Thus, in the preschool years, if different age groups are tested on the ToM Scale, total scale scores regularly and significantly increase with age across groups of 3-, to 4-, to 5-year-olds. In this way, the scale apparently gives a cross-sectional view of the sequence of understanding that any single child would go through as they grow older. But patterns of success and failure across many children do not definitively demonstrate individual longitudinal progressions. However, the same patterns, including important differences in both sequences and in timetables, are clearly captured in recent longitudinal data. That is, this ToM Scale has also been validated longitudinally by testing the same children repeatedly as they get older.

In this longitudinal research, Candida Peterson, Fuxi Fang, and I (Wellman et al., 2011) assessed almost 100 typically developing U.S. and mainland Chinese preschoolers as well as late-signing Australian deaf children on the ToM Scale. Each child was tested 2, 3, 4, or more times with approximately 6 months to 2 years between testing. Given the discussion in this chapter so far, this three-group comparison is particularly intriguing because it includes children who exhibit different progressions across culture (United States vs. China) and children who exhibit substantial theory-of-mind delays (late-signing deaf children of hearing parents).

The results showed that both English-speaking preschoolers and late-signing deaf children showed the exact same five-step sequence longitudinally that they had in cross-sectional comparisons: DD>DB>KA>FB>HE. And again Chinese children showed their distinctive sequence, DD>KA>DB>FB>HE, where knowledge access was especially early understood. Thus this particular scale provides a good cross-sectional approximation to longitudinal sequences, and thus also provides a useful methodological shortcut for tracking theory-of-mind developmental progressions more systematically.

Considering the U.S. and Chinese groups each in terms of *their own* standard sequence, then Figure 5.2 presents the longitudinal data. As clear there, almost all children proceed up the scale in order (i.e., in their respective orders); going backward was extremely rare (shown by the dotted lines). Proceeding out of order—by skipping ahead to pass a harder task while failing an "easier" intermediate task—was equally extremely rare. What about the deaf children? As also clear in Figure 5.2, these Australian deaf children (of hearing parents) displayed the same sequence as their English-speaking peers but again were substantially delayed in age at attaining each step along the way.

These longitudinal data provide additional findings and conclusions. For example, optimally, in a cognitive developmental sequence, early understandings do not just precede later understandings; they also longitudinally *predict* them. Indeed, in the longitudinal data, those children who were better on the earlier items (DD, DB, KA) as

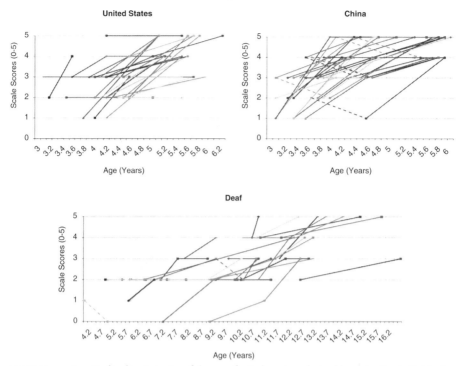

FIGURE 5.2 Longitudinal trajectories of theory-of-mind mastery derived by re-testing individual children on the ToM Scale. Each line shows one child's re-testings as measured by increases in their total ToM Scale score (which can range from 0–5) with increasing age.

3-year-olds became better on the later items (FB, HE) as 4-year-olds 1 year later. And more time between testings yielded larger increases in task successes.

Critical Period?

Note that because of their atypical conversational and social experiences as well as their clear theory-of-mind delays, deaf children of hearing parents are an important group for researching an intriguing and important question: Is there a critical period for theory-of-mind development? Deaf individuals have often been used to assess and confirm critical period hypotheses regarding language acquisition (e.g., Newport, 1991; Peterson, Pisoni, & Miyamoto, 2010). A critical period hypothesis for theory-of-mind development (Morgan & Shepard-Kegl, 2006; Siegal & Varley, 2002), more focally, could conceivably predict that those children (e.g., deaf children of hearing parents) who missed out on specific early experiences and inputs (e.g., discussions with family members of mental states such as knowledge and beliefs), and so are demonstrably and severely delayed in theory-of-mind acquisitions during a crucial preschool period, might be forever blocked in developing beyond some early level of understanding. The tasks in the ToM Scale were chosen to reflect preschool developments among normally developing children; so conceivably if a child failed to attain these insights during the preschool years, they might be unable to proceed beyond some early or intermediate point on the ToM Scale.

However, the deaf longitudinal data (Figure 5.2) demonstrate that, to the contrary, children can continue to make substantial progress on these "preschool" theory-of-mind insights well into adolescence. Virtually all of the late-signing deaf children in this sample were continuing to progress longitudinally through the scale at advanced ages. Jennie Pyers and Ann Senghas (2009) reported related data with still older deaf persons. Theirs was an intriguing longitudinal study of a unique group of eight Nicaraguan deaf adults who had grown up with no language other than a very restricted form of pidgin signing with no words or syntactic structures for expressing mental states. When first tested at a mean age of 22 years, most of these adults still could not pass standard false-belief tests. However, between the ages of 23 and 28 years, these adults joined a deaf social club and gained opportunities to converse and learn signs for mental states from a younger deaf cohort who had grown up using these terms. With this experience, the adults' false-belief performance improved substantially when tested 2 years later. Indeed, the older adults improved enough to equal the younger cohort. And they increasingly used mental-state discourse as well.

Sequences, Again

My preferred interpretation for the consistent sequential delays for the late-signing deaf children (as compared to native signing deaf children of deaf parents and for typically developing hearing children) is that this reflects socioconversational influences on theory-of-mind development. And similarly, conversational-experiential influences account for the difference in sequence between U.S. and Chinese children. But putting these two conclusions back-to-back highlights a conundrum: If socioconversational influences lead to differences in sequence (as evident in the Chinese case and that for Iran as well), then how are we to account for the identity in sequence across deaf children and their typically developing U.S. and Australian counterparts? To repeat, deaf children of hearing parents arguably live in very different socioconversational, even cultural worlds. Wouldn't such vast differences yield sequence differences as well? The answer is that they do; this just requires expanding the scope of investigation beyond the five tasks encompassed in the ToM Scale thus far.

Using this reasoning, Candida Peterson and I (Peterson & Wellman, 2009) expanded the five-item scale by incorporating a sixth task focused on children's understanding of social pretense. Why a focus on pretense? First, some understandings of pretense—for example, that persons who were away, and missed a change in the pretense that was instituted by others, will have old, outdated ideas about what is being pretended (Hickling et al., 1997)—clearly reflect understanding of others' mental states similar to understanding diverse beliefs or false beliefs, and comparable to understanding others' states of imagination, as I discussed in Chapter 2. In addition, social pretense stands out as important because childhood engagement in pretend play with others relates to and influences typically developing children's theory-of-mind understandings, as I discussed in Chapter 1. Thus, preschoolers' frequency of engaging in pretend play influences and predicts their developing false-belief competence, especially when the focus is socially shared pretense (Astington & Jenkins, 1995; Taylor & Carlson, 1997; Youngblade & Dunn, 1995).

If social experiences crucially influence pretense understanding and theory-of-mind development, there are reasons to expect that the experience of pretense, and thus the impact of pretense on theory of mind, might be quite different for deaf children. In fact, it is clear that deaf children (of hearing parents) are generally delayed in their pretense actions and interactions, just as they are generally delayed in their understanding of mental states such as beliefs and false beliefs (Brown, Prescott, Richards, & Paterson, 1997; Higginbotham & Baker, 1981).

However, granting overall delays in social-cognitive understanding, pretense understanding and experiences may be less delayed or less impaired in deaf children of hearing parents than understanding belief. For example, for these deaf children, sharing pretense enactments with others may proceed in largely nonverbal ways via gesture, pantomime, or toy manipulation. Indeed, simple social pretense might arguably occur as well via gestures as via words (e.g., by holding a banana to one's ear or pressing imaginary keys to simulate a cell phone). This could make nonverbal gestures (a strength of deaf children) a helpful medium for the social sharing of mental states with parents and playmates, within pretense. Via nonverbal exchanges of fictional states of mind with others during pretend play, deaf children might manage to "achieve the same increment in mental state understanding" (Harris, 2005, p. 80) as a language-advantaged child does through general conversation.

So, we (Peterson & Wellman, 2009) gave typically developing, hearing preschool children and late-signing deaf children, aged from 3 to 13 years, the five tasks in the "standard" ToM Scale discussed previously and a sixth task very similar in format, materials, and language that assessed shared pretense understanding. Our social pretense task was a version of the discrepant-pretense task outlined in Chapter 2 in which someone, Gail, was present for an initial shared pretense stipulation (e.g., that a red car was now pretend blue) but absent when the others subsequently changed that pretense. In a manner very like a false-belief format, the child then had to judge what Gail thought the color of the car was (vs. what the others thought *and* vs. what color the car actually was in reality).

Like prior studies, these deaf children from hearing families displayed delayed theory-of-mind understanding, including delayed understanding of shared pretense, relative to typically developing children. Moreover, these deaf children proceeded through the same five-step sequence first discovered for hearing preschoolers (Wellman & Liu, 2004) and first demonstrated for deaf children (Peterson et al., 2005). They progressed through the same developmental sequence of five steps, albeit at a slower rate than their hearing peers. But these data captured salient and intriguing differences not just in timetables but also in sequences.

Given the carefully chosen tasks, awareness of pretending as a subjective, socially shared mental process preceded false belief for both hearing and deaf children. But, whereas the sequence was DD>DB>KA>Discrepant Pretense>FB>HE for typically developing children, it was DD>DB>Discrepant Pretense>KA>FB>HE for the deaf children. So, comparing deaf with hearing children, understanding of socially discrepant pretense occurred at a later *age* for the deaf than the hearing, but earlier *within the sequence* of emerging understandings for deaf than hearing children. Such a difference is understandable, if we assume (a) that social-interactive experiences (and conversation) about pretense differ for deaf and hearing children and (b) that social-interactive experiences significantly influence the achievement of theory-of-mind understanding. Thus, nonverbal exchanges of fictional states of mind with others during pretend play might be an especially early and important venue for learning about mental states for deaf children: "early" in the sense that although deaf children are older on average when they evidence this understanding of pretense, it is earlier in relation to other theory-of-mind understandings for them.

Scaling Data Considered Further

One issue for scaling findings is the possibility that the task order obtained reflects more a logical dependence between tasks rather than a psychological-developmental progression. Perhaps, Task B (measuring *b*) succeeds Task A (measuring *a*) only because *b* is logically composed of *a* plus something more (Brainerd, 1978; Brandtstädter, 1987). However, the results for this scale speak against mere logical dependence because, for example, for U.S. and Australian children, DB is easier and comes before KA; but for Chinese and Iranian children, KA is easier and comes before DB. The fact that order of difficulty reverses for these tasks across groups argues against the possibility that one task or the other was intrinsically more difficult logically, or simply more difficult in terms of task demands or linguistic complexity. Similarly, whereas KA is understood before discrepant pretense for most children, for individuals with deafness, the order reverses to become discrepant pretense before KA.

It is important to emphasize that the empirical fact that theory-of-mind tasks are achieved in sequence does not necessarily imply a cause–effect relationship between earlier and later steps in sequence. The scaling data alone do not confirm that earlier desire understandings are necessary in shaping later theory-of-mind understanding (such as false belief or hidden emotion). However, longitudinal evidence, in particular predictive longitudinal relations of the sort established between the earlier scale steps as predicting later success on the later scale steps, help provide needed information. Even predictive longitudinal relations are not definitive; systematic training or experimental studies are needed to establish such causal conclusions, or better still a combination of longitudinal and intervention research (Bradley & Bryant, 1983).

Note in this vein that careful data as to consistent sequences (among carefully chosen, comparable tasks within a targeted domain of understanding) helpfully inform and constrain such experimental research. If understanding A reliably *succeeds* understanding B, it is implausible that it shapes and causes B; if it reliably *precedes* understanding B, it becomes a plausible causal candidate for further research. So, the ToM Scale is a particularly promising empirical tool for designing training research aimed at theoretical or practical concerns. The scale provides a blueprint of sequenced understandings that could be used to build on one another, and provides a reliable, extended measuring device for assessing systematic gains. The spread of the scale could prove especially advantageous for assessing short-term improvements in delayed groups (like late-signing deaf children or those with autism) who may require over 10 years to achieve the traditional ToM criterion (false belief) if untutored development is allowed to run its course. Indeed, in Chapter 6, I consider some recent training studies that combine together scaling, longitudinal, and microgenetic methods to address the mechanisms of development for theory-of-mind achievement in deaf and typically developing children.

UNIVERSAL SOCIAL COGNITION: CHILDHOOD THEORY OF MIND

Drawing together these various findings provides a way to address more precisely the universality of theory of mind and folk psychology. To begin, it is worth emphasizing how these scaling data reveal a mix of universally emerging understandings as well as culturally specific ones. That is, (a) in loose but important ways, "preschool" theory-of-mind developments reflect a near universal, progressive stream of conceptual insights; but (b) at the same time, cultural-social-conversational experiences shape children's developing theory of mind, resulting in notable differences in children's sequences and timetables for arriving at these conceptual insights.

These results thus mimic what some sage once said: All people everywhere are the same, *and* all people everywhere are different. The difficult task, however, is to properly understand how differences illuminate the universal human condition and how communalities frame the differences. Examining developmental sequences in theory-of-mind achievement helps specify the interplay between these forces, underwriting a perspective that emphasizes both cultural-conversational influences on the development of theory of mind as well as universal social-cognitive acquisitions during childhood. In my introductory chapter, I claimed that theory of mind constitutes a foundational human cognition and that foundational human cognitions help identify basic cognitive perspectives common to all humans. It is time to flesh out this claim more clearly.

Divergent Adult Folk Psychologies

All people and cultures cognize about themselves and others because they frequently encounter both normal and problematic agents and their activities: We think about everyday friends and everyday behaviors, but also mad, criminal, or antisocial persons and actions. We all have certain normal experiences of human life—say, sadness, or joy, or (for most of us) our own ordinary three-dimensional, color vision—but just as in Shakespeare's plays, we also encounter rage, insanity, hallucination, and blindness.

In trying to understand these varying phenomena, adult folk worldwide emphasize widely varying ideas about persons, actions, and human life. They come to differing folk psychologies. Here are some nonrandom examples:

According to Susan LeVine (1979, p. 358), the Gusii prefer to discuss overt behavior, and avoid talking about intentions and other aspects of mind:

> Their habitual mode of expression was to describe actions and events…leaving out personal reactions, opinions, judgments.

More radically, the anthropologist Jane Fajans (1985, p. 367) has claimed:

> The most challenging and interesting thing about the Baining [of Papua New Guinea], from the point of view of ethnopsychological studies, is that they appear not to have a folk psychology…. If [folk psychology] includes a concern with affect and emotions, concepts of person and self, theories of deviance, interpretations of behavior, and ideas about cognition and personality, the Baining manifest very little interest in these areas.

Returning to my prior discussion of Chinese understandings, Jin Li (2003, pp. 146–147) describes Chinese-Confucian versus Western-Socratic conceptions of knowledge, truth, and learning—things that would seem to be essential for understanding minds:

> Confucius was rarely if at all concerned about the notion of "truth" (or falsity)…. The Socratic model may be about truth finding…, but the Confucian model is about moral striving, which is very different from Western epistemology…. These differences are apparent in contemporary conceptions of learning…. [Comparing China and the United States]: *What learning means to members of these two cultures is substantially different to the degree that there is little conceptual overlap between them* [emphasis added].

These are three of many such ethnographic descriptions of other folk thinking about people and minds in ways that seem strikingly foreign (see Lillard, 1998). I admit it's not clear exactly what to make of all these claims. The most exotic ones are ethnographic accounts generated by "outsiders" to the cultural group in question, persons who might be especially interested in emphasizing and exaggerating the exotic and non-Western. But, I do not need to aggregate (or believe) them all to validly conclude that various ways of thinking about people exist—various folk psychologies exist—that are quite different one from another and different from my own. At the very least, conceptions of essential social actors and agents vary widely across cultures, encompassing people (of course, but also), cows, carved images, rocks, and dead ancestors: all manner of "counterintuitive" yet authentic social agents.

Nonetheless, I claim we should also validly conclude that everyday theory of mind is universal. That is, I argue both these things are true: Theory of mind is universal, but folk psychologies differ profoundly worldwide. How can that be so? The pieces of this puzzle assemble themselves around two clarifying themes. One concerns *levels of analysis*. We need to maintain a distinction between framework understandings versus detailed, specific ones, something like framework versus specific theories (as outlined in my introductory chapter). The other theme concerns *development*. We need to appreciate that and how theory of mind is both early achieved and also dynamic—it develops on the basis of experience. Theory of mind both constitutes universal social cognition yet allows vast differences in social cognition across cultures and societies. Here's how, I propose:

Framework Development

Children worldwide share a framework theory of mind. Accordingly, children tend to assume that people have subjective experiences and internal mental states. Such assumptions, strongly evident at ages 2 or 3 years, are themselves the products of earlier developments in infancy.

Levels of analysis and development both play important roles in this story. For levels, a general childhood expectation that people possess thoughts, wants, perceptions, and feelings provides only a very general framework; and children must engage in much specific instantiation of the framework, prominently including much culture-specific learning. The framework constrains the sorts of hypotheses that children make about people early on but leaves a great many details unspecified: Are cows as well as people belief-desire agents? (Yes, in India.) Should I privilege individualized beliefs over consensual knowledge? (Yes, in the United States.) Do cultures encourage "ideal" emotions that their members should show? (Yes, but the ideal is quite different in China as opposed to the United States, as I'll show later.)

As for development, an early theory-of-mind framework is dynamic and not static. In fact, it can revise and change to the extent of becoming in some parts and respects quite different from its initial form. An example of the extensive change possible is revealed in the momentous preschool changes represented by achieving awareness of false beliefs and hidden emotions, changes that require 10, 12, or more years to achieve in the case of deaf children of hearing parents.

My shorthand for this scenario is *framework development*; notably, the framework develops itself *and* it frames further development. Framework development predicts constraints on cultural variability in folk psychologies: not maturational constraints but developmental-learning constraints. After all, any specific folk psychology must be learnable by that folk's children. Cultural communities cannot sustain a specially developed construal of anything that their members cannot learn.

Constrained variability should be especially notable in childhood—when learning and development are in their early stages. Adults' conceptions of people can be much more dissimilar worldwide than childhood ones. Why? Because the initial framework is enabling (as well as constraining) precisely in that it is a general framework and it works developmentally. Initially, the framework provides a helpful ground for a community's members to communicate with their children. But, in part through this communication, communities teach and socialize their children into their group's practices and beliefs. In terms of individual development, cultural communities have many years (at the least from infancy to adulthood) in which to enculturate their children into their beliefs and worldviews. In terms of historical development, those groups have centuries in which to develop unique understandings of persons, selves, psyches, and societies. Resulting adult folk psychologies could be quite different from one another worldwide (and apparently are), although grounded in the initial framework assumptions of young children. A long path, studded with progressive novelties, connects early theory of mind to the profusion of divergent folk psychologies.

Framework development is different from other scenarios that dominate discussion of universality and variation in our conceptual thinking. One dominant alternative is *nativist knowledge*, according to which there are early, evolved understandings that don't change. Nativist knowledge scenarios (most recently, core knowledge and mental module accounts) privilege and easily account for universality. The other dominant alternative is *empiricist knowledge*, according to which young children begin ignorant and pick up—learn, match, and mirror—whatever their societies tell them. Empiricist knowledge scenarios (most recently, connectionist and dynamic systems proposals) privilege and easily account for variability in timetable and sequences. Framework development embraces, and accounts for, both universality and variability. It does so by emphasizing development and levels of analysis. If we insist there are several levels of analysis—framework versus specific—and if we insist there is developmental change, then the full pattern of the data make sense. Universal social cognition exists; if you want to see it, look at childhood theory of mind.

PROGRESSIONS IN EMOTION UNDERSTANDING

Data about progressions—sequences and timetables—are crucial for arriving at the preceding conclusions. But of course our ToM Scale (Wellman & Liu, 2004) is not crucial. The items in our scale were carefully devised to have the advantages of being comparable in testing format, few in number, easily understood by young children (to facilitate use with preschoolers and those with developmental delays), and to form a strict Guttman scale (where if a child passes a later item, he/she consistently passes all earlier ones as well). But as a consequence of these choices, those five tasks do not capture additional important aspects of theory-of-mind development, do not capture all the important theory-of-mind progressions, and certainly do not encompass all preschool theory-of-mind insights. Additional items (e.g., including pretense) and approaches are informative. Nicely, Francisco Pons, Paul Harris, and Marc de Rosnay (2004) provided a battery of items assessing childhood understanding of emotional states (largely neglected in the ToM Scale).

Preschoolers' earliest understanding of emotions as internal, subjective states (and inclusion of those insights in an early desire-awareness understanding of persons) was outlined in Chapter 4. And in Chapter 3, I noted that both understandings of mind, and relatedly understandings of emotion, predict preschoolers' social actions and interactions. Emotion understandings are various and complex (just as the understandings of mental subjectivity examined with the ToM Scale are various and complex), and even "preschool" emotion understandings encompass a progression of insights unfolding between 1 to 9 or 10 years. Pons and his colleagues (2004) summarized findings across multiple laboratories, studies, and countries as essentially reflecting the progressive developmental components outlined in Table 5.3.

Pons and colleagues (2003, 2004) then developed a series of emotion understanding tasks, one for each component in Table 5.3. Each task was roughly comparable in format, using similar, simple line drawings. For example, for assessing Component 4, *Belief*, a picture of a rabbit (face not shown) with a big juicy carrot was shown in a picture frame prominently including a fox that was, however, completely hidden from the rabbit's view by a bush. Children were then asked how the rabbit felt—scared, happy, angry, or just OK—with appropriate faces to choose from. The entire battery of tasks is called the TEC (Test of Emotion Comprehension; Pons et al., 2004).

When children from 3 to 11 years were tested (100 in Pons et al., 2004; 80 in Pons et al., 2003), the data showed significant progressions. Roughly, more children (and more younger ones) succeeded on the tasks for the earlier components, but fewer children and (mostly) only older ones succeeded on the later components. Like the ToM Scale, children's responses to the TEC revealed a significant Guttman scalability (Pons et al., 2004). Unlike the ToM Scale, the patterns of success and failure across the components in the Pons et al. (2004) battery overlapped substantially. However, a stricter progression emerged if the tasks were considered as falling into three larger clusters. *Cluster I* (Components 1, 2, and 5 from Table 5.3) was developmentally the easiest, and by the age of 5 years, the clear majority of children were able to correctly recognize different emotional expressions, correctly identify external causes of emotions, and understand the impact of reminders on emotion. Pons and colleagues say this cluster represents an "external" understanding of emotion (Pons et al., 2004). *Cluster II* appeared next (Components 3, 4, and 7); by 6 or 7 years, children were largely able to also understand the role of desires and beliefs in emotions as well as the possibility of hiding emotions. Pons and colleagues call this a "mental" understanding of emotion. Finally, mostly only

TABLE 5.3

Progressive components of emotion understanding (according to Pons et al., 2004)

1. *Recognition*: Visual recognition of facial expressions of the basic emotions (happiness, sadness, fear, and anger). Begins in infancy, and by approximately 2 to 3 years of age, children recognize and name several emotions.

2. *External Cause*: Understanding how external causes affect emotions. For example, by 2 to 4 years, if someone loses a favorite toy, children predict sadness; if someone gets a favorite toy, they predict happiness.

3. *Desire*: Appreciation that emotional reactions depend on the person's desires. By 2 to 4 years for simple situations (Repacholi & Gopnik, 1997; Wellman & Woolley, 1990), children understand that two people can have different desires about the same situation.

4. *Belief*: Understanding that a person's beliefs, false or true, will shape his or her emotional reaction to a situation. Understood between 4 to 6 years.

5. *Reminder*: Initial understanding of the relation between memory and emotion at least for negative events and emotions (e.g., events in a present situation can remind and reactivate past negative emotions; Lagattuta & Wellman, 2001). Understood between 4 to 6 years.

6. *Regulation*: Different strategies help control one's emotions. Younger children refer mostly to behavioral strategies; children 6 years and older start to acknowledge psychological strategies (denial, distraction, etc.).

7. *Display*: Understanding that the *expression* of emotions can be controlled, leaving a discrepancy between the outward expression of emotion and the actual, felt emotion. Understood 4 to 7 years.

8. *Mixed Emotions*: Understanding that a person may have multiple, even contradictory, emotions at the same time. Understood 7 or 8 years and after.

---

after 7 or 8 years of age were children able to understand mixed emotions, and the possibility of regulating emotion via cognition (*Cluster III*), said to represent a "reflective" understanding of emotion.

Some of these progressions reflect the specific way Pons and his colleagues tested children (2003, 2004)—for example, from Chapter 4 we know that the relation between desires and emotion can be very early understood (as in the broccoli-crackers task) and so more appropriate to *Cluster I* rather than on the later timetable apparent in the TEC data. Nonetheless, this research further shows the informativeness of considering theory-of-mind understandings in terms of systematic progressions, in this case by emphasizing and charting specifically emotion understanding.

Like the ToM Scale, longitudinal examination of a group of children ($N = 42$) showed that the cross-sectional levels of difficulty apparent across children on the TEC are roughly reflective of the progression that individuals pass through longitudinally (Pons & Harris, 2005). Again, this was more clear-cut for progressions among the three large clusters and much less clear-cut when considering possible step-by-step progressions among the nine specific components. And like the ToM Scale, the TEC has been translated and used in various countries, exhibiting similar progressions across many cultures (again essentially at the larger three-cluster level of analysis) as well as differences between cultures and communities in the age at which the majority of children succeed on the different TEC components (F. Pons, personal communication, January 10, 2014).

Besides data from using the TEC with children from various countries and language communities, children's emotion understandings have been studied cross-culturally in other research. Indeed, in part because emotion terms and emotional expressions differ widely across cultures and languages (Russell, 1991), emotion understanding has received considerable international attention. In this realm as well, studies have shown an informative mix between recurrent, near-universal acquisition and culture-specific development. Recognition of several basic emotions such as happiness, fear, disgust, anger, and sadness is at least "minimally universal" (Russell 1991, 1994; but see Barrett et al., 2009, for an alternative view). Similarly, young infants, apparently worldwide, evidence abilities to first distinguish positive and negative expressions of emotion (Termine & Izard, 1988) and then by as early as 10 weeks, to differentiate emotional expressions that reflect happiness, sadness, and anger and react to them appropriately (Haviland & Lelwica, 1987; Walker-Andrews, 1988). Then preschool children come to appropriately use their language's emotion labels to refer to (especially) these basic emotions (e.g., Widen & Russell, 2003).

However, culture-specific influences and acquisitions for emotion understanding are evident amid any such recurring trajectories. This is clear in Jeanne Tsai's (2007) consideration of Chinese and American children's understanding of a different key aspect of emotion control, *regulation* (part of *Cluster III*).

Ideal Affect

Tsai and her colleagues (2006, 2007) have focused on "ideal affect," cultural preferences for the sorts of "good" emotional feelings persons should cultivate. They distinguished preferences for high-arousal positive states (excited, enthusiastic) and low-arousal positive states (calm, peaceful) as contrasting ideal affects. They predicted that differences between (roughly speaking) individualistic versus collectivist cultural contexts could produce differences in such preferred ideal affects. In many individualistic cultural contexts, influencing others and others' actions is valued; and influencing others often requires excitement, enthusiasm, and animation, and consequently higher arousal. In such cultural circumstances, therefore, Tsai reasoned ideal affect tends toward high arousal (see, e.g., Tsai, 2007). Collectivist cultural contexts likewise value feeling "good" but at the same time consistently emphasize fitting in, adjusting to others, and maintaining equanimity and harmonious relations. Consequently, in these cultural circumstances, ideal affect tends toward (calm, peaceful) low arousal.

Work with Chinese and American adults largely supports such differences in ideal affect (Tsai, Knutson, & Fung, 2006). What about children? In a series of studies, Tsai and her colleagues (Tsai, Louie, Chen, & Uchida, 2007) began with an analysis of best-selling picture books for young children in the United States and Taiwan. Characters in U.S. books displayed more high-arousal emotional expressions and engaged in more high-arousal, stimulating activities (running, jumping). Characters in Taiwanese books displayed more low-arousal, positive-emotional expressions and engaged in more low-arousal activities (sitting, reflecting, resting).

Next Tsai and colleagues (2007) compared 4- and 5-year-old preschoolers in Taiwan and the United States on measures of their ideal affect. Taiwanese children clearly judged low-arousal, positive affect and activities as more preferred; whereas European-American children judged high-arousal, positive affect and activities as more preferred.

In a final study, Tsai and colleagues (2007) conducted a short-run experimental study where European-American and Taiwanese preschoolers were read carefully constructed picture books—either books about affectively excited or about affectively calm characters. In both groups, being read exciting stories led to increased preference for exciting (vs. calm) activities and excited (vs. calm) expressions, in an after-reading posttest. And, being read calm stories led to increased preference for calm activities and calm expressions in the posttest. At the same time, confirming the findings of their original preschool study, on average European-American preschoolers were more likely to prefer excited activities and excited expressions, whereas Taiwanese preschoolers were more likely to prefer calm activities and calm expressions.

When it comes to emotion regulation preferences, therefore, Western and East Asian children substantially differ by ages 4 and 5. These differences relate directly to adult cultural preferences and practices as well as cultural artifacts, such as picture books, designed for younger children. But at the same time, culturally specific understandings of ideal affect and emotional displays take their place within a developmental progression of various emotion understandings.

CONCLUSIONS

These accumulating data regarding extended developmental sequences have crucial implications for our understanding of theory of mind and its development in the foundational years from 2 to 7 or 8 (or until adolescence and adulthood in the case of delayed children). In sum, these data illuminate crucial sociocultural, developmental influences and variability on theory of mind. But importantly, this variability takes place against the background of common (but by no means identical), sequential patterns.

Worldwide, preschoolers make dramatic progress in discovering a key set of theory-of-mind insights, and they do so at an overall rate that is roughly similar from one culture to the next. Deaf children (of hearing parents) make consistent progress on these same insights as well, although over a much more extended time span. Against this backdrop, telling variability emerges, both within and between cultures and groups, in the actual sequential progression of theory-of-mind development. This variability in sequence and in timetable is predictably related to sociocultural-linguistic differences in childhood experiences; it is experience-dependent. And, as I noted in Chapter 3, this variability allows researchers to establish the real-world consequences of coming to a theory of mind. However, this variability takes its forms within more universal developmental progressions and frameworks.

6

Theory Theory

RECONSTRUCTING CONSTRUCTIVISM

JEAN PIAGET FAMOUSLY called for a "constructivist" theory of cognitive development (Piaget, 1970). The background idea is that we cognizers have coherent, abstract,
and highly structured representations of the world around us that allow us to understand the world and act within it. For example, we have a framework theory of mind just
as described in the last several chapters. Then, the core constructivist idea is that such
structures not only allow and engender learning, they are themselves learned—they are
constructed. Theory theory follows in this tradition. The claim is that our theories—
framework theories as well as more specific ones—arise and revise in the face of accumulating experience.

But how does this sort of constructivist learning work? For Piaget (e.g., 1952,
1983), children attempt to interpret new evidence within their current conceptual
framework (assimilation) while always making modifications to cope with new evidence (accommodation) until these modifications accumulate into adoption of a
new overall understanding (equilibration). Scholars have consistently described the
assimilation-accommodation-equilibration proposal as valiant but hopelessly vague.
It is valiant because to posit mechanisms that combine structure and change in this
inextricable way is intriguing (after all, scientific theories also seem to combine these
two forces for genuine scientific change). It is vague because the proposed amalgam of
structures that not only enable learning but are themselves learned seems like one of

those impossible, gerrymandered creatures of myth (centaurs and gryphons) rather than a natural, credible mechanism of mind.

This theoretical vagueness (along with empirical inadequacies) doomed the Piagetian account. Both during his time and today that seemed to leave only two other alternatives: empiricism and nativism. Traditional empiricist accounts—and more recently, connectionist and dynamic systems theories (Elman et al., 1996; Thelen & Smith, 1994)—deny that there actually are the kind of abstract, coherent structures that constructivists such as Piaget claimed. They see instead a distributed collection of specific associations between particular inputs or a context-dependent assemblage of various functions. Nativist accounts, including recent modularity and core knowledge theories (Pinker, 1997; Spelke, Breinlinger, Macomber, & Jacobson, 1992; Spelke & Kinzler, 2007), embrace the structure, coherence, and abstractness of our representations but deny that they could be learned. Theory theory is prey to these same challenges and tensions.

Computational scientists and statisticians wrestle with these issues as well. Crudely, one sort of computational approach has focused on general, knowledge-lean statistical mechanisms of inference. Statistical learning in this sense mines the data themselves to compute similarity, association, covariation, and the like—statistical metrics—which are empirical inductions then generalized to new samples. Baseball, "moneyball," statistical approaches show the nature and power of this statistical approach. Call this the bottom-up project. A second approach begins with knowledge-rich structures that constrain any learning or induction. For example, the modeler first limits the domain at issue—say medical diagnosis—then researches the ways in which experts (e.g., veteran diagnosticians) do this and the features they use. Then the modeler sets up computer programs that capture that know-how and also prestructures the input data into relevant features and factors. This is the top-down project in which, just as for mental modules, the key structures come from the "outside," that is, outside the system's own learning and inductions. For computational learning, the top-down, knowledge-rich structures come from the computer program's designer. For mental modules, the designer is evolution.

Recently, however, a new set of computational ideas aim for an alternative, constructivist form of machine learning. This new "rational constructivism" (Xu, Dewar, & Perfors, 2009) or "theory-based Bayesian learning" (Tenenbaum, Griffiths, & Kemp, 2006) uses the theoretical framework of probabilistic models and Bayesian learning. Alison Gopnik and I have argued that these ideas and demonstrations promise to "reconstruct constructivism" (Gopnik & Wellman, 2012). They thereby help underwrite theory theory as well, as I previewed in my introductory chapter. In this chapter, I focus on how these computational ideas can explain the development of our intuitive theories of the world and in particular theory of mind. (See Gopnik & Wellman, 2012, for an overlapping account that focuses less on theory of mind.)

THEORY THEORY REVISITED

Theory theory claims that several important conceptual structures constitute everyday theories and that cognitive development is like theory creation and revision (Carey, 1985; Gopnik & Wellman, 1994; Wellman & Gelman, 1992). In short, children construct intuitive theories of the world and alter and revise those theories based on new evidence. As prefaced in my introductory chapter, theory theory points to three distinctive aspects of intuitive theories: their structure, function, and dynamics.

First, theories have a distinctive structure encompassing coherent, abstract, and causal representations of the world. (For example, consider the structure outlined in Chapter 2, Figure 2.1, for theory of mind.) Often these representations include unobservable hidden theoretical entities (e.g., beliefs and desires). Moreover, theories have a hierarchical structure. Theories may describe specific causal phenomena in a particular domain, but these specific theories are also be embedded in more abstract "framework theories." Framework theories describe, in general terms, the kinds of entities and relations that apply in a domain rather than specifying those entities and relations in detail.

Second, theories have distinctive cognitive functions. They allow wide-ranging predictions about what will happen in the future. They also influence interpretations of the evidence itself. Moreover, theories are causal-explanatory enterprises. They promote causal accounts of the entities and relations in their domains that provide explanations of the nature of those things and events. These explanations and causal claims go beyond simple predictions about what will happen next.

Finally, and crucially, theories have distinctive dynamics that reflect a powerful interplay between hypotheses and data, between theory and evidence. In particular, unlike modules or "core knowledge," theories change in the light of new evidence, and they do so in a rational way. Moreover, unlike associationist structures, theories may change in their higher principles and not just in their specific connections and details. That is, framework theories can change too, yielding framework development.

The recent computational work, along with empirical evidence, has revealed further, significant aspects of these dynamics of theory change. In particular, theory change often relies on variability. In the course of theory change and cognitive development, children gradually entertain and change the probability of multiple hypotheses. Moreover, dynamically, this process of revision unfolds via a series of distinctive intermediate steps. As evidence leads children to revise their initial hypotheses and replace them with more probable ones, this yields a series of related conceptions that form a bridge from one broad theory to the next.

PROBABILISTIC MODELS AND RATIONAL LEARNING

Probabilistic models have become prominent in machine learning and artificial intelligence over the last 15 years (see, e.g., Glymour, 2003; Griffiths, Chater, Kemp, Perfors, &

Tenenbaum, 2010; Oaksford & Chater, 2007), and some of these have also been proposed as a model for theory-like cognitive development (Gopnik et al., 2004; Gopnik & Tenenbaum, 2007; Gopnik & Wellman, 2012). Two features of such probabilistic models are particularly important for theory theory. First, they describe structured models that represent hypotheses about how the world works. Second, they describe the probabilistic relations between these models and patterns of evidence in rigorous ways. As a consequence they both represent conceptual structure and allow learning.

Imagine some real structure in the world—especially relevant to theories, a network of causal relationships, for example, for theory of mind, the causal relations sketched in Figure 2.1. That structure gives rise to some patterns of observable evidence rather than others—statistical contingencies between events. A model or representation of that structure constitutes a hypothesis about what the world's structure is like. The right sort of representation would allow you to generate predicted patterns of evidence observable in the world, also allowing you to make new inferences accordingly. From a constructivist perspective on development, the really interesting question is how we might learn these representations. Critically, the systematic link between structure and evidence in adequate models also allows you to reverse the process and to make inferences about the nature of the structure from the evidence it generates. Vision scientists talk about this as "solving the inverse problem." In vision, the inverse problem is to infer the nature of three-dimensional objects from the reduced and noisy retinal images they generate. In theory development, the problem is to infer causal structure from the events you observe, learning about the world from evidence.

The idea that mental models of the structure of the world generate predictions about evidence to be observed, and that we can invert that process to learn the structure from evidence, is not new. Indeed, it is classically encompassed in one mathematical form by Bayes' rule. Here is the simplest version of Bayes' rule:

$$P(H/E)\alpha P(E/H)P(H)$$

Bayes' rule weaves together a hypothesized structure (H) and the evidence (E) that you see to yield (the inverse solution) the probability of H given E, or P(H/E). Therefore, Bayes' rule says that the posterior probability of your hypothesis (given the evidence) is proportional to the probability of the evidence given the hypothesis, P(E/H), and your initial estimate of the probability of the hypothesis, P(H).

P(H/E), the "posterior" probability of the hypothesis, is not the only part of Bayes' rule that has a conventional name. P(H) is the "prior," the probability of the hypothesis before you looked at the evidence. P(E/H) is the "likelihood," how probable it is that you would see the observed evidence if the hypothesis were true. So, according to Bayes' rule, the posterior is a function of the prior and the likelihood.

Here's a concrete example taken from the recent paper of Alison Gopnik's and mine (Gopnik & Wellman, 2012). Suppose Mary is travelling and she wakes up with a terrible pain in her neck. She considers three hypotheses about what caused the pain: perhaps she has a clogged carotid artery, perhaps she slept in an awkward position, or perhaps it was that lobster she ate last night that seemed a little "off." She goes online and discovers that both a clogged artery and awkward sleeping are much more likely to lead to neck aches than bad seafood. In fact, she reads that clogged carotids almost always lead to neck aches—the *likelihood* of a neck ache given a clogged carotid artery is particularly high. That sounds grim, but in fact it's unlikely in the first place that Mary has a clogged carotid artery and more likely overall that she slept awkwardly (or ate bad seafood)—awkward sleeping, in particular, has a much higher *prior* probability than severely blocked carotids. If you combined these two factors, the likelihood and the prior, you would conclude that a bad night in an awkward position is the most likely hypothesis.

Of course, eventually enough evidence could lead you to accept even an initially very unlikely idea. Evidence that the ache persists, that an X-ray shows blockage, and so on, can increasingly favor the initially unlikely clogged carotid diagnosis. This gives probabilistic Bayesian reasoning a characteristic combination of stability and flexibility. You don't abandon a very likely hypothesis right away, but you will if enough counterevidence accumulates.

The recent advances in computational modeling have integrated further ideas about probability into this Bayesian framework. If you think of a single hypothesis (the prior or the posterior) as deterministically related to evidence, and you think that the solution to the inverse problem is a decision of whether your hypothesis is right or wrong, then the inverse problem becomes extremely difficult to solve. This is because typically a great many hypotheses are compatible with any pattern of evidence. How can we decide on *the* right hypothesis? The task is arguably impossible. This conundrum concerning the indeterminacy of the data has led to nativist conclusions (e.g., Gold, 1967; Pinker, 1984).

Probabilistic Bayesian learning algorithms accept this indeterminacy and then exploit it. Rather than simply generating a yes or no decision about whether a particular hypothesis is true, probabilistic Bayesian learning considers multiple hypotheses and determines their posterior probability. Integrating probability along with variability still further into the process makes the learning problem more tractable. Although many hypotheses may be compatible with the evidence, some hypotheses can be more or less likely to have generated the evidence than others, and you can learn by adjusting the probabilities among multiple hypotheses.

To my mind, probabilistic Bayesian inference helps capture the piecemeal yet progressive way that development proceeds. (Empiricists also emphasize this aspect of development that is not easily accommodated by nativism.) At the same time, the generative power of structured models can help explain the abstract and general character of children's inferences. (Nativists also emphasize this aspect of development that is not easily accommodated by traditional associationist empiricism.) And the integration of prior knowledge and new evidence seems hauntingly like what Piaget had in mind when he talked about assimilation and accommodation.

Bayes' rule, by itself, is very general. In fact, it's too general to explain much without more information about the hypotheses and the likelihoods. Here is where the theories come in, and, to be applicable, the theories (the models) have to capture both causal relationships and the patterns of evidence they generate. The models are as important as the math. To allow use of Bayes' rule, the elements in Bayes' equation—the hypotheses (models), the evidence, and the likelihood—have to be specified so that the hypotheses systematically relate to evidence.

Causal hypotheses are particularly important both in science and in ordinary life; and, for theory theory, theories involve coherent and abstract representations of *causal* relationships (Carey, 1985; Wellman, 1990; Wellman & Gelman, 1998). So, it's causal models that must be specified in ways that link to causal evidence. Fortunately, as Alison Gopnik and her colleagues (Gopnik et al., 2004) first emphasized, over the last 15 years, computer scientists and philosophers have developed more precise models of causal relations that function in just this way. A good, illustrative set of models are known as "causal graphical models" or "causal Bayes nets" (Pearl, 2000; Spirtes, Glymour, & Scheines, 1993, 2000).

Causal Bayes Nets

Causal Bayes nets were first developed in the philosophy of science, computer science, and statistics (Glymour, 2001; Pearl, 1988, 2000; Spirtes et al., 1993). Scientists seem to infer theories about the causal structure of the world from patterns of evidence, yet philosophers of science found it very difficult to explain how this could be done. Causal Bayes nets helped because they provide a kind of logic of inductive causal inference. Clearly, scientists often infer causal structure both by performing statistical analyses and doing experiments. That is, they observe the patterns of relationships among variables and "partial out" some of those variables (as in statistical analysis); and additionally, they examine the consequences of interventions (as in experiments); and they combine these two types of procedures. Causal Bayes nets formalize these kinds of inferences.

In causal Bayes nets, causal hypotheses are represented by directed graphs such as the one in Figure 6.1. The graphs consist of variables, representing types of events or states of the world, and arrows (more formally, directed edges) that represent the direct causal relations between those variables. Figure 6.1 is a graph of the causal structure of the woes of academic conferences, again utilizing an example from Gopnik and Wellman (2012).

Given a particular causal structure, only some patterns of probability will occur among the variables. This means that from the Bayesian perspective, the graph specifies the likelihood of the evidence given the hypothesis (i.e., that particular graph). To illustrate how this works, consider a simple causal problem, partially embedded in the graph of Figure 6.1. Suppose that I notice that when I go to big conferences I often can't sleep when I've been to a party and drank wine. Partying (P) and insomnia (I) covary, and

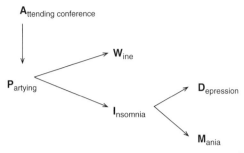

FIGURE 6.1 Causal Bayes net of academic conferences (and their consequences). Causal Bayes nets can connect any variables with connected edges. In this example, to keep things concrete, A = attending a conference; P = partying; W = drinking wine; I = insomnia; D = depression; and M = mania.

so do wine (W) and insomnia (I). Suppose further that I make some hypotheses about how these variables are likely to be related. There are at least two possibilities about the relations among these variables. Maybe parties cause me to drink wine and that keeps me awake (a causal chain). Maybe parties are so exciting that they keep me awake, and they also independently cause me to drink wine (a common cause). As shown in Figure 6.2, these possibilities can be represented by two simple causal graphs that include variables such as P+/− and I+/− but also specify the nature of the relations between them.

In these graphs P+/−, for example, conveys that partying can be present (+) or absent (−). P+/− → I+/− conveys the hypothesis that partying and insomnia are causally related, and P+ → I+ conveys the more specific hypothesis that more partying leads to more insomnia. So, maybe (Graph 1) parties (P+) lead me to drink (W+) and wine keeps me up (I+); or maybe (Graph 2) partying (P+) both keeps me up (I+) and leads me to drink (W+). The covariation among the variables—my noticing that I often can't sleep when I've been to a party and drunk a lot of wine—is consistent with both these structures.

However, these two graphs lead to different patterns of probabilities among the three variables, in particular different patterns of conditional probability. Or as statisticians put it, they test different relations between some variables when other variables are partialled out. Suppose I decide I'll keep a journal of all the times I drink and party and examine the effects on my insomnia. If Graph 1 (in Figure 6.2) is correct, then I predict that my journal will show that I'm more likely to have insomnia when I drink wine, whether or not I party (partialling out partying). If instead Graph 2 is correct, I will only be more likely to have insomnia when I go to a party, regardless of if I drink no, a little, or a lot of wine (partialling out wine).

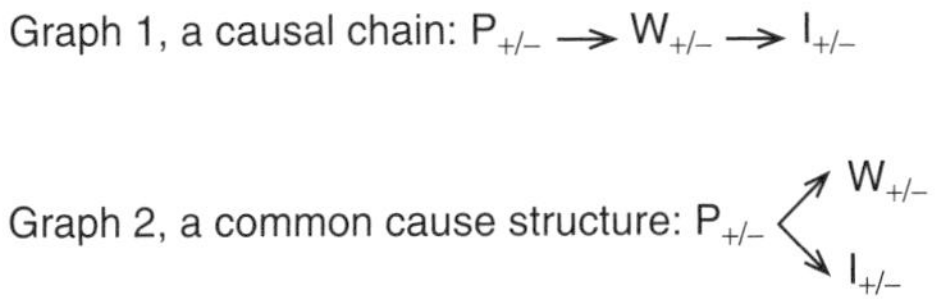

Graph 1, a causal chain: $P_{+/-} \longrightarrow W_{+/-} \longrightarrow I_{+/-}$

Graph 2, a common cause structure: $P_{+/-} \Big\langle \begin{array}{c} W_{+/-} \\ I_{+/-} \end{array}$

FIGURE 6.2 Simple causal graphs of two alternative causal relations between partying (P), drinking wine (W), and insomnia (I).

If I know whether the causal structure of my insomnia is indeed represented by Graph 1 (or Graph 2), and I know the values of some of the variables in the graph (+ or −), I can make consistent and quite general predictions about the probability of other variables. Note that the background notion of causality embedded in these directed graphs is more genuinely causal than just Humean covariation (see Gopnik & Wellman, 2012). In Bayesian terms, each graph tells us the likelihood of particular patterns of evidence given that particular hypothesis about the *causal* structure (the hypothesized arrows).

A Digression: Causal Maps

Allison Gopnik and her colleagues (2004) provided a useful analogy for thinking about causal Bayes nets in terms of everyday cognition. They used the construct of "causal maps" to help consider how causal learning and reasoning proceed. Causal maps can be understood on analogy to spatial cognitive maps. Spatial cognitive maps allow us "to represent geometric relations among objects in space non-egocentrically, generating new information and relations not previously directly experienced, and then to generate new spatial inferences" (Gopnik et al., 2004, p. 5). A novice cab driver who maps the spatial layout of London's streets from limited exposure to some of them can use this initial mental map to make new inferences about locations in London. On analogy to spatial maps, causal maps assemble specific experiences into a larger system that we use to infer new causally rich information as evident in future causal predictions and interventions.

Cognitive maps are clearly learned on the basis of the mapper's experience in his or her spatial environment, just as are London cabbies' knowledge of London's streets (Woollett, Spiers, & Maguire, 2009). In parallel, causal maps are arguably learned on the basis of causal cognizers' experiences in their causal environments.

Intriguingly, the philosopher of science Steven Toulmin (1953/1967) goes further to suggest a general analogy from maps to theories:

> We have seen how natural it is to speak of ourselves "finding our way around" a range of phenomena with the help of a law of nature, or "recognizing where on the map" a particular object of study belongs. In doing so, we are employing a cartographical analogy which is worth following up: for . . . the analogy between physical theories and maps extends for quite a long way and can be used to illuminate some dark and dusty corners in the philosophy of science. (Chapter 4, "Theories and Maps," p. 4)

Bayes Nets and Learning

Obviously, yet crucially, the apparatus of causal Bayes nets can be used to computationally solve the inverse problem—to learn about structure from evidence. We can learn the causal structure both by noting the evidence that results from the outcomes of interventions and/or by noting via observational evidence the conditional probabilities of events. For example, in the wine–insomnia example, how could I tell which hypothesis about my academic conference insomnia is the right one? How can I distinguish between the different causal hypotheses in Graphs 1 and 2 (in Figure 6.2)? Clearly, I could do an experiment. I could hold partying constant (consistently partying or never partying) and intervene to vary whether or not I drank wine; or I could hold drinking constant (consistently drinking or never drinking) and intervene to vary whether or not I partied. This reasoning underlies the logic of experimental design in science.

I might also use my journal to keep track of the relative frequencies of the three events. If I notice that I am more likely to have insomnia when I drink wine, whether or not I party, I can infer that Graph 1 is correct. If I observe that, regardless of how much or how little wine I drink, I am only more likely to have insomnia when I go to a party, I will opt instead for Graph 2. These inferences reflect the logic of correlational statistics in science. What I did with my journal, more or less, was to partial out the effects of partying on the wine/insomnia correlation and draw a causal conclusion as a result.

Probabilistic Bayesian modeling, then, coupled with tractable, specified hypotheses about causal systems, can (probabilistically) learn those causal systems that produce the evidence. Various Bayesian computational models actually do this given real-life data (see, e.g., Shipley, 2000).

Note that causal Bayes nets can also include unobservable variables—causal intermediaries not observed in any overt events but indirectly linked to overt events. Maybe the real culprit keeping me awake is an ulcer-like virus in my gut, one that flares up with drinking or loud music. So the real causal structure would be a graph such as Figure 6.1 but with an additional node. Crucially, there are Bayesian procedures for learning about such unobserved variables *from the data*. Gopnik et al. (2004) provided several clear examples. Theory theory, of course, proposes that children infer unobserved variables such as internal mental states from patterns of experience.

What About Children?

At a theoretical level, this modeling approach embodies a constructivist process, so at the least it provides plausible demonstration proofs that constructivist learning is possible. But this is "machine" learning. What about children? Do their causal learning and theory-building efforts look anything like these (computationally tractable) models? All children, according to theory theory, construct intuitive causal theories, including everyday theory of mind. Do children construct this knowledge in ways at all like these models do, and do the computational models do things like children do?

Over the past 10 years, a number of researchers have explored whether children can learn causal structure from evidence in the way that the Bayesian formalisms suggest. Most of this work has considered children's understanding of physical causation and used novel learning devices and situations to give children causal problems that they haven't already solved. So researchers have given children controlled evidence about new causal systems to see what kinds of causal conclusions they will draw. An early example of this sort of research, which spawned a lot of contemporary research with a variety of "blicket detectors," is shown in Box 6.1.

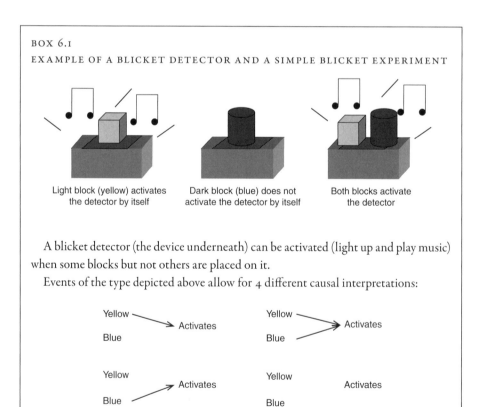

BOX 6.1
EXAMPLE OF A BLICKET DETECTOR AND A SIMPLE BLICKET EXPERIMENT

Light block (yellow) activates the detector by itself

Dark block (blue) does not activate the detector by itself

Both blocks activate the detector

A blicket detector (the device underneath) can be activated (light up and play music) when some blocks but not others are placed on it.

Events of the type depicted above allow for 4 different causal interpretations:

Yellow → Activates
Blue

Yellow → Activates
Blue →

Yellow
Blue → Activates

Yellow
Blue   Activates

Note: In this figure, light gray cubes are yellow; black cylinders are blue.

Social Cognition

However, we also need to know if these ideas can illuminate a child's typical knowledge of familiar causal generalizations and, in particular, apply to everyday social-cognitive learning. Moreover, do these ideas help characterize longer term developments, the kinds of changes in knowledge that cognitive developmentalists have charted as changes in children's intuitive theories? Theory of mind provides important data and claims about just these issues. To illustrate, I'll outline several areas of emerging findings within social cognition.

Infants

We know that even infants can detect complex patterns of probabilities and can learn from them. In fact, statistical learning has been one of the most important recent areas of developmental research on linguistic and perceptual learning (e.g., Gómez, 2002; Kirkham, Slemmer, & Johnson, 2002; Saffran, Aslin, & Newport, 1996; Wu, Gopnik, Richardson, & Kirkham, 2011). This includes the discovery that preverbal infants make use of probabilistic, statistical regularities in their experiences to make inferences about the structure of language and the physical world. This research shows that even young infants are sensitive to some of the statistical regularities in the data that would be necessary to engage in Bayesian causal learning at all.

Here is one relevant example. For infants' physical reasoning, Fei Xu and Vashti Garcia (2008) demonstrated that 8-month-olds were sensitive to statistical sampling patterns. An experimenter showed the infants a box full of white and red ping-pong balls, in an 80:20 proportion. Then she drew some balls from the box with her eyes closed. Assuming the draw was randomly generated, the distribution of balls in the sample should approximate the distribution of the balls in the box. Indeed, infants looked longer (showing a violation of expectation response) when a sample of mostly red balls was drawn from a box of mostly white balls than when a sample of mostly white balls was extracted.

These data indicate that infants are sensitive to statistical relations between samples and populations but do not indicate whether infants make causal inferences about the events nor, causally, what they think (if anything) about the person drawing the balls. Recent research goes further to demonstrate that children will integrate their prior knowledge with new evidence in a Bayesian way, to go beyond learning about observable variables to posit *unobservable* ones. They do this by inferring the agent's unobserved, causal-mental states, and in particular his or her intentions, desires, and preferences.

Here's an example. Imagine you saw a person repeatedly remove five blue balls from a box of many, many (80%) red ones and very few (20%) blue ones. You would easily see that this person drew a nonrandom, low-probability sample, and from that readily infer that this person *likes* blue balls or *wants* them for some reason. In contrast, what if you saw a different person take five blue balls from a box of 80% *blue* ones? Because that behavior largely reflects the underlying probabilities, it would provide you no (or unhelpfully ambiguous) information about that person's preference. If and when children understand this contrast—that the first person really wanted the blue ones—they have made a causal inference from the statistical data and done so in a psychological case: inferring the actor's preference.

Tamar Kushnir, Fei Xu, and I (2010) demonstrated that 20-month-olds can indeed interpret this sort of nonrandom sampling both causally and psychologically. In our research, a female experimenter took toy frogs from a box of almost all ducks (in the *minority* condition) or she took frogs from a box of almost all frogs (the *majority* condition). Then she left the room and another experimenter gave the child a small bowl of frogs and a separate bowl of ducks. When the original experimenter returned she extended her hand ambiguously between the bowls. The children could give her either a frog or a duck. In the minority condition (when the adult had originally taken frogs out of the box that was almost all ducks), children later gave her a frog. In this case, the toddlers concluded that she had wanted frogs. In contrast, in the majority condition (when she had taken frogs from a box of almost all frogs), children were equally likely to then give her a frog or a duck. In this case, these toddlers concluded that she had merely drawn a random sample from the box, rather than displaying a preference for frogs. So these 20-month-old had inferred an underlying mental state—a desire—from a statistical pattern. Note that in both cases toddlers saw the exact same overt behavior—the adult drew out five frogs. Yet they came to different causal hypotheses depending on the background probabilities of that behavior.

Not only do toddlers infer a preference from evidence of nonrandom statistical behavior (Kushnir et al., 2010; Ma & Xu, 2011), preschoolers do this as well (Kushnir et al., 2010). But what about still younger children, infants? Even toddlers have accumulated considerable information about persons' actions (Meltzoff, 1995) and desires (Repacholi & Gopnik, 1997), including verbally provided information from others (Bartsch & Wellman, 1995). Perhaps data from children this old show us one way that children can identify specific desires but don't show us that this is how younger children learn about the notion of desires in the first place. Testing still younger children could help here, so more recently we (Wellman, Kushnir, & Xu, 2014) tested preverbal 10-month-old infants in a violation-of-expectation paradigm to determine whether they can infer desires from such statistical patterns.

Consider Figure 6.3. As outlined there, two groups of infants saw a live actor remove five blue balls from a transparent box containing either 20% blue balls (minority condition) or 80% blue balls (majority condition). They saw this same action for multiple trials until habituated (looked for 50% less time on their last three trials than on their first three trials). After habituation, they saw one of two test events. In both events, the same adult was sitting halfway between two transparent bowls, one of red balls and one of blue ones. The adult looked at both bowls then reached her hand to grasp a ball in one of

Habituation Events

Person draws:

Minority (20%) Condition
ratio of blue to red balls: 5:20

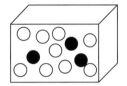

• Sample drawn intentionally

• From minority items

Majority (80%) Condition
ratio of blue to red balls: 20:5

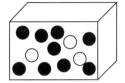

• Sample drawn incidentally

• From majority items

Test Events

       OR

Choose-Blue   **Choose-Red**

FIGURE 6.3 Depiction of how infants see a person draw out 5 blue balls, in habituation events, and the person then choosing a red or blue ball in the test events. In this figure, black circles represent blue balls; white circles represent red balls.

the bowls (red or blue) and at that point the action froze. Infants' looking times to this test event—choose red or choose blue—were the key measure.

In the minority (20%) condition, infants looked much longer at the choose-red than the choose-blue test event but not in the majority (80%) condition. In the minority condition, they expected the actor to exhibit the choose-blue test event, and so looked longer at her choose-red behavior. Note again that in habituation, infants in both conditions saw the same acts: the actor repeatedly took five blue balls out of the box. And at test, infants in both conditions saw the same acts: either a grasp of a red ball (from its bowl) or a grasp of blue (from its bowl). Both sets of actions were intentional—the actor looked at and reached into the box and carefully inspected and placed the balls—but the sampling process was different. The infants came to different conclusions—different posteriors—by considering how the acts relate to the (differing) background probabilities.

Moreover, these preverbal infants inferred a causal mental state—a desire or preference—from this statistical pattern of action: the actor's deliberate manipulation of the probabilities. Statistical learning, in a low-level, data-mining sense, could involve merely tracking frequencies and regularities; but our findings demonstrate that infants go beyond statistical associations alone to infer psychological causes.

This sort of social-causal statistical inference, available to preverbal 10-month-olds, could be a powerful contributor to childhood development of social cognition. More specifically, what may be crucial to causal learning in the psychological domain is that intentional actions characteristically violate physical probabilities. Just as deliberately drawing green frogs out of a box of almost all yellow ducks violates those physical prob-abilities, picking a toy up off the floor intentionally overrules its otherwise ongoing physical inertia, and sorting the pile of just-washed socks into pairs intentionally creates a randomly low-probability event out of an initial high-probability jumble. By hypoth-esis, it is by observing agents repeatedly violating physical probabilities in their actions that infants begin to posit that unobservable, causal psychological variables—the sim-plest being desires/preferences—may be warranted by the data. I believe that this sort of socially special, statistical learning shows us the beginnings of acquiring psychologi-cal concepts such as desires, preferences, and goals and eventually beliefs and thoughts as well.

Integrating Prior Knowledge and New Evidence

Bayesian inference combines evidence, likelihoods, and the prior probability of hypoth-eses. Do children take prior knowledge into account in a Bayesian way when they are making causal inferences? Several recent studies have shown that they do but that, also in a Bayesian way, new evidence can lead them to overturn an initially likely hypoth-esis. Again, these studies have mostly concentrated on physical causation—often using blicket detectors (Griffiths, Sobel, Tenenbaum, & Gopnik, 2011; Kushnir & Gopnik, 2007; Sobel, Tenenbaum, & Gopnik, 2004). A few revealing studies, however, have looked at psychological causation and done so in connection with physical or biological causation as well.

Laura Schulz and her colleagues (Schulz, Bonawitz, & Griffiths, 2007; Schulz & Gopnik, 2004) have explored whether children believe that causal relations can cross domains—that, for example, a physical cause could lead to a psychological effect or vice-versa. Many studies have suggested that children are initially reluctant to consider such hypotheses—they have a very low prior probability. For example, Laura Schulz and Alison Gopnik (2004) showed that 4-year-olds initially judged that talking to a machine—like the blicket detector in Box 6.1—would not make it light up and play. But then these 4-year-olds were given evidence, patterns of observable cause-effect dem-onstrations, and they used this statistical information to learn about this cross-domain causal relation. If children saw the appropriate links (conditional probabilities) between talking and activation, they became more willing to consider that talking would make the machine play: that is, they learned the cross-domain cause.

Given children's exposure to cell phones, intercoms, and so on in contemporary society, perhaps learning that talking to a blicket machine can activate it is a relatively likely rather than "less likely" prior hypothesis even for them. A more profound case concerns young children's inability to understand psychosomatic effects—where psy-chological causes (e.g., worry) lead to biological effects (e.g., stomach aches, ulcers). Preschoolers consistently and insistently deny that such effects are possible (e.g., Notaro, Gelman & Zimmerman 2001). So, in a series of experiments Laura Schulz, Elizabeth

Bonawitz and Tom Griffiths (2007) began with preschoolers who consistently denied psychosomatic effects and then gradually exposed them, via a sequence of storybooks, to more and more statistical evidence (within the storybook vignettes) supporting this cross-domain hypothesis. This systematically shifted children's inferences in precisely the way a Bayesian model would predict. As children got more and more evidence in favor of the hypothesis that worrying or fear can lead to tummy aches, they were more and more likely to accept it.

Intriguingly, in their first studies, this evidence-based revision of deep-seated prior beliefs worked for 4- and 5-year-olds but *not* 3-year-olds. This helps certify that for very young children, psychosomatic causation is a very unlikely prior hypothesis indeed. But then Elizabeth Bonawitz and her colleagues (Bonawitz, Fischer, & Schulz, 2012) took very young 3-year-olds and more systematically still, over the course of multiple sessions over 2 weeks, exposed them to evidence (through stories and skits). Young 3-year-olds who got this still more concerted diet of evidence began to revise their prior hypotheses (in gradual, progressive steps).

DYNAMIC FEATURES OF THEORIES

The results reviewed so far already tell us something about the dynamics of theory learning. They show that children are often learning about causal structure in a normatively correct way—given the right evidence, they draw appropriate causal conclusions. But now I want to look more deeply into the learning processes involved in developmentally more profound changes, such as those that are involved in theory change.

Sampling and Variability

The probabilistic Bayesian learner entertains a variety of hypotheses, and learning proceeds by updating the probabilities of these varied hypotheses. So variability among hypotheses becomes a necessary part and a crucial hallmark of the learning process. Developmental researchers have increasingly recognized that children also entertain multiple hypotheses and strategies at the same time. Children are typically variable. Individual children often perform correctly and incorrectly on the same task in the same session or employ two or three different strategies on the same task on adjacent trials. As Robert Siegler (1995, 2007) has cogently emphasized, this variability may actually help to explain development rather than being just noise to be ignored.

Siegler's examples typically come from number development. In his studies, children use variable strategies for exactly the same addition problems. But the same pattern applies to theory of mind. Consider standard changed-location, false-belief tasks. A child sees Judy put her toy in the dresser drawer and go away. Judy doesn't see that Punch then shifts the toy to the cupboard. Judy returns and the child is asked, "Where will Judy look for her toy? In the cupboard or in the drawer?" In one intensive study (Liu, Sabbagh, et al., 2009) almost 50 preschoolers were given 20 to 30 false-belief tasks. At one level of analysis, children were quite consistent: 65% of them passed more than 75% of these tasks, so they were consistently correct; and an additional 30% passed fewer than 25% of these tasks, so they were consistently incorrect—they said that Judy would look first in the cupboard, the "realist" answer. Only 3 children were in the middle, showing a fully mixed pattern. Such data help underwrite the firmness of young children's ideas—both their early unawareness of beliefs and then their later tenacious awareness of their power. But at the same time, when you examine the data in more detail, it becomes clear that there is enormous variability: All the children produced a mix of incorrect realism and correct false-belief answers.

Related data come from false belief explanation tasks. In these tasks, rather than asking for a prediction—"Where will Judy search for her toy?"—the experimenter shows the child that Judy actually goes to the place where the object no longer is (because it was switched to the cupboard) and then asks the child for an explanation: "Why is Judy looking in the drawer?" Young children offer cogent explanations; in fact, their explanations are often better than their parallel predictions (Wellman, 2011). But they produce a mix of very different explanations. On successive tasks, a typical child might answer "she doesn't want her toy anymore" (desire explanation), "it's empty" (reality explanation), "she doesn't know where it is" (knowledge-ignorance explanation), and "she thinks her toy's there" (belief explanation). Jennifer Amsterlaw and I (Amsterlaw & Wellman, 2006) tested 3- and 4-year-old children on 24 such false-belief explanation tasks over 6 weeks. Reality explanations were more prevalent early on, and knowledge-ignorance plus belief explanations were more prevalent later. But all the children were variable, often producing two or three different explanations on the same day.

Researchers who are interested in charting broad, long-term changes in children's thinking often treat this sort of childhood variability as if it is simply error variance and so uninteresting. But a probabilistic Bayesian approach says variability actually helps children learn. If children are sampling from a range of hypotheses, then variability is not noise, it's to be expected. And, variability can actually tell us something important about how broader changes take place. Moreover, if we additionally consider theories' hierarchical structure, variability has further aspects and further distinctive functions, as I discuss next.

HIERARCHICAL BAYES NETS: MORE THEORETICAL ADVANCES

Bayes nets are good representations of particular causal structures, even complex causal structures. However, according to theory theory, often children are not just learning particular causal structures but are also learning abstract, framework generalizations about causal structure. For example, in addition to learning that my desire for frogs causes me to take them out of the box, children may develop a broader generalization; they may conclude that desires are the kinds of variables that cause actions (although other mental states such as vague hopes or fictional imaginings do not).

In fact, "classic" theory theory research has shown that children develop more abstract, framework knowledge over and above their specific causal knowledge. When they make judgments about objects and people, children often seem to understand broad causal principles *before* they understand specific details (Simons & Keil, 1995; Wellman & Gelman, 1998). For example, at an abstract level, 3- and 4-year-olds, like adults, know that biological objects, such as a cactus or a pig, generally have different insides than artifacts, such as a watch or a piggy bank. They also know that those insides are important to identity and function. At the same time, however, such young children are notably inaccurate and vague about just what those insides specifically are (Gelman & Wellman, 1991). They say that biological objects have blood and guts (even a cactus) and artifacts have gears or stuffing inside (even a clothes iron). Similarly, in theory-of-mind tasks, children refer generally to agent's desires and beliefs, yet often they are amazingly vague and even circular about what those desires or beliefs are. "Look, Judy went to the drawer—why did she do that?" Because she wanted to. "Does she want her toy?" Yes. "Well, her toy is in the cupboard, why did she go to the drawer?" Because she wants to (Amsterlaw & Wellman, 2006; Schult & Wellman, 1997).

As noted before, broader generalizations are important in both scientific and intuitive theories. Philosophers of science refer to "overhypotheses" (Goodman, 1955), or "research programs" (Laudan, 1977), or "paradigms" (Kuhn, 1962) to capture these higher order generalizations. I prefer the term "framework theories" (Wellman, 1990; Wellman & Gelman, 1992). In their framework theories, children assume there are characteristic kinds of variables and causal structure (differing, e.g., for naïve psychology vs. biology vs. physics). Constructivists, including Piaget and theory theorists, insist that this more abstract causal knowledge could be learned. The Bayesian modeling described so far tells us how it is possible to learn specific causal structure. How is it possible, computationally, to learn these more abstract, overarching causal principles? How, computationally, could we actually get framework development?

Tom Griffiths and Josh Tenenbaum (2009; Tenenbaum, Kemp, Griffiths, & Goodman, 2011), inspired by both philosophy of science and cognitive development, have formulated computational ways of representing and learning higher order generalizations about causal structure. They call their approach hierarchical Bayesian modeling or also, nicely enough, theory-based Bayesian modeling (Griffiths & Tenenbaum, 2009; Tenenbaum et al., 2006).

In standard Bayesian modeling, a particular Bayes net represents a specific hypothesis about the causal relations among particular variables. Hierarchical Bayesian models (HBMs) stack up hypotheses. Two key insights are exploited. First, such structures can be seen as existing in hierarchies of specificity—from general "framework" theories down to the more specific "base-level" theories that describe and infer structure for a very specific set of data. The higher levels contain general principles that specify which hypotheses to entertain at the lower level. Thus these higher level structures can constrain the more particular hypotheses represented by particular Bayes nets. Moreover, and this is the second key insight, these higher level generalizations can themselves be learned by Bayesian methods.

More specifically, each pair of levels in the hierarchy captures an interplay between "data" and a "hypothesis space" (or theory). At the bottom are data or evidence, E, and first-level theory, H (just as in Bayes' rule). However, under this proposal, H is also, in turn, the data for Theory 1. So, one step up from E, H becomes the E for Theory 1, and Theory 1 is the hypothesis space for H. So, now there is E > H > Theory 1. In principle, then, if H can learn about the structure of its data, E, and make novel inductions about it, then Theory 1 can (via the same sort of principles) learn about the structure of its data, H, and make novel inductions about it. Of course, to do its job, Theory 1 can have some structure that already constrains it; that is provided by Theory 2. Thus, going up then back down the hierarchy, data revise/update their theories *and* theories constrain inductions over the data (i.e., make possible learning).

Recall that Bayesian reasoning means that we can solve the inverse problem and determine the posterior (the probability of the hypothesis given the evidence) by using what we know about the likelihood and the prior. P (H/E) is a function of P (H) and P(E/H). The insight behind hierarchical or theory-based Bayesian models of inductive learning

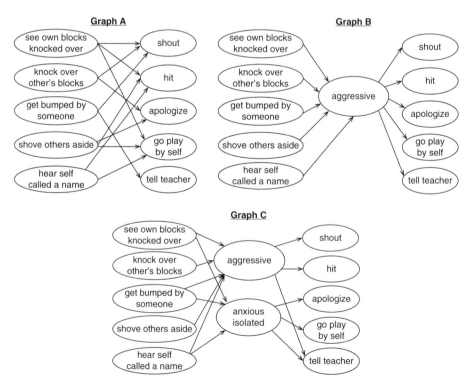

FIGURE 6.4. Three different causal Bayes nets of commonplace behavioral events.

is to not only let Bayesian learning operate between E and H but *also* between H and Theory 1, and *also* between Theory 1 and Theory 2, and so on.

Here is an example from naïve psychology, in this case, an example of behaviors and traits. Consider a family of causal graphs representing causal relations between certain "preschool" events such as knocking over blocks and bumping into people on one hand and reactions such as crying, telling the teacher, and apologizing on the other hand, as in Figure 6.4. Perhaps the relations might be captured by the causal graph of nodes and arrows on the top left-hand side of Figure 6.4, Graph A. Perhaps instead, the correct causal structure is Graph B or Graph C. In fact, something very like Graph B captures a simple trait conception, whereas something like Graph A would be more like the situation-action scripts discussed in Chapter 4.

Although Graphs B and C themselves differ, they are actually both versions of the same more abstract graph schema. In this schema, all the nodes fall into three general categories: Input Events, that is, situations that affect the child (someone bumps into them or knocks over their blocks); Reactions, that is, how the child reacts (hits, shouts); and internal dispositional Traits such as aggressive. Both Graphs B and C (in contrast to Graph A) have this general form but differ in specifics. Both could be generated from a simple higher order theory that goes something like this:

1. There are three types of nodes: Events, Traits, and Reactions.
2. Possible causal relationships only take the form of Event→Trait and Trait→Reaction, or in total Event→Trait→Reaction.

Note that Event→Trait→Reaction is more general and abstract than any of the more specific graphs in Figure 6.4. Event→Trait→Reaction is at a higher level in several ways. Event, Trait, and Reaction are not themselves any of the nodes in any of the graphs (which are instead "knock over blocks," "hit," etc.). Further, Event→Trait→Reaction does not itself directly "contact" the evidence, which would include dependencies between "gets bumped" and "hits" or "has blocks knocked over" and "tells teacher."

In Figure 6.4, we can think of Graphs A, B, and C as specific theories of human action. Event→Trait→Reaction is a higher level theory, not a specific theory. This "higher" theory generates some specific theories (e.g., Graphs B and C) but not others (not Graph A, e.g.). The higher level theory Events→Traits→Reactions does not directly contact the data. But because it generates some specific theories and not others, the higher level theory will indirectly confront the data via the specific theories it generates.

There are a variety of higher level theories just as there are a variety of specific theories and even more specific hypotheses. Bayesian inference lets one specify the probability of different higher level theories in a hierarchical stack. Indeed, computational work on hierarchical Bayseian models has shown that, at least normatively, hierarchical Bayesian learning can actually work. Higher level theories can indeed be updated in a Bayesian way via evidence that contacts only lower level hypotheses. Tom Griffiths and

Josh Tenenbaum (2007) provided several simple demonstrations, and Charles Kemp and colleagues (Kemp, Perfors, & Tenenbaum, 2007) and Noah Goodman and colleagues (Goodman, Ullman, & Tenenbaum, 2011) have provided more comprehensive and complex ones. These demonstrations show that it is possible, in principle, for learning to proceed at several levels at once—not just at the level of specific hypotheses or specific theories but, even more abstractly, at the framework theory level. At the least, these demonstrations provide intriguing thought experiments. They suggest that data-driven learning can not only change specific hypotheses but can also lead to more profound conceptual changes, such as the creation of more abstract theories and framework theories.

These computational thought experiments underwrite the feasibility of constructivist accounts that claim the dynamic interplay between structure and data can yield both specific kinds of learning and more profound development as well. Hierarchical Bayesian models (HBMs) provide a more detailed computational account of how this can happen. On the hierarchical Bayesian picture, local causal learning can, and will, lead to broader, progressive, theory revision and conceptual change.

Hierarchical Bayesian modeling also relies crucially on variability among hypotheses. This sort of probabilistic learning tests multiple specific theories and framework theories and updates the probability of those theories in the light of new evidence, just as probabilistic Bayesian modeling does in general. Moreover, from this hierarchical perspective, variability can be thought of not only "synchronically" (children adopt multiple approaches at one time) but also "diachronically" (different approaches emerge over time). This means that as hierarchical Bayesian learning proceeds over multiple iterations, intermediate transitional hypotheses emerge (Ullman, Goodman, & Tenenbaum, 2012). In particular, in the learning process, some abstract hypotheses progressively come to dominate others but then themselves become dominated by still others. HBMs, as they dynamically operate on evidence over time, result in characteristic progressions of intermediate hypotheses.

Progressive Learning in Childhood

If children are hierarchical probabilistic Bayesian learners, then they should also produce intermediate hypotheses, and those hypotheses should improve progressively. In fact, children's conceptual development does progress in this way. Indirect evidence of such progressions is available, for example, in studies of children's naïve astronomy (Vosniadou & Brewer, 1992) and naïve biology (Inagaki & Hatano, 2002).

More to the point for this book, think back to Chapter 5. Preschoolers don't just go from failing to passing false-belief tasks between ages 2 and 5. Instead they develop a series of insights about the mind. This transition involves a revealing, extended set of conceptual progressions captured in part by the ToM Scale (Wellman & Liu, 2004). If these progressions reflect hierarchical Bayesian learning, then they should vary depending on the learners' experiences. Chapter 5 demonstrated two kinds of crucial experience-dependent variation. First, differences in sequencing result from different childhood experiences. Thus, American and Chinese children, immersed in different languages and cultures, evidence appropriate differences in their early theory-of-mind progressions—their sequence of insights. And second, differences in timing result from different childhood experiences. Thus, hearing children and deaf children (of hearing parents) exposed to very different early communicative experiences evidence appropriate differences in their early theory-of-mind progressions—differences in timetables.

This extended series of developmental achievements fits the hierarchical Bayesian learning, theory-construction perspective because probabilistic Bayesian learning predicts that the sequence of hypotheses the learner develops depends on the learner's "diet" of evidence. Still more direct evidence is provided by microgenetic studies that track conceptual change longitudinally over days or weeks. Recent research on preschoolers' theories of mind employs this approach.

Microgenetic Evidence

One way to capture more precisely progressive developmental changes is through multiple closely packed sessions with the same children over a protracted transition, thereby achieving a microgenetic record of change and transition (Siegler, 2007). A few microgenetic studies have done this for the theory-of-mind preschool transition to an explicit understanding of false belief (Amsterlaw & Wellman, 2006; Flynn, O'Malley, & Wood, 2004).

Briefly, microgenetic studies are a special type of longitudinal study in which one samples behavior very frequently—to get a fine-grained picture of developmental change. Further, to experimentally capture change, some microgenetic research involves not just measuring change but intervening to accelerate it, in designs in which investigators "choose a task representative of the cognition in question, hypothesize the types of everyday experiences that lead to change, and then provide a higher concentration of these experiences than ordinary" (Siegler, 1995, p. 413).

Following this thinking, in an initial microgenetic study of theory of mind, Jennifer Amsterlaw and I (Amsterlaw & Wellman, 2006) focused on children's acquisition of an understanding of false belief. We began with young 3-year-olds for whom a pretest showed that they systematically failed numerous false-belief tasks as well as several other theory-of-mind tasks. In the course of everyday development, it takes such young children considerable time to go from consistent false-belief errors to consistent correct performance (see Chapters 2 and 5). Indeed, in our study, in a control group that received only pretests and posttests, after 10 to 12 weeks children made virtually no progress in false-belief understanding.

Focally, however, we took a comparable group of young children who consistently failed false belief and required them to make both false-belief predictions and explanations again and again over many weeks. So, in two sessions a week for a total of 12 sessions, they had to predict what would happen in a false-belief scenario (e.g., in Box 1.2 back in Chapter 1, predict where Judy would look for her candy); then they were shown what actually happens (Judy looked in the drawer) and asked to explain the characters' actions (Why did Judy do that?). One rationale for providing a higher concentration of these "everyday" experiences rested on data discussed in Chapter 2 showing that parents and children frequently ask for explanations of persons' actions and that variability in the frequency of explanations during everyday family conversations predicts individual differences in children's social-cognitive understanding. A second rationale was more Bayesian: Children's microgenetic experiences required them to note their predictive failures and explain them. Thus, in a Bayesian fashion, children were prompted to consider their priors (their failed predictions) and attempt to reconcile them with the evidence (via attempted explanations).

In this focal microgenetic group, there was significant improvement relative both to a pretest (that children consistently failed) and to two control groups (that also had repeated testing) where consistent failure persisted. Children in the focal microgenetic group went from initially making consistent false-belief errors (being incorrect 88% of the time) to later performing correctly 79% of the time. Moreover, on posttests these microgenetic children also improved on several other theory-of-mind tasks.

This first microgenetic study left several intriguing questions unanswered, however. One concern was how did children progress (e.g., through what steps)? A second concern was why did some children progress whereas others exposed to exactly the same microgenetic experiences apparently did not? For example, in the Amsterlaw and Wellman (2006) microgenetic study, using a criterion of 75% or better performance on multiple false-belief tasks, 9 of the 12 focal microgenetic children met this criterion at posttest (and 7 scored perfectly). But this means that 3 (25%) or 5 (42%) of the 12 did not. As another example, Heidemarie Lohmann and Michael Tomasello (2003) compared five different training conditions with young preschoolers, all of whom failed false belief at pretest. In the most successful condition (full training), on average, children performed substantially better at posttest on a set of three false-belief tasks; however, posttest success ranged from none to three among individual children.

Two rough but importantly distinct possibilities could account for such individual variations when children are exposed to the same conditions and some do but others do not learn. Perhaps general cognitive factors "external" to the domain of theory of mind account for why some children learned more—for example, some children were more attentive, thoughtful, interested, or had better memory. However, from a probabilistic Bayesian perspective, we should also consider factors "internal" to theory-of-mind conceptions themselves: Although all children consistently failed at pretest, some may have had a more solid or advanced conceptual foundation about persons and minds to begin with and so progressed more by building on these early insights. That is, Bayesian analyses of development and learning emphasize the relationship between new information (the evidence) and one's prior hypotheses. The result is incremental changes from prior to posterior probabilities. So, earlier conceptual status shapes later learning (beyond mere attention, executive skill, or general cognitive ability). Consistent failure on false-belief tests at pretest in a training or microgenetic study may nonetheless mask relevant conceptual differences. Novel mixes of scaling, training, and microgenetic-longitudinal methods better address these issues.

Combining Scaling Plus Microgenetic Evidence

Following these ideas, Marjorie Rhodes and I (2013) merged microgenetic and scaling approaches: We gave children the ToM Scale at pretest and posttest, accelerated their understanding via prediction-explanation microgenetic experiences, and examined how learning proceeds in terms of progressions of understanding. We also included a larger sample of focal children—29 (as opposed to 12 in Amsterlaw & Wellman, 2006)—to allow for some additional analyses and comparisons.

Just as in the original Amsterlaw and Wellman (2006) study, when given prediction-explanation microgenetic experiences many children progressed; but again in terms of false belief at the posttest, there was variability. Although 60% consistently passed false-belief tasks at posttest, essentially 40% did not. Importantly, children not only varied at posttest; they also varied on their ToM Scale performance at pretest. Although all 29 children in the microgenetic group consistently failed false belief at the start, some were further along the ToM Scale than others. Indeed, at pretest, essentially half had gotten as far as passing the diverse-belief task (DD and DB) and half had progressed as far as knowledge access (DD, DB, and KA). Call the first group the diverse-belief pretest group and the second the knowledge pretest group.

How did these two groups learn? For the knowledge pretest group, 75% became consistent at false belief; they passed three or four of four false-belief tests at posttest. Indeed, 50% were perfect: they passed four of four. Of the diverse-belief pretest group, *none* became consistent false-belief passers (and of course none passed all four posttest false-belief tasks). So the knowledge pretest children progressed to false belief understanding (given prediction-explanation microgenetic experiences) and diverse-belief pretest children did not, although they received the same microgenetic enhancement experiences.

What happened to the diverse-belief pretest children? On their posttest ToM Scale, many had progressed as well, in their case progressing beyond diverse belief to understanding knowledge access (KA) although still failing to understand false belief. A total of 43% of them made such progress. Thus, in a constructivist Bayesian manner, progress was dependent on where a child was to begin with (their priors). And children achieved a progression of intermediate understandings on the way to understanding false belief.

Microgenetic methods coupled with ToM Scale assessments also promote theory-of-mind progress for deaf children of hearing parents. In a recent training study, Candida Peterson and I (Wellman & Peterson, 2013) pretested and posttested deaf children of hearing parents on the ToM Scale plus on multiple false-belief tasks; we then trained 13 of them who consistently failed false belief at pretest in extended microgenetic sessions over 6 weeks and analyzed their progress. We reasoned that on average, these 9-, 10- and 11-year-olds would make progress, and given their overall theory-of-mind delays, that their protracted progress might give us a still more extended look at cognitive change in theory of mind over the period from pretest to posttest.

Two age-matched control groups who received the pretests and posttests did not change over a 12-week period, confirming that without intervention these children make very little change over such a period. Yet the focal group who had multiple intervening microgenetic training sessions did change—they became correct on 69% of their false-belief tasks at posttest. Not only did they gain understanding of theory-of-mind concepts focal to their training (the exact sort of false-belief task used in their microgenetic training sessions), they also generalized to other novel false-belief tasks as well. Moreover, they progressed significantly on the broader ToM Scale of theory-of-mind concepts.

Once again, however, not all children in this focal group came to understand false belief or progressed equally. What accounted for this variation? Although children systematically failed false belief at pretest, their "closeness" to false-belief understanding as measured by their position along the ToM Scale definitely influenced their progress. Children who were further along the scale (e.g., DD, DB, and KA) were more likely to make greater false-belief progress than those less far along (e.g., DD or DD and DB instead). In regression analyses, this was by far the largest factor accounting for posttest gain, even after language competence and age were controlled. Here again children's different theory-of-mind starting points (as measured on the ToM Scale) predicted differences in theory-of-mind progress among children, all of whom consistently failed false belief and were given the exact same intervention.

In total, these data help illuminate the mechanisms of cognitive change. They do so by manifesting three empirical signatures of constructivist learning, ones that are characteristic of probabilistic and hierarchical Bayesian learning as well: (a) Learning proceeds in orderly conceptual progressions; (b) both the sequences (in cross-cultural research) and timetables (for deaf children and in these experimental microgenetic studies) of the progressions are experience dependent; and, crucially, (c) prior conceptual knowledge influences the presence and amount of learning, both enabling conceptual change given some prior understandings and constraining conceptual change given others. For children closer to false belief on the ToM Scale at pretest, their (prior) knowledge enabled them to progress to an understanding of false belief. For those further from false belief to begin with, training did not engender an understanding of false belief, but rather it provoked other "earlier" theory-of-mind understanding instead.

BLESSINGS OF ABSTRACTION

So far it seems that hierarchical Bayesian models can provide computational accounts that explain how children might learn abstract framework theories from specific theories that are learned from specific evidence. This helps further characterize framework development as I began to outline it in Chapter 5. But that does not yet address the additional claim, and the related developmental findings, that children sometimes develop abstract framework theories *before* they develop detailed specific theories.

The conventional wisdom in psychology has been that learning at a lower level of generalization and abstraction—more concrete learning—must precede higher order, abstract, and general learning. This idea has been presupposed both by empiricists and by nativists. This is one reason why, when infants or very young children understand abstract structure, nativists conclude that this structure must be innate (see, e.g., Spelke et al., 1992). Although some developmentalists have stressed instead that young children often seem to learn abstract regularities and even do so before specific ones (Simons & Keil, 1995; Wellman & Gelman, 1998), this is a distinctively unconventional proposal and it might appear that this kind of learning just couldn't work.

However, recent work on hierarchical Bayesian modeling has shown that and how abstract generalizations can sometimes actually precede specific ones (e.g., Goodman et al., 2011). A simple example can illustrate this. Suppose I show you a pile of many bags of colored marbles and your job is to learn the color of the marbles in each bag. Now I draw some marbles out the bags. I start with Bag 1. I take out one, then two, then three, and then four red marbles in a row. Each time I ask you what you think will happen next. After a while you'll predict that yet another red marble will appear from Bag 1. Then I repeat this with Bag 2. This time I take out a succession of blue marbles. By Bag 3 you might well conclude, "I don't know the color, but whatever the first one is I bet all the rest in that bag will be the same color." You've learned an abstract regularity, and your knowledge of that regularity precedes your learning of the specific color in Bag 3 or, for that matter, any other remaining bag. Note that this abstract structure was certainly not innate; it was learned. Under the right circumstances abstract regularities (e.g., theory = all marbles in Bag 3 will be the same color) can be learned in advance of the specifics (H = all marbles in Bag 3 are purple). The philosopher Nelson Goodman (1955) called these more abstract principles "overhypotheses"—hypotheses about which hypotheses are likely.

Charles Kemp and colleagues (2007) demonstrated how overhypotheses can be learned in HBMs, and building on these ideas, Noah Goodman and colleagues (2011) used hierarchical Bayesian modeling to provide a striking set of computational results they call "the blessing of abstraction." They showed that, in hierarchical Bayesian models, it can be as easy to learn causal structure at several levels at once as it is to simply infer particular causal structure. Moreover, learning both higher level and specific structures from the data can be no slower (i.e., requires no more data samples) than having the abstract ones "innately" specified at the start and learning only the specific structures from the data. Probabilistic hierarchical Bayesian learners thus learn abstract structures alongside and even before the specifics that those regularities subsume. Children do the same thing.

CONCLUSIONS

According to theory theory, there is a deep kinship between childhood cognitive development and science: Both involve learning about the causal structure of the world, and both involve learning that depends on the interplay between theory and evidence. However, science may seem a suspect phenomenon to compare to children's learning. After all, although analogies between science and cognitive development were among Piaget's legacies, science is practiced by a small minority of the human species, mostly only in recent history. Science is supported by advanced degrees and advanced technologies (e.g., microscopes, neural scanners, particle accelerators); and contemporary science focuses on phenomena that were unimagined just centuries ago (e.g., space-time relativity, Darwinian evolution, quarks).

More basic for theory theory, however, scientists engage in certain key knowledge-generating processes, cognitive practices further illuminated by contemporary computational learning models:

- They inductively, probabilistically infer general conclusions from small samples of evidence.
- They infer causal relationships from such evidence.
- They use both experimental and statistical inference to infer causal relations.
- They seek explanations and revised hypotheses for anomalous or surprising data.
- They propose unobserved variables to explain anomalous data.

It is these knowledge-generating practices that are essential to scientific inquiry and progress (and not, e.g., practices of publication, peer review, or grantsmanship). *And*, according to theory theory, it is these practices that are crucially characteristic of childhood conceptual development as well. At least these theory-building practices are characteristic of childhood conceptual development in certain foundational domains such as naïve physics, naïve biology, and focal for this book, naïve psychology or *theory* of mind.

Summary

New computational ideas coupled with new theory-of-mind research provide crucial support for theory theory. The new computational research relies on probabilistic Bayesian learning and hierarchical theory-based modeling. The new theory-of-mind research examines sequences of childhood conceptual learning. Both sets of research show how sampling and variability lead to progressively more accurate intuitive theories. The theory-of-mind research does so with studies of children who grow up in different sociocultural circumstances and who evidence differing sequences of theory-of-mind advancements. It does so as well with more experimental, microgenetic research. Together these advances provide a more empirically rich and theoretically clear version of the theory theory as manifest in theory-of-mind development.

7

Alternatives and Extensions

THEORY THEORY, AND the related constructivist, Bayesian approach, are not the only accounts available attempting to explain theory-of-mind developments. How do different accounts fare and compare? This is a complex question because the various accounts are constantly evolving. And the different accounts rarely square off directly, complementing one another on some points while contradicting one another on others, engendering differing studies that do not compare and contrast neatly. Nonetheless, the rich data outlined to this point are useful for theory comparison and development. No one position has all the merit; yet in the end, theory theory remains an especially empirically validated, and in some ways indispensable, account.

EXPLANATORY ACCOUNTS

One way to carve up the theoretical terrain is into, roughly, accounts that are domain general versus domain specific. Perhaps general developmental changes—such as changes in IQ, executive functioning, or increasingly complex cognition—completely account for developmental changes on theory-of-mind tasks. Or, perhaps knowledge and processes specific to the social-psychological domain not only result from but shape theory of mind (processes that also inevitably yield fundamental differences between naïve psychology and naïve physics or naïve biology).

Domain-General Accounts

A baseline possibility is that social cognition and its development simply reflect general intelligence—IQ—and its development. Smarter kids know more and develop faster, and that is what the data on theory of mind are showing us, full stop. But that is too general. Theory-of-mind achievements (such as understanding false belief) do correlate significantly with verbal IQ in children in the preschool years (e.g., Carlson & Moses, 2001; Happé, 1995); nonetheless, theory of mind makes independent contributions to analyses of preschool social cognition beyond verbal IQ and beyond other constructs, such as age, which also correlate with IQ (Carlson & Moses, 2001; Sabbagh, Xu, Carlson, Moses, & Lee, 2006). Moreover, individuals with autism have marked deficits in theory-of-mind understandings, even when they have high IQs (Happé, 1995).

Here is a nice example of this dissociation. Children who grow up with older siblings (rather than as first born or alone) are better (on average) at false-belief understanding and develop this theory-of-mind milestone faster than children who are only children or first born (e.g., Perner et al., 1994; McAlister & Peterson, 2007). The *opposite* pattern is true for IQ. As has been shown in many studies over many years (e.g., Zajonc & Mullally, 1997), it is children who are singletons or first born that have (on average) higher IQs.

IQ is a very imprecise and encompassing construct—measured by an amalgam of vocabulary, memory, factual knowledge, spatial reasoning, and quantitative tasks. Domain-general processes can be more precise than that, such as accounts that focus on the development of executive functions.

Executive-Function Accounts

Executive functioning (EF) has been proposed to be a basic component of all information processing (Miyake & Friedman, 2012), and changes in executive functioning have been proposed as accounting for cognitive development generally (Zelazo & Müller, 2011) and for theory-of-mind development in particular (Frye, Zelazo, & Palfai, 1995; Müller, Zelazo, & Imrisek, 2005). And indeed, at the time that sizable developments are occurring in preschoolers' mentalistic understanding of persons, executive functions are dramatically improving.

Executive functioning refers to processes involved in the control of action, emotion, and thought. Executive functions evidence both diversity and unity (Zelazo, Carter, Reznick, & Frye, 1997): They include the separable components of cognitive flexibility, inhibitory control, and working memory that cohere moderately into a sensible overarching construct (Miyake & Friedman, 2012). This means there are several overlapping possibilities for how theory-of-mind developments might be explained by more general executive-function developments (Apperly, 2011).

For one specific example of the more general case, consider inhibitory control. Several theory-of-mind accounts focus on inhibitory control (e.g., Leslie, German, &

Polizzi, 2005; Luo & Baillargeon, 2010); and in some research, inhibitory control has demonstrated particularly strong relations to theory of mind (Carlson & Moses, 2001). *Inhibitory control* refers to the capacity to suppress actions or thoughts that are irrelevant to performance on some task. After several years of keeping the salt on the table, you move it to over the stove; then you often find yourself beginning to go to the table to get the salt (when you know full well it's above the stove), and having to inhibit the tendency to go there, sometimes stopping yourself in midstride. Changes in inhibitory processing have been argued to be the explanation for a variety of cognitive changes—including general increases in cognitive competence in childhood and complementarily general cognitive declines in aging (Dempster, 1992).

Ability to inhibit salient thoughts (e.g., not to think about your birthday presents so as to wait more patiently for the time to open them) and inhibit typical or prepotent responses (e.g., not to go to the table to get the salt) develop markedly in the preschool years, and thinking about mental states recruits some of these same processes. Thinking about mental states typically requires thinking about two things at once—desires versus behaviors, feelings versus emotional displays, beliefs versus reality, self versus other— and requires properly considering some things over others, as needed, for example, to privilege a person's beliefs over reality in predicting their mistaken, false-belief-based actions. Performance on inhibitory control tasks correlate highly with performance on false-belief tasks even when age and language ability are partialled out (Carlson, Mandell, & Williams, 2004; Carlson & Moses, 2001).

Learning about and reasoning about mental states of the sort apparent in the preschool years undoubtedly requires executive-function resources. So, a first question to consider is whether advances in theory of mind reflect essentially just general advances in executive functioning as applied to the world of persons and their actions. Executive function *expression* accounts claim so; but empirically, executive-function developments alone seem insufficient to account for many of the most important differences and developments within an understanding of mind. As reviewed in Chapter 3, false belief, for example, still significantly predicts aspects of children's conversations, their social interactional skills, their engagement in pretense, their interactions with and popularity with peers, and their participation in games like hide-and-seek in studies in which executive functioning is controlled and factored out (e.g., Peskin & Ardino, 2003; Razza & Blair, 2009). Although, to reiterate, theory of mind is much more than just understanding false beliefs, nonetheless an initial focus on false belief is warranted because some executive-function theorists have argued that false-belief reasoning in particular presents an extra layer of executive control problems. According to this perspective, it is false belief that is especially difficult (Birch & Bloom, 2007; Mitchell, 1996; Russell, Jarrold, & Potel, 1994), and it is false-belief competence that might especially reflect executive-function competence.

Suppose for a moment that false-belief performance does represent just executive-function achievement. Then those children who early achieve better executive functioning should equally attain better early false-belief performance. This hypothesis was explored by Mark Sabbagh and his colleagues. Intriguingly, there is evidence that in East Asia (e.g., Oh & Lewis, 2008), and specifically in China (Sabbagh et al., 2006), children have earlier developing executive-function skills relative to their Western peers (probably because parents and teachers place particular emphasis on the socialization of self-control). But this earlier competence at executive function does *not* translate into better or earlier false-belief understanding. In precise comparisons between preschoolers in Beijing (Sabbagh et al., 2006) and the United States (Carlson & Moses, 2001), Chinese children were consistently and significantly advanced in executive functions (on eight different executive-function tasks); and yet at the same time for the same children, there were no theory-of-mind differences between the Chinese and U.S. children at 3½, 4, or 4½ years on four different, standard, preschool false-belief tasks. (See the Liu et al. 2008, meta-analysis discussed in Chapter 2 for related U.S.–Chinese comparisons.)

Beyond false belief, further telling evidence is outlined in Box 7.1, including ToM Scale data. To sum up, as concluded in Chapter 3, executive function *expression* accounts (which claim theory-of-mind tasks are more or less just varieties of executive tasks) fall short of explaining theory-of-mind development. An alternative perspective is sketched in executive function *emergence* accounts: Changes in executive functions promote the emergence of increasingly insightful theory-of-mind conceptions (Moses, 2001). As one example, to recognize that persons can have not only different desires about the same object but also different beliefs about it requires some capacity to flexibly shift between and remember alternatives. In emergence accounts, then, theory-of-mind conceptions themselves importantly develop, and increases in executive functioning play a permissive role—they permit the child to more effectively engage in conceptual theory building.

Because all explicit, preschool theory-of-mind tasks require some executive resources for execution, various task contrasts can, of course, primarily vary in executive-function difficulty. Consider a variation of a changed-locations task—a variation on the task schematized in Box 1.2—where in this case an *undesirable* item is hidden—a doll for boys or a truck for girls—in the drawer. The other container—the cupboard—has a toy too. Judy knows that but never sees what that toy might be; she just sees the truck hidden in the cupboard. Then Judy goes away, and while she can't see, the two items are switched. Judy returns wanting an item to play with and desiring to avoid the truck. Where will she look for a toy to play with? Children find it significantly harder to judge for the case in which Judy has a desire to avoid (e.g., avoid the truck) than for the standard case in which Judy has a desire to obtain (Cassidy, 1998; Friedman & Leslie, 2004; Leslie et al., 2005; Leslie & Polizzi, 1998). Pretty clearly the additional executive-function resources needed to inhibit a desire (desire to avoid) does make this sort of belief-desire reasoning more difficult.

Conceptual Versus Execution Issues

Nonetheless, more generally, executive functions fall short of explaining preschool theory-of-mind development—preschool theory-of-mind performances do not just

BOX 7.1
FURTHER CONSIDERATION OF HOW EXECUTIVE FUNCTION DIFFERENCES
RELATE TO THEORY-OF-MIND TASK DIFFERENCES

Diverse Desires Versus Diverse Beliefs

In a diverse-beliefs task (see Chapter 4), children may well have to inhibit a prepotent consideration of what they know to be true to consider what the other person believes. But, similarly, in a diverse-desires task—such as Repacholi and Gopnik's (1997) broccoli-crackers task—children have to inhibit their own prepotent preference to attribute to the adult a different preference.

- Yet children judge correctly for desires at 18 months, but only do so for beliefs at about 3 years of age. In a meta-analysis of many related studies, understanding diverse desires was consistently easier than understanding diverse beliefs (Wellman & Liu, 2004).

- Even when tasks are designed to have closely comparable demands and formats, the same 2- and 3-year-old children can attribute different desires to self versus others, but not different beliefs (Flavell, Flavell, Green, & Moses, 1990), and can attribute failed (frustrated) desires to self and others but not failed (outdated) beliefs (Gopnik & Slaughter, 1991).

In spite of equivalent, inhibitory control demands, this developmental difference in theory-of-mind understanding remains.

ToM Scale Data

Not only diverse-desire and diverse-belief tasks, but all the scale tasks on the Wellman and Liu (2004) scale appear to have very similar executive function and cognitive complexity demands.

- All deal with two alternatives, and one alternative must be inhibited to correctly choose the other. For diverse beliefs, inhibit my belief to answer based on the other's belief; for knowledge-access, inhibit my knowledge/reality to answer based on the other's lack of knowledge; and so on.

In spite of such similar inhibitory demands, the five tasks all differ in their developmental sequence.

Incremental Executive-Function Improvements?

Could the progression of five tasks in the five-step scale sequence represent more extended childhood increments in executive function? Stephanie Carlson (e.g., Carlson & Schaefer, 2012) has been developing an executive-functions scale, a short (~10 minute) assessment of various executive-function skills (prefigured by an examination of a large variety of preschool tasks in Beck, Schaefer, Pang, & Carlson, 2011).

The battery encompasses seven levels of difficulty and reveals gradual increases in executive functions in the preschool years. Conceivably, such a measure might show that gradual increases in executive function account for progressive preschool increases in theory of mind. However:

- Data showing *reversed* ToM Scale sequences for children growing up in the United States versus those growing up in China (or Australia vs. Iran) argue against this possibility. If some step-by-step increments in executive functioning accounted for the detailed, five-step U.S. data (e.g., that the knowledge-access task requires more inhibition than the diverse-beliefs task), it could not then account for the Chinese data.

  Sequence reversals (e.g., for diverse beliefs and knowledge access for Chinese vs. U.S. children) contradict any claim that inhibitory control differences across the tasks can fully account for the focal theory-of-mind differences.

  These task comparisons address not only inhibitory control issues but also closely related executive-function ones such as working memory or cognitive flexibility.

reduce to executive-function performances. Of course this does *not* imply that executive function is unimportant for theory-of-mind development. The execution of theory-of-mind reasoning in most situations involves more than just theory-of-mind conceptions. Ian Apperly (2011, 2012) cogently argued that much of everyday theory-of-mind reasoning—in ongoing conversations, in "reading" a playground squabble between two peers, in summing together multiple cues (a person's speech, actions, and emotional expressions) to read their beliefs and desires, in attempting to teach someone else—requires effortful, thoughtful, online processing to inform social interactions in quick-paced, everyday exchanges. So, social cognition necessarily recruits executive-function resources to interact within the social world. Theory of mind is something that we do as well as something that we know, "and an adequate account of ToM should explain how we do it" (Apperly, 2012, p. 829). I agree. Moreover, I would argue that executive-function developments, along with other factors, can hasten the emergence of preschool theory of mind in the first place; children use these resources not only to employ their theory-of-mind concepts but to learn about the social world as well. At the same time, although executive-function processes are used to employ theory-of-mind conceptions, the findings I have just reviewed show theory-of-mind conceptions have their own nature, power, and development beyond executive function alone.

Cognitive Complexity

A related domain-general analysis focuses on increases in cognitive complexity as accounting for the progress of theory-of-mind development. Often cognitive complexity is thought to go along with executive functioning, as in the proposals of cognitive complexity and control (CCC) theory advocated by Phillip Zelazo and his colleagues (Zelazo, Müller, Frye, & Marcovitch, 2003).

For cognitive complexity in general, the idea is that different tasks with their different demands require solutions embodying different levels of cognitive inference and insight. Of course, tasks do vary in cognitive complexity—167×43 is more complex than $3 + 2$. But is there a general analysis of cognitive complexity that applies across all tasks irrespective of their domain-specific contents? And can that analysis account for the developmental changes we have seen in theory of mind? Douglas Frye and colleagues' (1995) application of CCC theory to false-belief reasoning illustrates the general approach.

In Frye and Zelazo's CCC analysis (e.g., Frye et al., 1995; Zelazo et al. 2003), responses to false-belief tasks are claimed to require flexible, "embedded-rules" reasoning such as this: If the focus is reality, then the item is in the cupboard; but, if the focus is the character's belief, then the item is "in the drawer." But again consider the ToM Scale tasks as well as results with parallel tasks such as diverse desires and diverse beliefs as outlined in Box 7.1. For diverse beliefs, if the focus is your belief, then the item is "in the cupboard"; but if the focus is my belief, then the item is "in the drawer." But then diverse desires seem to require equal embedded rules reasoning: If the focus is my desire, crackers are the attractive object; but, if the focus is the other person's desire, broccoli is the attractive object. However, these tasks, which seem so equivalent in cognitive complexity and control, nonetheless consistently yield developmental differences.

Moreover, as outlined in Box 7.1 for executive functions, the reversed and alternative ToM Scale sequences, as evident, for example, for the United States versus China, make it implausible that focal theory-of-mind progressions simply represent childhood increments in cognitive complexity. Any cognitive complexity analysis proposed to account for the detailed U.S. data (e.g., that knowledge access requires more complex reasoning than diverse beliefs) would be challenged by the Chinese data. Any such analysis proposed to account for the Australian data would be challenged by the alternative progression evident for children from Iran.

As was true for executive-function considerations, of course some theory-of-mind tests do differ primarily in terms of cognitive complexity. One clear example is the difference between first-order and second-order false-belief tasks. A first-order false-belief task is like the one sketched in Chapter 1 in Box 1.2. In comparison, a second-order false-belief task, such as the ones first devised by Josef Perner and Heinz Wimmer's (1985), goes something like this: Dad looks in the door while Mary and Gary settle down for a rest. Mary is on the bed, Gary is on the recliner chair. Gary is called away by Mom, and Dad sees that while Gary is away, Mary moves to the recliner. Now, where does Dad think that Mary is, the bed or the recliner (first-order *true* belief)? Where does Dad think that Gary thinks Mary is, the bed or the recliner (second–order *false* belief)? The second-order task requires recursive understanding of one character's belief about another's belief and is a frequently used individual-differences measure of older children's theory of mind.

To set up a task about thinking about thinking, such as Perner and Wimmer's (1985) necessitates an extended narrative and sequence of events (with numerous essential test and control questions). So, along with recursive second-order thinking (a cognitive complexity issue), the added linguistic and memory demands seem to require advanced executive-function competences to follow the procedure. These total demands—recursive thinking, executive functioning, advanced language—make the second-order false-belief tasks' difficulty mostly a product of cognitive complexity and control irrespective of their theory-of-mind demands. In fact, this non-theory-of-mind interpretation is underwritten by Helen Tager-Flusberg and colleagues' findings (Sullivan, Zaitchik, & Tager-Flusberg, 1994) that 4- and 5-year-olds often passed a modification of Perner and Wimmer's task with multiple reminders, prompts, corrections, and story repeats to reduce its domain-general (non-theory-of-mind) cognitive burdens. The point here is that cognitive complexity can sometimes differentiate between some theory-of-mind tasks versus others; indeed, it may account for much if not all the developmental differences between first- and second-order false belief. But that does not mean that theory-of-mind developments are just cognitive complexity developments.

Another informative example comes from Glenda Andrews and her colleagues (Andrews, Halford, Bunch, Bowden, & Jones 2003). Using Graeme Halford's relational complexity theory (e.g., Halford, Wilson, & Phillips, 2010) as an alternative way to think about cognitive complexity, Andrews and her colleagues outlined stepwise increments in cognitive complexity that they used to examine comparisons between related tasks. In one study, for example, these authors used their complexity analysis to devise two different versions of several theory-of-mind tasks. To illustrate, they created two different changed-locations tasks, one—the more complex one—was a changed-locations false-belief task, again of the sort sketched in Box 1.2. But the other was a less cognitively complex *non-false-belief* task that also involved changed locations. Indeed, young children were likely to fail the more complex and pass the less complex versions.

Note, however, that this analysis would not be able to explain the more extended ToM Scale results. By Halford's relational complexity analysis (e.g., Halford et al., 2010), diverse desires and diverse beliefs would both be at one "easier" level of complexity, whereas knowledge access and false beliefs would be at another more complex level. Nonetheless, diverse desires and diverse beliefs developmentally *differ*. And so do knowledge access versus false beliefs. Therefore, changes in theory-of-mind reasoning and conception occur that are not merely changes in cognitive complexity; rather, they are changes in theory-of-mind conceptions themselves.

In short, developments in cognitive complexity, just as those for executive function, seem to be best thought of in terms of a permissive-execution role. Increases in cognitive complexity can permit and promote theory-of-mind conceptual advances as well as enable theory-of-mind conceptions to be employed in various reasoning situations. Increases in cognitive complexity (and executive function) undoubtedly impact children's understanding of mental states; but additional, domain-specific conceptual work is needed. To my mind, constructivist theory building is needed.

To summarize, a key issue is really the same one I raised in discussing microgenetic research in Chapter 6. Most generally, what accounts for theory-of-mind progress? Perhaps general cognitive factors "external" to the domain of theory of mind—attention, memory, executive control—could sufficiently account for theory-of-mind changes. But empirically they fail to do so. So, alternatively, factors "internal" to theory-of-mind conceptions themselves—concepts and processes inherent to and distinctive for thinking about agents, actions, and minds—are needed to account for theory-of-mind changes. From a constructivist, theory theory perspective, earlier conceptions of persons and minds constrain and enable later ones by providing building blocks within the conceptual domain of psychological cognition. On this account, theory-of-mind development represents processes of content-specific conceptual development at least as much as increases in more general capacities or systems.

Domain-Specific Accounts

In contrast to (or complementary to) domain-general accounts, all domain-specific accounts assume that human propensities to understand people mentalistically stem from special knowledge, processes, and/or mechanisms specific to *social* understanding and learning. At the very least, humans as a species do seem especially prepared for and adept at social information acquisition (Banaji & Gelman, 2013)—learning about the world indirectly via information and affect from other persons (Harris, 2012), from pedagogy (Csibra & Gergley, 2009), and from conversation (Gelman, 2009). Moreover, there is little doubt that by 3 or 4 years of age, children's knowledge about psychological versus physical phenomena contrasts in several distinctive ways (Fodor, 1992; Hirschfeld & Gelman, 1994; Wellman & Gelman, 1992, 1998). Briefly, as outlined in Chapter 2, by that age children insist that mental and physical entities differ, that physical mechanical forces account for changes in the physical world, but that a very different set of forces—beliefs and desires—account for intentional actions and experiences.

It is no longer surprising to claim that naïve psychology, naïve physics, and naïve biology distinctively differ, in part because it has become generally accepted that cognition can differ substantially in different areas or domains (Cosmides & Tooby, 1994; Fodor, 1983; Hirschfeld & Gelman, 1994; Wellman & Gelman, 1992, 1998). However, the notion of specific, distinguishable cognitive domains admits of several separable interpretations captured in three differing classes of theoretical account: theories, modules, and expertise.

Theory Theory

Theory theory is essentially a domain-specific account. Scientific theories carve the world into different domains of understanding. Current understandings of astronomy, for example, specify that stars are massive bodies, each similar to the sun existing in a space–time continuum of enormous extent. Because of this, celestial mechanics provide the key causal-explanatory frame for understanding the interrelations of these celestial entities—and hence provides explanations for days, seasons, tides, eclipses, and the like. In contrast, economics carves out a very different domain where the entities are consumers, producers, goods, gross national product, and the like and where microeconomic and macroeconomic forces, such as supply and demand, monetary liquidity, market constraints, and government regulatory pressures, provide the relevant causal-explanatory factors. In these ways—both with regard to the entities in the world they encompass and with regard to the causal-explanatory frameworks they employ—scientific theories carve the world into very different domains of understanding. So too, according to theory theory, do everyday theories such as theory of mind versus naïve physics.

Modules

"Theory of mind" is a catchy phrase that aptly points toward a distinctive sort of cognition—not just social cognition but the mentalistic appraisals so central to that cognition. But for some theorists, "theory of mind" is a misnomer; it is catchy but wrong.

For modular theorists, in particular, theory-of-mind processes stem from no theory; they stem instead from the computations of an innate mental module. Mental modules, as described initially by Fodor (1983), generate representations of perceptual inputs, as in the 3D representations of spatial layout achieved by the visual system (Marr, 1982). Such perceptual modules are innately specified, their processing is mandatory and encapsulated, and thus they are essentially unrevisable—no amount of training or counterexperiences would cause us to perceive the world in terms of two dimensions rather than three. Claims of other theorists regarding modularity have varied in at least two respects: whether modularity is restricted to perceptual processes or affects central cognitive processes (such as theory of mind) as well and whether modularity is innate or constructed. Modularity need not imply evolved innate modules (Karmiloff-Smith, 1992), but for theory-of-mind accounts it has, and that is the sort of modularity I focus on. Those accounts (e.g., Leslie, 1994; Scholl & Leslie, 2001) have proposed a theory-of-mind module (ToMM) that is central (not perceptual), that mandatorily and automatically takes certain forms of inputs (e.g., perception of an animate agent), and computes relevant mental states (the agent's beliefs, desires, intentions). These constitute the module's (and the organism's) innate representations.

It is important to distinguish the general claim that there is innate knowledge from the stronger claim that there are innate modules (e.g., Carey, 2009; Gopnik & Wellman, 1994; Wellman & Gelman, 1998). Certain representations could be innately specified yet fail to be modular, either because the knowledge is domain general or because it is readily revisable on the basis of new experience. All sorts of knowledge, including expertise or naïve theories, may include or begin from a base of innately specified representations.

A crucial difference between nativist modular accounts and others, therefore, concerns the nature of the interplay between experience and conceptual structure. Modular processes are mandatory in the sense that, assuming they come online (and are not impaired), they result in conceptions that are necessary conversions of the relevant inputs into the special representations, specified by that module (Leslie, 1994).

Expertise

Clearly, expertise can carve out domain-like knowledge and skills because with enough practice at a task (e.g., chess, reading, mnemonics), an ordinary person reorganizes knowledge into complex hierarchical systems and develops rich networks of causally related information (Chi, Hutchinson, & Robin, 1989). These abilities cannot be explained as individual differences in the general processing talents of experts. The same individual who is remarkable on the chessboard shows mundane performance on tasks outside the skill domain. For example, the chess expert's memory for a string of digits is quite ordinary (e.g., Chi, 1978). It seems, then, that these abilities are domain specific, at least in some sense of domain.

The notion of skill domains molded by expertise is distinct from modularity. With the former, there is no appeal to innate modules, innate constraints, or evolutionary forces (although there may well be appeal to innate cognitive building blocks). The classic example here is reading. Homo sapiens did not evolve in a world full of print, but contemporary persons can become expert at it; and, when expert, reading becomes a distinctive domain of cognition with distinctive neural substrates. Moreover, expertise in the domain then influences further learning, attention to, and understanding of new domain-related information.

One domain-specific expertise account—simulation theory—uniquely applies to theory of mind. In contrast to theory theory, simulation theory contends that ordinary reasoning about persons and minds proceeds *not* via conceptual constructs or abstract representations but instead by way of our own firsthand experiences (Goldman, 1992, 2005; Gallese & Golman, 1998; Harris, 1992, 2000). Because we are creatures who have mental-state experiences (e.g., beliefs and desires), we certainly come to refer to such states; but our capacity to do so does not depend on developing concepts and representations. Rather, we simply experience and report our own mental experiences. Attributing such experiences to others, relatedly, requires not a series of conceptual constructs and inferences but instead a process of simulation. To think about others' minds, we project ourselves into the other person's situation (perhaps, arguably, via mirror neurons; see Chapter 11), experience what we would feel in that situation ourselves, and then attribute that (simulated) experience to the other. Simulation is domain specific in being specifically anchored in first-person mental experiences. Expertise is needed as well because in this process, children must learn not to attribute their own states to others but to simulate others' states from *their* situation.

Data Relevant to Modules

To begin, it is clear that a nativist-modular perspective has promoted important, informative research, which was, at least initially, not promoted by other accounts. The large, obvious example concerns research with individuals with autism.

From a nativist, modular perspective, the rapid development of person understandings apparent in normal children worldwide, such as the acquisition of an understanding of false belief, depends on a specialized theory-of-mind mental module (ToMM) "coming online" in early development. From their inception, such accounts began with a neurological-maturational framework for thinking of modules (Leslie, 1994; Baron-Cohen, 1995). And from this perspective that module—ToMM—could come online early in development *or* it could be impaired. This reasoning inspired modular theorists to initiate the influential theory-of-mind research with individuals with autism (Baron-Cohen, 1995). Indeed, numerous studies have since shown that individuals with autism, even those who are very high-functioning otherwise, find theory-of-mind reasoning inordinately problematic (Baron-Cohen, 2000). Moreover, such difficulties are accompanied by abnormalities of the neural substrates that characterize the human "social brain" (see Chapter 11).

At the same time, such modular accounts entail additional implications. One implication of positing theory-of-mind modules is that individuals who are *not* impaired in the relevant modules—for example, who do not have autism—should achieve mental-state understandings on a roughly standard maturational timetable. Here is where the complementary studies of deaf preschool children raised by hearing parents have been so revealing. As outlined in Chapter 5, those studies show delays and deficiencies on theory-of-mind tasks comparable to those of children with autism. Yet these deaf children have not suffered the same sort of neurological damage that autistics have. Their damage is peripheral—in the ears, not the mind. This is clear in the fact that deaf children raised by deaf parents do not show theory-of-mind delays. Findings such as these challenge accounts of theory-of-mind development relying heavily on neurological-maturational mechanisms.

Innate modules, as well as autistic children's difficulties with theory of mind, have also suggested important genetic influences on theory of mind and theory-of-mind development. So too do the impairments of children with William's Syndrome and the social-cognitive impairments found in girls with Turner's syndrome, a clearly delineated chromosomal disorder (Skuse et al., 1997). To address possible genetic influences, Claire Hughes and her colleagues (Hughes & Cutting, 1999) reported the first behavioral-genetic twin study of individual differences in typically developing children's theory of mind, studying 119 pairs of 42-month-old twins. Analyses showed that 60% of that sample's variance in theory of mind could be attributed to genetic (rather than environmental) factors. Such a finding seemed to support modular accounts that insist on an innate basis for early theory-of-mind development (Baron-Cohen, 1995; Leslie, 1994).

However, Hughes and Cutting (1999) noted at the time that their original study encompassed a small, potentially nonrepresentative (volunteer) sample for behavioral-genetic twin analyses. So Hughes and her colleagues (Hughes et al., 2005) then conducted a more definitive study of theory-of-mind differences in a nationally representative sample of 1,116 pairs of young twins in England. Behavioral genetic models of those data "showed that environmental factors explained the majority of variance in theory-of-mind performance" (p. 356). In fact there were strikingly large individual differences in theory of mind: 44% of the variation in theory-of-mind scores was accounted for by theory-of-mind-specific nonshared environmental influences and 20% by theory-of-mind-specific shared environmental influences. An additional 21% was accounted for by common shared environmental influences on theory of mind and verbal ability, presumably reflecting the influential role of semantic-conversational factors of the sort revealed by, for example, the deaf data. Only 15% was accounted for by common genetic influences. These findings argue strongly against a nativist, coming-online, maturational account for theory-of-mind developments, under the assumption that any such maturational development would be similar across genetically related children and especially similar for monozygotic (identical) twins.

Data Relevant to Simulation

Simulation accounts have also generated their own novel and needed findings. Simulation theory focuses especially on pretense and imagination as skills of young children that support simulative projections from self to other (rather than mental states concepts and inferences). For example, Paul Harris (2000) argued that pretend play, so frequent in young children and so rare in adults, never really disappears: It manifests itself throughout life in our abilities to empathize and understand the lives of others. This work on pretense and imagination has certainly been informative and important. Further, according to simulation theory, it is increasing expertise in other-oriented imagination that produces increases in theory of mind. Because of this, simulation theory predicts empirical links between preschoolers' engagement in social pretense and their success at theory-of-mind tasks. This link is well confirmed in various studies (e.g., Astington & Jenkins, 1995; Lohmann & Tomasello, 2003; Schwebel, Rosen, & Singer, 1999; Youngblade & Dunn, 1995).

However, simulation theorists' more detailed developmental account of theory-of-mind achievements fails to square with the data outlined in this book. To repeat, according to this account, in the course of development, children must learn not to attribute their own states to others, but to simulate others' states from information about that person's situation—"They must view the world through the eyes of another person" (Harris, 2000, p. 54). Simulation involves creating a "situation model" (Harris, 2000) *for the other* and then reacting as if in that situation. Creating such a situation model (for the other) poses several difficulties. Thus, Harris accounts for children's difficulty with false-belief attributions as follows (1992, 2000). Children's situation models and their simulations operate against a backdrop of two default settings, the mental states of the self and the real state of the world. Simulations are more or less difficult depending on how many defaults the child must override. Suppose a child does not know what is in a box but thinks it holds a doll. To simulate the belief of someone who thinks it holds a toy truck, the child must override her own belief and simulate the other's contrasting belief. So, to simulate someone else's diverse belief (or diverse desire), for instance, one must ignore one's own state and imagine the state of the other. An understanding of false beliefs, however, requires the child to override not only her own mental stance but reality as well. Thus, if the child *knows* the box holds a doll and must simulate the thought of someone else who mistakenly believes it holds a truck, then the child must set aside her own state *and* known reality to imagine that other person as having a different thought altogether.

Note that according to this proposal, attribution of desires *and* beliefs to others should be equally easy as long as only one default must be overridden, as in the previous example of attributing diverse beliefs to others. False beliefs should be remarkably more difficult because in this case, two defaults must be overcome. However, as noted when discussing executive-function accounts, the empirical data, and focally the ToM Scale data, have consistently indicated that attributing diverse desires is considerably easier than attributing diverse beliefs—a difference that challenges simulation proposals. A comparison between understanding knowledge access and understanding false belief is similarly problematic for this account. When the child knows what toy is in the box, to simulate ignorance for someone else should require the child to override both her own mental state and reality as well, just as for false belief. So, according to the logic of Harris' simulation account, both should be equally difficult. Yet the ToM Scale (as well as the meta-analysis by Wellman & Liu, 2004) shows that false belief is consistently more difficult than knowledge access.

Conceptually, a simulation account casts "theorizing" and "imaginative projections" as incompatible—firsthand experiences involve no theoretical constructs, we just have them. But such an opposition is misleading. When Einstein utilized thought experiments such as imagining how a clock would report time inside a vehicle traveling at the speed of light, he was engaged in simulation but also theory construction and application. The use of imaginative projections is complementary with, indeed typically encompassed by, rather than antithetical to our theories.

This applies to childhood theory of mind as well. For example, to understand everyday behavior (or to answer an experimenter's questions, or to understand story protagonists' actions) via simulation, children might simulate a character's heartbeat or respiration or hunger or any of a number of states and sensations that the child can experience themselves in a situation (or situation model). Why do they so often focus on beliefs and desires? Children concentrate on some "simulatable" things (beliefs and desires) and not others (respiration, itches) because of their role in causal-explanatory reasoning framed by their belief-desire framework theory. Just like Einstein's, everyday simulations themselves are theory driven.

Firsthand experiences themselves are additionally theory saturated. Simulation—recourse to the child's own first-person experiences to understand others—is undoubtedly important for theory-of-mind development and its utilization. But one's own first-person experiences present problems as well as aids. Children's (and adults') firsthand observational-experiential database is large and immediate, yielding immense numbers of experiences in many intermingled episodes and events. Children must develop a coherent conceptual framework to organize and make sense of these experiences. They must organize some sort of generalities, such as beliefs and desires, out of the ongoing stream of specific personal experiences that indiscriminately interleaves this particular idea, that specific want, these and those sensations, emotions, and so forth. What organizes these experiences for children in such a fashion that they are able to simulate another's desires instead of, for example, their ever-present stream of consciousness, their flow of intermingled sensations, pains, hungers, and so on? Children achieve orderly imaginings because they have recourse to a commonsense framework theory. This is one important function of theories, both scientific and everyday ones: to derive and impose conceptual order on a wealth of chaotic observations.

Thus, the story in regard to simulation can also be understood as parallel to the story for executive functions. In theory-of-mind reasoning, theory-of-mind conception must often be employed in various fashions. Simulation processes aid in the employment of theory-of-mind conceptions but cannot substitute for them.

Data Relevant to Theories

Human cognition must encompass robust procedures for inferring generalized knowledge from discrete experiences. This feat is crucial, it would seem, for learning in a narrow sense and for development in the broader sense. It is crucial as well, I believe, for developing theory-of-mind conceptions.

As should be clear by now, the knowledge creation processes of theory discovery and construction distinctively predict that children achieve an extended set of understandings, with early ones assisting the creation of intermediate ones that set the stage for further ones and so on. So, just as modular approaches inspired research on theory of mind in autism, and simulation accounts inspired research on imaginative perspective taking, theory theory has inspired research on progressions of understanding, research not tackled by others. It is this account, moreover, that predicts the three empirical signatures of constructivist learning I showed to characterize theory-of-mind development in Chapter 6: (a) learning proceeds in orderly conceptual progressions; (b) both the sequences and timetables of these progressions are experience dependent; and (c) prior conceptual knowledge influences the presence and amount of learning.

Similarly, theory theory has inspired novel research on explanation. According to theory theory, our everyday folk psychology is an everyday theory about people and minds—deserving the phrase *theory* of mind. Theories explain phenomena; explanation thus, by this account, is central to theory of mind. Consider instead an innate modular account of theory of mind. A ToMM "spontaneously and post-perceptually processes behaviors that are attended, and computes the mental states which contributed to them" (Scholl & Leslie, 2001, p. 697). Modular accounts do not emphasize explanations, but rather they emphasize the modularized computations that lead to mental state attributions. In fact, current evolutionary accounts of modular cognition focus exclusively on how specialized information processors increase the organism's ability to solve adaptive problems by making accurate predictions of the environment and responding accordingly. In this account, understanding and providing explanations are unnecessary (or at the least unmentioned) for solving adaptive problems (Cosmides & Tooby, 1994). Explanations play no crucial role in simulation accounts either, which concentrate instead on children's developing abilities to engage in attribution by simulation. As with modular accounts, the central focus of simulation accounts is simply solving the problem of attribution. Development follows the child's increased ability to simulate.

Theory theory predicts a fundamental and motivating role for explanations in development and insists that explanations provide part of the mechanism underlying development. And, as I have reviewed, such emphases nicely match the empirical data: Explanations provide a motivating role in children's thinking about people; indeed, as reviewed in Chapter 2, children are particularly motivated to ask questions about people in comparison to physical objects and biological processes. And explanations influence how development proceeds; recall the microgenetic experiments outlined in Chapter 6 where an increased diet of child explanations produced theory-of-mind gains, whereas predictions alone did not.

THE ROLE OF LANGUAGE AND COMMUNICATIVE EXPERIENCE

Learning about the mind recruits cognitive structures and experiences. Both first-person and second-person experiences contribute. Language and communication are plausible, potent sources of relevant structures and especially potent sources of relevant experiences. Indeed, one set of empirical facts that require incorporation within any comprehensive account of theory of mind is the interplay between theory-of-mind development and language. Much evidence shows that children's success on explicit theory-of-mind-tasks, such as preschool false-belief tasks, is related to their performance on various tests of language. Generally, better language skills and richer communicative experiences both correlate with and longitudinally lead to better theory of mind. I will not comprehensively review these many studies; Janet Astington and her colleagues have done so in an edited volume (Astington & Baird, 2005) and in a meta-analysis (Milligan et al., 2007).

But it is useful to consider which aspects of language play what roles in theory-of-mind developments.

Syntax

Jill and Peter de Villiers (2000; de Villiers & Pyers, 2002) have emphasized that verbal statements about mental states such as thinking and knowing use a specific syntactic construction: embedded complement clauses as in "John thinks that Obama is a Republican." In that sentence, "John thinks..." is the main clause, under which is embedded the complement clause, "*that* Obama is a Republican." In English, statements about desires also use embedded clauses but use a different construction: "John wants Obama to be Republican." It is sentential *that*-complements, in particular, that allow the truth of "John thinks that X" to be independent of the truth of X. So "John thinks that Obama is a Republican" can be true, despite the fact that Obama is a Democrat.

The syntax of complementation provides a language of embedded propositions and the de Villiers argue that learning this special syntax provides the *necessary* basis for children to think about beliefs and other related propositional mental states (de Villiers & de Villiers, 2000, see pp. 195–197). Moreover, different constructions for beliefs over desires account for belief understandings developing later than parallel desire understanding. This is a very strong claim about language's impact on theory of mind and a strong claim about the developmental role of one syntactic structure.

Children's understanding of this focal *that*-complementation has been tested by (simply) having them remember embedded complement constructions that are false (e.g., de Villiers & Pyers, 2002). So the child hears, "Really the candy is in the cupboard. Jill thinks that the candy is in the drawer." The test question then asks, "What does Jill think?" Answering this question correctly ("Jill thinks that the candy is in the drawer") arguably does not require the child to make any inference about what Jill thinks; rather the child needs simply to attend to the complement utterance ("Jill thinks that the candy is in the drawer") and repeat it back. Nonetheless, the complementation task is difficult for 3- to 4-year-olds, and not much easier, if any, than standard false-belief tasks (de Villiers & Pyers, 2002; Flavell et al., 1990; Wellman & Bartsch, 1988).

More to the point, success at repeating these complement sentences can statistically account for false-belief competences on standard tasks. Most telling, perhaps, Jill de Villiers and Jennie Pyers (2002) tested the same children on multiple occasions and found that children's performance on this embedded complements test at an earlier point in time predicted their performance on various false-belief tasks at a later point in time. In contrast, early false-belief performance was not systematically related to later performance on the embedded-complements task.

It is unlikely, however, that such syntactic competence is necessary for, or causes, theory-of-mind competence. For example, diverse-belief tasks and false-belief tasks both require the same sort of complement language and "embedded" reasoning. For diverse beliefs, "John thinks that the fruit (hidden in the bag) is an apple, but Mary thinks it's a banana." For false beliefs, "John thinks that the fruit is an apple, but really it's a banana." Why would "complement competence" cause early understanding of diverse beliefs yet still fail for false beliefs—that is, on a complement analysis, why would these not both be developed at the same time?

Moreover, other non-English languages require little such complementation in ordinary conversation (Chinese, American Sign Language) or vary in the sorts of complements required (German). For example, in German (but not English), some *want*-sentences obligatorily take the same grammatical *that*-complement as *think*-sentences do (and as *think*-sentences in English do). Yet, Josef Perner and his colleagues (Perner, Sprung, Zauner, & Haider, 2003) found that the lag between understanding desires and only later understanding beliefs was the same in German children as in English-speaking ones, and this was true even for desire versus belief tasks that used exactly the sort of *that*-complement constructions emphasized by the de Villiers.

Chinese provides a complementary case. In Mandarin and Cantonese, it is possible and typical to use the same relatively simple grammatical construction (one with a very abbreviated embedded construction) to talk about beliefs and desires. Yet Twila Tardif and I (Tardif & Wellman, 2000) found a much earlier and higher frequency of desire talk than belief talk for Chinese children, very similar to the English data (Bartsch & Wellman, 1995). Thus, contrary to the de Villiers' position, children talk about desire earlier than belief even when their native language provides the facility to communicate about belief without complex *that*-complement constructions (Chinese) or when desires as well as beliefs utilize the same *that*-complement construction (German).

Note as well that the de Villiers' assessment of "predicate complement" competence requires repeating back predicate complement statements that are semantically false: "Really the candy is in the cupboard. Jill thinks that the candy is in the drawer. What does Jill think?" Him Cheung has shown that it is the meaning—what is actually said in the embedded clause—not syntactic structure that affects how Chinese children's language correlates with their false belief performance (e.g., Cheung, 2006). And Ted Ruffman and colleagues (e.g., Slade & Ruffman, 2005) also demonstrated that semantic instead of syntactic abilities correlate most with false belief for English-speaking children.

Semantics

In everyday conversation, people talk widely about their own and others' mental states and do so with and without complex syntax. They do so in particular by using a set of mental verbs—*think, know, remember, want, need, feel*. Intriguingly, early conversational experience with such words predicts concurrent and later theory-of-mind understandings. For example, when parents talk more to their child via such terms early on, the child comes to do better on false-belief reasoning (Ruffman et al., 2002). Moreover, English-speaking children (Bartsch & Wellman, 1995), Chinese children (Tardif &

Wellman, 2000) and deaf children (Anderson & Reilly, 2002) all talk about people using "desire" and "feel" terms before coming to talk about people in terms of "think" or "know."

Semantics includes how languages carve up the world, including the world of mental states, and in particular how languages do so in their lexicons, in the words they use. The linguist Anna Wierzbicka (1993) claims that *all* the worlds' languages lexicalize the related concepts "think," "want," and "feel" into mental verbs such as *think, want,* and *feel.* If so, that might show us a remarkable imprint of theory-of-mind conception on semantics. Regardless of whether that strong claim does or does not hold true (and it is strongly contested), different languages package mental-state verbs in different ways and these provide ways to study the influence of mental-state semantics on mental-state understanding. English, for example, has several ways of talking about the mental states of thinking and knowing, including *think, believe, guess, know*, and so on, each of which involves differences in the thinker's certainty and other aspects of their mental states (Moore, Bryant, & Furrow, 1989). Other languages also carve up the domain of mental life into various linguistic terms, some of which are very similar to English and some of which are different. One window onto the role of such lexical constructions for theory-of-mind understanding comes from "think falsely" verbs.

In English, belief terms such as *believe* and *think* are neutral with respect to whether the person's belief is true or false. If told that "John thinks Obama is a Republican," Obama may be Republican or Democrat. Some languages, including Chinese languages, include terms to designate beliefs that are decidedly false. The appearance of such terms could have several plausible influences. Most generally, there is the possibility that acquiring a language that lexically marks beliefs as false may generally and profoundly aid children in coming to understand false belief, and in particular the divergence between beliefs and reality. At the extreme, children learning such a language might never evidence difficulty with false belief because their language clearly marks this distinction. Alternatively, however, understanding false belief may be enhanced, but more modestly. Or, of course, the presence of explicit false-belief terms may provide no enhancement whatsoever.

Suppose enhancement occurs; then the hypothesis of a general enhancement effect implies that children's understanding and performance could be enhanced on tasks that use the explicitly marked false-belief term but also on tasks that do not use the term. Alternatively, the hypothesis of a limited modest enhancement implies that such terms might well facilitate false-belief performance only when they are used in the task. Twila Tardif and her colleagues (Tardif et al., 2004) along with Kang Lee and his (Lee et al., 1999) tested these possibilities for children learning Chinese languages and exposed to those languages' explicit false-belief verbs.

In both studies, one for Cantonese (Tardif et al., 2004) and one for Mandarin (Lee et al., 1999), growing up speaking Chinese did *not* result in generally coming earlier to an understanding of false belief. The Chinese-speaking children were very similar in their false-belief understanding to the almost 200 studies of English-speaking children examined in our (Wellman et al., 2001) meta-analysis. The more focused meta-analysis of Liu and his colleagues (2008) specifically comparing Chinese-speaking and English-speaking children confirmed this more precisely: The presence of marked false-belief verbs in Chinese certainly did not mean that very young Chinese children were especially facile with false belief. Instead the data demonstrated a limited, specific, rather than a general, effect. Getting a false-belief task presented with terms explicitly marked for false belief helped Chinese children perform somewhat better for *that* task. Having a marked term for false belief provided no benefit more generally for tasks in which the term was irrelevant or not used.

A cross-linguistic study by Marilyn Shatz and her colleagues (Shatz, Diesendruck, Martinez-Beck, & Akar, 2003) showed the same pattern. Children who spoke languages with explicit false-belief terms (Puerto Rican Spanish and Turkish) passed only certain false-belief tasks earlier than children who spoke languages that do not mark false belief explicitly (English, Brazilian Portuguese). Specifically, the false-belief tasks they passed were the ones that use the marked false-belief term in the test question (i.e., "falsely think" vs. "think"), whereas the children's performance on other false-belief and theory-of-mind tasks showed no relative advantage.

Summing up so far, a mental-language *expression* account is no more tenable than an executive function *expression* account. It is not generally the case that theory-of-mind competences are achieved early independent of language and only await specific semantic or syntactic acquisitions for their expression. At the same time, it is also not the case that children quickly and simply acquire those mental-state notions marked in their language. The relation between language and theory of mind is more complex than that and includes large doses of actual theory-of-mind conceptual development.

Pragmatics, Conversation, and Social Experience

Communicative interchange (and even verbal meaning) is more than the sum of syntax and semantics. Even apparently simple sentences, such as "That's the blue one," can have very different meanings depending on whether the listener can see the items or not (e.g., is blindfolded, listening to that utterance on the phone, etc.). Deriving the meaning behind the message requires sensitivity to social context (what the listener knows/sees) and what Herb Clark (e.g., 1996) calls "common ground"—how a listener and speaker are (or are not) privy to the same events. Attention to social context and common ground is laced with theory-of-mind features. Pragmatic conversational interchange could thus prompt children to attend to and learn about theory of mind.

Summarizing a large number of studies, Judy Dunn and Marcia Brophy (2005) suggest that the total amount of conversational experience, how much that experience includes talk about mental states, and the quality of the relationship between the child and their conversational partner, all affect children's current or subsequent theory-of-mind abilities. The edited volume by Janet Astington and Jodie Baird (2005) presented still further discussion of these language-dependent experiential features. And Michel Deleau (2012) summarized several studies showing that conversational experiences and the child's pragmatic competences predict children's developing false-belief understandings. How do such experiences work to impact theory of mind? It is easy to imagine at least two ways: by providing rich semantic evidence for the acquisition of theory-of-mind concepts (concepts such as "think" and "know" via use of the terms *think* and *know*) and by highlighting theory-of-mind notions via the pragmatic requirements of conversational exchanges.

In the data I have reviewed in prior chapters, it is the findings from deaf children of hearing parents that most clearly underwrite and add to these claims. A conversational-communicative (Astington, 2001; Harris, 2005, 2006) interpretation of the deaf data seems reasonable for several reasons. Deaf children who grow up in hearing families do not usually acquire sign language until school entry and, until then, typically have no one at home who can converse freely with them about unobservable thoughts, feelings, and other mental states (e.g., Vaccari & Marschark, 1997; Moeller & Schick, 2006). Despite sometimes heroic efforts to learn sign, when their children are young, hearing parents are only able to communicate with them via short, one- and two-word utterances, typically about overt here-and-now objects and actions (Spencer & Harris, 2006; Vaccari & Marschark, 1997). So, most hearing parents have too little proficiency in sign language to converse about unobservable referents such as others' beliefs. In fact, hearing mothers of deaf 2- and 3-year-olds communicate primarily through verbal *speech* to their deaf children, and the children typically do not attend (Lederberg & Everhart, 1998). Usually in hearing families, communication is didactic rather than conversational, limiting social-communicative interactions still further. I just noted that for typically developing children, rich exposure to conversational-communicative input about persons' minds (via parental mental-state talk and the like) correlates with more rapid theory-of-mind development (e.g., Dunn & Brophy, 2005; Ruffman et al., 2002). This is true for deaf children of hearing parents too (Moeller & Schick, 2006). In addition, as noted earlier, typically developing children's performance on theory-of-mind tests is significantly related to their number of siblings and to the number of older children and adults with whom they regularly interact (Lewis et al., 1996; Perner et al., 1994; Ruffman et al., 1998). The paucity of such social-conversational experiences for deaf children growing up in a hearing household is an obvious barrier to mentalistic understanding.

Finally, recall that nature has provided a controlled comparison. Even though most deaf children are born to hearing parents, a small minority of about 5% have a deaf parent and grow up in signing family environments from birth, conversing as early and as naturally in sign with parents and siblings as hearing infants and toddlers do in speech. Intriguingly, these native signers have been found to achieve false-belief understanding (e.g., Courtin & Melot, 1998; Schick, de Villiers, de Villiers, & Hoffmeister, 2007) and

ToM Scale milestones (e.g., Peterson et al., 2005; Peterson, Wellman, & Slaughter, 2012) on the same early timetable as hearing children. Thus, the severe theory-of-mind delays consistently reported for deaf children with hearing parents are not a consequence of deafness per se but rather of growing up deaf in the closed conversational world of a hearing family.

Paul Harris (2005) argued that a critical role for conversation is in highlighting perspective differences between the child and their interlocutor, and the training study by Heidemarie Lohmann and Michael Tomasello (2003) apparently confirms this. Of course, to reiterate, communicative social interactions are not merely conversationally pragmatic; they often include specific talk about mental states (via *think, know, want, feel*, and the like), hence adding to a semantic evidence base. Deaf children of hearing parents more often engage in conversational experiences that are much less rich in utterances about internal psychological states *and* much less rich in the ordinary perspective-shifting, back and forth of conversational interchange.

CONCLUSIONS

From a Bayesian, constructivist perspective all this makes sense. Conversational-communicative experiences, through their frequent focus on persons' mental states and intentional actions—via mental-state terms and references and via the turn-taking social exchanges that are also involved—provide crucial evidence needed to form and revise children's mental-state hypotheses and in turn to form and revise their developing theories of mind. Critically, nothing in this conclusion entails that domain-general preschool advances in language competence *or* executive functioning *or* in cognitive complexity are unimportant to children's developing theories of mind. All are known, potent influences. But these domain-general cognitive changes are not the full story or even its central story line; conceptual insights specific to subjective, mental-state understandings are also required for the progressive attainment of theory of mind. I maintain that constructivist learning, of the sort emphasized in Chapter 6 and inherent in theory theory, increasingly, precisely captures essential features of the sort of learning that underpins and characterizes theory-of-mind development. It crucially helps specify how we "make minds."

A big issue, relevant for understanding theory-of-mind development and for comparing theoretical positions, left hanging until now, concerns infant false-belief results. Alan Leslie originally proposed that ToMM came online in late infancy (Leslie, 1994). But at that time and for many years after, it was problematic for such a modular position that there was no evidence of understanding beliefs and false beliefs until later in the preschool years (Wellman et al., 2001). But, of course, demonstrations of infant recognition that actions can be shaped and constrained by false beliefs, if valid, would be completely consistent with his position. They seemingly provide a confirmation of his originally theoretical proposals (Leslie, 2005).

For theory theory, however, demonstrations of infant recognition that actions can be shaped and constrained by false beliefs, if valid, seem to challenge an account based on the progressive construction of new concepts built from a process of evidence-based revision of prior less-complete conceptual networks. Certainly demonstrations of early, infant understanding of false belief would overthrow the more specific proposal that early preschool understanding is totally bereft of an understanding of belief (Wellman et al., 2001). So, data on potential infant understanding of false belief is of keen import to our understanding of theory of mind and its development. I take up these issues along with the infant "false belief" data next, in Chapters 8 and 9.

8

Infants, Actions, and Mental States

"THE BABIES—HERE THEY come!" was an ad for a quasi-documentary called "The Babies" that aired recently (2010) in major theaters in the United States. It was a feel-good production that contained largely sensible footage of babies in four families: one each in the United States (San Francisco), China (Inner Mongolia), Africa (a village in Namibia), and Japan (Tokyo). By focusing on some comparable situations (eating, bathing, interacting with parents or with other family or with other children) and milestones (grasping, smiling, rolling over, crawling, walking, babbling, talking), the footage brought to life the saying cited in Chapter 5—all humans everywhere are different; all humans everywhere are the same. Infancy is a period when differences in childrearing practices are immense (sleeping alone vs. cosleeping; being constantly carried vs. being constantly "strollered"; being often or seldom left alone; being positioned largely face to face vs. outward facing to the world; being interacted with actively and vocally vs. with special quiet and calmness). Because infants are especially socially dependent and socially parented, infants in particular may be especially subject to socialization practices and differences. At the same time, however, infancy is a period when human universals, including emerging understandings of persons, can be especially obvious.

INFANT THEORY OF MIND IN DEVELOPMENTAL CONTEXT

Research on infant social cognition is booming, providing welcome insights into the early steps that prime the pump for the rich understandings of toddlers and preschoolers. The work is undeniably creative but patchy, both richly informative and in its infancy.

From prior chapters the following are clear:

1. There is a progression of theory-of-mind understandings that unfold in early childhood (Chapters 4 and 5).
2. Several coherent levels punctuate this unfolding progression, but generally during the preschool years, children come to evidence a broad cognizance of persons and minds that reflects a belief-desire understanding with many facets (Chapter 2)—understanding beliefs (true and false), understanding nonmaterial mental entities, understanding fictitious mental entities, understanding various desire- and belief-based emotions, and so forth.
3. These developing mentalistic understandings are demonstrably impacted by children's social and conversational experiences (Chapters 5 and 7) and demonstrably impact children's social actions and interactions (Chapter 3).
4. These developments are launched by infants' attention to persons' internal mental states (and not just external acts and events)—in particular, infants clear and impressive construal of persons in terms of their intentions and attentions (Chapter 1).

To understand theory of mind as a developmental achievement, it is crucial to capture foundational infant understandings. No single infant competence defines foundational social cognition, but here too (mimicking the early days of research with preschoolers) a pivotal question has become do infants (not just preschoolers) attend to persons' beliefs and false beliefs? As intriguing as the infant "false-belief" work is, and it is my primary focus for this chapter, it can only be understood in developmental context. So I begin by outlining several levels in the infant understanding of agents and actions.

Attention to Agents: Very young infants specially attend to intentional agents (prototypically humans), agents that act intentionally and encounter the world perceptually and experientially. Thus, young infants look at faces, imitate persons, attend to others' eye gaze, and attend to biomechanical movements. Nothing in this attention to agents requires that infants understand agents as intentional (or mental) beings; more simply, the special perceptual features of such agents and their acts (their faces, biomechanics, eyes, and movements that are interactive with and contingent on the infant's own) are highly attention worthy for even very young infants.

Understanding Goals and Referents: Then, infants understand various acts and actors as goal or object directed (not just animate but as directed toward specific goal objects). Initially, this may be a teleological rather than intentional understanding (Gergely & Csibra, 2003); infants may well understand agents as directed to and acting for certain external objects but still lack an understanding that the agent has *internal* states, goals, and experiences.

Understanding Internal States: Regardless, by the last half of the first year, infants understand persons in terms of at least some internal states, especially an agent's goals/desires and perceptual experience. Indeed, infants track agents' changing experiences yielding a sense of the agents' awareness and lack of awareness, including that an agent's awareness fails to include certain things the infant himself or herself is aware of.

Infants' early attention to faces, voices, and animacy (attention to agents) is fascinating in its own right. But I'm simply going to remind us that that is so (see also Opfer & Gelman, 2011). Further, I'll merely remind us of the important data on infants' emerging understanding of goal-directed agency in the first 12 months of life (understanding goals and referents) outlined earlier (especially Chapter 1).

This gets us to understanding internal states, which includes at a minimum infants' understanding of the intentions behind even unsuccessful action and their capacity to infer agent's preferences (including inferring those preferences from statistical information; Chapters 1 and 6). A pressing question with regard to understanding mental states is whether infants at about 12 to 18 months understand others' beliefs and false beliefs. Do they, and if so in what sense? In Box 8.1, on the next page, I outline the methods of the first, now-classic infant false-belief study by Kristine Onishi and Renée Baillargeon (2005). In many ways this study directly parallels the events used in preschool change-of-location, false-belief tasks (see Box 1.2 in Chapter 1). Presented with an agent who did not see the target object move from the dark to the light box, infants looked significantly longer at the Light box test events (where the agent reached to the light box to retrieve the object). It was as if they expected the agent to falsely think the object was still in the dark box and so should search there. Indeed, Onishi and Baillargeon concluded that by 15 months, infants understand how false beliefs constrain actions.

This initial study led to numerous other ones, so in Box 8.2, I outline another compelling infant false-belief study, this one by Rose Scott and Renée Baillargeon. In the Scott and Baillargeon (2009) study, as shown in Box 8.2, on the test trials 18-month-old infants looked significantly longer when the agent reached for the transparent container than when she reached for the opaque one. Scott and Baillargeon interpreted their results as showing that infants attributed a false belief to the agent: the agent falsely thought the penguin she could see (in the transparent box) was the one-piece penguin, so she went to the opaque box to find the disassembled two-piece one instead.

These are clever studies. But do we need to attribute to infants an understanding of the agent's false belief from these data? And if so, what level or type of understanding? There are—at least—three plausible perspectives on these results and others like them. One is that, indeed, infants understand false belief in the same sense that preschoolers (and adults) do. In that case, apparent failure to understand false beliefs later in

BOX 8.1
OUTLINE OF ONISHI AND BAILLARGEON'S 2005 STUDY

Recent research claims that the intention understanding of 1-year-old infants also includes false-belief understanding. The initial and most well-known demonstration comes from Onishi and Baillargeon (2005) in a familiarization-test paradigm schematized here. In essence, paralleling standard tasks (see Box 1.2 in Chapter 1), infants see that the agent places the object in one location—the dark box—and does not see the object switch locations—to the light box. If infants expect the agent to search in the prior location (on the basis of a false belief), they should look longer at the Light box test event (not expecting her to search at the correct, new location): 15-month-old infants do consistently look longer at Light box test events.

(a) Familiarization: Agent puts toy in dark box

(b) Change: Agent doesn't see toy move to lighter box

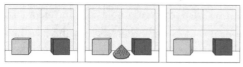

(c) Test events: Infant sees agent search, in either:
    Light box   Dark box

Onishi and Baillargeon also used several other carefully contrasting conditions. For example, in a true-belief condition, infants saw the same events except that in Phase B they saw the agent watch the object move to the lighter box. In that condition, infants looked longer at the Dark box test event (rather than the Light box event).

Note, however, that understanding false belief requires more than just understanding ignorance. So, alternative interpretations are possible based on an infant understanding of ignorance rather than false belief. For example, if infants understand the agent is unaware (and thus ignorant of the location of the object), that understanding could be sufficient for them to see the Light box test event as novel or unexpected. In essence, the infant might reason "She can't know where it is," and so find it unexpected and attention worthy that she searches in the correct box.

(Figure modified from Baillargeon, Scott, & He, 2010)

preschool is a ruse: Young preschoolers' ability is masked by task demands. Thus, Leslie (2005) argues that young children, including infants, show their false-belief competence in "tacit," looking-time, false-belief tasks but fail if the tasks require considered, verbal judgments. They fail because "early competence…is later obscured by failures in inhibition of prepotent responses" (Leslie, 2005, p. 460). The prepotent response at issue is that "people's beliefs about everyday matters typically are true" (p. 460) so children can only respond correctly to preschool false-belief tasks if they inhibit this beliefs-are-true response.

A second possibility is that the infant "false-belief" tasks require a simpler attribution from infants than false belief. Perhaps infants can solve such tasks by attributing to agents intentional action and attention—desires and awareness—rather than beliefs. If so, then preschoolers go further than that and come to understand belief and false belief. In this case, infants' understanding is an abbreviated, partial form of agent understanding that needs to expand to become that of preschoolers by incorporating an understanding of belief.

A third possibility is that two very different sorts of understandings are at issue—dual system accounts. That is, one cognitive system allows infants to expect agents to act in terms of their "beliefs," but another different system is required to reason about beliefs when it comes to predicting and explaining a person's actions and minds in the way that preschoolers (and adults) can. Perhaps, infant understanding is implicit, and fast but limited, whereas preschool understanding is additionally explicit, flexible, and expansive. And it is explicit, flexible, systematic judgments that are required, and revealed, in preschool tasks. With their limited conceptions, for example, infants are not tracking mental-state constructs that are entrenched in belief-desire reasoning and seen by the child as nonmaterial, mental, and representational. Only preschoolers begin to evidence this second reasoning system.

All these perspectives are similar in accepting that infants know some important and intriguing things, things overlapping with a full-bodied understanding of beliefs and belief-desire psychology. They are equally similar in accepting that young preschoolers fail standard false-belief tasks. Thus, each perspective attempts to reconcile infants' success and preschoolers' failings in their alternative fashions. At present, no decisive evidence definitively adjudicates between these several perspectives. Nonetheless, we can weigh their merits and thereby better understand what the findings tell us about the origins and the nature of theory of mind understandings.

I'll begin quickly with the first account just outlined, and specifically Leslie's (2005; Leslie, German, & Polizzi, 2005) inhibitory performance versus false-belief competence proposal. This is an executive function *expression* account. Yuyan Luo and Renée Baillargeon (2010) also advanced an executive function expression account. As I argued in Chapter 7, executive function expression accounts cannot fully explain preschool false-belief development. At the very least, recall that preschool theory of mind predicts preschoolers' social actions and interactions even when executive function is partialled out.

Moreover, a hidden assumption for both Leslie (2005), as well as Luo and Baillargeon (2010), is that infant false-belief tasks must *not* require executive functions. But, why not? Let's say that the young child's prepotent, default understanding is a reality orientation ("beliefs are typically true") as claimed by Leslie. Then, to correctly attribute false

BOX 8.2

OUTLINE OF SCOTT AND BAILLARGEON'S 2009 RESEARCH

Familiarization trials (6-part sequence)

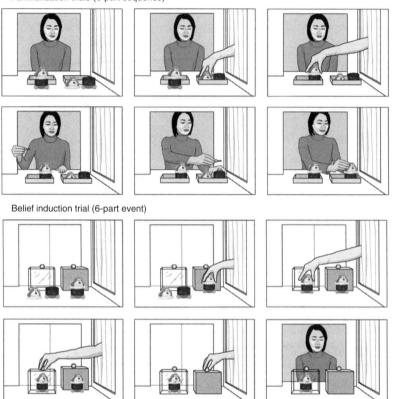

Belief induction trial (6-part event)

Test trials (either of these two events)

Transparent-cover event   Opaque-cover event

In the false-belief condition of Scott and Baillargeon (2009), the infants received four familiarization trials involving two containers (shaped abstractly like toy penguins) that were identical except that one could come apart (two-piece penguin) and one could not (one-piece penguin). As a female agent watched, an experimenter's hand placed the one-piece penguin and the pieces of the disassembled two-piece penguin in shallow containers. The agent then placed a key in the bottom piece of the two-piece penguin, stacked the two pieces, and paused.

During belief-induction trials, while the agent was absent, the experimenter assembled the two-piece penguin, covered it with a transparent cover, and then covered the one-piece penguin with an opaque cover. The agent then entered the apparatus with her key. For the final test trial, the agent then reached for either the transparent cover (transparent-cover event) or the opaque cover (opaque-cover event), and paused.

Scott and Baillargeon reasoned that for the test events, the infant inferred the agent wanted the two-piece penguin (to hide things), expected that there would be one disassembled two-piece penguin and one solid one-piece penguin (because that is how familiarization always began), could see an entire penguin under the transparent cover, and believed that meant the disassembled two-piece penguin must be in the opaque box instead. This false belief (because the two-piece penguin was already assembled and under the transparent box) would lead her to go to the opaque box, expecting the disassembled two-piece penguin to be there. If so, infants would look longer at the unexpected, Transparent-cover event.

In Scott and Baillargeon's (2009) experiment, this "false-belief" scenario was compared to a "true-belief" one where the agent was present throughout the six-part belief-induction phase. So the infant saw the agent witness the two-piece penguin assembled and put in the transparent box. Indeed, 18-month-olds in the "false-belief" condition looked longer at the Transparent-cover test event, whereas in the "true-belief" condition, they instead looked longer at the Opaque-cover test event.

Moreover, there was a third "ignorance" condition where everything was the same as in "false belief" except that on test trials, the agent was faced with two opaque boxes. Here infants looked equally at either scenario.

(Figure modified from Baillargeon, Scott, & He, 2010)

beliefs, infants, just like preschoolers, have the task of inhibiting that reality expectation, in this case the expectation that the agent will reach to the locale where the sought-for object really is. So, executive-function demands are at issue within infant tasks, not just preschool ones.

In short, it is extremely unlikely that infant "false-belief" tasks show us unvarnished theory-of-mind competence, and preschool errors are simply executive function performance errors. That leaves the two other possibilities to consider in more detail.

DESIRE-AWARENESS ATTRIBUTIONS

What about the possibility that infants may be construing people in terms of their intentional actions and experiences and doing so in rich intriguing fashions sufficient to perform correctly on many infant "false-belief" tasks but without an attribution of false belief? The version of such an account that I think deserves most consideration, and indeed that I think is at least partly and importantly true, is that infants construe persons in desire-awareness ways (rather than belief, false-belief ways).

To be clear, I am not suggesting here that infants simply cognize about people in tasks like Scott and Baillargeon's (2009) in terms of behavioral rules (Ruffman & Perner, 2005) or mere bottom-up statistical regularities (Ruffman, Taumoepeau, & Perkins, 2012)—for example, people search for things where they last saw them. Infants' understandings are more psychological than that, albeit failing to encompass a conception of beliefs.

Tracking Others' Awareness or Engagement

To flesh out this alternative account, let's back up and begin with infants' ability to track an agent's engagement with events. Briefly recall a few key studies. In one study by Michael Tomasello and Katharina Haberl (2003)—outlined in Chapter 1—infants interacted with three unusual objects and critically, a target male adult joined in these interactions for two of the objects but not the third. After these initial interactions, the three objects were shown together on a tray, and the target adult said to the infants, "Oh, wow! That's so cool! Can you give it to me?" while gesturing ambiguously in the direction of the objects. All three objects were now old for the infant, but one was new to the target adult. Infants gave the target adult the object that was new *for him*. By giving him that object, 12- and 18-month-old infants showed some understanding of, and tracking of, the target adult's experiences. And this required recognizing something of the subjectivity of these experiences, recognizing that the adult's prior experiences critically differed from the infant's own—"the object of interest, albeit old for me, is new for him." (See Moll, Carpenter, & Tomasello, 2007, for related results.) In doing this, infants demonstrate they track agents' awareness/unawareness of events, and this encompasses something like a rudimentary sense of knowledge-like (old for me) and ignorance-like (new for him) states.

Betty Repacholi and Alison Gopnik (1997) provided a different example of infant appreciation of individuated, subjective experience in their broccoli-cracker task. In the focal mismatch condition, the female adult looked at, tasted, and liked the broccoli and disliked the cracker, mismatching the child's preference. Then the adult held her hand halfway between the two snacks and said, "I want some more, can you give me some more?" Their 18-month-olds overwhelmingly gave the adult more of what she, the adult, had liked, demonstrating an understanding of desires as subjective—realizing that the adult wanted broccoli, contrary to their own preference for crackers.

In these studies, infants track the other person's awareness of or engagement with various objects and events and distinguish that from their own. Indeed, 7-month-old infants track someone else's experiences at the same time as accumulating their own. Angela Kovacs and her colleagues (Kovács, Táglás, & Endress, 2010) showed 7-month-olds videos of a series of events—for example, a ball rolling onto a table, then behind a screen that was on the table, then from behind the screen to off the table. The videos also included another character, a bystander, who, across different conditions, was present for some things and not others. In a final set of test events, the infants then saw the table with the screen, whereupon the screen dropped down revealing either (a) the ball behind it or (b) nothing behind it. How did infants look at these test events, given their prior experiences with the stimuli?

Given what we know about infant understanding of objects (e.g., Spelke et al., 1992; Baillargeon & Wang, 2002), as expected, infants responded with greater attention if their own experience suggested the ball should not be there—for example, they had just seen the ball roll from behind the screen and depart—but when the screen dropped, there it was. Here, the ball's presence mismatched the infants' own experience and they looked longer.

More novel and crucial, infants looked longer as well if the ball's presence mismatched the *other agent's* experience. For example, suppose the agent was not present to see the ball depart even though the infant was; so if the screen dropped, the agent would not know the ball was gone (even though the infant knew). Here too infants looked longer. Kovacs et al. (2010) claimed that in this case, their 7-month-olds were automatically tracking the other agent's beliefs. But that is unclear to me and seems an overinterpretation. What does seem clear is that infants were tracking something important about their own *and* the other's experience with the ball events, noting, for example, that the bystander did not see the ball leave (so its absence behind the screen was noteworthy to him) even though they themselves had seen it leave. If the event would be noteworthy for themselves *or for the other*, they looked longer.

It is worth stressing how intriguing these studies are. Classic accounts of infancy, and particularly Jean Piaget's (e.g., Piaget, 1952), portray infants as deeply egocentric—caught in their own experiential world with no recognition of that or how their experiences could be different from others. In contrast, the studies I have discussed here show that infants are registering others' experiences too—even when different from their own. They are seeing the world through others' eyes, not simply their own. Indeed, remarkably, from as young as 7 months, they seem to automatically track some key aspects of the other's experience in relation to how it is similar versus different from their own. In the Kovacs et al. (2010) study, the video was saliently about the ball and its action; the other agent was not central to the events, he was merely a bystander (or not) as the events unfolded. But infants tracked whether he was connected to certain key events anyway, and his experience—not merely their own experience of the ball—influenced their reactions to the test events.

This automaticity in tracking others' experience reveals itself in word learning as well. Infants 12 months old who hear an adult provide a name for an object the infant is looking at will learn the label as the object's name. But they only do so if the adult is looking at the object too. If the adult is looking elsewhere, the baby won't learn the label as the name of the object (e.g., Baldwin, 1991). In general, infant word learners seem to determine which aspects are and are not referential for the adult and use that to engage in and to avoid word learning (Baldwin, 2000).

In this section, I call this infant tracking of others' experiences a sense of the other person's awareness or engagement. Given how adults often use the term "awareness" to refer to a person's richly mental apprehension, a narrower understanding of awareness, denoted by "engagement," is more the idea. In this usage, I am following the proposal of Daniela O'Neill (1996) who, in a nifty set of studies with young 2-year-olds, prefigured contemporary research with infants. In her research, for example, a desirable toy was in a container on a shelf too high to reach, so 2-year-olds had to ask a parent for help in retrieving it. The parent was either present, along with the child, during the relevant events (e.g., when the toy was placed into the container) or was not present. Toddlers communicated with their parents quite differently if the parent had or had not been present. For example, children specifically pointed to the relevant location much more if their mother had not witnessed the toy's original placement in the container at that location and also provided more location-specific (rather than merely general) verbalizations.

These results were novel and surprising at that time and O'Neill (1996) strove to neither overinterpret or underinterpret them. The interpretation she settled on she titled "engagement + updating." In her opinion, toddlers were tracking their parent's past engagement and disengagement with an item and attempting to update the parent's awareness later. Importantly, in this interpretation, the parent's experience was *not* updated simply because the infant's experience changed. The parent's experience was updated (in the toddler's mind) only by further experiences—apprehension that the toy was in the container or seeing the container pointed out—on the *parent's* part. O'Neill distinguished an "engagement + updating" account from a (full-fledged) "see + knowing" or "seeing = believing" account. Indeed, note that engagement is not essentially or necessarily about visual experience. Although parents who did not witness the toy being hidden lacked visual information, engagement from the infant's point of view could be broader than vision or any specific perceptual modality—it arguably included a host of possible features (and in some situations vision would be neither necessary nor sufficient for engagement).

It is natural to think of the infant as tracking two individual things, her own experiences and separately the other's experiences. But, conceivably, the infant may be tracking something more communal and social than that—something like *our* experiences and not-*our* experiences. *We* jointly experienced X, *we* did not jointly experience Y (I did but she didn't; see Moll et al., 2007, and Stack & Lewis, 2011). In any case, the upshot is that the infant has a sense of the others' engagement (or not) beyond just their own. For simplicity, I will refer to this infant understanding of engagement as tracking knowledge or knowledge-like experiences. If something happens and the agent is appropriately engaged with it, she is aware of it and in that limited sense knows of it; if it happened and she was unaware, she does not know. I do not think such young children track knowledge exactly as adults more fully understand knowing. But on this account, they do track awareness in this way that is sensibly knowledge like.

A key point I want to emphasize is that an understanding of desires and awareness coupled with some understanding of intentional action would provide infants a powerful mentalistic social cognition, even *without* an understanding of beliefs. This is the same point I made in Chapter 4 about toddlers' mentalistic understandings, but here I elaborate it and also apply it to infants. So, in what follows next, I outline some of the extent and power of plausible infant understandings of engagement along with desires and actions (including, in particular, actions to search and find things). The focal question here is what the infant thinks will happen when the agent is ignorant. What will she do?

Desires and Awareness/Unawareness

The infant research always includes someone involved in some focal intentional acts, and essentially searching for an object, as in the Onishi and Baillargeon (2005; Box 8.1) and Scott and Baillargeon (2009; Box 8.2) studies. Intentional acts are overt and so, methodologically, can be straightforwardly presented to infants for their consideration. This means that infant inferences are constrained by both their understandings of desires and awareness *and* understandings of searching for objects. Here are some related things that someone (an infant) with a desire-awareness understanding of people can predict agents will do when searching for desired things:

1. If an agent wants an object and sees it, she is aware that it's there (the agent has engaged the object's presence and thus knows about it) and so she (often) goes for it. That is, she can act intentionally to get it. Indeed, agents often attempt to get things they desire.

2. Because agents attempt to get things they desire, then, if an agent wants the object but doesn't see it and is otherwise unaware (ignorant) of where it is, she (often) searches for it. Because she is unaware of its location, she does not know where to look (or what item to choose) and so can search randomly. (But stay tuned, she can do a lot more too.)

These two principles alone help provide an interpretation of Onishi and Baillargeon (2005). Look again at Box 8.1. From a desire-awareness/unawareness point of view, if the agent can't know where the toy is, why does she search directly in the correct box? Infants find this correct search for an agent whose awareness has not been appropriately updated—someone who is ignorant—noteworthy.

These two understandings are a beginning, but desire-awareness reasoning allows more:

3. If the agent in Principle 2 just outlined searches in Location 1 of several locations for her desired target object and she finds it there, she (a) is happy

or satisfied and (b) stops searching (see discussion of wanting-finding in Chapter 4).

4. Complementarily, if she searches in Location 1 and doesn't find her target object, she (a) is unhappy or unsatisfied and so (b) searches further in another location.

5. If the agent is unaware of the object's whereabouts, and so she doesn't know where to search or which item to consider, someone else can show her. (Agents can be influenced by others' direction of their attention and management of their awareness.)

   (a) A simple case: Someone who is aware (does know)—for example, someone who has seen where the object is—can point out and/or show the agent the correct location or correct item (as in O'Neill's, 1996, study).

   (b) A less straightforward case: Someone can show the agent which *order* to search/try in.

6. If the agent doesn't know where to search, she can (under appropriate conditions) search where she last saw it put. A desire-awareness infant can make this inference *not* because of a low-level rule (agents always search where they saw the item placed last) and not because of an understanding that the agent *thinks* it's there, but rather by inferring that because the agent is unaware (ignorant), yet must search someplace, then (under many conditions) searching where you last engaged the object can be an appropriate first search. Infants themselves, when they do not know an object's immediate location, often search where they last saw it (Wellman, Cross, & Bartsch, 1986). Moreover, an appropriate search tactic can be to search where the object is regularly kept or found; that is, an ignorant searcher might search where the object "belongs." In infant "false-belief" tasks, if the infant and the agent see the object placed (often several times) at a first location, they could easily infer that that signals where the object belongs and so is likely to be.

7. Searching can occur actively but also by less-active, perceptual (e.g., visual) inspection. This is because agents are actors *and* attenders. So (a) awareness can come from visual information or from information generated by more active/interactive search (or from others, as in Principle 5). Thus, relatedly, (b) unawareness can come from lack of more active/interactive access as well as lack of visual access.

I'll call these Principles 1 through 7 of a larger desire-awareness reasoning system. I don't think a desire-awareness reasoner must separately distinguish, list, and reason through all these principles—they are just sensible implications of thinking of agents' search actions as reflecting their desires and awareness/unawareness. I have gone into this much explicit detail, however, to adequately characterize what I think infants can infer and do with just this level of understanding. Moreover, outlining the sense and extent of such a conceptual system distinguishes this proposal from merely a set of ad hoc, low-level behavioral rules.

Part of the point of this exegesis is to clarify that if a desire-awareness agent is ignorant, she or he does not merely or always do nothing nor act randomly nor act wrongly. Because of this, if an infant predicts the agent will act in a directed, nonrandom way, that prediction does *not* necessarily signal an understanding of the agent's beliefs or false beliefs; all sorts of directed, nonrandom action can stem from awareness and unawareness plus sensible searching. In many infant "false-belief" studies, I believe, the infant's expectation of an agent's directed, nonrandom action is taken, too simply and too easily, as an index of false belief.

A Desire-Awareness Explanation for Scott and Baillargeon (2009)

Return to the Scott and Baillargeon (2009) study outlined in Box 8.2. In their false-belief condition, the desire-awareness infant would take the agent to be looking for the disassembled two penguin parts (just as Scott & Baillargeon also claim). But, consider the test events further. For the transparent-cover test event, the infant can clearly see that the agent sees (visual search) that the disassembled two-part penguin is *not* in the transparent box (Location 1); and so the infant should expect a desire-awareness agent to then go on to search at the other location (the opaque box) instead. This follows from Principle 4 as just outlined. So, the infant should expect the desire-awareness agent to search at the opaque-cover location and not at the transparent-cover location, and indeed that is how infants behave: In Scott and Baillargeon, infants look longer at the transparent-cover event than the opaque-cover event.

As outlined in Box 8.2, Scott and Baillargeon (2009) also ran an ignorance condition. Here there were two opaque boxes. Therefore, the searcher could not see the contents of either box. In this case, a desire-awareness agent could first search at either location (as follows from Principle 2 outlined before). And indeed, in Scott and Baillargeon's ignorance condition, infants looked equally at a reach to either opaque-cover box.[1]

Another Example

David Buttelmann, Malinda Carpenter, and Michael Tomasello (2009) reported a clever approach to infant/toddler "false-belief" understanding via an active–interactive paradigm rather than a looking-time paradigm. (See also Southgate, Chevallier, & Csibra, 2010.) This has advantages in that, as outlined in Box 8.3, interpreting looking-time experiments is not always, or typically, as straightforward as assumed. Indeed, within the infant development literature there are serious debates about how to interpret such looking-time studies and in particular what constitutes the needed (often missing) controls (Aslin, 2007; Cohen, 2004). Moreover, converging evidence across paradigms with different method-specific features and demands is always important, even crucial.

In the Buttelmann et al. (2009) paradigm, the infant interacted with an adult male experimenter who (a) dealt with two boxes (that could each open if a nonobvious catch

BOX 8.3

INTERPRETATION OF DATA FROM LOOKING TIME METHODS

Baillargeon (2004) calls Scott and Baillargeon (2009) and Onishi and Baillargeon (2005) violation of expectation (VOE) tasks. VOE looking-time tasks have their own logic, an asymmetric logic (and this is importantly related to whether the infant is attributing engagement or something more). If an infant looks longer at test event A than B (given proper familiarization/habituation, plus control conditions, etc.), we can infer that he did *not* expect A. We can *not* infer that, in contrast, he did expect B. The infant might have no expectation about B (but still look longer when seeing A because he did not expect that).

Glosses of infants' thinking often ignore or go beyond this asymmetry, I believe. For example, for the "false-belief" task of Scott and Baillargeon (2009), the one depicted in Box 8.2, the authors say that for the transparent cover test event, the infant (based on his analysis of the agent's belief) expected the agent to search in the opaque box and so was surprised when she searched in the transparent box instead.

This is not quite right (or sufficiently precise). More precisely, the gloss should be "the infant did *not* expect the agent to search in the transparent box and so looked longer when she did." This is a crucial difference. The infant may actually have *no* expectation about the opaque box (in this example) or certainly not so definite an expectation as that the agent thinks the object is there or should look there. We have no evidence as to the infant's expectation about the opaque box *because* the increased looking is toward the transparent box.

Rephrased in this (I believe more appropriate) way, it is much less seductive or convincing to interpret these, and other VOE, data definitively in terms of false belief. For Onishi and Baillargeon (2005), for example, an interpretation focused on the box that garnered the longer looking might be, "She can't know where it is, but, wow, she's searching X (where it is), that's attention worthy." This clearly contrasts with the authors' preferred interpretation: "She thinks it's in Y but is searching X, wow, that's attention worthy."

was released) that could contain and conceal things; (b) desired a toy; and (c) either did or did not witness a crucial part of the sequence of events. The task took advantage of the ordinary, strong infant motivation to help others succeed at their goals (as in Warneken & Tomasello, 2006). Again, as in many of these studies, there was a focal "false-belief" condition and a contrasting "true-belief" condition. In addition, crucially, for these tasks the infant, and *not* the adult, knew how to undo the catch to unlock either box.

In Buttelmann et al.'s (2009) false-belief condition, the adult agent interacted with a desirable toy, saw it hidden in one box, left the room, and while away did not see it transferred to the second box. He then returned wanting something to play with. On his return, the adult went to the original box, attempted to open it but could not, then sat forlornly between the two boxes. At this point, the 16-, 18- or 30-month-olds were encouraged to help him. These young children significantly went to open up the new box, where the toy actually was, rather than the old box, the one the adult had just visibly tried to open. Infants at all ages, even 16-month-olds, did this about 75 to 80% of the time.

Buttelmann and his colleagues (2009) argued that the infant understood the adult wanted the toy, thought (falsely) it was in the old box, and hence the adult tried to open that. But, helping him get the toy he really wanted required opening the other box. From a desire-awareness perspective (including Principles 1–7 outlined before), however, the infants could have done exactly the same helpful thing (with no attributions of belief). Instead, the infant would reason, the adult wants the toy but is unaware of where it is (indeed he has just demonstrated, by going to the empty box, that he is searching incorrectly). To help him get what he wants, the infant would help him open the correct box (i.e., the *other* box).

Buttelmann et al. (2009) attempted to rule out that infants are merely trying to directly help the adult get the hidden toy. They tackled this he's-unaware-so-I'll-help interpretation with their true-belief condition. In that condition, the adult saw the toy in one box then transferred to a new one (and the child was explicitly directed that the adult was watching attentively). Then after a brief delay (with the adult still present and *no* further object movement), the adult went to the old box where the toy was not (as in *false belief*) and attempted to open it unsuccessfully. In this case, the children helped him to open that old box and not the new one (that had the toy). So in this condition, the infant did not just go get the toy for the adult. Why not? In this case Buttelmann et al. reasoned the infant understood the adult had a true belief (i.e., knew) about where the toy was, so the adult must not desire the toy and must want to play with something from the other, old box instead. So they helped him achieve that *alternative* desire.

Again, however, a desire-awareness interpretation could suffice. The adult is aware of where the toy is, but he wants something else (the same attribution about an alternative desire that Buttelmann et al., 2009, assumed the infant held), so infants help with this alternate desire.

Buttelmann et al. (2009) acknowledged that "a key interpretive challenge is to distinguish an understanding of false belief from an understanding of knowledge-ignorance" (p. 341). I agree. They argue that their tasks do so because, as the true-belief condition shows, the natural "helping" response is to aid the adult to open the box he tried to open. But infants do not do that in false belief. "What makes it a study of false belief, in our opinion—is that without an understanding of the [adult's] false belief children cannot help him appropriately" (p. 341). But, clearly in my opinion infants can help the adult appropriately *without* an understanding of his false belief, and they would do so appropriately with only a desire-awareness understanding: In the false belief condition, he desires the toy, he's played with it and likes it, but he's gone to the box that is empty (because he isn't aware of where the toy is). I'll help him get the toy; period. And in the true-belief condition, the adult wants something else (and not the toy)—I'll help him get *that*. Such a desire-awareness alternative interpretation of Buttelmann et al. requires no attribution of beliefs.

These interpretations of both Buttelmann et al. (2009) and Scott and Baillargeon (2009), of course, make clear that just because authors call something a false-belief condition does not mean that it requires false-belief attribution and reasoning on the part of the infant; it could instead, more simply, require desire-awareness reasoning. In essence, the infant tracks "agent knows" or "agent can't know" and this, *along with key understandings of intentional searching*, determine the infant's expectations for the agent's actions.

It is worth emphasizing that these studies do show infants' cogent understanding of persons in terms of their knowledge-like (aware) or ignorance-like (unaware) states in the service of searching for objects. That is, they evidence an extensive grasp of desire-awareness reasoning, including Principles 1 through 7. Here is one further example. Diane Poulin-Dubois and her colleagues (2013) gave 14- and 18-month-old infants looking-time presentations very much like Onishi and Baillargeon (2005; Box 8.1) with a few key modifications. Their first study was as in Box 8.1 except that the two boxes were completely transparent. In this case 14- and 18-month-old infants looked longer on test events in which the female adult reached to the empty box where the object had been but no longer was. As prescribed by Principle 1, if the agent wants the object and *can see it*, she should search where it is. So, when she goes to the empty box instead, that is attention getting.

Note this study rules out certain simple rule-based accounts of infant behavior, for example, that infants merely predict the agent will look where *she* saw the object last placed (Ruffman & Perner, 2005). In this Poulin-Dubois et al. (2013) study, the adult last saw it placed in the now empty (transparent box), but infants predict she will look in the full one. Presumably, à la Principle 1, the agent will look there because she can see where it is. In a second study (Poulin-Dubois et al., 2013, Study 2), the setup was the same except the agent was now blindfolded. Here the infants looked equally if the agent searched at either box. À la Principle 2, if she can't see, she's unaware where it is and searches randomly.

All this, plus what infants do in Scott and Baillargeon (2009) as well as Buttelmann et al. (2009; as well as Onishi & Baillargeon, 2005) is very impressive social cognition, way beyond simple low-level behavior rule following. But it does not require the infant to attribute false beliefs.

DUAL SYSTEMS

Despite the plausibility of a desire-awareness account, there are reasons for thinking it is not the full story. First, although it can account for much of the infant "false-belief" results, it requires more stretching to account for anticipatory-looking results such as those of Victoria Southgate (Southgate et al., 2007) with 2-year-olds, or the related anticipatory-looking results from Neumann, Thoermer, and Sodian (2008) with 18-month-olds. In these tasks, infants do more than react with longer looking to various search actions; they anticipate the actor's actions by looking to one location or another in advance of the actor reaching to either. Predicting ahead of time more narrowly reveals the infant's sense of the agent's states.

More important, however, a desire-awareness account may falsely suggest both too much continuity *and* too much discontinuity between infant and preschool capacities. For continuity, a desire-awareness account suggests that infants have a pretty solid, preschool-like conception of ignorance-like states and only need to extend that to an understanding of belief states. For discontinuity, a desire-awareness account suggests that preschoolers no longer do what infants do—they've *replaced* desire-awareness reasoning with belief-desire reasoning instead. Dual-systems accounts of the sort I consider here[2] instead propose that infant successes and preschool successes are both more similar and more discontinuous. Both are similar in honoring something like beliefs (or belief-like states). But they are discontinuous in reflecting two separate systems that operate at very different levels of cognitive process: a lower level, "implicit," automatic system that allows infants to track precursor, knowledge-like, and even belief-like states, and a second conceptually rich, "explicit" reasoning system that allows older children and adults to infer and systematically reason about a coherent network of mental states including beliefs, knowledge, and more—that is, develop a theory of mind of the sort I describe in Chapter 2.

To justify such a dual-system account, Ian Apperly (2011) noted that adult theory of mind needs to do two fairly incompatible things: In some situations, we need to quickly and efficiently read someone's mental states. Is the basketball player opposite me faking a dribble to the right to deceive me, or does he really intend to go right? In other situations, we need to come to a considered, deliberate decision about someone's mental states. Did the defendant knowingly put the poison in the tea, to deceive the victim into ingesting poison (and is only saying that he thought it was sugar to deceive the jury into thinking it was an accident)?

Quick and efficient (fast) decisions versus deliberate and considered (slow) inferences are both important (Kahneman, 2011). But according to Apperly (2011), they are also incompatible—one system cannot do both—so they could best be solved by two different "mind-reading" systems. Flexible, expansive, and conscious (but inefficient) theory of mind underwrites preschool reasoning of the sort outlined in Chapter 2 in standard theory-of-mind tasks; efficient, narrow, inflexible theory of mind underwrites infants' responses. Importantly, for Apperly, the quick, efficient system allows infants to simply track the agent's registration of (or awareness of) an object at one location, *including* that the agent can hold onto that exact registration even when things objectively change. Arguably, such a system could be useful for adults (and so evolutionarily adaptive enough to be favored) and available to infants as well (accounting for the infant "false-belief" findings).

To propose that a fast (inflexible) tracking of an agent's belief-like cognition under-writes infant responses (system 1), rather than considered (flexible) belief-desire rea-soning (system 2), is plausible. But it is also vacuous (or circular) unless something else distinguishes the former from the latter. In principle, a system that is fast and efficient in some ways would also be distinctively limited in other ways. Indeed, Apperly (2011) hypothesized (on analogy to infant number conceptions) that an implicit, efficient, belief-like, theory-of-mind system would also be rigid or inflexible; and in this rigid-ity, it should exhibit some signature *limitations*. Unfortunately, however, the burgeon-ing infant "false-belief" literature has rarely considered infants' limits (other than that infants presumably, like young preschoolers, would fail preschool false-belief tasks). Studies report infant successes in tasks and situations in which infants respond sensibly. Considerably less is known about limitations and errors in infants' social cognitions. But, conceptually, here are three key directions in which to look for limitations.

First, there might be limits in the nature of the sort of mental states a fast, rigid system might track: when it comes to "epistemic" states in particular, the system would be lim-ited to belief-like states (e.g., object registrations, as discussed further in what follows) rather than full-fledged beliefs. Second, even that limited notion must integrate together with something like desire states to create its inferences about actions. An initial system might be limited in the sorts of desires it tracks and relatedly in the sorts of desire-based actions it can apply to. Third, to be at all rational, even a limited, rigid system needs to take into account something of the information access that yields the focal belief-like states. Thus, the initial system, to achieve fast, relevant inferences, might be limited in the way it processes the agent's information access.

Object Registration

Arguably, the infant's belief-like notions—its fast, efficient awareness-tracking system—may track something like an agent's *registration* of *objects* rather than an agent's beliefs per se, a distinction advocated by Apperly (2011). If this distinction is valid, then there should be crucial limits with regard to the first system's (system 1) registration of the *objects* involved. The targets of full-fledged beliefs are like the example from Chapter 7 of "He thinks that *Obama is a Republican*." The targets of belief states are not fully the real object (Obama = Democrat) but "objects" under a representational description ("Obama = Republican"). The objects in a belief-like (quick, inflexible) registration, however, could conceivably be essentially the physical objects themselves. Apperly (2011) and Jason Low (e.g., Low & Watts, 2013) have referred to this as tracking objects versus representing identities.

More clearly to my mind, this is the same distinction John Flavell first described in researching Level-1 versus Level-2 understandings of perception. As I outlined in

Chapter 4, in a Level-1 understanding, infants and young children understand that others can see different objects. If a toy robot is on the table in front of a barrier for the child but in back of the barrier for me (because I'm sitting opposite), very young children know they see the robot but I don't. Or if there is no barrier, then we both see the robot. What if the robot is two colored, so that it is red on one side but blue on the other—that is, looks red from one profile but blue from the other? Young children know both they and I see the robot (Level-1 understanding) *but* fail to know that while they see it as red, I'll see it as blue. If we reverse positions, they'll say they see it as blue and I, too, see it as blue. Older preschoolers know they see it as blue, but I see it as red (Level-2 understanding of perception). Very young children understand persons as registering or not registering objects, but fail to understand them as perceiving identities.

One way to depict this difference is along the lines of Figure 4.2 in Chapter 4. In the top panel of that figure, the agent has a Level-1 connection to the object. So, if the object is that apple, the agent registers *that*. At the bottom, the agent does not just register the object (as is) but represents it as one way and not the other. That is, the agent represents the object as having an identity, "a red apple," maybe even something like "a tasty red apple." Let's say the apple object actually turns out to be a deceptively red-painted orange (that looks like an apple). If the cognizer is only tracking an agent's registration, the agent registers *that object*, where that object is an orange. But, if the cognizer is ascribing a representational mental state, the agent represents "an apple." The object as registered is an orange; the identity as represented is "a red apple." So a signature limit of belief-like registration might be this focus on objects not identities.

Jason Low and Joseph Watts (2013) tackled this possible limitation of system-1 (vs. system-2) reasoning by examining whether the efficient belief-like system could register an agent's belief-like tracking of objects but err in not representing identities. These researchers did not study infants, but reasoned, clearly enough, that in a dual-system proposal, 3-year-olds, 4-year-olds, and adults as well should also have the fast efficient system—with its signature limits—not just infants. Only beginning in the preschool years would people have that system *and* the other, slower, considered, explicit one as well. So, Low and Watts looked for signature limits in the rapid efficient processing of 3- and 4-year-olds and adults.

Low and Watts (2013) conducted a complex study using looking and eye tracking (to measure anticipatory looking), and red-blue two-sided toys, but the key idea is straightforward. Children watched an agent see a symmetrical-shaped robot colored blue on one side but red on the other. As in typical false-belief tasks, the robot was placed in a box (red side forward to begin with), Box A, and then the agent saw the robot move to another box, Box B, and then return again to Box A. However, the agent did not see the robot turn around side to side within Box B, now presenting its blue side instead of its red side. Because of a cutout window on the side of Box B that faced the child, children could see the original robot turn around but the agent could not.

The key idea here was that if children (via a flexible, considered system 2) construed the agent as tracking represented identities, then when the robot turned sides, because the agent could not see that, he or she would believe some new blue robot had left Box B and not the original red one; so the red one must remain in Box B. In that case, the agent could be expected to search for the original robot in Box B. However, if the child (via fast, rigid system 1) construed the agent as tracking registered objects, then *the* robot had returned to Box A and so the agent should search for it there. Low and Watts (2013) then had two measures: a verbal explicit inference ("where will the agent search?") and an eye-gaze measure (when the agent first begins to reach, where do the child's eyes anticipate the agent will first search?). The explicit verbal inference should require system-2 reasoning; the implicit eye gaze should reveal automatic system-1 tracking of the agent's registration.

The data were clear: 4-year-olds and adults answered the explicit question correctly (he'll search Box B), but not 3-year-olds (who answered Box A). In contrast, all age group's anticipatory gazes were "incorrect," going quickly to Box A. In short, the implicit system 1 tracked objects, whereas the explicit system 2 could track identities. System 1 quickly and efficiently tracked an agent's belief-like registration of objects, but this quick tracking of agents' registrations failed to include representation of identities. That system was limited to registering belief-like states; it tracked Flavell's Level-1 perceptual objects. The explicit system could take account of states that were like Flavell's Level-2 perceptual identities.

Simple Desires

Consider Figure 4.2 in Chapter 4 again. In the top panel of that figure, the agent is depicted as having a very simple desire—wanting *that* object, the apple. As just noted, this is a sense of desiring equivalent to registering the object; and so if the object is a tasty, red apple, the agent wants *that*. In parallel to the system-1 belief-like states just described, this is a system-1 desire-like state. It is not an adult (system 2) mature sense of desires, because in the adult case, if you want an apple, but the thing you are apprehending is not really an apple (its just a deceptively red-painted orange), you don't want *that*; you want an apple in all its identity. So a signature limit of system 1 would include a limited registration of objects, not identities, for desires as well as beliefs. Thus, only some sorts of desires could be operative for system 1.

Moreover, I suspect that system 1 desires—focused on desirable, preferred things—are more limited still in focus. For comparison, in flexible belief-desire reasoning, desires encompass much more than desires for preferred objects, they encompass desires to be president, desires for self-improvement, desires to manage one's own baser desires, and so on. By hypothesis, system 1 would be limited to objects. Not only could system 1 be limited to desires for objects, this limitation would also entail limits to the desire-based actions that system 1 focally could reason successfully about. The limited initial system may only apply to actions that involve an agent searching for preferred objects. In this, all the principles outlined previously for desire-awareness searching would apply, but only these sorts of search actions would be predicted by this system.[3] The infant research thus far essentially only takes place in the context of infant understanding of agents' searching for preferred objects. More comprehensively examining the scope of desire-based action that infants can reason about would be a clear direction in which to look for signature limits.

Information Access

Finally, consider that in a standard change-of-location false-belief task, the protagonist has a false belief because that person did not see the exact critical set of events; the protagonist did not see that the object was moved to the cupboard and so is no longer in the drawer (as in Box 1.2 in Chapter 1) or did not see the toy move from the dark box to the light one (as in Box 8.1). This means that subsumed within false-belief understanding is a "seeing leads to knowing" understanding. And, indeed, preschoolers who pass preschool false-belief tasks in fact pass many related seeing-knowing tasks as well. They judge that a person who saw an object but did not touch it might know its identity but not its "feel"; whereas a person who touched but did not see might know much about the object but not its color (O'Neill, Astington, & Flavell, 1992). They judge that a person who looks inside a closed container would know what's inside, but a person who touched the container or lifted it but did not look inside would not know (Pratt & Bryant, 1990). They judge that a person who saw a deceptive object (e.g., a sponge that looks like a rock) but did not explore it further would not know its true identity and instead have a false belief about that (Tardif et al., 2004). Relatedly, preschoolers who pass false-belief tasks judge correctly that someone who saw very little *but saw the critical transfer event* would know, whereas someone who saw a lot but missed the critical transfer event would not know (and so believe falsely).

Conceivably, however, a fast, limited infant system registering belief-like states quickly (and crudely) might not include some (or much) of these understandings. Belief-like (or knowledge-like) registration resulting from an agent's engagement with objects is not the same thing as attributing beliefs resulting from an agent's informational experiences of events.

Beate Sodian and Claudia Thoermer (2008) tackled some of infants' "seeing leads to knowing/believing" responses. The four conditions they contrived are in Box 8.4. Sodian and Thoermer began by replicating two Onishi and Baillargeon-type (2005) findings (as outlined in Box 8.1) for 16-month-olds. In a baseline true-belief condition, shown at the top of Box 8.4, an agent watched as a toy moved across a table and went into one of two containers (gray or white) located just off the right or left sides of the table. Once the toy went into a container it was out of sight. After some familiarization with these events, then the infant saw either of two test events: The agent reached

BOX 8.4

OUTLINE OF SODIAN AND THOERMER'S 2008 RESEARCH

Each row represents an extended event the infant sees. For example, for True Belief, the infant sees an agent (smiley face) watch while a ball rolls into (and is hidden within) a box. Infants see only one of the tests events at a time, where the agent is present (smiley face) and reaches into either the gray or white box. In test events, the agent reaches but then the action freezes with her hand halfway into a box, and no object is visible or retrieved. A smiley face means the agent is present, looking. A crossed-out face means the agent is absent (and cannot see).

into the correct (gray) box or the agent reached into the other, incorrect (white) box. As expected, infants looked significantly longer at incorrect than correct test trials.

A contrasting ignorance condition (second task in Box 8.4) showed the expected results as well. In the same setup, the agent was first visible and saw the toy on the table but then went away and did not see the entire toy movement and hiding. After this two-part presentation, then again the infants saw either of the two test events. Here infants looked equally at correct (reach gray) and incorrect (reach white) trials, again showing that the infants understood the ignorant person would not know which of the two boxes was correct and so could appropriately search in either place. This parallels the findings from the ignorance condition of Scott and Baillargeon (2009) discussed previously.

The key conditions come next, true-belief-delay conditions. These are indeed true-belief conditions, but with a two-part presentation phase parallel to *ignorance*. As shown in Box 8.4, similar to *ignorance*, for one part of the two-part event the agent was present and for one part absent. Note, however, that the agent was always present for the critical part of the hiding—present and watching as the toy went into the (gray) box. In both of these conditions, however, infants looked equally at reach-gray or reach-white test events.

Thus 16-month-olds acted as if these true-belief-delay conditions were the same as ignorance conditions (an ignorant agent could search either place) and not the same as the other, original, true-belief condition. The infants' ability to register ignorance was, thus, clearly limited. It was appropriately linked to the agents' absence in the ignorance condition, but inappropriately, similarly linked to the agent's absence (at noncritical points) in the true-belief-delay conditions. Thus, sufficient absence was a cue to "ignorance" even though the agent saw the critical event. In some sense, then, infants seemed to be tracking and considering whether the agent had sufficient *engagement* with the object/event or not, rather than if they had information-based knowledge in the adult sense.

One might be worried that in the first true-belief-delay condition, where there is a delay between the agent's seeing the critical event and then searching, the delay just interfered with the infants' memory of the critical agent-viewing event. So maybe the delay just confused infants who then displayed null results (they looked at both test events equally). This is unlikely because in the other true-belief-delay condition, the delay is before the critical events, and no more time passes between the critical agent-viewing event and the test events than was there for the original true-belief condition (where infants responded appropriately). The combination of both before and after delay conditions makes several other alternative interpretations unlikely as well.

Of course, it remains true that data that yield null effects—equal looking at both test events—present some worries. (Perhaps in some way or other infants just got confused in these delay conditions.) Fortunately, James Stack and Charles Lewis (2011) conducted a complementary study focusing on false belief (whereas Sodian & Thoermer, 2008, focused on true belief vs. ignorance). You will see also that, where for Sodian and Thoemer's focal conditions the agent was *absent* for some noncritical part of the events, for Stack and Lewis the agent was *present* for a noncritical part of the events.

The key conditions are outlined in Box 8.5, false belief and ignorance false positive. In each there is a four-part initial presentation, followed by two test events. *False belief* is almost identical to Onishi and Baillargeon (2005). The target male agent sees a toy move into the gray box, the agent goes away, and first is absent for a moment while the toy remains in the gray box, and moreover remains absent while the toy is transferred to the other white box. In ignorance false positive, the agent is absent for an identical amount of time as in false belief, but at a different, noncritical part of the transfer sequence. As shown in Box 8.5, the four-part sequence here is the following: The agent is present and

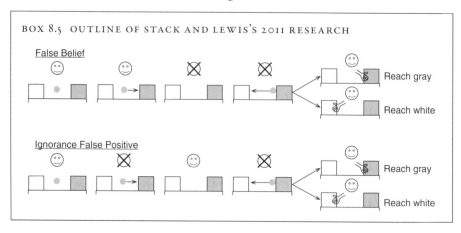

BOX 8.5 OUTLINE OF STACK AND LEWIS'S 2011 RESEARCH

sees the toy, but the agent does *not* see the toy move into the gray box; then he reappears briefly while the toy *remains* hidden in the gray box; then he goes away and is absent for the transfer of the toy to the white box.

So on the basis of belief alone (reflected in seeing leads to believing or knowing), infants should look longer at reach-white events in the false-belief condition (expecting instead the agent to search at gray on the basis of her false belief). But in ignorance false positive, as the agent is ignorant, infants should look equally at reach-gray and reach-white event (just as they do in the ignorance conditions of Sodian & Thoermer, 2008, and also Scott & Baillargeon, 2009). In fact, 14-month-olds and 18-month-olds responded to *false belief* and *ignorance false positive* identically. In both cases, they looked longer to reach-white events. Presumably, engagement for equal amounts of time by both agents when the toy was in the gray box led infants to read both agents' "knowledge" similarly. Both were engaged with the object at gray, and neither saw it move to white; as a result, neither should expect the object to now be at white (and so the infant looks longer when the agent reaches to white).

Of course, to us adults, the false-positive agent should not know the toy was in gray or white; he did not see it hidden anywhere, he is ignorant. He was, however, engaged for awhile with the situation while the toy was in the gray box (before its moving to the white box).

Note here that the infants in the contrasting ignorance-false-positive condition do not provide null results—they do not look equally at both the reach-gray and reach-white test events (as they did in Sodian & Thoermer, 2008). They respond systematically—just as in *false belief*, infants in *ignorance false positive* look significantly longer when the agent reaches to white. But from a full-fledged belief understanding, this is inappropriate. Again, the infant's (fast, crude) tracking of an agent's belief- or knowledge-like states evidences clear limits; it erred.

CONCLUSIONS

Infant beginnings are undoubtedly crucial to any developmental account. At the same time, regardless of what the infant data show, preschool understandings, as they emerge and change in the preschool years, are demonstrably important. Crucial, foundational theory-of-mind understandings are evident in infancy (although we are still discovering their nature and limits) and additionally evident in the belief-desire understandings of 3-, 4- and 5-year-old children. At the least, emergence in the years 2 to 6 of more full-fledged and considered understandings predicts various everyday childhood social actions and interactions (as shown in Chapter 3). It is preschool theory of mind—full-fledged, flexible, belief-desire reasoning and explanation—that shapes social action.

That said, the infant false-belief research is intriguing and important. It is also notably incomplete. It focuses almost completely on infants' successes, leaving us with little information as yet about infants' errors and the limits to their initial conceptions. In fact, I suspect the published data encompass a "file drawer" problem: Successful demonstrations of infant "false-belief" understandings are published; unsuccessful ones are in various file drawers, unpublished. Regardless, more comprehensive data on infants' errors and limits would clarify their successes.

The infant false-belief work is also, I believe, overinterpreted. Infants can do much with only a desire-awareness understanding, including perform correctly on most, perhaps all, infant "false-belief" tasks. Moreover, as I have argued throughout this book, we need detailed developmental data and comparisons to understand the key issues; the infant false-belief studies, however, almost always examine infants in some single age group—13-month-olds in this study (Surian et al., 2007), 15-month-olds in that one (Onishi & Baillargeon, 2005), and 18-month-olds in still another (Scott & Baillargeon, 2009).

In spite of these crucial omissions in the available infant database, I think a fuller developmental account is emerging from the empirical mists. So, in the next chapter, I will sketch a proposal—a theory theory proposal—for understanding infant developments and for tying together infant beginnings and later developments.

NOTES

1. Scott and Baillargeon (2009) attempted to rule out a knowledge-ignorance (i.e., desire-awareness) interpretation in their Experiment 3. The specific "ignorance" hypothesis they tackle, however, is that infants of this age will reason that if the agent is ignorant, she will search *incorrectly*, and she'll be wrong. They show instead that if the agent is ignorant, infants seem to expect she will search randomly. This is fine; in fact, Principles 1–7 appropriately work so that infants could expect the ignorant agent to go to either location first.

Of course, some have claimed that infants' and children's early understanding of ignorance does imply an ignorant agent will act incorrectly (Fabricius & Khalil, 2003; Southgate, Senju, &

Csibra, 2007). That is, for infants and young children an ignorant actor must *necessarily* choose wrong. I, like Scott and Baillargeon (2009), think this is unlikely; and indeed, in ignorance conditions, this is not how infants behave.

2. Luo and Baillargeon (2010) proposed a very different sort of dual-systems account, essentially similar to Leslie's (1994) ToBy (theory of body) versus ToM (theory of mind) account.

3. System 1 could sensibly apply not only to an agent searching for objects but also naming objects. The agent would be construed as registering the object then naming it. Infants could also check to see if the namer was registering an object at all. If the agent was not registering an object, the infant would not take the agent's verbalization to be a naming event. (Desire-awareness understanding of agents would similarly be adequate and helpful for guiding the infant's word learning.)

9

Origins and Development

HOW DO INFANT and childhood theory-of-mind research and developments fit together? That is, having distinguished infant and preschool understandings as substantially different (e.g., one dealing with desire-awareness, the other with belief-desire understandings; one dealing with quick belief-like registrations, the other with belief representations), how do the two systems relate? Indeed, more generally, how does early infant understanding relate to later cognitive acquisitions? This is a key contemporary question for theorizing about all cognitive development. Research on theory of mind is a crucial forum for addressing, and understanding, this issue.

To begin with, empirically, it is now clear that infant social-cognitive understandings do predictively relate to later preschool ones. Several studies have now shown that infant attention to intentional action in looking-time studies predicts later theory of mind (Aschersleben, Hofer, & Jovanovic, 2008; Wellman, Phillips, Dunphy-Lelii, & LaLonde, 2004). In essence, how long infants attend to intentional action, in displays very much like those in Box 1.1 in Chapter 1, predicts their later performance on false belief as well as other preschool theory-of-mind tasks.

We know, however, that infant attention to perceptual-object displays (such as familiar vs. novel objects and images) in looking-time studies predicts later IQ (Bornstein & Sigman, 1986; McCall & Carriger, 1993). These perceptual-attention findings are consistently interpreted as demonstrating developmental continuity in general information processing, such as memory encoding or executive function. Do the predictions from infant intention understanding to preschool theory of mind simply reflect continuity in such general cognitive processing, or are they more specific to a domain of social cognition? In the most comprehensive study to date, my colleagues and I showed that infant attention to intentional action at 10 to 12 months predicted later theory-of-mind understanding in the same children at 4 years (essentially false-belief understanding on standard tasks) even when IQ, language competence, and executive functioning were factored out (Wellman et al., 2008). Moreover, infant attention to physical-action displays does not predict later theory of mind (Yamaguchi, Kuhlmeier, Wynn, & van-Marle, 2009).

Thus, social-cognitive understanding evidences distinctive infant-to-preschool continuities; infant understanding of persons in terms of their intentions is not only early achieved, it is formative for further developmental advances in theory of mind. In fact, Claudia Thoermer and her colleagues (Thoermer, Sodian, Vuori, Perst, & Kristen, 2012) recently showed a direct link between infant performance on infant "false-belief" tasks and later theory of mind. In their study, infant looking at displays very much like those in Onishi and Baillargeon (2005; see Box 8.1) at 18 months (looking measured via eye tracking in this study and not merely total looking time) longitudinally predicted preschool false-belief performance at 4 years.

Establishing that infant and preschool understandings relate is important. For example, a strong, separatist version of a dual-systems proposal, such as Ian Apperly's (2011), envisions that the two systems do not relate much at all. The fast, efficient, implicit system 1 works its own way (and appears early); the slow, considered, explicit-reflective system 2 works in its own separate way (and emerges later). In principle, system-2 inferences are dissociated from the system-1 registrations; the two systems run parallel to each other. Yet empirically, the systems, instead of being completely separate, have some demonstrable, longitudinal links. At the least, in some fashion, the initial (rigid, registration) system seems to be contributing to or setting up the later (flexible, inferential) system. So, echoing a point from Chapter 8, we want an account that predicts neither too much continuity nor too much discontinuity. Moreover, I think we want an account that honors domain separation (between early naïve psychological understanding vs. understandings of the physical world, e.g.) but does not claim too much separation either.

CORE KNOWLEDGE?

To sketch an account of the sort I think we need, I begin, in contrast, with Elizabeth Spelke's influential formulations about core knowledge (e.g., Spelke, 2003). Core knowledge provides Spelke a way to describe the major, differing sorts of things that infants understand: their initial systems of knowledge. Her characterization also uses the infant understandings to splice together human cognition with that of other mammals and to splice together infant knowledge with adult knowledge and minds. This is an ambitious project, and a needed one, and for this reason alone Spelke's core-knowledge proposals deserve serious attention. But I believe core knowledge as Spelke describes it, although providing a serviceable characterization of several infant beginnings that shape human conceptual development, does so at the expense of too much discontinuity (between infant core and later understandings) and too much separation (e.g., between infant understanding of intentional agents and infant understanding of inert, physical objects). That is, Spelke claims her systems of core knowledge are rigidly separate, are not only apparent in infancy but remain unchanged over the course of development, and indeed are shared by humans with all mammals. Core knowledge constitutes understandings that are "evolutionarily ancient" and that "persist over human development" (Spelke & Kinzler, 2007, p. 90). In contrast, I think that early infant theory-of-mind understandings cannot be so easily divorced from various physical understandings, can change remarkably over human development, and cannot be granted so easily to all primates, let alone all mammals. Thus, I prefer the phrase foundational knowledge (rather than core knowledge) for what I mean (see, e.g., Wellman & Gelman, 1998).

INITIAL REPRESENTATIONS AND LEARNING MECHANISMS

Any developmental account must specify both initial states of the organism and mechanisms of development—origins and development. You can't do without either of these, although of course you can have richer or leaner starting states and richer or leaner development. Any account, such as theory theory, that emphasizes developmental learning must include initial states and learning mechanisms that change the initial states into later ones. So, the crucial questions concern how we characterize the starting state and the learning mechanisms. Spelke (e.g., 2003), in her core-knowledge account, provides characterizations of both sorts.

Initial Representations

I agree that human cognition cannot merely reflect "a single learning system that copes with all the diversity of life," nor can human cognition reflect a huge collection of "myriad special-purpose systems and predispositions" (Spelke & Kinzler, 2007, p. 89). Human cognition does not begin with fully domain-general learning or with massive modularity. Instead, "humans are endowed with a small number of separable systems" (Spelke & Kinzler, 2007, p. 89), perhaps the ones Spelke has called core knowledge. Roughly, Spelke often identifies four core-knowledge systems, ones for representing objects, agents, numbers, and places. That is, core knowledge includes understanding inanimate, material objects and their mechanical interactions; understanding agents and their intentional actions; understanding sets and their numerical relationships of enumerating, adding, and subtracting; and understanding geometric relationships including certain forms of spatial layout and localization (Spelke & Kinzler, 2007, 2009). These encompass a near-enough shorthand list of systems that are important, separable, and that appear early in development.

A first and crucial question concerns how separate are these systems? Very separate, according to Spelke (2003), to the extent that the entities in each domain (e.g., material objects vs. intentional agents) and the processes that account for interactions among entities within each domain (e.g., mechanical causation vs. intentional causation) do not intersect. Core-knowledge systems are "*encapsulated*: the internal workings of each system are largely impervious to other representations and cognitive processes" (Spelke, 2003, p. 291). And they are "*isolated* from one another: representations that are constructed by different systems do not readily combine together" (Spelke, 2003, p. 291).

Agents Versus Objects

To illustrate, Elizabeth Spelke and Katherine Kinzler (2007) began by describing a core system that represents material objects and their interactions that "centers on the spatiotemporal principles of cohesion (objects move as connected and bounded wholes), continuity (objects move on connected, unobstructed paths), and contact (objects do not interact at a distance)" (Spelke & Kinzler, 2007, p. 89). Then they described a "second core system [that] represents agents and their actions" (p. 90). Because these systems are defined as encapsulated and isolated from one another, "spatio-temporal principles do not govern infants' representations of agents, who need not be cohesive, continuous in their paths of motion, or subject to contact in their interactions" (Spelke & Kinzler, 2007, p. 90).

Clearly, an initial understanding of intentional agents cannot completely overlap with that of merely physical objects because intentional actions are not merely physical actions within the object world—they are goal directed—and intentional agents are propelled into action not merely by object contact—their actions can be self-initiated. Moreover, intentional agents can influence other agents at a distance via language, imitation, pointing, and the like. Research with infants shows that they know that agents and intentional actions work in these not-merely physical ways.

Importantly, however, for adults, intentional agents, although not merely physical, are nonetheless prototypically physical (and biological) entities too. (Adults can think of nonphysical agents, such as ghosts; but ordinary human and animal agents are physical and biological entities as well as psychological-intentional ones.) Force contact (e.g., winds), gravity, continuity, and solidity (e.g., inability to ooze through physical barriers) apply to human agents just as they do to (most) physical objects because even thinking-wanting, human agents are material objects, albeit very special ones. This is clear not only to adults but also to 3- and 4-year-olds (Hickling & Wellman, 2001; Schult & Wellman, 1997). Spelke's claim (e.g., 2003; Spelke & Kinzler, 2007) for infancy, in contrast, is a radical, "separatist" one: This sort of integrated, intersecting understanding (that human agents are also physical objects) does not apply to young infants whose core-knowledge systems are fully isolated and encapsulated.

One study Spelke has often cited favorably (e.g., in Spelke & Kinzler, 2007) in support of her contention that, for infants, human agents are not also physical objects is that of Valerie Kuhlmeier and her colleagues Paul Bloom and Karen Wynn (Kuhlmeier, Bloom, & Wynn, 2004). In that study, in a physical-object condition, 5-month-old infants understood that a single physical object (a small solid block) could not go behind an occluding barrier then jump through time or space across a visible gap to appear emerging from behind a second separate barrier. Instead, in the case of such apparently discontinuous motion across a physical gap, infants infer there must be two identical objects rather than one—one that moved behind the first barrier and a second one appearing from behind the second barrier. Following this reasoning, when shown continuous object motion, infants expected one object (not two); but when shown discontinuous object motion, infants expected two objects. In contrast, 5-month-olds apparently did not make the same inference for human agents; when a person went behind a first occluding barrier, did not appear within the gap, but then reappeared from behind the second screen, infants seemed not to infer that there were two identical people rather than one.

Note, however, that to be realistic, the test events for human agents in this study used a pair of identical twins. Surely, individuating and inferring the presence of two identical twins is more difficult and odd than individuating and inferring two identical blocks. Physical objects often look alike (identical cars, socks, forks, blocks); 5-month-olds rarely (if ever) encounter identical twins; and infants are specially oriented to individuating people as different, via their differing faces, voices, hair, and manners. Moreover, human movements, albeit continuous, are often indirect, and so can appear to be (sensibly) discontinuous, as when a person goes out one door but returns via another.

A better study to consider, to my mind, is that by Rebecca Saxe and her colleagues (Saxe, Tzelnic, & Carey, 2006). Saxe, Tzelnic, and Carey (2006) examined infants' understanding of the solidity of objects. Their 5-month-olds were habituated to either a toy train or a human hand moving behind an occluder that hid part of its path of motion. Then for test events, a solid wall was ostentatiously placed behind the occluder. There were two conditions constituting two types of test events: one with a narrow solid wall (narrow enough so that a hand or train could remain behind the occluder yet bypass the wall) and one with a wide solid wall (wide enough that it touched the back of the occluder, so nothing could go around it). For both physical objects and humans, understanding solidity meant understanding that the train, or human hand, could pass behind the occluder for the narrow-wall test event (expected event) but could not pass behind the occluder for the wide-wall test event (unexpected event).

These 5-month-olds looked significantly longer at the unexpected event *both* for the toy train (a physical object) *and* for the human hand (an intentional agent). Thus, they expected both objects and human agents to be physically solid and so unable to move through another solid physical object. Saxe, Tzelnic, and Carey (2006) concluded that "the challenge for infants…may not be in perceiving that humans are simultaneously intentional agents and material objects… but in seeking to understand how they can be so" (p. B7).

In this vein, it's informative to consider a different set of studies by these same authors (Saxe, Tzelnic, & Carey, 2007). In these studies, 9-month-olds saw an inert physical object (a beanbag) repeatedly fly out on a curvilinear path from behind a screen and land in the middle of a small stage. At test, infants were shown two potential causes of the event: a human hand or a physical toy train. If infants understand that a hand can easily cause small inert objects to loft into the air, but a toy train cannot, they should look longer when the beanbag's flight appeared to be caused by the train (unexpected) than when it appeared to be caused by the hand (expected). This is what they did.

This study takes its place among several (e.g., Meltzoff, 1995; Woodward, 1998) that have shown infants can distinguish agents (hand) and physical objects (train), but this study further showed that infants see agents as physically causing the motion of physical objects—the hand launched the beanbag. Indeed, Alan Leslie (1982) showed that a crucial piece of this knowledge was available to 5-month-olds, who understand that hands can lift and shift physical objects *and* that physical contact is needed as part of such intentional action. In some sense, that infants understand agents causally affect material objects is unsurprising—as noted in Chapter 6, intentional actions routinely intervene on the physical world. But, in the extreme, on the strong, agent-object, separatist construal apparently encompassed by core knowledge, because agents are conceptually isolated from the physical object causation core-knowledge system, it should be argued that infants have no clear expectations as to agents as causes of physical object motions at all. Yet they do.

In sum, I am convinced that infants do *not* have entirely different modes of construal for physical objects and intentional agents. For infants, human agents are not merely physical objects; but they are physical objects nonetheless. Intentional actions require intentional agents but agents with physical properties whose actions have material (as well as intentional) consequences. Contrary to Spelke's claim of strict isolation, representations of intentional agents, or at least intentional human agents, readily combine with those of material objects in that agents as material objects easily interact causally with other material objects (even inert physical objects).

An Alternative Proposal

Rather than core knowledge's strict segregation of intentional agents and material objects, it seems more correct to me that infants see agents and objects as integrated, crosscutting entities. In what senses might they do this? In part, I think agents and objects are integrated for them via the overlapping causal roles they can assume. To flesh this possibility out more concretely, consider first the linguistic roles of causal agent and causal patient encompassed in numerous semantic systems. In the sentence "John hit the truck," John is the causal agent and the truck is the causal patient. In the sentence "The truck hit John," the truck is the causal agent and John is the causal patient. For the current discussion, it is potentially confusing that there are two different uses of the term *agent* to contend with here: There are thinking, intentional beings, which I'll call intentional agents in keeping with the discussion to this point; and there is the semantic role of the causer of a causal interaction, which I'll call the causal agent. Intentional agents, but *also* mere physical objects, can be causal agents; intentional agents, but also mere physical objects, can be causal patients.

Within such a semantic system, it is clear that intentional agents and mere physical objects are distinctive sorts of entities. Nonetheless, they overlap in that both can play the role of causal agent (and causal patient). Moreover, they are connected in that intentional agents (in the role of causal agents) can intervene on physical objects (as their patients) and vice versa. I think babies understand something like this; in a larger causal terrain, intentional agents and physical objects are distinctively different yet (partly) overlapping in kind and clearly connected in interaction.

I use this example to make two points. First, minimally, this example underwrites the claim that understandings of intentional agents and physical-material objects need not be (and are not) isolated and encapsulated in the way core knowledge describes; not for infants, just as not for children and adults. Second, more expansively, I use this example to begin to outline an alternative view from which infant's recognition of the distinctions *and* connections between agents and objects may be understood. In short, infants are not simply fixated on the differences between intentional agents and physical objects; they are aware of crucial overlaps and connections as well, and in particular causal connections.

Agents Versus Social Partners

Given overlaps and connections between infants' understanding of agents and objects, it is useful to consider an overlap between infants' understanding of agents with a different candidate "core knowledge" system: infant understanding of social groups and partners. Here, Spelke and Kinzler (2007) asked

> Are there other core knowledge systems, with roots in our evolutionary past, that emerge in infancy and serve as foundations for learning and reasoning by children and adults? Recently, we have begun to investigate a fifth candidate system, for identifying and reasoning about potential social partners and social group members. (p. 91)

In investigating this fifth system, Spelke and her colleagues have focused their research on the overt cues infants use to assign persons to groups—race, gender, and common language. Using such cues, infants categorize persons as us or them and prefer others who are categorized as like them (Kinzler, Dupoux, & Spelke, 2007; Shutts, Roben, &

Spelke, 2013)—"my in-group, or us" versus "that out-group, or them" (Spelke & Kinzler, 2007, p. 92).

For Spelke, the status of this sort of social reasoning as a core-knowledge system remains provisional and not fully characterized; it is a hypothesis in need of further tests (see Spelke & Kinzler, 2009). But she is not alone in hypothesizing a knowledge domain referring to social groups and social actions, beyond a domain of psychological agents with intentional actions and minds. Thus, Scott Atran (1996) states, "People from a very early age and throughout their adult lives seem to think differently about different domains, including the domains of naïve physics, naïve biology, naïve psychology, and naïve sociology" (p. 217). In distinguishing naïve psychology from naïve sociology, Atran follows Larry Hirschfeld (1996, 2013); and in this account, naïve psychology, or theory of mind, is based on attribution of "intentional relationships to one another's beliefs, desires, and actions" (Atran, 1996, p. 217), whereas naïve sociology is based on "group assignments (e.g., kinship, race) that specify a range of deontological obligations and contractual actions" (Atran, 1996, p. 217; see also Kalish, 1998).

Deontic reasoning concerns what someone may, should, or may not, should not, do, and so includes sociomoral conceptions of good and bad social actors, actions, and groups (us vs. them) as well. Somewhat similarly, several scholars have argued for an innate "moral faculty" (Harman, 1999; Hauser, 2006) separate from an innate psychological faculty. It certainly is conceivable that there could be separable core knowledge systems for reasoning primarily about intentional agents and intentional actions versus reasoning about social actors and sociomoral interactions. Again, however, a key question is how separate are these core (or, better, foundational) knowledge systems?

Joan Miller and I (Wellman & Miller, 2008) argued at length that, conceptually, the sociomoral could not be easily or neatly distinguished from the intentional—they overlap. Moreover we reviewed considerable evidence that by the preschool years, children and adults see the two as inextricably interlinked. Again, however, à la Spelke (2003), the initial systems could potentially be rigidly separate in infancy. At the time of our article (Wellman & Miller, 2008) there was surprisingly little research on infants' social understandings of sociomoral actions or preferred social partners. This has changed strikingly over the last few years, however, with an outpouring of research on the sociomoral understandings and preferences of infants (Banaji & Gelman, 2013). Research by Kiley Hamlin and her colleagues Karen Wynn and Paul Bloom (see Hamlin, 2013, for a review) has been seminal in this effort.

In a prototypic study, an infant sees little morality plays, such as a scenario in which a target puppet tries but fails to achieve a goal, and then a Helper aids or a Hinderer obstructs the target's success. To be more concrete, say a pig tries to open a box to get a treat and a Helper frog aids the pig to open the box, or a different-looking Hinderer frog slams the box shut. Infants as young as 3 months prefer Helpers over Hinderers—for example, they choose the Helper frog puppet to play with themselves (Hamlin, Wynn, & Bloom, 2010). And by 6 months, infants positively evaluate Helpers—choosing to have the experimenter reward Helpers—and negatively evaluate Hinderers—having the experimenter punish them or scolding the Hinderers themselves (e.g., Hamlin, Wynn, & Bloom, 2007; Hamlin, 2012).

Adults of course do not just evaluate actors in terms of the surface help–hurt features of their acts, but in terms of the agents' intentional-mental states: for example, whether the Hinderer frog intended obstruction or whether the Helper frog was aware or unaware of the consequence of his social actions. This is a key way that the intentional and the sociomoral overlap—only voluntary, knowing acts are subject to certain forms of praise or sanction, obligation, or permission (Wellman & Miller, 2008). And preschoolers as well as adults understand this.

Do infants consider actors' mental states when evaluating or partnering with them? By 10 months they clearly do. Hamlin (2013) showed infants a scenario in which the target puppet (e.g., the pig) repeatedly liked one toy of two available toys. Then the pig lost access to both toys; each was secured behind its own closed door. At this point, two frogs opened the doors, one each. In one condition, these two frogs had been onstage from the start and so had seen the pig's preference. In this case, infants preferred the door-opening frog that allowed the pig access to his preferred object. In the other condition, both frogs had been offstage, so neither could see the pig's initial preferences; the door openers were ignorant. In this case, infants preferred both door openers equally—the one who provided the pig access to his preferred toy as well as the one who provided access to the other toy instead. So, even 10-month-olds understood that the nature of sociomoral acts depend on the mental-intentional states of the actors; they categorized, as well as preferred, social partners accordingly. Thus, intentional-agent reasoning overlaps with sociomoral, social group reasoning, just as intentional-agent reasoning overlaps with physical-object reasoning.

I want to reiterate that Elizabeth Spelke's aim in characterizing infants' initial conceptual building blocks is extremely important (e.g., Spelke, 2003; Spelke & Kinzler, 2007). As I argued in my introductory chapter, such building blocks, if empirically validated and properly described, reveal to us the early architecture of the human mind. Moreover, I agree with Spelke that these building blocks (foundational knowledge in my terminology) are both moderate in number and separable to the extent that they carve out initial domains for infant understanding of the world. However, a rigidly separatist view of these initial domains, as not only separable but fully encapsulated and isolated, is conceptually and empirically problematic; it pushes aside rather than solves crucial questions of how infant cognizers reason about humans as agents *and* objects, reason about humans and objects as causes and patients, as well as reason about intentional agents as individual but also social-relational entities.

Learning

Beyond encapsulation and isolation, Spelke has claimed that core knowledge systems appear early, because they are innate. And in at least one article with Kinzler she has specified that in her view, "*innate* means *not learned*" (Spelke & Kinzler, 2009, p. 96). Moreover, Spelke has consistently specified that core knowledge systems do not change in the course of development; they work for adults as they do for infants. In total, according to Spelkian core knowledge, the crucial, early knowledge systems are not learned (not learned rapidly in early infancy, e.g.) and not revised via developmental learnings. "The core knowledge systems found in infants exist throughout human life" (Spelke, 2003, p. 291).

Originally (e.g., Spelke et al., 1992), Spelke claimed that the initial human core knowledge systems were uniquely human, and thus they accounted as well for the uniquely human cognitions we see in science, mathematics, tool manufacture, and the like. More recently, however, Spelke (e.g., 2003) has contended instead that core knowledge is shared with most other mammals, and so she has proposed that distinctly human cognitive achievements require a different source:

> The core knowledge systems found in human infants exist throughout human life, and they serve to construct domain-specific, task-specific encapsulated, and isolated representations for adults as they do for infants. With development, however, there emerges a new capacity to combine together distinct, core representations. This capacity depends on a system that has none of the limits of the core knowledge systems…, for it allows representations to be combined across any conceptual domains that humans can represent and to be used for any tasks that we can understand and undertake. Its representations are neither encapsulated nor isolated, for they are available to any explicit cognitive process. This system is a specific acquired natural language….Natural languages provide humans with a unique system for combining flexibly the representations they share with other animals. The resulting combinations are unique to humans and account for unique aspects of human intelligence. (Spelke, 2003, p. 291)

In short, humans exploit the compositional properties, and in particular, the compositional semantics, of their natural languages to reason across core-knowledge domains, thereby creating new constructs (space–time, antimatter, infinite progressions, and the like).

This proposal encompasses important forms of learning, but it is undermined by a mystery as to just how such learning is supposed to take place. Indeed, it is difficult to see how the compositional properties of language alone could lead to the needed transformations. Suppose I combine the terms (and notions) *natural* and *selection*. This may be helpful, but it leaves unspecified how that leads me to understand Darwinian natural selection. Combination of the terms fails to tell us about the conceptual processes that actually and constructively led Darwin to his insights, or the processes required for a child to come to understand evolution when instructed about it (e.g., Evans, 2001). The linguistic structure affords many, many combinations (such as space–time, or antimatter, or cell phone, but also green idea, hour-long arm, and more); how do we construct and grasp sensible new conceptual visions afforded by the combinations?

Deferring to the compositional possibilities of language, however potent, suffers from the same problem I addressed in Chapter 6 for constructivism: characterizing the learning processes in more precise terms that demonstrably, computationally work. An obvious possible solution is to propose that we need no more than, but no less than, the probabilistic and hierarchical Bayesian algorithms that help resolve the vagueness of constructivism. Those processes, designed to address the creation of new (abstract, theoretical) knowledge, can account for creation of new cross-domain knowledge as well.

Note, however, that unlike Spelke's core-knowledge vision, hierarchical Bayesian learning processes could yield revisions not only across core-knowledge domains but within core-knowledge systems themselves. If subject to those processes, then human foundational knowledge is not unchangeable; it is revisable. It develops. Moreover, this learning could, in principle, be operative in infancy, accounting in part for the establishment of foundational knowledge and the progressive revision of foundational understandings, instead of operating only postinfancy when language comes into play. Why not? Only an insistence that by definition core knowledge is itself unlearned stands in the way.

Infant Social-Cognitive Learning, Again

Under a core-knowledge construal, early core understandings do not depend on experience-dependent learning; they are innate. Especially pertinent to the focus of this book, research on infant false-belief understandings typically takes this same interpretative stance. Thus, according to Alan Leslie (2005), "mental state concepts ('theory of mind') emerge from a specialized neurocognitive mechanism that *matures* [emphasis added] in the second year of life" (p. 459). This is an "automatic, modular, 'instinctual' mechanism" (Leslie, 2005, p. 462). In short, from this perspective, a theory-of-mind mechanism comes online in infancy via maturation rather than by learning (although it influences further learning, e.g., learning of what exact preferences X has or beliefs Y has).

This nativist stance, apparent in core-knowledge accounts and also in infant false-belief research, has an initial appeal. It is tempting to think of young, novice humans as revealing our innate foundations. Crucial to these accounts is that infant understanding of false belief will be apparent if that understanding is assessed via "spontaneous" nonverbal tasks, such as infant looking time or anticipatory-looking tasks (Luo & Baillargeon, 2010; Leslie, 2005). Given that it is assessed in such implicit and less reflective manners, because it is unlearned, then basic implicit false-belief awareness should be apparent early on for all manner of human infants (save, probably, those with autism). Such strict nativist interpretations are reflected in and encouraged by a paucity of findings about how infant social cognition develops and changes in response to experience. But a neat recent study by Marek Meristo and colleagues (Meristo et al., 2012) provides some needed empirical evidence.

Meristo and his colleagues (2012) used anticipatory-looking methods to test the spontaneous false-belief inferences of both hearing infants (19- to 20-month-olds) and, crucially, deaf infants of hearing parents (17- to 26-month-olds). On nativist accounts (a core-knowledge account, a ToMM modular account, etc.), hearing infants' "false-belief" understanding reflects early, innate computations (not experience-dependent learnings). Relatedly then, the understanding of deaf infants should do so as well. This is because those infants have peripheral hearing loss and not the central-neural deficits that might delay maturational timetables in the case of autism.

Intriguingly, however, the findings for the deaf infants in Meristo et al. (2012) were in sharp contrast to such maturational predictions. Hearing infants in that study expected agents' search-actions to be guided by their false beliefs, just as in earlier anticipatory-looking findings for 25-month-old hearing infants (Southgate et al., 2007) and 18-month-old hearing infants (Neumann, Thoermer, & Sodian, 2008). Deaf infants of hearing parents, however, tested with the same implicit and nonverbal anticipatory-looking methods, displayed impairment in their responses—they did *not* anticipate agents' search actions to be guided by their false beliefs.

To account for their findings, Meristo and his colleagues (2012) straightforwardly refer to the differences in communicative and interactive experience that characterize the deaf and hearing infants. Recall that for hearing children, mothers' use of mental-state talk with and about their young infants predicts children's future theory of mind performance on preschool verbal tasks (Meins et al., 2002). But in comparison to hearing infants, direct communication between deaf infants and their hearing parents can be significantly different and impoverished even in the 1st year of life (Moeller & Schick, 2006; Vaccari & Marschark, 1997). Moreover, deaf infants cannot learn indirectly from overhearing mental-state conversations (Akhtar, 2005) among others either.

In sum, the data by Meristo and his colleagues (2012) attest to the impact of experience-dependent learning even on infants' implicit, system-1 understandings of mental-state driven action. And these data, along with the studies of infants' statistical learning within the social-cognitive domain (e.g., Kushnir et al., 2010), suggest more broadly that infant foundational understandings can reflect learning as much as native endowment. In short, even in infancy, children engage in foundational theory-of-mind learning.

A constructivist, Bayesian-learning account of the sort detailed in Chapter 6 provides a needed framework here, and a framework that potentially encompasses both starting state knowledge plus learning mechanisms. Bayesian approaches insist you can't have learning without some initial priors (initial hypotheses) *and* consideration of evidential experiences. From this perspective, infant beginnings provide key raw materials (not unrevisable knowledge systems) for forging increasingly insightful social-cognitive theories.

To be fair, just as all domain-specific accounts can include a base of innately specified representations, all contemporary accounts (modular, core knowledge, and theory

theory) can include a place for learning. Spelke's (2003) core-knowledge account clearly does—via (unspecified processes afforded by) the combinatorial properties of natural language. Contemporary nativist modular accounts also embrace certain forms of learning. Some sorts of modules, modular theorists insist, are to be seen as dynamic learning mechanisms and not merely static computational mechanisms. Leslie (e.g., 1994) began by emphasizing the computational mechanisms needed for ToMM (ToMMechanism). He later claimed that ToMM is also, in part, not merely a computational mechanism; it is a learning mechanism (e.g., Leslie, 2005).

> Experience undoubtedly plays a key role in infants' learning about specific goals (e.g., learning why Mommy sometimes holds a small box over her ear), dispositions (e.g., learning that Daddy prefers coffee over milk), or informational states (e.g., learning about blindfolds or dark glasses). (Leslie, 2005, p. 460)

Fair enough.

Still, important distinctions about forms of learning can be made. In particular, not all accounts embrace anything like constructivist, hierarchical Bayesian learning of the sort explicated in Chapter 6. Only when acquiring knowledge in some domain embodies special hierarchical, constructivist learning processes, then the learning in question is theory-based learning. Only when new knowledge emerges from prior beliefs that are revised on the basis of the interplay between hypotheses and evidence is the learning in question theory-based learning. This is the sort of learning that allows for framework development (Chapters 5, 6) not merely learning of specifics. Thus theory-based, hierarchical Bayesian learning, as outlined in Chapter 6, helps delimit the sort of learning distinctive to theory theory in particular.

GOING FROM SYSTEM 1 TO SYSTEM 2

At the start of this chapter, I summarized the longitudinal data showing that infant looking-time responses predict later preschool theory-of-mind achievement. Thus, infant system-1 registrations must set up preschool system-2 inferences in some fashion. System-2 representations are not simply parallel to system-1 registrations (as Apperly's dual-process model implies), system-2 representation could be inspired and constrained by system-1 registration. How might that work? A Bayesian interplay between hypotheses and evidence that involves both earlier understandings (priors) and accumulating experiences (evidence) that shape later understanding suggests two ways in which the first, efficient system could help shape the second, more explicit system. The first system could both (a) provide prepackaged evidence for, and (b) provide a source of hypotheses for learning and revising the complex, causal network that characterizes preschool theory of mind.

First consider the fast, efficient system's role in prepackaging evidence. Infant understandings, as reviewed in Chapter 8 (as indicators of the first system), have been revealed mostly by examining infants' attention. This is more than just a useful method. Infant attention, as shaped by the early, fast system, determines infants' observations of the social world (their evidence). By looking longer at some things rather than others (e.g., human object-directed actions more than merely biomechanical movements; puzzling actions that violate some initial but limited intentional understandings rather than other actions), young children attend to some social evidence rather than others. This, in turn, shapes the sort of evidence most readily available for preschool theory-building efforts.

Next consider hypotheses. Here (as outlined in Chapter 6 and further considered in Chapter 10), a key issue concerns the learner's formulation of new hypotheses and search through a pool of alternative hypotheses. One source of alternative hypotheses could conceivably be the child's consideration of his or her own implicit hypotheses and preferences. This would constitute a form of something like Annette Karmiloff-Smith's (1992) "representational redescription." For redescription to provide preschoolers with hypotheses, this means that some parts of the second, learned, explicit system must have (at least partial) access to the representations of the first system. Fine. Nothing (other than insisting that the first system is, by definition, encapsulated like a Fodorian mental module or like Spelkian core knowledge) mandates that the fast, efficient system is fully inaccessible to later knowledge building. At a minimum, instead, the second system could inspect the products of the first system. For example, system 2 could in part simply attempt to categorize and understand the child's own social-interactive behaviors and experiences, behaviors and experiences shaped at first by the infant "implicit" system. Any such categorization would provide fodder for more explicit hypotheses.

CONCLUSIONS

Theory of mind is a developmental achievement, an achievement that crucially begins in infancy and also continues in important ways in typically developing children in the preschool years. Achieving theory-of-mind understandings evidences constructivist learning processes, and this is true initially in infancy as much as in later development. Origins and development are not two separate stages, one (e.g., core knowledge) characterizing the prelinguistic and the other characterizing the postlinguistic child. Origins and development merge, and a helpful way to envision this merger is provided by hierarchical Bayesian learning, which integrates hypotheses and evidence along with prior and posterior hypotheses.

Important achievements and learning also take place beyond infancy, and beyond preschool, evident in more advanced theory-of-mind understandings as well. Looking ahead, I discuss these later achievements in Chapters 13 and 14.

10

Evolution, Chimps, and Dogs

NICHOLAS HUMPHREY, IN a provocative series of essays published in 1984, claimed humans should not be characterized as Homo sapiens but as *Homo psychologicus*:

> The ability to do psychology, however much it may nowadays be an ability possessed by every ordinary man and woman, is by no means an ordinary ability . . . [Yet] far from being something which baffles human understanding, the open discussion of one's inner experience is literally child's play to a human being, something which children begin to learn before they are more than two or three years old. And the fact that this common-sense vocabulary is acquired so easily suggests that this form of description is natural to human beings. (Humphrey, 1984, pp. 5, 8)

Humphrey (1984) then went on to tell an evolutionary "just so" story. He claimed that the platform for human intelligence was not bipedalism or a manual facility for dealing with the physical world—tool use—rather, it was increasing facility for thinking about the social world. Humphrey called this the "social intelligence" hypothesis, but it is now usually called the "social brain" hypothesis (Dunbar, 1998). The claim is that human intelligence arose because humans lived in an increasingly complex social world, a social world that formed an escalating impetus for a cognitive arms race whereby increased social life among close groupmates placed a premium on better understanding them (including one's allies and competitors), which promoted further increases in social life and social reasoning.

The best empirical data driving this social brain hypothesis probably comes from studies of the relationship between the volume of brain neocortex and its relation to intelligence and to sociality when species are compared over mammalian and, especially monkey/ape, taxa (e.g., Barrett, Henzi, & Dunbar, 2003, Dunbar, 1993). Much of this research has been conducted by the comparative anthropologist Robin Dunbar and his colleagues.

But research on brain volumes does not directly reveal the evolution of theory-of-mind capacities themselves in our primate forebears. Comparative cognitive-behavioral research with nonhuman primates, and other species as well, however, can shed light on this issue. It can address questions such as what is distinctively human about human cognition? To what extent is theory of mind primarily human or apparent in other animals? And is theory of mind a key to distinctively human cognizing? Comparative cognitive-behavioral research addressing these questions has had an intriguing history over the last 25 years.

BACKGROUND

Historically there have been two competing views of the social-cognitive savvy of non-human primates: rich and lean. Much of the focus has been on chimpanzees who (along with bonobos) are particularly genetically close to humans. So, for illustrative purposes, I focus mostly on chimpanzees. To begin, 30 to 40 years ago, there were fragmentary data coupled with provocative claims by scholars such as Jane Goodall (and her descriptions of chimpanzee "culture"; 1971) and Frans de Waal (and his description of chimpanzee "politics"; 1982). Nifty television programs of Goodall's chimpanzees looking deeply into Jane's eyes, grooming one another, and apparently making tools evoked a clear image of chimpanzees as our brothers. This was a vision reinforced by the first wave of ape language learning studies and pictures from those. There was Washoe, the female chimpanzee, on film, seemingly using almost 300 signs from American Sign Language to talk fluently with Beatrix and Allen Gardner about things, people, and herself. These investigations fostered a wide-ranging belief in profound similarities between humans and apes with regard to social cognition, tool use, the emergence of cultural traditions, and more.

But, Then

However, an accumulating set of rigorous and clever laboratory experiments with chimpanzees, especially by Daniel Povinelli and his colleagues and by Michael Tomasello and his colleagues, resulted in a more detailed, and much leaner, picture. To illustrate, Povinelli and his team conducted an influential series of studies aimed at assessing seven adult chimpanzees' understanding of the psychological causes of behavior, such as perception, intentions, and beliefs (outlined in Povinelli & Eddy, 1996). The research on chimps' understanding of perception—what others see—was the most systematic and telling. Originally designed as a steppingstone to launch further research on understanding of intentions, knowledge, and beliefs, instead the data kept showing little, if any, understanding even of seeing.

Povinelli's many studies (Povinelli & Eddy 1996; Povinelli & Preuss, 1995) had a basic format based on chimpanzees' natural begging gestures—an outstretched hand used by chimps in trying to acquire food from one another. Originally, the apes were trained to enter a laboratory testing room (from their outside exercise yard) and gesture to a familiar trainer seated behind a clear Plexiglas wall separating trainer from chimp. There were several holes in this clear wall but the apes were supposed to use the hole directly in front of the trainer. When they gestured with a begging gesture through that hole, then the trainer praised them and gave them a food reward. All the apes quickly learned to beg through the correct hole to the trainer.

This was unsurprising, but the real purpose of this initial training was to then assess the apes when there were two trainers: one who could see them and one who could not. When faced with trainers who could patently see or not see from a human perspective, would the apes use seeing and not seeing to direct their gestures? So, after their initial training, the apes were tested on a series of contrasts. For example, in one pair of trainers, (a) there was one who sat facing toward the chimp and one facing away (*front vs. back*). In others, (b) there was one with a bucket covering her head and one with the same bucket held beside her head (*buckets*); or (c) one trainer had her hands over her eyes, the other had her hands over her ears (*hands*); and so forth.

In essence, for the front-back contrast, apes gestured to the person facing forward more than chance, but in none of the other conditions did they do so. In this way they were unlike 2- and 3-year-old human children who consistently distinguished numerous varieties of seeing versus nonseeing when tested on very similar tasks.

Povinelli's original studies (e.g., Povinelli & Eddy, 1996), as well as additional ones, seemed best interpreted as indicating that although the apes were clever learners, apt at learning about behavioral regularities, they knew essentially nothing about the mental states (in this case the mental state of perception) that lay behind the behavioral regularities they tracked. For example, consider the front-back comparison again, the one that originally might have seemed as if apes were homing in on the trainers' perception, if any of the comparisons did. Povinelli and his team (in Povinelli & Eddy, 1996) cleverly presented apes a comparison of two trainers, *both* of whose bodies were facing away from the ape, but one with her head twisted forward (looking over her shoulder). The chimps were at chance begging from these two, although to us humans one could obviously see them (head-over-shoulder trainer), and one could not. Apes seemed clearly to have picked up on a regularity that body position could be a cue to being fed (e.g., in the original front-back comparison) but not that *seeing* was the critical factor (still operative for the head-over-shoulder trainer even though the trainer's body was facing away).

In many of these tasks, Povinelli and his colleagues gave the apes numerous trials; and on each trial, the apes got the food reward only if they begged to the "correct" (e.g., seeing, looking-over-shoulder) trainer. For some comparisons, apes could learn who was correct, but it was laborious slow learning that took many, many trials. Children were successful on their very first trials. And in some conditions, even numerous trials did not provoke above-chance performance in chimps. An intriguing comparison of this sort proved to be one trainer with a black blindfold tied over her eyes and another with the same black cloth tied over her mouth (*eyes vs. mouth*). Chimps begged equally to both trainers over many, many trials where they were rewarded only if they begged to the "mouth" trainer. Further studies indicated that as long as equal amounts of the face were covered, apes chose randomly. It did not matter that for one person specifically the eyes were covered.

These apes were clever learners, and they were motivated, often finding some cue to use to their benefit after many trials of effort. But this only further contributed to a compelling picture of chimpanzees as achieving a laborious storehouse of learned regularities, regularities that told them much about others' behavior but failed to penetrate to the underlying minds involved. Essentially, if we utilize the ideas outlined in Chapter 6, we could say that apes engaged in statistical data mining of behavioral regularities rather than anything like theory-based, causal understanding. They used statistical covariations between surface features of the experimenters' behaviors to achieve "shallow" empirical generalizations in the social realm. But they neither achieved nor evidenced theory of mind—they patently failed to understand others' behaviors in terms of understanding mental states. Both Daniel Povinelli, and from their own independent research Michael Tomasello and his colleagues (as summarized in Tomasello, 1999), concluded chimpanzees learned much about the physical and social regularities that governed their worlds, but little if any about the causal principles underlying agents, tools, and events. Indeed, their understanding of the physical world did not rest on underlying causal constructs either (Povinelli, 2000; Tomasello & Call, 1997). The high-water mark of this skepticism was evident in the extensive summary of research from many labs and observations provided by Michael Tomasello and Josep Call in their book, *Primate Cognition* (1997).

Then, Again

Further, clever research, however, turned the tide once more. Much of this research emerged from the efforts of Michael Tomasello and his colleagues (e.g., Hare, Call, Agnetta, & Tomasello, 2000; Tomasello, Call, & Hare, 2003) overturning their own prior, careful, studied skepticism. One now-famous experimental paradigm that helped compel a sea change utilized the setup depicted in Figure 10.1. Two chimpanzees—one a dominant and one a subordinate—were behind doors across an inner room from each other. Food was placed in the inner room, and the doors could be cracked and occluders could be placed so that one or both animals could see the food placement. Shortly after

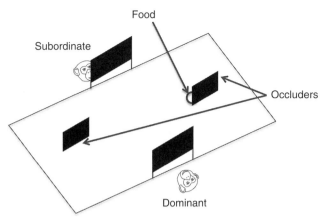

FIGURE 10.1 Depiction of the kind of competitive situation used in research with chimpanzees by Tomasello, Hare, Call and their colleagues (e.g., Hare et al., 2000, 2001). The chimpanzees can see under their half-open doors but not enter until the doors are fully open. The subordinate sees food placed and can also see the dominant. To begin, consider two conditions: informed—the dominant also sees the food placed; uninformed—the dominant cannot see food placed because his or her door is closed. When the doors are opened, the subordinate gets a small head start (not enough to avoid the dominant if the dominant has seen the food placed, but enough to get to the food first if the dominant hasn't seen it).

the food was placed, the doors were fully opened. In short, a piece of food was hidden between a dominant and a subordinate chimpanzee and, as a result of the positioning of certain obstacles, the chimpanzees had different visual access to the food.

This situation was a food competition situation based on the background idea that when dominants and subordinates compete directly for food, the subordinates lose out and defer to the dominants. But in this case, the competition could be controlled. In particular, on some trials the subordinate could see food hidden but the dominant could not versus trials where both saw. Would subordinates respond appropriately to exploit their advantage when they (but not the dominant) had seen, in contrast to their typical deferral when both had seen?

A first crucial result was that when the subordinate could see two pieces of food and the dominant could see only one, the subordinate preferentially targeted the less-risky food that the dominant could not see (Hare, Call, Agnetta, & Tomasello, 2000). Does this mean that chimpanzees can adjust their behavior on the basis of what the other can see—their states of perception and attention? Additional information and control conditions increasingly made it seem that they could and did. For example, recall in Povinelli's experiments described previously, if successful at all, mostly chimps only learned the critical contrasts over many reinforced trials. But in the food competition experiments, subordinates adjusted to the dominant's ability to see (or not see) from the very first trial and in a variety of different situations.

And, as opposed to Povinelli's experiments, where additional conditions (e.g., head-over-shoulder) increasingly ruled in ways that the chimps were just attending to low-level behavioral cues, in the food competition experiments, additional conditions increasingly ruled *out* such low-level hypotheses (as summarized in Tomasello, Call, &

Hare, 2003). For example, first, perhaps in the experiments in which both animals saw one piece of food (and saw the other animal see that food) but only the subordinate saw the other piece, a dominant's mere association with the one piece of food "tainted" it, leading the subordinate to prefer the other one. But in conditions where the dominant saw the food, but then did not see it being hidden, subordinates would go directly for it. Clearly a dominant's association with that food had not tainted it. Moreover, consider a condition in which one dominant had not only seen the food but seen it at Location 1 (maybe tainting any "food-at-location-1"). But, in a control condition, after these initial events, then the dominant's door was completely closed and that dominant chimp was swapped for another dominant. In that case, subordinates would happily go for the food at Location 1. It was not tainted; instead, it was nicely unseen by the relevant dominant and so up for grabs. Second, perhaps it was not vision but mere physical obstruction that chimps were tracking. But in conditions in which the "occluder" was actually transparent, subordinates would not search. That food was obstructed but not invisible to the dominant. Third, Daniel Povinelli, given his expertise with chimps, suggested that in a layout like that in Figure 10.1, for example, the critical cue for the chimps was not whether the food could or could not be seen but whether it was physically close to or in the shadow of an edge (Povinelli, 2000). In the wild and in captivity in large enclosures, chimps avoid foraging at edges and in shadows (perhaps because those are good places for predators to lurk). But in variations of the competition layout that varied seen and not seen but did not employ edges and shadows, seeing and not seeing governed chimps' responses anyway.

Why did this new paradigm show such competence whereas so many prior ones had shown only laborious learning of cue-based regularities? A key ingredient seemed to be competition versus cooperation, a factor I return to later.

PRIMATE SOCIAL COGNITION

Having forged ahead with this particular paradigm, I want to now step back to take a systematic look at contemporary research on nonhuman primates' social-cognitive understanding. First, there is research on their understanding of intentional actions; then their understanding of intentional states of attention or perception; then knowledge; and last belief. From here on, I'll use the term *primates* to refer to nonhuman primates, to keep a simpler terminological contrast with *humans*. For the most part, the primates that have been studied are old world monkeys and great apes.

Primate Intention Understanding

Recall that discoveries about infants' understanding of others' internal states began with demonstrating their understanding of intentions as manifested in observable actions.

Understandings of intentional action are an important point of departure for considering primates as well. Reconsider Box 1.1. Following familiarization with events in which a human agent reaches in an arcing path over a barrier that separates him from a goal object, infants look longer at the indirect than the direct test events. This, in conjunction with several control conditions, demonstrates an understanding of the agent's actions in terms of the agent's intentions. Following familiarization with such barrier events, macaque monkeys also looked longer at the indirect than the direct test event (Rochat, Serra, Fadiga, & Gallese, 2008). In control conditions, after familiarization with actors displaying the same acts with no barrier, macaques looked equally at the indirect and direct test events. These findings support the view that, like human infants, monkeys and apes possess a basic understanding of the goal directedness of action.

For human infants, complementary data came from more active/interactive paradigms that added to the conclusions from looking-time research. As one example, recall the unwilling-unable paradigm described earlier for infants. Tanya Behne and colleagues (Behne et al., 2005) engaged infants in a game in which a woman gave them toys across a table. Interspersed were trials where she held up a toy but did not give it over, sometimes because she was unwilling to do so and sometimes because she was "unable" (e.g., could not extract the toy from a transparent container). Nine- to 18-month-olds behaved more impatiently (e.g., reaching, turning away) when the woman willfully kept the toy than when she was making good-faith efforts to pass it along, although the surface behaviors and outcomes were parallel in both conditions.

This study was actually designed to have a version for chimps as well as human infants. And, similarly, chimpanzees produced more begging behaviors and left the testing room earlier when an experimenter was unwilling to give them food (e.g., offering and withdrawing a grape teasingly) than when she was unable but trying to give them food (e.g., repeatedly dropping the grape; Call, Hare, Carpenter, & Tomasello, 2004). Indeed, in research from a different laboratory, capuchin monkeys left the testing station sooner in response to the actions of an unwilling compared to an unable experimenter (Phillips, Barnes, Mahajan, Yamaguchi, & Santos, 2009). Although the experimenter's actions were remarkably parallel on the surface, chimpanzees and capuchins recognized a difference between the actor's underlying intentions in the two cases. (See Call & Tomasello, 2008, and Rosati, Santos, & Hare, 2010, for reviews of still other related research.)

Primate Understanding of States of Attention

Many primates spontaneously follow the gaze or head orientation of conspecifics or humans. Although it is unlikely that most primate species follow gaze because they understand the nature of visual experience, great apes probably do. In controlled situations, chimpanzees, bonobos, gorillas, and orangutans all follow gaze to distant locations and around barriers (even when it requires physically reorienting their bodies) and visually check back to verify the direction of the looker's gaze (Rosati et al., 2010), just as human 9- to 12-month-olds do (see Chapter 1).

For chimpanzees in particular, the food competition experiments described earlier, utilizing setups such as that in Figure 10.1, tell us still more convincingly that and how chimps assess others' perception and attention.

These abilities to track others' vision in competitive situations are probably not unique to chimpanzees. Rhesus monkeys also show impressive sensitivity to human experimenters' perception and perceptual experiences in competitive food-getting situations (Flombaum & Santos, 2005).

Primate Understanding of Knowledge

Studies further suggest that chimpanzees, in particular, demonstrate an understanding of something about the link between seeing and *knowing*. In extensions of the food-competition situation outlined in Figure 10.1, chimpanzees adjust their behavior not only on the basis of what others currently can and cannot see but also on the basis of what others have and have not seen in the past—what others know or do not know. Subordinates preferentially targeted an occluded piece of food that the dominant was ignorant of (had never seen) or misinformed about (had seen in one place but had not seen moved; Hare, Call, & Tomasello, 2001). So, subordinates took account of the other chimpanzee's past and cumulative visual experiences, beyond just what the dominant chimpanzee could see right now.

To recap, in early research using cooperative-communicative paradigms (in which an experimenter's goal was to share food with the chimpanzee), primates performed poorly and failed to demonstrate awareness of the internal mental experiences of others (as in Povinelli & Eddy, 1996). In paradigms involving competition for food, however, great apes and even monkeys perform much better (as in Hare & Tomasello, 2004). The data are particularly prevalent for, and convincing for, chimpanzees.

Limitations

The overlap between infants and primates in early social-cognitive understandings, often based on very similar tasks and measures, provides good reason to interpret the understandings of humans and nonhuman primates as more deeply, rather than merely superficially, similar. At the same time, although chimpanzees (and some monkeys) understand action as intentional and understand something about the visual experience and even knowledge of others, primates' understandings fall short of children's.

Importantly, there is no evidence that apes go beyond the distinction between knowledge and ignorance to represent the false beliefs of others. This is true even when the false-belief tasks involve competitive situations and require no understanding of communicative intentions (Drew, Ruiz, Mukerji, Goddu, & Santos, 2011; Kaminski, Call, &

Tomasello, 2008; Krachun et al., 2009). Moreover, in the human case, social-cognitive understanding and theory of mind are revealed in numerous, robust acts of pointing, showing, and teaching (Gergely, Egyed, & Király, 2007); yet there is sparse evidence, and only for limited, partial efforts, for anything like teaching in monkeys or apes.

Finally, recall that in the human case, early infant abilities are predictive of older children's more complete mentalistic reasoning (see Chapter 9). These infant predictive findings help validate their earlier social-cognitive abilities as containing true seeds of the later ones, in human ontogeny. Because, 2-, 3-, and 4-year-olds show increasing understandings of agents' perception, desires, knowledge, and beliefs, empirically linked to their earlier understanding of agents' intentions, this provides further reasons to consider their earlier understandings as going beyond mere surface behavioral regularities and penetrating to underlying psychological states. We have no such evidence for apes.

Development

This last observation leads to another factor worthy of serious attention in a book about development: We know next to nothing of the ontogenesis of nonhuman primates' social-cognitive skills. In fact, we know almost nothing about the social-cognitive understandings of juvenile chimps or monkeys, let alone how juvenile understandings develop into adult ones.

Sometimes, demonstration of similar abilities in primates and infants leads scholars to claim innateness. Elizabeth Spelke, in her claims about core knowledge as reviewed in Chapter 9, takes this stance. Thus, according to Spelke's view, infants' capacity to represent and understand agents (and also objects, numbers, etc.) is equivalent to that of primates (e.g., Spelke & Kinzler, 2007). To be clear, however, current comparative analyses are based on essentially three groups: human adults, human young (infants, young children), and primate adults. Yet, full comparisons require at least four groups: primate adults, human adults, human young, and primate *young*. Michael Tomasello and Malinda Carpenter (2005) provided some nice initial findings for three juvenile chimpanzees. But their findings emphasize how little information is available. What if comprehensive research found that for primates, social-cognitive understandings were mostly late-developing, mature insights often limited to animals with extensive training or life experience? Such a finding, intriguing in itself, would change our sense of how to best understand the phylogenesis and ontogenesis of social-cognitive understanding. Perhaps primates, with very reduced competence for theory-based, hierarchical Bayesian learning of the sort described in Chapter 6, require lifespan efforts to come to social-cognitive understandings, and at best come to reduced understandings in reduced contexts, such as food competition. Yet, clearly for humans, social-cognitive understandings begin early and extend widely; they are readily apparent in even quite young humans.

Evolution

Of course, throughout this book, I've argued that human social-cognitive learning requires protracted, cumulative social input and experiences. Perhaps chimps could come to human-like, social-cognitive understandings if they received similar intensive experience; it's just that the needed social input and experiences are more broadly and consistently available for humans. But this can't be the key explanation. Chimps that are raised from birth in human homes, with human "parents" and parenting—so called enculturated chimps—fail to achieve anything like preschoolers' theory of mind. Enculturated chimps are sometimes reported to be better than their chimp-reared cousins on social-cognitive and language tasks (Tomasello, 1999) but nowhere near as competent as even human 2-year-olds.

Although this is often overlooked, evolutionary considerations themselves do *not* point to an innately fixed infant social knowledge system for the human or the primate case. To the contrary, many researchers who actually conduct comparative-evolutionary studies (as opposed to dominant voices within evolutionary psychology such as Cosmides & Tooby, 1994; 2006) have emphasized that the great apes, and even more extremely humans, are distinguished by a long period of immaturity where learning, especially social learning, accumulates in the individual. To emphasize the importance of this point, we need only return to the social brain evolutionary hypothesis. In essence, that idea is that living in complex, close-knit social groups provided an advantage for those species' members who could better track the social "marketplace"—how others can advantage and disadvantage you and your offspring.

But tracking the social marketplace requires tracking a changing social landscape. For example, in matrilocal groups, sisters (who will continue to be in your group) provide better long-term allies than brothers (who at maturity must relocate to a different group). Moreover, if some competing group member has more, or more useful, sisters, this is worth calculating, and it requires much more than a single obvious calculation because someone's sisters might die or be demoted in rank as dominance hierarchies shift over time. Further, it's not just sisters who are visible and obvious right now (ascertained by looking around) but also sisters who are away—for example, foraging—but who will be a force to be reckoned with in the future when they return.

As Robin Dunbar (2013) acknowledged, effective tracking of the social marketplace encompasses a capacity for social learning:

> While it might seem reasonable for the neurological machinery for perceptual processing (e.g., pattern recognition, color recognition) to be modular and hard-wired (after all, the properties of the physical world remain more or less constant), this makes much less sense for something that is inevitably both more serendipitous and more likely to change through time. Who knows how many brothers and sisters you might end up having, and yet the balance between them can radically

affect an individual's optimal social strategy: Sisters might normally be the best allies to have, but if you happen not to have any, then you need to find an alternative substitute among what is available to you (presumably brothers)....If you live in a social world where alliances of this kind are important to either your survival or your ability to reproduce successfully, then you need to be phenotypically more flexible....The only sensible solution is to use experience as a guide for behavior...[and] this involves learning. (pp. 4–5)

In fact, the social brain hypothesis and data fit with an evolutionary emphasis on development and learning (rather than, say, an emphasis on hardwired ToM modules or innately framed, unchanging core knowledge). Humans not only have especially large neocortexes; hand in hand with that we have a specially prolonged period of cognitive immaturity that affords learning and development. And indeed, not only does close-knit sociality predict neocortex volume across species, the proportion of time spent as a juvenile does as well (Joffe, 1997): "In response to increased social complexity...evolution has favored an extension in the amount of time primates spend as juveniles (Joffe, 1997, p. 603).

In short

While the social brain hypothesis offers a functional (i.e., evolutionary) explanation for the evolution of unusually large brains in some species, it inevitably slides over the fact that...learning and social experience must play an important role....Thus, there is an inevitable and important developmental aspect to the social brain hypothesis that has, as yet, received very little attention....In some ways, this is surprising because the whole emphasis of the hypothesis is on managing complex social environments. We would not expect these kinds of capacities to be neurologically hard-wired because the social world is both complex and dynamic. (Dunbar, 2013, p. 4)

SHARING AND HELPING VERSUS ACQUIRING

The food competition situations of Tomasello, Hare, and Call (Hare et al., 2001; Hare & Tomasello, 2004) differ from the food-begging situations of Povinelli (e.g., in Povinelli & Eddy, 1996) in that the two protagonists are not engaged in communicative exchanges (e.g., one chimp does not gaze fixedly or point to an object or location to inform the other), and one protagonist is not trying to help the other (e.g., providing food for the other). In natural situations, chimpanzees rarely share food. Chimpanzees will tolerate others taking food from them, even other nondominants, but essentially only when food is difficult to monopolize anyway ("passive sharing"; Boesch & Boesch, 1989; Gilby, 2006). Mothers will occasionally more actively share food with their own youngsters (Ueno & Matsuzawa, 2004), but this is much rarer than you would think if you based your expectations on the human case in which food sharing is rampant from mother to child, child to mother, and child to child.

In laboratory situations, cooperation between chimps can be "engineered" (Melis, Hare & Tomasello, 2008). For example, two chimps can pull together on a board-like device if that is the only way to get the food positioned on it. But, if the food is positioned in one clump (not predivided), cooperation unravels because one chimp (the dominant) will then typically hog all the results. Very young children will frequently cooperate; and if they cooperate and the spoils are not predivided, they actively attempt to divide them equally (Moore, 2009).

In communicative situations, very young children use gestures (and words) to inform others. In "proto-declarative" communication situations, children simply point things out, and their goal is to get the other to notice rather than to prompt the other to do something for them—in contrast to "proto-imperative" communication (Bates, Benigni, Bretherton, Camaioni, & Volterra, 1979). Proto-declarative communications greatly outnumber proto-imperative ones in very young children (Carpenter et al., 1998). This is so ubiquitous in the human case it almost can go without notice. Young humans from 12 months on even engage in pointing and showing to help *the other person* rather than themselves (Liszkowski, Carpenter, Striano, & Tomasello, 2006). Consistent with the research in Chapter 8 showing that infants track others' knowledge and ignorance, 12-month-olds not only point helpfully to others; they point appropriately and differently to help knowledgeable versus ignorant others (Liszkowski et al., 2006).

In contrast, virtually all ape communications are self-serving. When chimpanzees communicate with humans by pointing, they almost always are trying to get the human to give them (the ape) something or otherwise provide help. Their communications are imperative about 95% of the time (Rivas, 2005). A potential exception might seem to be communicative calls that result in food sharing:

> However, in recent interpretations, even these vocalizations are considered mainly self-serving. Thus, when chimpanzees find food they call so that they can have company while eating, as protection against predators....Importantly, these vocalizations are also given when the entire group is already there and so not in need of any information about the situation—so their function is not to inform. (Warneken & Tomasello, 2009, p. 397)

Helping

A natural forum for informing and sharing is helping more generally. In a series of studies, Felix Warneken and Michael Tomasello have dramatically shown how often and easily very young children help others. In Warneken and Tomasello's early research (e.g., Warneken & Tomasello, 2006), for example, 14- to 18-month-olds interacted with an adult in a quasi-naturalistic situation. Embedded in the interaction were situations like these: The adult dropped an object from a desk and couldn't easily reach it; the adult, with his hands full of books, was stuck at a closet door that he couldn't swing open; the adult couldn't retrieve an object from a closed box, but on the child's side (unknown to the adult) the box was fully open. In these situations, toddlers consistently help—they retrieve the toy, they open the closet door, they point to the hidden opening (Warneken & Tomasello, 2006, 2007, 2008). They do this whether they are praised or not and even if they have to interrupt their own fun activity to help the adult instead. Indeed, even 6-month-old humans discriminate between actors who are "helpers" versus those who are "hinderers," and *prefer* helpers (Hamlin, 2013; Hamlin et al., 2007).

In comparable situations, chimpanzees rarely help (Warneken & Tomasello, 2006). In recent studies, Warneken (2013; Warneken & Tomasello, 2009) has shown, however, several situations in which chimpanzees will help humans (e.g., retrieve an out-of-reach item for a trainer). Notably, such helping occurs in relation to blocked intentional actions directed at objects (and not for food) and involves direct action from the chimpanzees (and not declarative gestures such as pointing). Nonetheless, spontaneous helping is not a uniquely human response.

As Warneken and Tomasello (2009) put it, "From an early age human infants and young children are naturally empathic, helpful, generous, and informative" (p. 401). Understanding others' intentions, actions, desires, and informational situations underpins these robust human activities. The story is different for our nearest primate kin. Both theory of mind and helpful behavior are much more minimally apparent. Chimpanzees do understand others' intentions, actions, and informational states, in part, and especially within competitive situations. Yet chimpanzee helping is vastly less apparent than even the helping of human infants and, when apparent, chimpanzees engage largely in passive rather than active helping. Chimpanzee communication is almost totally imperative; and unlike even the very early communications of human children, is rarely (if ever) declarative. Chimpanzees seek to acquire rather than inform. In total, the data suggest that theory of mind is specially, if not uniquely, human. Moreover, anything like a helpful, communicative theory of mind (e.g., as described by Harris & Lane, 2013, for infants) has a special human trademark.

DOGS

The primate data, and especially how it emerges best from studies of competitive situations with conspecifics rather than situations of cooperation, raise intriguing questions about the distinctively communicative-cooperative flavor of human theory of mind. Intriguingly, recent research with dogs sheds light on this issue.

Whenever I give talks or classes on theory of mind, some dog owner inevitably asserts "my dog understands my mind." I used to be skeptical, thinking that dogs were like "clever Hans"—scrupulously, behaviorally tuned to their owners' cues, an attunement requiring many years of close cohabitation with someone who provides all the opportunities for food, affection, and bonding. The story, however, turns out to be a lot more intriguing.

In brief, dogs are surprisingly good at reading the social and communicative signals of others (humans and conspecifics). For example, they easily read where someone points to show them food, where someone is gazing, and understand the referential meaning of various words and gestures (Hare & Tomasello, 2005; Kaminski, Call, & Fischer, 2004). Dogs do so in controlled situations where a person might walk toward one location but point to another; they avoid forbidden food when the person's eyes are open but not when closed; and they interpret gaze as referential when it is directed at an object/location but not when someone is gazing off in space above that object/location (Hare et al., 2005; Soproni, Miklósi, Topál, & Csányi, 2001). Dogs read such social-communicative intentions correctly on the first trials of novel tasks, and here is a crucial developmental point: They do so as puppies (Hare & Tomasello 2004).

These skills resemble in several ways those of human infants, who correctly read points, gestures, and eye gazes; engage in communicative interactions; and otherwise decode the intentional meanings of others by their first birthday (Harris, 2006; Harris & Lane, 2013). These skills contrast with the inabilities of wolves and chimpanzees on similar tasks. Chimpanzees prove capable of reading others' intentions and attentional reference in situations of competition over food and resources, as just discussed, but are poor in comparison to dogs (let alone humans) in cooperative-communicative situations (Hare & Tomasello, 2005; Povinelli & Eddy, 1996). These skills also contrast with those of wolves, dogs' predomestication ancestors. To be clear, dogs' social-cognitive skills are distinctly limited. They evidence special attention to humans, and to human communicative gestures, much like year-old infants do. But they evidence nothing like the comprehensive blossoming of theory-of-mind capacities that even 2- and 3-year-old children display.

In several papers, Brian Hare and Michael Tomasello (2005; Hare, 2007) have argued that the human-like social-communicative skills of dogs, resembling the initial theory-of-mind capacities of human infants, represent a case of convergent evolution traceable to the domestication of dogs in their long history within human communities. Specifically, they propose a "social-emotional reactivity" hypothesis whereby wild canines who were less fearful of and nonaggressive toward humans were selected by domestication processes over generations. A product of that process was dogs' social-communicative capacities of a more human-like sort. Because dogs/wolves become reproductively mature in 1 to 2 years (instead of 15–20 for humans), then even 500 years of cohabitation with humans would encompass 200–300 generations for dogs (or wolves). That would be plenty of cycles in which evolution could select for and change behavioral (and biological) capacities. This is a multiplier effect exploited by dog breeders, of course.

In fact, a critical piece of evidence for the emotional-reactivity, temperament-evolution hypothesis comes from an intriguing breeding study. The research here utilized a rare population of domesticated foxes selectively bred on a simple criterion—whether they less fearfully and nonaggressively tolerated approach and handling by humans (Belyaev, 1979). In essence, generation after generation of caged foxes had kits on a fur farm facility in Siberia. Each generation of kits was divided into two populations. In the target population, foxes were tested and, in each generation, those that were less fearful of and less aggressive toward their human attendants were bred together. Then their kits were tested, and the least fearful and aggressive of *that* generation were interbred. And so on, again and again. Other, control foxes continued to be bred randomly in this regard.

After generations, the target population displays little fear or aggression to humans, naturally enough. But additionally these foxes show other signs of dog-like domestication. Crucially, fox kits from this population, tested on basic pointing and gaze-following tests, were as skilled as age-matched puppies in using human social cues (Hare et al., 2005). Control foxes performed poorly (although as well as domesticated foxes on a non-social-cognition task). In short, domestication involved, centrally, attainment of a special temperament, and a *by-product* of that temperament was special communicative-cooperative, social-cognitive skills. By hypothesis, a special temperament might help account for the trademark helpful-communicative theory of mind in humans too.

It is difficult to test this hypothesis in any evolutionary-historical sense. But the hypothesis leads to a related, developmental hypothesis that is intriguing in its own right. Perhaps, parallel or similar temperament factors might aid children in the ontogenetic achievement of theory of mind. Of course, there is a big difference between "in evolution, X caused Y" and "in ontogeny, X causes Y." Yet one can inspire hypotheses about the other. The relation of temperament to human social reasoning and development is intriguing at several levels, but until recently largely unaddressed.

One way to shed light on these issues would be to ask whether children with certain types of temperament become more skilled than others in social understanding. Using longitudinal data, my colleagues and I did just this (Wellman et al., 2011). We explored the predictive contribution of several specifically chosen temperament dimensions for the achievement of a key theory-of-mind milestone in the preschool years—false-belief understanding.

Temperament and Theory of Mind

Temperament differences, along varied dimensions, are apparent in infancy with continuity and change occurring over development. Temperament variation influences children's social interactions and social adjustment (among other things), especially in the preschool years (Rothbart & Bates, 1998). Because social interactions contribute to and shape childhood theory-of-mind understandings, children's social-interactive temperaments might also influence their acquisition of theory of mind. For example, because increased participation in social interactions can inform children about persons and minds, then even negative interactions (e.g., aggression) might aid children's theory-of-mind development. If so, then aggressive-externalizing temperament might positively predict later theory of mind; and shy-withdrawn temperament might negatively predict later theory of mind. Equally, however, perhaps heated, reactive social interactions (as in aggression) are negatively related to later, more sophisticated theory-of-mind understanding; whereas a shy-observant, less reactive approach to social interaction could conceivably aid children in more reflectively understanding others and, in comparison, themselves.

This discussion shows that there might be numerous possible relations between temperament and theory-of-mind development. But, following from the dog research and its emotional reactivity hypothesis, my colleagues and I specifically hypothesized that certain forms of social-emotional reactivity (e.g., aggressiveness, fearfulness) would interfere with childhood development of theory of mind. Conversely, a less reactive, more observant temperament could enhance theory-of-mind understanding.

We assessed almost 150 preschoolers at age 3½ and then again at age 5½ years (Wellman et al., 2011). At 3½, mothers completed a series of temperament questionnaires; and at 3½ and again at 5½, children took theory-of-mind tests (essentially false-belief tests) and also, for control purposes, they had an often-used measure of verbal IQ (WPPSI Vocabulary; Wechsler, 1989) and several executive function (EF) tests.

To make a long story short, temperament at age 3½ predicted theory-of-mind achievements at age 5½ and did so after numerous controls. In particular, aggressive temperament predicted relatively worse theory-of-mind development; and shy, observant temperament predicted relatively better theory-of-mind development. These predictive relations held even when various control factors (verbal IQ, EF) were included as well. Other temperament factors—such as sheer activity level—did *not* predict later theory of mind (but activity level at 3½ did predict worse executive functioning at 5½).

It is important to emphasize that the kind of shy, observant temperament that related positively to theory-of-mind achievement was *not* fearfully, avoidant shyness (e.g., Kagan & Snidman, 2004). It was instead socially interested but observant temperament rated in such items as "prefers to watch rather than join play," "comments when a parent wears new clothing," and "acts shy around *new* people."

Temperament itself, and particularly aggressive and shy-withdrawn behaviors, undoubtedly have a neurohormonal substrate (e.g., Kagan & Snidman, 2004). And domesticated foxes evidence related neurohormonal changes in comparison to their undomesticated counterparts (Belyaev, 1979). Thus, phylogenetically, human theory of mind might depend in part on "domestication" of the human neurohormonal, stress-related system that mediates interaction with others (Hare & Tomasello, 2005). At the same time, the findings we reported suggested important cognitive and social-interactive mechanisms through which temperament influences theory of mind in human childhood. A nonaggressive, observant-reflective stance on social interactions could certainly provide enhanced opportunities for coming to understand how actions and expressions are shaped by persons' underlying mental states. The immediate fray of social interaction might often be a relatively more difficult arena for children to extract such regularities, because in immediate, ongoing interactions (especially aggressive ones), overt behavior and emotion themselves can loom so large.

Indeed, in further research headed by Jonathan Lane (Lane, Wellman, Olson, et al., 2013), we used cortisol measures of physiological stress reactivity to differentiate two types of shy children, in both U.S. and Chinese samples. One group was socially withdrawn and physiologically reactive; the other included those who were also socially withdrawn but low in reactivity. It was the shy but nonreactive children that were advantaged in theory-of-mind skills, in both the United States and China.

In sum, specific early temperament characteristics—lack of aggressiveness and a shy but observant nonreactive stance to interacting with others—predict children's more advanced theory-of-mind understanding in the preschool years. To be clear, these findings are not strictly or rigidly "biological." Temperaments emerge early but also change in the course of childhood developmental interactions. Temperament influences social interactions; social interactions inform theory of mind. More generally, information acquisition can benefit theory-of-mind developments, however achieved. Indeed, our temperament findings intriguingly relate to research that shows the richest parent–child conversations about emotions (referring to the causes, consequences, and connection of emotions to other mental states) occur not about current emotional upheavals but more reflectively about past emotional episodes (e.g., Dunn & Brown, 1994; Lagattuta & Wellman, 2002). An observant-reflective stance on human events helpfully advances theory-of-mind understandings whether the stance is induced temperamentally or conversationally.

CONCLUSIONS

Theory-of-mind research with humans shaped theory-of-mind research with other animals, which then shaped theory-of-mind research with humans (at the least, via the "emotional reactivity hypothesis"). More generally, the comparative-animal research sheds great light on both the evolution *and* development of human theory of mind. Theory of mind in humans reflects beginnings we owe to our nonhuman ancestors and so are apparent in part in great apes as well. Nonetheless, human theory of mind is distinctive. It is broad; theory-of-mind understandings impact almost all human social cognition and social interaction (and not just competition for resources). Human theory of mind is massively developmental; it evidences an accumulation of more and more advanced mentalistic insights over a long progressive developmental trajectory. Human theory of mind is also especially helpful and communicative in nature. Even infants insistently deploy their social-cognitive insights to help and communicate with others. Our closest animal kin, the great apes, rarely do.

11

The Social Brain

NEURAL REGIONS DEVELOPED FOR THEORY OF MIND

NEUROSCIENCE INVESTIGATIONS—ESPECIALLY METHODS for imaging the intact, functioning, human brain as it works on some task—have exploded in the last years. They impact scientific and everyday understandings; images of brains with one area or another activated, "lit up," are now frequent in scientific journals, newspapers, magazines, and TV documentaries. Recall the NBCNews.com story outlined at the start of Chapter 1 where German investigators used functional neuroimaging to "read the minds" of their participants.

Theory of mind, like any cognition, functions within and depends on the brain, and research has begun to inform us about the neural processes involved. However, deep questions remain, including, in particular, how neural substrates developmentally shape, result from, and support theory-of-mind reasoning. Most behavioral research on theory of mind is developmental research with children, of the sort reviewed extensively in prior chapters. But most neuroscientific studies addressing theory of mind have been conducted with adults. Nonetheless, I want to emphasize development.

At its most general, the question I address concerns what kinds of functional brain changes, if any, occur during theory-of-mind development? To begin basically, are the brain regions that correlate with theory-of-mind reasoning in adults the same or different for children? Additionally, paralleling questions addressed earlier about domain-specific versus domain-general processes, does theory-of-mind reasoning recruit essentially general-purpose brain systems (e.g., those serving memory, language, and executive functions), or are there brain systems that seem specially dedicated to theory-of-mind reasoning? Are there, perhaps, even special cells—mirror neurons—dedicated to theory-of-mind reasoning? And, what is the relation between neural and behavioral developments for theory of mind: What paces what? Even partial answers to these questions are proving intriguing and informative.

There will also be some intriguing questions I do not address. The key example here concerns what happens in infancy. To extend the discussion from Chapters 8 and 9, in principle, neuroscience evidence could help us know how to characterize infant theory-of-mind understandings. That is, neural mechanisms underlying infant (fast, automatic or system-1) reasoning could be compared with those for older children to address how infant mental-state understanding relates to the belief-desire understanding demonstrated in preschoolers. Unfortunately, to date no neuroimaging studies have compared infants and preschoolers, let alone compared them on appropriately contrasting tasks.

Considering the other direction of development, and to preface Chapter 13, children's performance reaches ceiling on standard, behavioral theory-of-mind tasks at roughly age 6 or 7 years, yet theory of mind surely develops beyond that. Neuroscience data do help us understand theory-of-mind development postpreschool. In contrast to infancy, there are emerging neuroscience data with older children (and even some with preschoolers) that begin to shed light on later developments. Primarily, I tackle those data here, beginning with research from adults and moving backward in development.

Functional magnetic resonance imaging (fMRI) and event-related potentials (ERP) are the two most used methods for collecting functional neuroscience data from children (and adults) and the ones I consider here. Box 11.1 contrasts those techniques on several features. Potentially, MEG (magnetoencephalography) and fNIRS (functional near-infrared spectroscopy) could also be used in the future, but no current theory-of-mind research has employed those methods.

NEURAL CORRELATES OF THEORY OF MIND IN ADULTS

Cognitive neuroscientific investigations with adults demonstrate that theory of mind involves a network of neural regions, primarily those noted in Figure 11.1: the medial prefrontal cortex (PFC) and the left and right temporoparietal junctions (TPJ) most consistently; but also the precuneus, as well as the superior temporal gyrus/sulcus (STG/STS); and, relatedly, the temporal poles (see Apperly, 2011; Carrington & Bailey, 2009, for recent reviews). These regions are recruited when adults engage in multiple mental- and social-reasoning tasks in functional neuroimaging (e.g., fMRI) and electrophysiological (e.g., ERP) studies alike.

To illustrate, consider adult decoding of mental states. Adults showed increased blood-oxygen-level-dependent (BOLD) signal (the hemodynamic response that indexes neural activation and is tracked by fMRI; see Box 11.1) in the left PFC and the left STG

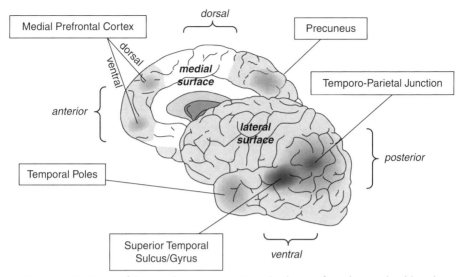

FIGURE 11.1 Depiction of the neural regions comprising the theory-of-mind network. Although shown here on only one hemisphere, research demonstrates that each of these regions are recruited bilaterally for theory-of-mind reasoning in adults and children.

(as well as the medial frontal gyrus) when inferring mental states from photographs of eyes (e.g., desirous, thoughtful, confused) versus determining the gender of the eyes (Baron-Cohen et al., 1999). When this task was adapted to ERP methods, adults showed increased electrophysiological activity in frontal and middle scalp locations, roughly corresponding to prefrontal cortex (PFC) and temporal cortex (STG), respectively (e.g., Sabbagh, Moulson, & Harkness, 2004).

Beyond mental-state decoding of simple static images, theory-of-mind neural regions are recruited when processing descriptions of more complex social interactions and scenes. In an illustrative study, adults showed increased BOLD signal in the bilateral TPJ, anterior STS, and medial frontal cortex when hearing mental-state descriptions in contrast to nonmental *human* descriptions (e.g., nonmental descriptions of people's appearances; Saxe & Kanwisher, 2003).

Reasoning about a specific type of mental state—beliefs—activates the theory-of-mind neural network as well. When attributing true and false beliefs to cartoon characters, adults show activation in the TPJ, prefrontal cortex, and precuneus—showing more activation to false-belief attribution compared to attribution of true beliefs (Sommer et al., 2007). In an ERP study, David Liu, Mark Sabbagh, Bill Gehring and I (Liu, Sabbagh, et al., 2009) found that when adults reasoned specifically about beliefs contrasted with reality, they showed electrophysiological activation in both mid-frontal and right-posterior scalp regions, roughly corresponding to medial PFC and right TPJ locations.

As a methodological aside, these studies exemplify a typical neuroscience subtraction methodology. The focal neural activations for theory of mind (e.g., mental-state inferences) are those that remain after some informative contrast activations (e.g., those

BOX 11.1

Functional Magnetic Resonance Imaging (fMRI)	Electrophysiology (EEG/ERP)
• Uses magnetic principles to detect changes in blood oxygenation in the brain (an indirect correlate of neuronal activity).	• Uses electrical sensors placed on a participant's scalp to detect the electrical potentials that are a direct consequence of underlying neuronal activity (termed *electroencephalographic* data or EEG). Neurons activate via chemo-electrical changes, and EEG records the scalp emanations of this electrical activity.
• Oxygenated and deoxygenated blood hemoglobin have different magnetic properties. Thus, participants lie surrounded by large magnetic coils that generate magnetic fields, which detect changes in hemoglobin concentrations.	• Many functional electrophysiological studies use event-related potential (ERP) methods. *ERP methods* detect the electroencephalographic activity associated with processing a particular event (e.g., viewing a target image). They result in characteristic wave forms of electrical activity time locked to that particular event.
• Critically, hemoglobin concentrations change systematically as a function of neuronal activity. This neural-dependent blood-flow change is termed the *hemodynamic response function* (HRF), which peaks ~ 5 seconds after a neuronal event.	• Temporal resolution (the time course of the electrical wave forms that result) is on the order of milliseconds (given how quickly electrical potentials propagate from the neuronal source to the scalp surface).
• The HRF is used to derive the blood-oxygen-level-dependent (BOLD) signal, which can then be compared across conditions and populations as an indirect correlate of neuronal activity.	• Spatial resolution of raw EEG data is associated with the number of sensors placed on the head. But even dense-array systems use only 100 or so sensors spaced around the head, so spatial resolution is on the order of centimeters (rather than mms) and is somewhat ambiguous (given several scalp sensors could measure activity from one neuronal source or one sensor could measure activity from several neuronal sources).

- fMRI has a spatial resolution of ~1–3 mm (because the magnetic field penetrates deep into the brain to detect blood-flow changes very close to the site of neural activity).

- Temporal resolution is ~1–5 seconds (given the lag between neuronal events and corresponding HRF).

- Source localization methods (e.g., sLORETA; Pascual-Marqui, 2002) can more precisely statistically estimate the location of underlying neuronal sources (via assessment of activity patterns across the scalp sensors and calculations of electrical conductivity of blood, bone, and tissue), given a variety of background assumptions.

Another EEG method uses spectral power analyses. *Spectral power analyses* measure changes in the amplitude and frequency of the electrical potentials to estimate regions of activity and neural maturation of differing brain regions. Spectral power analyses are often used in a task-independent way as a measure of "baseline" or "resting" brain activity, which can indicate functional connectivity and neural maturation. (It can also be used to measure activation patterns across conditions as an index of neural activity associated with different cognitive tasks.)

for mechanical inferences, those for reality) are subtracted. The logic is that both tasks would require inference, memory, and so forth, but the mental-state inferences would also reveal theory-of-mind specific processes over and above the more general cognitive processes. Task contrasts are a general methodological feature of most theory-of-mind research; a general concern for neuroscience research, in particular, is whether the target and contrast or subtraction tasks are well matched and to what extent the target task taps mental-state reasoning.

To summarize to here, although much is unknown about the neural underpinning of theory of mind in adults, there is now substantial evidence that theory-of-mind reasoning consistently recruits a network of specific neural regions including the left and right TPJ, medial PFC, precuneus, and STS/STG. Identification of "neural signatures" such as these help to address larger and more complex questions of cognitive processing.

Theory of Mind and Executive Functioning

As I've discussed in prior chapters, behavioral findings demonstrate links between executive functions (e.g., attention, inhibitory control, working memory) and theory-of-mind performance and can do so even when controlling for age and general intelligence (e.g., Carlson & Moses, 2001). Recall from Chapter 7 that one account of theory-of-mind development posits that advances in mental-state understanding reflect domain-general maturation of executive-functioning skills; these domain-general skills develop, and conceivably this development might fully explain children's emerging ability to make mental-state attributions (e.g., Leslie, 2005; Luo & Baillargeon, 2010). Questions about the role of such domain-general cognitions as involved in theory-of-mind reasoning (surely they often have some role to play) have received attention in adult neuroscientific investigations. The general subtraction methodology addresses this issue, in part, by showing that specialized theory-of-mind neural regions activate above and beyond contrast tasks that also have memory and executive-functioning demands. But, more specifically, researchers have investigated whether neural substrates recruited for theory of mind are dissociable from those recruited for executive functioning. Dissociable substrates would provide additional evidence for domain-specific theory-of-mind processes.

For example, in an fMRI study of adults, Rebecca Saxe and her colleagues (Saxe, Schulz, & Jiang, 2006) compared brain regions activated by performance on an executive-functioning task (i.e., learn a series of rules to track a moving object), a belief-attribution task (i.e., infer a character's belief after reading a short story), and a combined social-cognition task that required both executive functioning and belief attribution. Brain regions recruited during the executive-functioning task (bilateral intraparietal sulcus, frontal operculum, middle frontal gyrus, and middle temporal gyrus) did not overlap with any regions recruited for the belief-attribution task (left and right TPJ, medial PFC, and anterior STS). Such results show there are distinct, domain-specific cognitive processes for theory-of-mind reasoning (e.g., in medial PFC and right TPJ), further supporting the conclusions I drew from behavioral data in Chapters 3 and 7. The combined task appropriately recruited both "ToM" and "EF" regions. So, these results also provide evidence that theory-of-mind reasoning on many ordinary tasks can require executive-functioning skills as well.

Similar conclusions resulted from a more recent study from other investigators (Rothmayr et al., 2011), who also found common neural regions for both executive functioning and belief attribution in adults but additionally domain-specific theory-of-mind activations in the TPJ and PFC (albeit left dorsal regions of PFC in this study), independent of executive-functioning activations. Thus, both studies strongly indicate that theory-of-mind reasoning recruits neural regions that are specific to mental-state attribution, beyond those that overlap with executive-functioning processes. They thereby underwrite the idea that theory-of-mind tasks target domain-specific cognitions, although they often recruit domain-general cognitive processes as well. Questions remain, of course, about precisely how executive functioning and theory of mind differ and relate in development.

Reasoning About Different Types of Mental States

Rebecca Saxe in particular has accumulated considerable converging evidence that posterior brain regions (i.e., TPJ) are likely specialized for processing mental states, and particularly for processing beliefs. Saxe and Wexler (2005) demonstrated that adults selectively recruited the right TPJ for processing mental states but not for processing other socially relevant facts about a person (i.e., marital status, family relations, cultural background). Moreover, none of the other regions typically recruited in theory-of-mind reasoning (i.e., medial PFC) showed such a specified role. Saxe and Powell (2006) then found that activations in the TPJ and posterior cingulate were selectively associated with reasoning about beliefs but not with reasoning about other socially relevant facts such as a person's appearance, or about other specific nonmental internal states such as bodily sensations.

As I've emphasized all along, however, theory-of-mind reasoning encompasses understanding of and reasoning about multiple distinctly different *mental* states, including desires, intentions, and emotions and not just beliefs. Yet, these adult neuroscientific studies typically examine mental-state reasoning generally, or even more commonly, belief reasoning by itself (in comparison to personal appearance, family role, etc.). Consider an early fMRI study by Rebecca Saxe and Nancy Kanwisher (2003) that primarily examined false-belief reasoning by contrasting it with reasoning about non-mental representations (i.e., false photographs). Indeed, TPJ regions were involved in false-belief reasoning in contrast to false-photograph reasoning. In this study, Saxe and Kanwisher also included mental stories about desires along with beliefs, but the data for processing desires specifically were not mentioned or analyzed further. More generally, Saxe's research studies have not contrasted desires with beliefs. In fact, for adults, there are almost no data available on the neural correlates of reasoning about desires or reasoning about desires in contrast with beliefs. Yet, neuroscientific investigations that directly contrast desire reasoning and belief reasoning could be particularly important from a developmental perspective. This is because, as reviewed in Chapters 4 and 5, one especially clear progression of mental state understandings apparent in behavioral research is that development of desire understanding precedes development of understanding beliefs (see, e.g., the meta-analysis in Wellman & Liu, 2004).

To shed further light on the mechanisms that might underlie this developmental progression, David Liu, Andy Meltzoff, and I (Liu, Meltzoff, & Wellman, 2009) recorded ERPs as adults performed diverse-desires tasks (requiring reasoning that different persons can have different desires for exactly the same thing) and diverse-beliefs tasks (requiring reasoning that different persons can have different beliefs about the exact same situation). These tasks were very similar to the matched diverse-desire and diverse-belief tasks used in the ToM Scale (Wellman & Liu, 2004) discussed in Chapter 5. As a control, participants performed parallel diverse-physical tasks (requiring reasoning about where different things go). In our results (Liu, Meltzoff, et al. 2009), a late slow ERP wave with mid-frontal scalp distribution was associated with desire *and* belief judgments (with peak activations at about 900 msec, almost 1 second poststimulus). That is, mid-frontal regions activated for both desire and belief judgments (and did so equivalently) beyond any activation for the physical control. However, a late slow wave with right-posterior scalp distribution was associated *only* with belief judgments—beyond any activations not only for physical but also for desires. This neural dissociation between desires and beliefs was even more striking considering behavioral accuracy for the judgments in the two conditions was identical.

The mid-frontal activations of course correspond loosely to medial PFC neural regions, and the right posterior activations correspond loosely to right TPJ. However, any inferences about localization from ERP data are indeed loose in two senses: (a) Regional scalp electrophysiological recordings come from areas that are spatially large (on the order of several centimeters rather than the several millimeters identified via the voxels for fMRI, as outlined in Box 11.1); and (b) electrical activity recorded at the scalp cannot definitively be attributed to specific underlying brain regions. Nonetheless, the rough correspondence across methods in identifying both mid-frontal and right-posterior regions as active for theory of mind is comforting and revealing.

Note, at a broad level, these results demonstrate how neurocognitive data can provide distinctive information when behavioral data do not; they revealed underlying neural differences despite behavioral equivalences in terms of accuracy. More specifically, these findings demonstrated neural overlap as well as critical differences in reasoning about desires and beliefs. Thus they point to a possible explanation for the progression from understanding desires to understanding beliefs seen in children: Children may need to recruit additional neural resources (within posterior parietal regions) for reasoning about beliefs beyond a common neural system (within medial frontal regions) for reasoning about mental states more generally. Neuroscientific data with adults, thus, can shed indirect light on development.

Only one other neuroscientific study with adults has directly compared desire versus belief reasoning (Abraham, Rakoczy, Werning, von Cramon, & Schubotz, 2010). As a consequence, it is difficult to definitively conclude that right posterior parietal regions (e.g., right TPJ) are specifically specialized for belief reasoning, over and above recruitment of mental states such as desires. Indeed, the role of the right TPJ as specific for beliefs is debated by some researchers (see Mitchell, 2008; Rothmayr et al., 2011). So here too, current adult literature is helpful but not yet conclusive.

Interim Summary

Executive functioning and a belief-desire progression are just two examples in which adult data shed indirect light on developmental aspects of theory of mind. Another example addresses frequent characterizations of theory-of-mind processes as necessarily fast and automatic. For example, Alan Leslie in advocating that theory of mind is an early appearing mental module, often has claimed, "Consistent with this modular interpretation…the interpretation of people in terms of their mental states appears to be fast and irresistible" (Scholl & Leslie, 2001, p. 697). In this respect, Leslie has often characterized theory of mind as similar to vision. Potentially, then, if it was indeed the reflection of an innate mental module, online theory-of-mind processing might be perception like in its speed and automaticity.

Adult findings with standard "preschool" theory-of-mind tasks shed considerable doubt on such a claim. Recall that in our study (Liu, Meltzoff, & Wellman, 2009), the focal activations distinguishing adult belief reasoning from desire or physical reasoning occurred in a late slow wave peaking at about 900 msec. This is quite different from the activations of 200–300 msec that characterize automatic perceptual processes. Although ERP data are imprecise in terms of spatial localizations (as noted earlier), they are quite precise in terms of charting the time course of neural activations. In a related study, David Lui and colleagues (Liu, Sabbagh, Gehring, & Wellman, 2004) used ERP to compare adult judgments about false beliefs versus about reality. A late slow ERP component again differentiated judgments about belief from those about reality in the range of 900 msec. With this late peak and extended time course, it seems extremely unlikely that the online neural processes that result in standard belief and desire reasoning are modular and perception like in their automaticity. Instead the findings are more in line with Ian Apperly's (2011; Apperly & Butterfill, 2009) analysis of standard tasks as representing a slower, more flexible, system-2 form of reasoning. Perhaps system-1 tasks would evidence "perception-like" automaticity, but this has not yet been tested.

The adult findings contain an emerging consensus as to an adult theory-of-mind neural network, amid continuing debate and ambiguities. However, even if the adult findings were definitive, it is not possible to address development from adult data alone. An understanding of neurocognitive correlates in cognitively expert adults does not translate to an understanding of cognition earlier in development. *Developmental* neuroscience data are needed, at the very least because theory of mind is a deeply developmental achievement. Moreover, as I have argued all along, theory of mind is a product of constructivist learning and development. Some sort of "neuroconstructivist" account (see, e.g., Westermann et al., 2007) may well be indicated.

Thus, I turn next to the emerging studies that have applied neuroscientific methods to children as well as adults, and to children at different ages. At the least, such studies can provide important additions to behavioral investigations. For example, they can reveal underlying similarities where behavioral data show differences, as well as underlying differences in processing where behavioral data show performance similarities (as occurred in Liu, Meltzoff, & Wellman, 2009).

NEURAL CORRELATES OF THEORY-OF-MIND DEVELOPMENT

Initial Investigations of Children

In an early investigation of children's theory-of-mind neural correlates, Matthew Mosconi and his colleagues (Mosconi, Mack, McCarthy, & Pelphrey, 2005) used fMRI to examine intention understanding in typically developing children 7 to 10 years old. Intention-understanding measures for this study consisted of viewing a character shift her eye gaze toward a target image (an action with a clear intention of viewing a target object), contrasted with viewing the same character shift her eyes away from the target image toward an empty space (an action with a less-clear goal). The STS, middle temporal lobe, and inferior parietal lobule showed increased activation in the "shift-toward" condition compared to the "shift-away" condition. Thus, this study provides evidence that the STS is recruited for intention understanding in children as young as 7 years of age.

Note that neuroscience methods pose certain difficulties for working with children. This results in less total studies, smaller samples, and also in examining less precise age groupings than in behavioral theory-of-mind research. The focus on a relatively broad 7- to 10-year-old age span in the Mosconi et al. (2005) research is only one example.

Takashi Ohnishi and his colleagues (2004) similarly used fMRI to examine action-intention understanding but additionally to examine mental-state attribution in typically developing children aged 7 to 13 years of age. They compared neural activation in action-intention conditions (viewing purposeful hand actions such as grasping a cup of the sort often used in infant research) to mental-state attribution conditions (in this case, viewing triangles moving in "mentalistic" ways such as one triangle jumping out to "surprise" another triangle). In this way, Ohnishi and his colleagues attempted to investigate the relation between intention understanding and "higher level" theory of mind. The action-intention and mental-state attribution conditions both yielded neural activation in the bilateral STS, temporal lobes, and fusiform gyrus. This was roughly comparable to the investigation by Mosconi and colleagues (2005). However, activations in the right-medial PFC and the right TPJ (as well as the right inferior parietal cortex) were unique to the mental-state attribution condition.

This pattern of overlap and distinction promotes a hypothesis that neurally, as well as behaviorally, theory of mind may develop from an earlier capacity to infer intentions to a later capacity to engage in more complex, mental-state inferences. At the least, the data indicate that even in childhood, substrates in the medial PFC and right TPJ are recruited to support the more complex mental-state reasoning.

In an intriguing study, Mark Sabbagh and his colleagues (Sabbagh, Bowman, Evraire, & Ito, 2009) measured neural correlates in preschool children, at a point in development when behavioral tasks demonstrate stark, outward change (i.e., transitioning from failing to passing standard false-belief tasks). These researchers used dense-array

(128-channel) EEG recordings to investigate how 4-year-olds' resting EEG alpha coherence (a variant of spectral power analyses; see Box 11.1) related to their theory-of-mind development (e.g., performance on false-belief tasks). This is clever methodologically because by using task-independent EEG (baseline/resting data), neural data were collected from preschool-age children in just 6 minutes (in contrast to the 30 minutes or more often needed to collect multitrial, task-dependent data in ERP or fMRI studies with children). Resting EEG alpha coherence does not provide task-related neural activation (like ERP or fMRI) but does provide a measure of functional maturation of underlying neurocognitive systems (e.g., Nunez & Cutillo, 1995). Sabbagh and his colleagues (2009) then related this EEG measure of neural functioning to theory-of-mind task performances in the same children via standard theory-of-mind tasks administered in a different session. Moreover, in their study, besides theory-of-mind tasks, children's executive-functioning performance (e.g., response conflict, inhibition) was also measured as a covariate.

Source localization (as outlined in Box 11.1) of the EEG alpha showed that increased functional maturation of the medial PFC and the right TPJ predicted increased theory-of-mind performance in these young children. Importantly, this relation held even after statistically controlling for children's executive-functioning performance. These findings extend adult ones by providing evidence that even early in development, theory of mind includes domain-specific substrates (e.g., substrates that correlate with theory-of-mind development independent of any common relation with executive functioning). And they show involvement of both medial PFC and right TPJ in theory-of-mind performance in preschool children.

Other research has examined children's neural correlates of mental-state reasoning more directly, albeit with older children. In an fMRI study, Rebecca Saxe and colleagues (Saxe, Whitfield-Gabrieli, Scholz, & Pelphrey, 2009) measured neural activation as typically developing children (6–10 years old) listened to stories in three conditions: (a) a mental condition (descriptions of people's mental states including intentions, desires, and beliefs), (b) a people condition (nonmental descriptions of people's appearance and interactions), and (c) a physical condition (descriptions of physical scenes). Children showed greater activation in the bilateral TPJ, precuneus, and medial PFC for the mental condition relative to the physical condition. Additionally, as children aged, specifically the right TPJ was found to increase in selectivity for mental-state reasoning (in comparison to *both* processing physical descriptions and descriptions of people's appearance and interactions). Thus the data demonstrated continued neural development beyond the childhood age at which children's performance reaches ceiling on behavioral measures of theory of mind.

Summing up across these studies, child neuroscience findings implicate regions involved in theory-of-mind reasoning that are similar to those found in adults, even for children as young as 4 years of age (i.e., Sabbagh et al., 2009). Comparisons between child and adult neural data could certainly have turned out differently; conceivably, the adult data could have shown neural activations only for expert, fluent, well-developed social cognition—activations that were different from child activations needed to learn about theory-of-mind concepts in the first place. However, two of the adult neural regions, in particular, are also implicated in the development of social-cognitive reasoning from early on—PFC and TPJ. Thus the data illustrate some important neurodevelopmental continuities. There is also initial evidence for developmental change, again often with regard to the amount and specificity of activations in PFC and TPJ. However, comparisons across separate studies, which have used different methods, give only the loosest measures of developmental continuity and change. Studies that include children and adults on the same tasks and methods are needed for firmer developmental conclusions.

Investigations of Children and Adults Together

One clear possibility is that early in theory-of-mind development, tasks may fail to activate adult theory-of-mind neural regions at all, potentially confirming a nonmental (or less-mental) interpretation of the target tasks by young children. David Liu and colleagues (Liu, Sabbagh, et al., 2009) found this pattern in their ERP study examining children's developing false-belief judgments on standard "preschool" tasks (in comparison to judgments about reality) in 4-, 5-, and 6-year-olds and adults. The key finding was that the children divided into two clear groups: those who were consistently correct on false-belief tasks (correct on 75% or more of 40 false-belief trials)—the "passers"—and those who were consistently incorrect (correct on less that 25% of those trials): the "failers." Although in this study, the child passers and failers were carefully selected to be equal in age, on average, of course, failing is evident early in the preschool years and yields to passing false-belief tasks later in the preschool years. Adults (who consistently passed) and child passers displayed the same patterns of activations described earlier: a late slow ERP wave differentiating belief reasoning from reality reasoning in frontal scalp regions (corresponding roughly to medial PFC) and peaking at about 800–900 msec for adults and even a bit later at 1200–1400 msec in the children. Child failers, however (even at the same ages as child passers), evidenced no ERP activations distinguishing beliefs versus reality.

A different pattern often occurs when comparing child and adult neurocognitive activity, whereby children show greater (and more diffuse) activation compared to adults (Casey, Giedd, & Thomas, 2000). Bregtje Moor and colleagues (2012) found this pattern in fMRI activity when adults, early adolescents (ages 10–12 years), and mid-adolescents (ages 14–16 years) inferred mental states from images of eyes. At all ages, activation was observed in the posterior STS. However, only the youngest age group (10- to 12-year-olds) showed additional involvement of the medial PFC. Regression analyses showed decreasing activation of medial PFC as age increased in these later childhood years.

Medial PFC figures in other developmental studies as well. Thus, in their fMRI study, Monika Sommer and her colleagues (2010) had adults and children (ages 10–11 years) view cartoons depicting characters' true and false beliefs. Both age groups showed increased activation in the dorsal-medial PFC for false-belief reasoning compared to true-belief reasoning; however, the activation in the dorsal-medial PFC was significantly greater in children versus adults, whereas the activation in the TPJ for false-belief versus true-belief reasoning was significantly greater for adults than for children.

A similar pattern of results was found recently in a study by Hyowon Gweon and her colleagues (Gweon, Dodell-Feder, Bedny, & Saxe 2012). FMRI activation was measured as adults and children (5–11 years of age) listened to descriptions of people's mental states (mental condition), people's appearance and social interactions (social condition), and physical scenes (physical condition). Both adults and children showed greater activation for the mental versus the physical condition in the left and right TPJ, the dorsal-medial PFC, and the precuneus. However, adults showed higher *selectivity* for specifically mental-state processing (relative to social and physical processing) in the TPJ and precuneus (but not in the medial PFC) compared to children. Moreover, correlation analyses showed that mental-state selectivity in both the left and right TPJ increased with age, and mental-state selectivity in the right TPJ positively correlated with children's behavioral theory-of-mind performance.

Emerging Developmental Patterns

From behavioral studies, we can imagine (at least) two possible patterns for theory-of-mind neural development. First, the theory-of-mind network and its key regional components (e.g., medial PFC and TPJ) might already be functioning maturely very early in life. A strict interpretation of recent infant data (e.g., that reviewed in Chapter 8) might imply this—if even infants can reason correctly and fully about beliefs and knowledge and not merely desires and intentions, we could expect their neural activations to mimic adults. A strict core-knowledge interpretation should entail this pattern as well because according to Spelke (e.g., Spelke, 2003; Spelke & Kinzler, 2007), core knowledge persists unchanged across development. Alternatively, however, in line with a more protracted progressive timeline for theory-of-mind development, these regions might still be developing and changing within the preschool years and even beyond.

The data for the studies reviewed here suggest that functional changes in the relevant brain regions (a) are observable in the preschool years (4, 5, and 6 years) when behavioral changes on standard theory-of-mind tasks are dramatically apparent, and moreover (b) are further observable after 5 and 6 years as well even though accuracy on standard theory-of-mind tasks is often at ceiling. Such prolonged functional change in theory-of-mind regions, as well as definitive distinctions between neural regions used for theory of mind versus those recruited for executive functions, argues against a strict, nativist or core-knowledge account of theory-of-mind development from preschool on.

Moreover, both medial PFC and right TPJ regions figure consistently in this prolonged theory-of-mind development. Results from Gweon et al. (2012), Sommer et al. (2010), and Saxe et al. (2009) demonstrate that the TPJ in particular increases in selectivity for mental-state processing as children age from as early as 5 years old to adulthood. Gweon et al. confirmed that this selectivity increase is correlated with increased behavioral performance on belief-reasoning tasks.

There is complementary evidence for a prominent role of the medial PFC in children's theory-of-mind reasoning as well. Moreover, and intriguingly, there is initial evidence suggesting that perhaps medial PFC may have a more prominent role for *younger* versus older children and adults. The medial PFC is recruited for processing thoughts and beliefs more strongly in children (10–14 years) compared to adults (Pfeifer et al., 2009; Sommer et al., 2010). And it is related to theory-of-mind reasoning in 4-year-olds, independent from any common associations with executive functioning (Sabbagh et al., 2009) but does not show this domain specificity in adults (Saxe, Schulz, et al., 2006), whereas right TPJ does.

In short, one intriguing hypothesis is that earlier in development (potentially as early as 4 years of age and roughly up to 14 years), the medial PFC plays a more prominent role in general mental-state reasoning, including belief reasoning; but later in development (after roughly 12–14 years), its role in these types of reasoning is diminished or becomes more specialized. In contrast, the TPJ plays a more and more prominent role as development proceeds; it becomes increasingly selective for processing mental states and especially beliefs as children age and become more accurate in their belief-desire reasoning.

However, a key element is missing in these studies so far. Just as in the studies of adults, these child studies have narrowly focused on belief reasoning, or on mental-state reasoning in general. Theory of mind (belief-desire naïve psychology) involves understanding multiple causally interconnected mental concepts—and especially both belief states (which represent the world) and desire states (which motivate particular actions within the represented world, to get what one wants).

So, in a recent study, Lindsay Bowman, David Liu, Andy Meltzoff, and I (2012) directly examined the neural correlates of belief *and* desire reasoning in children. We recorded ERPs when 7- and 8-year-olds performed diverse-desires and diverse-beliefs tasks, as well as physical-reasoning tasks as a control condition. The tasks, methods, and EEG acquisition system were identical to those used in the Liu, Meltzoff, et al. (2009) ERP study with adults described earlier. This enabled direct comparisons between child and adult ERP data. Both adults and children showed frontal neural activations for belief and desire reasoning that equally differentiated from activations for the physical control but did not differentiate from each other. And as noted before, adults also showed neural activation that was specific to belief reasoning, distinct from both physical *and* desire reasoning in right posterior scalp regions. Crucially, this pattern was also emerging in children. When all child ERP trials were included in analyses (as was done for the adult data), no right posterior, belief-desire distinction was evident. However, when analyses included only the trials in which children judged correctly (adults were almost always correct), right posterior activations for belief reasoning emerged as distinctly greater than activations for desires.

Thus, by ages 7 and 8 years, children had already developed neural specializations for reasoning about beliefs and desires that were distinct from the neural activations for physical reasoning—neural patterns that are similar to those found in adults and located in similar mid-frontal scalp regions. And these same children recruited right posterior regions for reasoning about beliefs over and above reasoning about mental states more generally, although children showed this selective activation for belief over desire reasoning only when analyses were restricted to correct trials.

These results more directly support the hypothesis that neuromechanisms for mental-state reasoning, and in particular for belief reasoning, are still developing in childhood (e.g., see Gweon et al., 2012; Saxe et al., 2009; Sommer, Meinhardt, et al., 2010) and indeed beyond early childhood. More specifically, they and the false-belief data from Liu, Sabbagh, et al. (2009) point to a mechanism whereby developmental increases in *accuracy* for inferring complex mental states contribute to the development of the neural specialization that supports social-cognitive understanding.

MIRROR NEURONS AND SELF-PROJECTION

Mirror Neurons

Any contemporary discussion of the neural bases of social cognition—including understandings of intentional action, goals, and desires as well as beliefs—has to say something about mirror neurons. Mirror neurons, like brain research more generally, are much in the news. As an early example, see the *New York Times* article by Sandra Blakeslee titled "Cells that Read Minds" (2006).

Interest began in mirror neurons (MNs) when Italian scientists found that some neurons in the macaque premotor cortex (technically, in frontal area F5 in macaque brain anatomy) that were already known to activate when the monkey engaged in a goal-directed action (e.g., picked up a peanut) fired similarly when the monkey merely passively watched someone else engage in that action. These data came from single-cell recordings, and according to the most detailed early study (Gallese, Fadiga, Fogassi, & Rizzolatti, 1996), mirror neurons comprised about 20% of the cells they sampled within F5. The cells did not fire to visually presented objects (e.g., a peanut), to faces, to body parts, or to bodily movement without a clear goal object.

A straightforward interpretation of the function of such cells might have been that they support direct imitative actions. But monkeys rarely imitate. And to reiterate, mirror neurons did not activate to body movements in the absence of target objects (e.g., arm motions such as waving), although those actions are often imitated by humans.

Thus, these Italian researchers increasingly interpreted the function of those MN cells as providing "intentional action understanding" (Gallese, Keysers & Rizzolatti, 2004; Rizzolatti & Fabbri-Destro, 2008): When these cells fire as the animal sees someone else's action, it allows the animal to map that action on to its own intentional action repertoire and in that sense "immediately" understand it. Spelke (see Spelke & Kinzler, 2007) from her core knowledge position, applauds this approach to thinking about the core system of knowledge for reasoning about agents because it specifies commonalities across humans' and monkeys' agent representations. "Goal-directedness…contingency…and gaze direction provide signatures of agent representations that allow for their study in non-human animals and in human adults…. These…accord well with the physiological signatures of 'mirror neurons' observed in captive monkeys" (Spelke & Kinzler, 2007, p. 90).

In the Blakeslee (2006) *New York Times* article, one of the key Italian scientists, Dr. Rizollati, stated "Mirror neurons allow us to grasp the minds of others not through conceptual reasoning but through direct simulation. By feeling, not thinking" (p. F1). This sort of claim was quickly promoted by theorists who had proposed that theory-of-mind reasoning proceeded by way of simulation (see Gallese & Goldman, 1998; Goldman, 2009), as that perspective was outlined in Chapter 7. This was an expanded claim that mirror neurons formed the basis for a larger mirror system (MS), a system that also operated in humans (the use of "mirror neurons allow *us* to grasp the minds of others…through direct simulation" as in the previous Rizzollatti quote). So, expanding still further, it was claimed that MNs, as crucial to an MS, provide the neural substrate that allow human empathy, imitation, and theory of mind.

It is important to enumerate all the steps involved in this sort of expansive mirror neuron thinking (and popularized science reporting): (a) Mirror neurons exist in monkeys (which fire similarly for seen as well as self-produced actions) and (b) allow direct action understanding of others' intentional actions; and (c) homologous neurons play a fundamental role in a more expansive human mirror system that includes but goes beyond motor-action understanding to underpin (d) empathy, (e) projecting oneself into others' activities, (f) imitation, and (g) attributions of mental states like desires and beliefs (beyond action goals), and (h) when impaired lead to the characteristic social-cognitive, social-learning, and social-action deficits of individuals with autism (the "broken mirror" theory of autism). Once we get past step (a), however, there are difficulties and lack of empirical evidence for all the other steps in this argument chain.

Consider, for example, that only one study (with 21 seizure patients implanted with intracranial electrodes for clinical purposes) has provided single-cell recordings from humans of cells (in various neural locations it turns out) that appear to fire identically for observed and executed simple actions (Mukamel, Ekstrom, Kaplan, Iacoboni, & Fried, 2010). All other studies have used noninvasive (e.g., fMRI) procedures that track entire clusters of cells 1 to 3 mm in area and so representing the activity of hundreds of thousands of cells. These fMRI studies (with adults) have yielded evidence for neural regions specially activated for intentional action understandings. But such studies have revealed a network of locations (partly overlapping with the ones I described as the theory-of-mind network), only one of which is (sometimes) localized in a similar part of human brain, Brodmann's area (e.g., BA 4, 6, 9, 46), as the frontal F5 area from monkeys. "Mirroring" as actually studied in humans more clearly involves coordinated brain regions rather than special single cells.

Moreover, recall that key evidence for monkeys was that F5 mirror neurons only fired to actual goal-directed actions, not objectless acts such as waving or actionless states such as simply desiring (but see, e.g., Rizzolatti & Fabbri-Destro, 2008, for increasingly broad claims about the sorts of actions that will fire mirror neurons). However, in humans, somehow, that is exactly what a mirror system is claimed to do—for example, allow attribution of actionless mental states (such as desiring, dreaming) and objectless intentional actions (waving, or objectless pretending) and moreover account for human imitation.

Many researchers thus question a mirror neuron theory for action understanding, or especially for mental-state understandings, in humans (Cook, Bird, Catmur, Press, & Heyes, 2014; Hickok, 2009). And they question a mirror neuron theory for human imitation, and certainly question a "broken mirror" interpretation for autism (Southgate & Hamilton, 2008).

In Chapter 7, I outlined many problems for a pure simulation account of theory of mind, if simulation is taken to mean anything like a process to "allow us to grasp the minds of others not through conceptual reasoning but through *direct* simulation" (as in the prior quote from Rizollatti; see also Gallese et al., 2004, p. 396). In understanding others, humans clearly can and do at times use their own minds as an important source for understanding the internal experiences of others. But this amounts to theory-driven simulation and not conceptually barren "direct simulation."

Nonetheless, it seems reasonable to accept mirror system data in humans as helping to localize the network of regions employed when humans engage in something like "action understanding" in the sense of encoding intentional actions that occur in response to seeing action stimuli. Given that, we can then ask how these regions relate to the network of regions discussed in this chapter as the theory-of-mind neural network. In an interesting meta-analysis, Frank Van Overwalle and Kris Baetens (Van Overwalle & Baetens, 2009) did just that. In their meta-analysis of over 200 fMRI studies, they looked for consensus evidence of the neural regions involved in the human "mirror" and "mentalizing" systems. Once again, fMRI studies of mentalizing indicated regions in medial PFC and the right TPJ. FMRI analysis of the "mirror" system, however, indicated three different regions: premotor cortex (PMC), the anterior intraparietal sulcus (IPS), and the posterior STS. Van Overwalle and Baetens (2009) concluded that the mirror system helps compare directly observable biological motions (especially of the hands and mouth) to "one's own behavioral repertoire and the most common goals associated with it" (p. 567). But, "the mirror and mentalizing systems are two distinct systems" (p. 579), and, "there is no evidence for involvement of a mirror system in the inference of more abstract and complex forms of intentionality and mentalizing" (p. 567). Thus, just as in the study described earlier by Ohnishi and colleagues (2004), lower level action-goal understandings separate, neurally, from higher level theory-of-mind understandings.

Yawning

Contagious yawning illuminates the operation of the mirror system as encoding directly observable behaviors in others in ways that overlap with one's own action tendencies. Spontaneous yawning is an evolutionarily old behavior. But contagious yawning—where viewing someone else yawn makes you yawn too—is evolutionarily young. It is common in humans and monkeys (macaques, baboons, chimpanzees) but little evident elsewhere. Spontaneous yawning occurs in human infants, but contagious yawning seems not to appear until the 2nd year of life (Anderson & Meno, 2003; Provine, 2005). In fMRI research, contagious yawning—evoked by watching videos of others yawn—activates specific portions of Brodmann's area (BA 9), a region within the human mirror system (Haker, Kawohl, Herwig, & Rössler, 2013). Brain areas linked to face perception are also activated, but the contagious-yawning mirror system activations appear after subtracting out activations to neutral videotapes of the same persons when not yawning.

Recall the research in Chapter 10 about dogs' special social-cognitive skills at attending to and reading human gestures and actions. Intriguingly, dogs evidence contagious yawning as well, in their case yawning in reaction to *human* yawns. Dogs yawn more when seeing their owners yawn than when simply seeing them open their mouths. And dogs yawn considerably more when seeing their *owners* yawn than when seeing other, unfamiliar humans do so (Romero, Konno, & Hasegawa 2013).

Development

Current research on mirror neurons provides a further opportunity for repeating an emphasis of this whole book: development. The mirror neuron research with monkeys has all been done with adult monkeys (of undetermined or unknown developmental history). Hence, it is not clear whether the neural structures detected are innate and apparent at birth or the product of long histories of experience-dependent learning. Richard Cook and his colleagues (2014), in an insightful recent review, argued that the complex patterns of mirror neuron data, including differences in function for animals apparently raised with different learning experiences, only make sense if we view mirror neuron functions as learned outcomes. And recall, if contagious yawning serves as a marker of the operation of a human mirror system, it does not appear early in infancy (when spontaneous yawning does) but only after about 1½ years of postnatal development.

Self-Projection

In total, neuroscience data show that the human mirror system plays little direct role in most mentalizing tasks (Van Overwalle & Baetens, 2009). As noted in Chapter 7, however, clearly humans do employ a strategy of understanding others' minds on analogy to their own. This raises the additional interesting question of how the theory-of-mind neural network, broadly construed, incorporates such specific processing. Jason Mitchell and his colleagues have provided intriguing data on this. Mitchell and his colleagues have been careful to call such self-projection strategies *an* important source of understanding minds (e.g., Waytz & Mitchell, 2011) but not claim that such strategies are the inevitable or fundamental or only source of understanding minds.

Mitchell and colleagues (Mitchell, Macrae, & Banaji, 2006), using fMRI subtraction methods, attempted to track what happens when adults reason about the mental states of self and others and relatedly when we reason about the mental states of others similar to ourselves versus others who are quite different. Two findings emerged. First, the active regions for self and other mental-state reasoning are similar in both being roughly in medial PFC—one of the key regions consistently part of the theory-of-mind network. But given that, the subregion most active for thinking about the self (and others similar to the self) is located more precisely in ventral-medial PFC; whereas mentalizing about others, and especially dissimilar others, engages a separable more dorsal region of medial PFC.

The rough overlap of these regions as within medial PFC encouraged Mitchell et al. (2006) to affirm "the plausibility of 'simulation' accounts of social cognition, which posit that perceivers can use knowledge about themselves to infer mental states of others" (p. 655). Indeed, adults can. The nonoverlap, however, additionally suggests that often theory-of-mind reasoning about others can proceed without reliance on self-referential engagement. Adult theory of mind is not necessarily or constitutively simulative. Indeed, recall that Waytz and Mitchell (2011) asserted that individuals use several different mechanisms for engaging in mental-state inferences.

CONCLUSIONS

In total, extant developmental neuroscience outlines a developing theory-of-mind neural network focused on the same neural regions as implicated in adult theory-of-mind research but evidencing considerable long-term development. In particular, results suggest a neural system for reasoning generally about mind and action, including reasoning about desires as well as beliefs, in mid-frontal regions. Accordingly, the medial PFC is consistently implicated in child studies measuring mental-state reasoning more generally, including beliefs but also desires. In addition, a growing specialization of right posterior brain regions (e.g., right TPJ) emerges developmentally for belief reasoning specifically, beyond reasoning for other mental states more generally, and in particular beyond reasoning about desires.

More speculatively, medial PFC and right TPJ may be undergoing somewhat complementary development in older children: increasing activation of TPJ for mental-state reasoning (for beliefs specifically) and decreasing activation of medial PFC (for reasoning about mental states generically). Perhaps as specialization of the TPJ increases for belief reasoning specifically, some computational load is transferred away from the medial PFC, potentially contributing to the decrease in medial PFC activation seen in older children and adults.

One clearly important task for future research is to disentangle the role of maturational factors and experience in accounting for theory-of-mind changes. Mark Sabbagh, who helped me to conduct my first developmental neuroscience investigations, also first conveyed to me a felicitous phrase for describing current research: We are beginning to chart the neural correlates that "pace" theory-of-mind development. This is apt because we are charting the neural developments that go hand in hand with, and help elucidate, theory-of-mind development. But pace is nicely ambiguous. Think about it in racetrack terms. If one horse paces another, it can mean pace from ahead (pulling the other along), go along side by side (in step with each other), or even follow quickly on the heels of. Given adult data alone, it has been tempting to assume that biologically driven brain maturation "pulls along" improved behavior performance. And relatedly, infant behavioral data have encouraged the conclusion that the crucial brain systems may be largely mature very early in life, set to pull behavioral accomplishments along behind them. In contrast, it is now clear that theory-of-mind brain activations change throughout childhood development in step with behavioral theory-of-mind changes; they co-occur. And, these changes do not co-occur alone in developmental time. The changes are also paced by changes in performance accuracy. When accuracy changes with age, neural activations change; when same-age children differ in accuracy, their neural activations also differ. To my mind, the triangular relations between age, performance, and neural activations suggest important experience-dependent links among theory of mind and the theory-of-mind neural network.

Theory-of-mind neural networks and neural development have not been commonly explained in experience-dependent ways. However, it is undeniable that experience shapes neural organization. Developmental neuroscientists, such as neuroconstructivists but others as well, increasingly stress the variety of ways in which brain development is experience dependent and plastic (e.g., Lillard & Erisir, 2011). So too, theory-of-mind development is experience dependent as I show in Chapters 5, 6, and 9. And recall from Chapter 10 that Robin Dunbar (2013) insisted that the human social brain has evolved to require not simple maturation but ontogenetic learning. I favor, and I believe current data favor, a very large role of experience in shaping neurofunctional as well as behavior change in theory of mind. Increasingly precise *developmental* cognitive neuroscience research will further elucidate the intermingled contributions of intrinsic and experiential factors in theory-of-mind development.

Fortunately, as reviewed here, data are already emerging about the development of theory-of-mind reasoning and brain processes. Summing up, those data yield three clear conclusions:

1. Too little is known about infancy and early development.
2. From preschool on, theory-of-mind reasoning recruits some of the same neural regions that adult theory-of-mind reasoning recruits—in particular, the medial PFC and TPJ are early recruited portions of what will become the adult theory-of-mind network.
3. Neural structures supporting theory-of-mind reasoning change with development, and they do so even postpreschool when children are largely at ceiling behaviorally on the theory-of-mind reasoning tasks (e.g., false belief, belief vs. desire) that have been explored.

12

Searching, Learning, and Listening

EXPLORATION, PEDAGOGY, AND TESTIMONY

TWO CLASSIC TRUISMS about childhood cognition are that children are (often) active learners—as evident in their play and in their questions—and that children are (often) social learners—as evident in their learning from parents, teachers, and peers. Nowhere are these processes more apparent or more useful than in social cognition— learning about the social world. Constructivist, theory-theory perspectives on learning embrace these truisms and go further to describe and explore them.

Chapter 6 outlined how theories emerge and change on the basis of an intriguing but comprehensible interplay between hypotheses and evidence, yielding revised posterior hypotheses. Indeed, contemporary probabilistic Bayesian learning models describe how hypotheses and evidence constrain and enable learning, and even lead to abstract framework learning. Integral to this process are several sorts of theory-based searching: rational modes of exploration that shape learning. One sort of search problem, consistently addressed by much Bayesian machine learning, concerns searching through hypotheses to home in on the most probabilistically likely ones. A probabilistic Bayesian learner can even hypothesize unobservable, hidden variables or constructs to best account for the evidence. But, equally, a learner can actively search for new evidence and search for explanations. How do children engage in such exploration? Do they do so haphazardly, or—as befits a Bayesian, constructivist learner—more rationally? A variety of contemporary research sheds light on these questions, thereby shedding light on children's processes for making knowledge. This research also illuminates children's processes for making minds because such exploration is not merely cognitive; it is social cognitive—saturated with developing understandings of agency, persons, and minds.

Probabilistic Bayesian approaches overlap with theory theory in particular for the case of causal learning. One of the insights of this approach to causal learning, noted in Chapter 6 for starters, is that deliberately intervening on the world—and observing the outcomes of those interventions—is a particularly good way to figure out the causal structure of the world. The philosopher of science Frederick Eberhardt, using Bayesian models, has mathematically explored how interventions allow you to infer causal structure from data (Eberhardt & Scheines, 2007; see also Cook, Goodman, & Schulz, 2011). It turns out that by intervening yourself you can rapidly get the right evidence to eliminate many possible hypotheses and thus to narrow your search through the remaining hypotheses. That is, just as scientists believe, intervention facilitates exploration of the evidence, which then shapes searching through hypotheses. In this way, the probabilistic Bayesian approach formally explains the scientific intuition that experiments tell you more about causal relationships than simple observations do.

Exploratory Play

Could it be that childhood intervention—as in active play perhaps—can also work in this fashion? Children's play has been studied for many years and, historically, Piaget, Montessori, Bruner, and most preschool teachers have agreed that children learn through play (see Hirsh-Pasek & Golinkoff, 2003; Lillard, 2005). Anyone who watches young children has seen how they ceaselessly fiddle with things. In play, children intervene on things, and in this way children's play can look like informal experimentation. However, could it actually function as experimentation, helping children rationally explore causation?

Recent research has begun to address these issues. The upshot of these studies is that children's exploratory play, although certainly not structured like the ideal experiments of science, nevertheless can be sufficiently systematic to help children discover causal structure.

In an illustrative series of studies, Laura Schulz and Elizabeth Bonawitz (2007) assessed how preschool children explored a new "jack-in-the-box" type of toy. The toy had two levers that produced two effects (a duck and/or a puppet could pop up). Crucially, Schulz and Bonawitz compared two conditions. In both, an adult and a child interactively played with the toy; but in one condition, the causal structure of the toy was ambiguous, and in the other it was clear. In the *confounded* condition, the adult and the child each pushed a lever and did so simultaneously. As a result, both effects appeared. With this demonstration, it was completely unclear how the toy worked. Maybe one lever produced the duck, and the other produced the puppet; maybe one lever produced both effects; maybe both levers produced both effects; and so on. In the *unconfounded* condition, on the other hand, the adult pushed one lever, and it systematically produced a single effect; and then the child pushed the other lever, which systematically produced the other effect. In this unconfounded condition, the causal structure of the toy was clear.

After manipulating the toy interactively with the child (in either the confounded or unconfounded manner), the experimenter then placed this old toy and a new toy (a novel but simpler, single-lever toy) in front of the child. Then she left the child alone, free to play with either toy. The backdrop to this free-play contrast is that often, after children have played with one toy, they then prefer to play with a new toy; in play, as in other regards, children often prefer novelty. So if children's play is driven by desire for novelty, in this case they should prefer the new toy *in both conditions*. But, if children's play is driven by a desire to explore and understand causal structure, then they should behave differently in the two conditions. Given a desire to explore causal structure, in the confounded condition, they should be especially likely to explore the old toy. This is because in that condition, the old toy's causal structure is unclear, and further intervention could help reveal it. In the unconfounded condition, however, interventions will have no further benefit because the initial manipulations already revealed the toy's causal structure.

Indeed, 3- and 4-year-old children systematically explored the old toy rather than the new one in the confounded condition but not the unconfounded one. Moreover, after they had finished exploring the toy, children in the confounded condition showed that they had figured out how the toy worked. This research shows not only that children actively seek out new evidence, they do so rationally in two senses: in the sense of attempting to disentangle confounds and in the sense of generating evidence sufficient to draw the correct conclusions. In short, when given a causally puzzling toy to play with, young children spontaneously produced interventions on that toy—intervened in ways to produce new evidence—generated relevant evidence, and drew the correct conclusions from the evidence they generated (see also Cook et al., 2011).

So, children's play-based actions can represent effective search for causally relevant and informative evidence. But, of course, there is also the equally convincing observation that children's play is often just that—playful; that is, undirected and unsystematic. Indeed, children's play has most often been viewed as whimsical and messy, cute but capricious. Surely childhood play does not achieve well-controlled experimentation; in fact, other research has demonstrated that even older children and naïve adults are bad at explicitly designing causally informative experiments (Chen & Klahr, 1999; Kuhn, 1962). This leads to a conundrum. If children's playful explorations are so messy and unsystematic, how could they actually lead to rational causal learning?

A less obvious, but to me even more intriguing, result from Frederick Eberhardt's Bayesian calculations (e.g., Eberhardt & Scheines, 2007) helps explain this: Informative interventions need not be the systematic, carefully controlled experiments of science. Eberhardt's formal work shows that even less controlled interventions on the world can be nicely informative about causal structure. For example, in many situations, multiple simultaneous interventions (confounding several factors together) can be as effective as intervening on just one variable at a time. Moreover, "soft" interventions, where the experimenter simply fiddles with the value of a variable, can be as effective as more controlled interventions, where the experimenter completely fixes that value. In short, what scientists disparagingly call a "fishing expedition" can still tell us a great deal about causal structure—you do not necessarily need the full apparatus of a randomized controlled trial. Eberhardt's calculations show that for machine learning, and for scientists, playing around can effectively reveal causal structure via exploratory interventions. This is so for children too.

Exploration via Explanations

Recall from Chapter 2 that young children actively seek explanations: They request them from others and actively formulate them on their own. They not only seek explanations, they learn from them. As one example, in the microgenetic research highlighted in Chapter 6, when children must provide explanations for actors' actions, then they more quickly make theory-of-mind progress, learning more than a variety of control groups. Cristine Legare (e.g., Legare, 2012) has provided recent research that links children's learning from explanations directly to their exploratory interventions as well.

To set the stage, Cristine Legare, Susan Gelman, and I (2010) initially showed that anomalous events inconsistent with children's prior knowledge trigger their explanations. In our research, children saw two sorts of different-appearing objects and how several of them influenced a blicket detector (similar to the one depicted in Box 6.1 back in Chapter 6). Several objects of one sort (e.g., green triangular blocks), called "tomas," always lit up a blicket detector; but several objects of another sort (e.g., yellow heart-shaped blocks), called "daxes," never lit up the detector. After these preliminaries, then in a focal test event, both a green triangle and a yellow heart were placed on the detector simultaneously, and the device failed to light. At this point the adult pointed ambiguously to the entire detector with both blocks on it and asked (nonspecifically), "Why did that happen?" Children overwhelmingly attempted to explain the inconsistent event (the green triangle that failed to light the detector) rather than the consistent event (a yellow heart that, like the prior yellow hearts, failed to light the detector). In their explanations, they essentially either offered *category-switch* explanations (e.g., it looks like a toma but it's really a dax) or offered *causal* explanations (e.g., that toma must be broken, its batteries must be dead, etc.). So, this research showed that children particularly seek and offer explanations for anomalous occurrences.

Cleverly, in subsequent research with young children ranging in age from 2 to 6 years, Legare (2012) did essentially the same thing but then asked children if they wanted to play with the materials—a pile of the two different-appearing objects and the detector. All of them wanted to, and so she then left them free to do so.

Children eagerly engaged in exploratory play with the objects (as they did in the Schulz & Bonawitz, 2007, research), and moreover their earlier explanations shaped their explorations. Children who gave category switch explanations typically sorted the pile of objects into its two apparent types and then checked to see if other tomas seemed to work like daxes. In contrast, children who gave causal explanations looked for some sort of malfunction. In fact, children had given two subtypes of causal explanations originally: *causal function* explanations (e.g., the machine is broken, the ones that work are probably heavier) or *causal action* explanations (e.g., you set the toma on its wrong side, you didn't push it down hard enough). If they had given causal function explanations, their explorations were aimed at the functions (were some tomas too lightweight, was the machine plugged in, etc.). If they had given causal action explanations, they tried rotating the "malfunctioning" ones, pushing them harder on the machine, stacking two up on the machine, and so forth. Observations led to explanations, explanations led to interventions and explorations, and one rationally led to the other as children fiddled and played.

Exploration via Pretense

Notably, most childhood play is emphatically social, much more so than mere child–adult comanipulation of objects. By hypothesis, playful exploration of the evidence might extend especially to the social world and provoke social learning as well as object learning. This is where children's play impacts their theory of mind most directly. Social pretend play, for example, is often described as trying on social roles: "You be the mommy, I'll be the daddy." From a Bayesian experimentation-exploration perspective, social pretense seems to give children a special place for experimenting with social-mentalistic causality, a laboratory for social-causal explorations and interventions. If so, then, following causal-models reasoning, engagement in pretense should yield insight into the causal structure of social agents; it should link to development of theory of mind.

Neatly, the links between pretense and enhanced theory of mind are clear: Children's increased participation in pretend play is associated with learning about persons and minds (although see Lillard et al., 2013, for some skepticism about the definitiveness of this research). Marjorie Taylor and Stephanie Carlson (1997), for example, found that 3- and 4-year-olds with extensive fantasy experiences—such as play with imaginary playmates and frequent pretending—were more likely to pass false-belief tasks. But, more specifically, the link is between *social* pretend play and theory of mind (Harris, 2005; Kavanaugh, 2006). Thus, more frequent engagement in social pretense with parents (Astington & Jenkins, 1995) and role-playing games with siblings and peers (Schwebel et al., 1999; Youngblade & Dunn, 1995) predicts children's false-belief understandings.

Collaborative plans and assigning roles are ways to intervene socially and are hallmarks of childhood play. In social play, collaborating on a social narrative and discussing what characters do and think is frequent (Dunn & Brophy, 2005). And a higher frequency of such play is related to theory-of-mind competences (Howe et al., 1998). In social play, assigning roles to self and other and making shared plans for joint pretense is frequent. And, engaging in conversations that assign roles and that organize shared pretense is related to false-belief performance (Jenkins & Astington, 2000). Such connections appear not only in research in which pretend play and theory of mind are assessed concurrently, but also in research in which these two factors are assessed longitudinally (Jenkins & Astington, 2000).

Deaf children provide additional evidence for links between pretend play and theory of mind. In general, deaf children of hearing parents are delayed not only in theory-of-mind achievement (as outlined in Chapters 5 and 6) but also engage in dramatically reduced amounts of pretend play. For example, when two scientists observed a group of orally communicating, deaf 4- and 5-year-olds, they found that solitary pretend play was infrequent and social pretense was almost nonexistent (Higginbotham & Baker, 1981). Whereas hearing preschoolers spent 25% of their free time in social pretend play (and 42% of it in pretense of all kinds), corresponding percentages for the deaf children were only 3% and 25%, respectively. Similarly, a more recent study (Brown et al., 1997) found that whereas hearing preschoolers communicated about pretense events frequently in free play with peers (averaging 20 such utterances per hour), an age-matched deaf group did so rarely (averaging 2 or 3 utterances per hour or, for many children, none at all). By implication, then, in their paucity of pretend play and in their altered social interactions more generally, young deaf children of hearing parents have fewer opportunities to explore social roles, search for and through social evidence, and intervene on their own and others' actions. This yields delayed social learning.

Summary

As adults we often seek knowledge to exploit it; our motives are often pragmatic. But we also sometimes just seek, out of curiosity, simply to understand, divorced from any pragmatic goal. Basic scientists and adventurers exemplify this exploration motive. So do children. Unfettered, children deploy a wide-ranging curiosity as is clear in their questions: "What does it do?" "Why did she do that?" "What's its name?" "Why do people eat snails?" "Can I try?" "Is it alive?" (Chouinard, 2007; Hickling & Wellman, 2001; Callanan & Oakes, 1992). The explorations of scientists and children are not haphazard; often they "fish" and fiddle, but as much rationally as randomly. Their active exploration of and intervention on the world provides important information about the causal properties not only of objects but also of people. It is often not in the service of something "practical"; it is in the interest of theory building.

LEARNING FROM OTHERS: IMITATION, PEDAGOGY, AND OBSERVATION

Imitation and Pedagogy

A straightforward means of learning from and about others is not only playing with them but imitating them. Even infants imitate (Bauer, 1996; Meltzoff, 2011).

When most people first think of imitation they think of straightforward, direct mimicking—faithful copying of someone else's acts. Yet imitation is not so simple; rather, it both requires and reveals children's causal learning and in particular causal learning about agents and minds. For example, recall from Chapter 1 that infants "imitate" unsuccessful actions; and when they do so, they enact the actor's unseen, intended goal and not the actually seen, failed act. Recall also that infants don't imitate obviously accidental acts ("Whoops") but do imitate obviously intentional acts ("There"). These results already show that children, even infants, do not just imitate what they see—what they imitate depends on their analysis of agents' causal intentions.

A further, neat demonstration of imitation as a window onto children's causal understandings additionally shows an important interplay between exploration and imitation. Elizabeth Bonawitz and her colleagues (2011) showed children a single function of a novel toy that could behave in many different and nonobvious ways (pressing a button made it beep, squeezing a bulb made it light up, etc.). When the demonstrator said that she was showing the child how the toy worked, saying "Look at this toy. Look what it does," then in a subsequent free-play situation, children would simply imitate the action the demonstrator performed. However, when the demonstrator activated the toy accidentally, saying "Look at this toy, oops, look at that," then in the free-play opportunity, children would explore the toy and discover its other causal properties.

This study demonstrates, again, children's active playful explorations; but it also, in reverse, helps exemplify children's receptivity to pedagogy—others' intention to teach them something. When the adult intentionally demonstrated something to them, children constrained their interventions to the ones demonstrated. Indeed, a particularly powerful, and early, forum for social-causal learning is others' teaching—usually for young children informal (not formal) pedagogy. Csibra and Gergely (2006) in particular have insisted that even infants are sensitive to pedagogy and make different inferences when evidence comes from a teacher. For Csibra and Gergely, this is the result of an innate set of cues pointing to pedagogical intent, such as the use of child-directed speech ("motherese") and eye contact, which automatically lead children to make particular kinds of inferences. But, alternatively, others argue that infants and children are often making deeper analyses of others' intention to teach (Gopnik & Wellman, 2012; Shafto, Goodman, & Frank, 2012). That is, children are not blindly privileging pedagogy; rather, they are more rationally judging the causal implications of teachers' intentions and demonstrations.

Voluminous research on "overimitation" helps illustrate children's analyses. In these imitation studies, children see another person act on the world in a complicated way to bring about an effect. For example, an adult leans down and presses his forehead to a blicket-detector type of box to activate it. Sometimes in these circumstances, children simply reproduce exactly the sequence of actions they see the experimenter perform even when some of the modeled actions are irrelevant to the causal effect—they overimitate (Horner & Whiten, 2005; Lyons, Santos, & Keil, 2006; Meltzoff, 1988; Tomasello, 1993). Sometimes, though, children act rationally, reproducing the most causally effective action (Gergely, Bekkering, & Király, 2002; Southgate, Chevallier, & Csibra, 2009; Williamson, Meltzoff, & Markman, 2008), for example, using their hand not their head to press on and activate the box. In one case, children seem to be following a social-causal analysis—this is the way one is supposed to act in regard to this object (in our social group; see, e.g., Harris, 2012). In the other case, they follow a physical-causal analysis—activation requires pressing on the top of the device.

In general, sensitivity to implicit pedagogy is an enormous asset for learning; it helps direct one's search for evidence and hypotheses. It allows children to focus on just the hypotheses and evidence that are most relevant and significant for their culture and community or for this task and device. Others are presorting the relevant hypotheses and evidence for the child, short-circuiting some or most of the exploration needed to find them.

On the other hand, implicit pedagogy also has disadvantages. As in the Bonawitz research (Bonawitz et al. 2011), it may lead children to ignore some causal hypotheses; as in the overimitation research, it may lead children to assume irrelevant causal features are relevant. In that Bonawitz research, for example, given a "pedagogical" demonstration, children spent most of their time exercising the demonstrated function. As a consequence, they failed to explore more broadly and so failed to discover that the toy had other functions and operations as well. In contrast, in the nonpedagogical condition (e.g., the accidental condition), preschoolers explored more broadly and learned additional ways in which the toy operated. Daphne Buchsbaum and her colleagues (Buchsbaum, Gopnik, Griffiths, & Shafto, 2011) provided very similar findings. And, children overimitate most when adult models are being most obviously pedagogical, for example, when they use more directive language (e.g., "look"). As another example, 3- to 6-year-olds imitate still more faithfully (they "stick to the script") if they see two adults model the same act rather than just one (Herrmann, Legare, Harris, & Whitehouse, 2013).

Observing Others

I began this chapter by outlining how children learn causal structure from their own interventions in exploratory play, in pretending. So we can learn about causation by experimenting ourselves, and crucial for children, experimenting just by playing around. But we can also learn about causation by watching what other people do, and what happens as a result, as occurs in childhood imitation and children's receptivity to pedagogical demonstrations. These are instances of social learning, social learning shaped by and resulting in causally relevant explorations of social evidence. However, not all social-causal learning concerns imitation or pedagogy. We engage in other forms of causal learning about and from others, and these provide examples as well of learning via interventions, in this case, simply observing others' interventions.

As I have argued throughout this book, a crucial social-cognitive feature of people, understood early on by young infants and children, is that they are intentional agents. Moreover, intentional actions constitute interventions on the world; all intentional actions attempt to produce causal effects by intervening on background probabilities (the box full of mostly yellow ducks), biomechanical dynamics (moving one's hand), or object mechanics (moving a toy). According to the causal Bayes Net framework, one can learn causal structure effectively from the interventions of others as well as from one's own. By implication, then, young children, as rational causal learners, should be alert to others' interventions as a special source of causal information. All kinds of causal covariation information are informative, but causal covariations that result from the direct actions of people could be especially causally informative.

A clear example was provided by Elizabeth Bonawitz and her colleagues (2010), who showed 4-year-olds and also 2-year-olds correlations between two events that were and were not the outcome of human action. In one case—human intervention—children saw an actor push a box that moved and collided with a second box several times. Each time the second box would light up, and then the propeller on a toy plane a few inches away would spin. In a second case—object intervention—the first box spontaneously moved and collided with the second box, and again each time the second box would light up and a toy plane would spin. So, in both conditions children saw a first box collide with a second and then the propeller on an adjacent toy plane would spin. The only difference was that in one condition (human intervention) a person initiated this sequence, and in the other (object intervention), no one did. After viewing these events, children were then asked to make the plane's propeller spin themselves. The obvious course of action is to push the first box against the second.

In both conditions, 4-year-olds spontaneously pushed the first box against the second when asked to make the plane spin. And they also looked toward the plane as soon as they did so. The key developmental result, however, was that 2-year-olds were strikingly unlikely to spontaneously move the box to make the plane go in the *object intervention* condition. Although they would happily move the box if they were specifically asked to do so, even then they did not look toward the plane and anticipate the result. However, these younger children were much more likely to spontaneously act themselves and to anticipate the result when they observed a human agent bring about exactly the same events. That is, in the human intervention condition, when they saw an experimenter push the first block against the second to make the plane spin, 2-year-olds would both push the block themselves and anticipate the result.

Using different stimuli and additional controls, Andrew Meltzoff and his colleagues (Meltzoff, Waismeyer, & Gopnik, 2012) tested 24-month-olds on a task where the child sat between two light boxes that flanked a nifty marble dispensing device. The child saw a consistent sequence of events where when one of the boxes lit up, then the marble dispenser emitted a marble; but when the other box lit up, no marble was forthcoming. One group of children saw this sequence when an adult clearly activated the light boxes—the human intervention group. And a second group saw the same sequence of events but when the light boxes lit up on their own—the natural covariation group. The 2-year-olds were especially likely to make causal inferences from these events when the events were the result of human actions. Indeed, often for these very young children observing the events as resulting from deliberate intervention was necessary for them to infer the causal connections. Again, as in the findings reported by Bonawitz and her colleagues (2010), when Meltzoff and his colleagues (2012) tested older children, in this case 3- and 4-year-olds, they could make the inferences in the natural covariation as well as the human intervention conditions.

Summary

Children explore, fiddle, and play. Intriguingly, they do so in ways that aid discovery of causal regularities, ways that effectively narrow their search for causal hypotheses and evidence. Passive observation of naturally occurring covariations between events can provide evidence of causal structure. However, experimenting yourself can provide especially rich information about causal structure. These interventions help home in on just the statistical relationships that are most likely to support causal inferences. Indeed, attending to the interventions of others can also point children in the right direction, and very young children particularly attend to and learn from human interventions. Understanding when those interventions are pedagogical adds still more information, and young children are specially attuned to pedagogical demonstrations. Moreover, young children search for evidence and search through hypotheses by actively seeking and generating explanations. Empirical work shows that these natural proclivities of very young children align with the search and learning approaches that computational causal models highlight as particularly effective ways to learn about causality.

These information-gathering activities of childhood are very often social activities. And, they very often lead to social learning, to theory-of-mind insights. Children not only learn *via* play, human interactions, pedagogy, and explanation. They learn *about* acting, teaching, learning, and explaining; and they learn *about* agents, teachers, learners, and explainers.

LEARNING FROM TESTIMONY

A chapter on children's explorations of, and learning from and about social sources, would be deficient without consideration of the burgeoning literature on children's receptivity to testimony. From others' testimony, we acquire information ranging from the mundane—today's date or someone's phone number—to information that cannot be easily observed or assessed—the presence of germs, the existence of God, the atomic structure of matter (Harris & Koenig, 2006; Lane & Harris, 2014). Given young children's limited firsthand experience with the world, seeking, listening to, and learning from testimony is an invaluable source of information for them (Gelman, 2009; Harris & Koenig, 2006). Attention to testimony is necessary, for example, for as important a childhood task as learning names; and classic "testimony" tasks have explored children's learning of name for things.

In an example of a standard testimony task, children are shown two characters, typically hand puppets or real people on video (Clément, Koenig, & Harris, 2004; Koenig, Clément, & Harris, 2004; Pasquini, Corriveau, Koenig, & Harris, 2007), who differ in their demonstrated accuracy (e.g., their correct or incorrect naming of common objects), and children choose to ask one character to learn something new (e.g., the name of a novel object). Then both characters offer conflicting information (testimony), and children choose which character's testimony they believe by endorsing one or the other. Most of the burgeoning work on children's receptivity to testimony examines children's selective "trust" in this sort of testimony (Harris, 2012).

A consistent finding is that when learning the names of novel objects, 4-year-olds prefer to endorse object labels provided by accurate informants (Clément et al., 2004; Jaswal & Neely, 2006; Koenig et al., 2004). In related tasks in which children choose who to ask to learn the name of a new object, they ask previously accurate informants (Koenig et al., 2004). Although 3-year-olds often do not consistently preferentially endorse accurate informants' testimony in these tasks, even 3-year-olds will selectively endorse informants when presented more data about them. Take a comparison in which young children see one informant is consistently accurate across four instances, and the other informant is inaccurate across four instances. Then, even 3-year-olds trust testimony provided by the previously accurate informant (Birch, Vauthier, & Bloom, 2008; Pasquini et al., 2007; Scofield & Behrend, 2008). However, if both informants are wrong at least once—even though one is correct 75% of the time, whereas the other is correct only 25% of the time—3-year-olds no longer demonstrate selective trust; 4-year-olds do (Pasquini et al., 2007). Thus, 3-year-olds in particular seem to require more consistent, error-free evidence about informants' tendencies to shape their trust in testimony.

I will not review the large literature that has emerged researching children's responses to testimony (see instead Harris, 2012). But it is worth emphasizing, for a book about making minds, that learning from testimony, although of course social, is not merely minimally social: It is saturated with theory-of-mind features and understanding. To see this, consider that accuracy could be thought of as an "objective" feature of a person's testimony—what he or she said accorded with reality. From the point of view of theory of mind, however, the "subjective" features of testifiers are further and especially relevant and important. Some people unknowingly offer inaccurate information because of their own misperceptions or ignorance. Others intentionally (perhaps malevolently) provide false information. And so on. Because of this variability in informants' knowledge and intentions, they are differentially trustworthy. To be appropriately selective in whom they choose to learn from, children need to penetrate to testifiers' intentions to inform (e.g., to be helpful or to mislead), testifiers' knowledge or ignorance, and their epistemic traits (e.g., that X is a consistent liar or that Y is consistently honest). Although less research on children's trust in testimony has targeted these subjective qualities, when it has, even preschool children appreciate these aspects of testimony as well.

Considering Informants' Knowledge

In particular, testimony research has begun to reveal how young children are appropriately sensitive to informants' knowledge, at least in certain scenarios. For example, if faced with a scenario in which one informant accurately labels common objects and the other informant consistently says "I do not know," 3-year-olds prefer to ask the accurate informant for the label of a new object, and 4-year-olds prefer to both ask and to endorse labels provided by the accurate rather than the avowedly ignorant informant (Koenig & Harris, 2005). Four-year-olds are also more accepting of information provided by informants who are confident in their knowledge (Moore et al., 1989). For example, they believe information provided by someone who says, "I know it is in the red box" versus someone who says, "I guess it is in the red box" (see Jaswal & Malone, 2007; Sabbagh & Baldwin, 2001). And children as young as 3 years of age are less willing to believe the testimony of someone who lacks visual access to relevant information and so who should be uninformed (Robinson, Champion, & Mitchell, 1999).

This sensitivity to knowledge and beliefs, of course, accords with 3-, 4-, and 5-year-olds' blossoming understanding of these representational mental states, the sorts of understandings and advances discussed in Chapters 2, 4, and 5. As such, the data add to the discussion in Chapter 3 explicitly reviewing how childhood belief-desire understanding, their theory of mind, impacts preschoolers' social lives. In this case, childhood belief-desire understanding impacts their selectivity in learning from others, an activity that constitutes one of the premier social interactions in young children's lives.

Of course, would-be teachers and testifiers can be knowledgeable but deceptive or intentionally unhelpful, even mean. Thus, in several studies, Oliver Mascaro and Dan Sperber (2009) attempted to examine the influence of informants' kindness and honesty on children's trust. In one of their studies, 3-year-olds clearly preferred the testimony of a nice informant rather than the testimony of a mean informant. Jonathan Lane, myself, and Susan Gelman (2013) found the same thing. In our research, children aged 3 through 6 years were told about two boys, one of whom was nice ("Neal is a boy who does nice things for people. Look, Neal sees another boy struggling to carry a big plant; Neal helps the boy carry the plant. Neal is nice."), and one of whom was mean ("Mike is a boy who does mean things to people. Look, Mike sees another boy struggling to carry a big plant; Mike pushes the boy and his plant falls and breaks. Mike is mean."). Children then saw a closed box and were asked (a) to decide who they wanted to ask to find out what was inside (*ask* question). Then both Neal and Mike stated opposing contents for the box and children were asked (b) what they themselves now thought was in the box (*endorse* question). Children at all ages consistently chose both to ask the nice Neal and to endorse his answer over that of the mean Mike.

What about characters who lie? Lying is a feature of testimony that seems still more clearly linked to childhood understanding of theory of mind, as discussed in Chapter 3. Mascaro and Sperber (2009), in their research, had an informant (e.g., a frog puppet) provide young children with erroneous testimony about the location of candy. In the case of lying, the informant was described as a "Big liar! He always tells lies. Watch out!" Then children were presented two boxes, and the informant made a claim that the candy was in one of the boxes. By 4 years (see their Study 2), most children avoided the box indicated by the deceptive frog. However, these results may not reflect children's consideration of informants' honesty in particular. In Mascaro and Sperber's study, children were told the puppet was a "big liar" but also warned about him ("watch out"), so it is not clear if 4-year-olds' appropriate choices reflect the warning, the lying, or both.

Our research headed by Jonathan Lane (Lane et al., 2013) improved on this. In parallel to the contrast between Neal and Mike, who were nice and mean as just described, children also heard about other pairs such as Tom and Larry. "Tom is a boy who tells the truth. Tom is truthful. Look, Tom accidentally threw his ball through the window. His mom asked him, 'Tom, did you break the window?' and Tom said 'Yes'. Tom is truthful." In contrast for Larry, "Larry is a boy who tells lies. Larry is a liar. Look, Larry accidentally threw his ball through the window. His mom asked him, 'Larry, did you break the window?' and Larry said 'No'. Larry is a liar." Then as in the nice–mean comparison, children saw a closed box. Children 4 years of age and older consistently asked Tom not Larry, the truth-teller not the liar, what was in the box, and consistently endorsed Tom's not Larry's statement about what was in the box (Lane et al., 2013). The 3-year-olds were less consistent; but crucially, considering all the children, children's preference for asking and trusting the truthful informant was related to their performance on a separate theory-of-mind task that assessed their understanding of knowledge and ignorance.

Sensitivity to the importance of knowledge and beliefs is important for learning about the world from others more generally—beyond others' provision of testimony per se. Recall from the prior section that preschoolers use information from others' interventions—namely, their intentional actions—to make causal inferences. The knowledge states of others as interveners can be as important as the knowledge states of testifiers. Tamar Kushnir, Susan Gelman and I (Kushnir, Wellman, & Gelman, 2008) showed that 3- and 4-year-olds understand this.

Preschoolers saw a blicket detector (that lit up when some but not all types of blocks were placed on it) and saw two actors—two puppets, "squirrel and monkey"—place a block each, simultaneously, on the machine, which then lit up. One actor (squirrel, let's say, although this was counterbalanced across children) was introduced as someone "who has seen the machine before," "knows all about it," and "knows which blocks make the machine go." The second actor (monkey, let's say) "has never seen the machine before," "doesn't know anything about it," and "doesn't know which blocks make the machine go." Squirrel and monkey each picked a block from a pile of various blocks and placed it on the machine at the exact same time. Then the child was asked which block made the machine go. Children consistently chose the knowledgeable puppet's (squirrel's) block.

In this same study, children also demonstrated they understood that actors not only had to have knowledge; their knowledge had to actually cause their relevant actions. So in a control condition, the knowledgeable puppet and the ignorant one were given blocks randomly by the child (who didn't know which blocks were effective) and placed *those* blocks on the machine simultaneously. Now when asked which block had made the machine light up, children chose randomly or said they couldn't tell. And in another control condition, squirrel and monkey chose their own blocks but did so blindfolded. Again in this control, children did *not* pick the knowledgeable puppet's block. In total, these children understood the knowledgeable puppet's block indicated the specially relevant intervention only when that puppet both had knowledge and could use it—could intentionally choose his own block and could see what he was choosing (Kushnir et al., 2008). Social understandings based on evaluating persons' epistemic states are crucial in accepting (or rejecting) others' testimony and intervention as specially informative about the world; and by 3 and especially 4 years, preschoolers know this and exhibit this in their learning from others.

THEORY THEORY, AGAIN

According to theory theory, there are deep and telling parallels between childhood cognitive development and science. Paul Harris (2012), in his recent book about children and testimony, says

> I am skeptical about this analogy. Scientific communities and their distinctive
> modes of investigation are extreme latecomers, when viewed against the protracted

backdrop of human history. It would be odd if cognitive development were to mirror such a recent and distinctive institution. (p. 206)

But the point, for theory theory, is not that childhood cognition mimics science; it is that both mimic each other in certain, but only certain, crucial fashions. Thus, at the end of Chapter 6, I noted that when learning about the causal structure of the world, scientists and children not only both exploit the crucial interplay between theory and evidence; they engage in requisite cognitive practices that allow and constrain theory construction:

- They infer causal relationships from evidence.
- They inductively, probabilistically infer general conclusions from small samples of evidence.
- They use both experimental and statistical evidence to infer causal relations.
- They seek and generate explanations and revised hypotheses for anomalous or surprising data.
- They propose unobserved variables to explain anomalous data.

From this chapter, we see that children, along with scientists, engage in additional, important, knowledge-generating practices as well:

- They not only attend to evidence, they generate it, and they actively search for evidence.
- They attend to the evidence that others generate in addition to their own investigations.
- They seek knowledgeable and helpful others as teachers and informants.
- They seek knowledgeable and helpful others as collaborators.

In short, young children actively explore and experiment; and they see themselves as part of a community of knowers, and thus learn from others, not just nature. For theory theory, and for children, theory construction is not a passive cognitive activity; it is active and experimental. Theory construction is also not a solitary cognitive activity; it is socially saturated. It takes place with others, informed and guided by them both directly and indirectly.

It is a caricature of science to envision a lone investigator learning and theorizing about the world, just as it is a caricature of childhood theory building to envision an individual child constructing knowledge of the world. Think instead of an alert graduate student learning within an interdisciplinary, collaborative laboratory group: attending to evidence others generate, using that to shape his or her own emerging investigations, seeking knowledgeable teachers to apprentice with, seeking collaborations as much as seeking evidence, and learning from the lot. Processes of theory construction must account for each individual's theory learning, but the overall epistemic process is characteristically collaborative and social as well. We scientists have always engaged in such social epistemic practices, but we increasingly utilize them in this era of collaborative, interdisciplinary science. In this way our scientific practices have increasingly come to mimic the socially saturated cognitive practices of children.

13

Further Developments

FOR ADULTS, EXTRAORDINARY agents, like God, are distinctively different from ordinary agents, even famous powerful agents like Mao Zedong. For adults, the brain is distinctively different from the mind. Are god concepts different from ordinary person concepts for children? If so, when and how? Are brain concepts different from mind concepts for children? If so, when and how? My thesis for both sets of questions is that brain concepts and god concepts similarly represent later developments, built on a platform of preschool theory of mind—those concepts explored and explained in Chapters 2, 4, and 5.

So, to begin, I briefly recap some of the key preschool achievements that set the infrastructure for constructing these later ideas and do so by describing them as achievements of a naïve childhood dualism, just as in Chapter 2. This childhood achievement is apparent in our own adult everyday psychophysical dualism. Everyday dualism, apparent even by 3 and 4 years of age, encompasses several subjective–objective distinctions:

1. Thoughts differ from things: A thought about ice is mental; ice itself is physical, concrete, cold, and slippery.
2. Mental attitudes subjectively differ across individuals: I can think a 10-story building is really tall, someone else might think it is short.
3. Private mental acts and events can differ from external expressions and events: A person's desires, thoughts, and feelings can be hidden and at odds with

objective reports, expressions, and acts. I can be deeply unhappy, but smile and laugh anyway.

4. Mental acts differ from bodily behaviors: Intentions, desires, and beliefs are not physical movements. I can think correctly and act mistakenly, and vice versa.

Quite young children appreciate many of these distinctions via understandings entrenched within their everyday theory of mind. What happens after these preschool accomplishments? Many things, including the consolidation and automatization of "preschool" understandings I described in Chapter 11. But here I consider new, quite different sorts of ideas that older children and adults wrestle with and embrace.

FROM INTUITIVE UNDERSTANDING TO REFLECTIVE IDEAS

For preschoolers, ordinary understandings of agents, minds, and intentional action provide rich yet intuitive concepts for apprehending mentality and intentionality. Moreover, preschool concepts provide the groundwork for reflective ideas that extend beyond intuitive experience. The intuitive-reflective distinction I employ here is imprecise, and different authors draw different lessons from it (see, e.g., Baumard & Boyer, 2013; Sperber, 1996, 1997), but it is an important vehicle for thinking about further developments. So, what, in my view, are intuitive versus reflective ideas about the mind, and how do they differ?

Preschool concepts of mentality and intentionality, the early developments I described in Chapters 2 and 4, although themselves advances beyond infant (fast, initial) understandings, are usefully distinguished as intuitive in the sense of constituting an immediate, taken-for-granted way in which mentality (and agency) is directly understood. That is, based on the early developing ideas discussed so far, to the young child the mental, no less than the physical, appears to be an indubitable part of experienced reality. Children, via their initial theories of mind and object, assume (without reflective cogitation and effort) that there are psychological agents "in here" and physical objects "out there." It is at this basic level that children are psychophysical dualists. Mental as well as physical kinds of things appear to them to be directly given in external or internal perception (e.g., sight vs. introspection), and these kinds of things clearly differ. These childhood ideas have been derived from an intricate inferential interplay of data and hypotheses, reality and framework theory. But to the child at 3 or 4 years, there is no further awareness of these underlying conceptual frameworks, or any gap between what is so and their ideas about it. In this sense there is no reflection on their own ideas.

Reflective ideas, in contrast, are more "second-order," marked by further notions about these intuitively known, given realities. Reflective ideas require some extra reflective cogitation and effort, along with developmental learning. With age and experience, differentiations emerge, ideas *about* the first-order realities emerge; preschool indubitable realities can be questioned, and extensions and alternatives can be entertained.

(To be clear, then, even if we adopt a dual-process account of infant and preschool theory of mind, preschool theory is still intuitive and not reflective. Preschool ideas may represent system-2 cognition in comparison to system 1, but preschool ideas still provide the child an immediate, direct impression of what's what. Reflective ideas go further to justify, to comment on, to explain, and to explicitly question prior intuitions.)

In sum, early in development, constructivist inferential processes provide for the development of organized conceptual systems (intuitive theories) that serve to explain and predict ordinary actions, objects, and events and serve to distinguish mental states from physical ones and intentional actions from mere bodily movements, just as described in Chapters 2, 4, and 8. Reflective ideation, in contrast, takes these "first-order" concepts—intentional belief-desire actions, mental entities, in the case of theory of mind—as its object and then more consciously constructs conceptual systems about them. Of course, philosophers engage in rigorous efforts to critically examine and systematize these intuitive and reflective ideas still further. I am not talking about that. I'm talking about the everyday, less rigorous, less systematic but nonetheless reflective ideas of older childhood.

In fact, to consider this developmental trajectory further, compare the everyday reflective ideas of older children and adults with the further elaborated ideas of philosophers. Philosophers attempt to systematically conceptualize how mind could actually be instantiated in the bodily brain, devising notions such as supervenience, compatibilism, and epiphenomenalism. Theologians attempt to systematically explain how Jesus could be both divine and human, ordinary and extraordinary. I believe that these still more systematic reflections of philosophers, theologians, and the like stem in the first place from the everyday reflective ideas of typical children and adults, which themselves depend originally on the intuitive ideas of early childhood.

In his early work, Jean Piaget (1929/1967) attempted to distinguish his interest in older children's reflective ideas as separate from the intuitive understandings of younger children (see Johnson, 2000). He termed children's spontaneous yet reflective tendencies, "children's philosophies." Piaget contrasted children's emerging fragmentary reflective notions, apparent to begin with in school-age children (those with concrete-operational competence), as different both from the more systematic, formulated ideas of adults, but also from the basic intuitions of younger children. It is these more reflective ideas of middle childhood that are my focus in this chapter.

Developmentally, I think it is clear that reflective ideas arise from both *spontaneous reflection*—the child's own reflective musings—and from *collective ideas*. Paul Harris (e.g., Harris & Koenig, 2006; Harris, 2012) has argued that children's knowledge about the world beyond their experience is indelibly the product of collective ideas transmitted by others. Such knowledge is derived from testimony; having no direct experience with things such as brains and souls, children rely on information from others. Collective ideas are undoubtedly important, and testimony is undoubtedly important, but so too are children's own spontaneous ideas, even at the level of middle childhood reflective thought. If children relied "exclusively on information from others...their assimilation of all sorts of ideas introduced to them via the testimony of others (e.g., God's omniscience) would proceed more rapidly than it actually does" (P. Harris, personal communication, October 29, 2013). To my mind, childhood acceptance of (or misunderstanding of) collectively presented ideas and notions is a constructive process, a process that requires a background of spontaneous inferences. Moreover, crucially, I am convinced that children's reflective ideas about *mind, brain, soul,* and *God*—whether inspired spontaneously or collectively—arise from a groundwork of early achieved, intuitive, mental-state understanding.

Reflective processes extend children's (and adults') understanding beyond the groundwork of intuitive mental-state understandings in at least two directions. On one hand, preschool understandings frame later more reflective ideas about the mind and brain. Here, children develop a more elaborate and explicit everyday or folk psychology distinguishing brain from mind and wrestling with how the immaterial mind causally depends on the physical brain. On the other hand, in a second more exotic direction, children extend initial ideas about ordinary, limited mental states and processes to consider ideas about extraordinary mentality, wrestling with spontaneous and collective ideas about supernatural beings, gods, souls, and omniscience.

IDEAS ABOUT THINKING, MIND, AND BRAIN

During the preschool years, children become highly competent in making inferences about the interplay of intentions, perceptions, desires, and beliefs in understanding human action and in distinguishing thoughts from objects or from overt actions. In middle childhood, this intuitive theory expands into the development of explicit ideas about the nature and function of the *mind*, and complementarily of the *brain*. Here children achieve reflective ideas that go beyond intuitive ones but are not themselves counterintuitive (as children's reflective ideas about God, omniscience, and the like may become).

What are childhood concepts of mind (beyond their conceptions of various mental states)? And how are they built on an earlier database (the earlier intuitive understandings)? In part, children's increasingly rich and reflective ideas about the mind depend on their increasingly rich and aware ideas about thinking.

Thinking

As described in Chapter 2, 4-year-olds know that thinking is an internal mental event that is different from seeing, talking, or touching and that the contents of one's thoughts (e.g., a thought about a dog) are not physical or tangible. Relatedly, from 2 to 6 years of age, young children come to grasp much about the subjectivity, and thus diversity, of thoughts. For example, if 3-year-olds do not themselves know what is in a box, they are able to understand that while Mary thinks the box has a doll in it, Bill thinks it contains a teddy bear (Wellman et al., 1996).

Intriguingly, however, as outlined briefly in Chapter 1, such young children seem to have little or no understanding of the constant flow of ideas and thoughts experienced in everyday life and involved in actively, consciously thinking. This seems like an undeniable part of mental life to adults. Like the experiences of characters in a James Joyce novel, mental life is an ever-present stream of thoughts, impressions, self-awareness, and so on that make up our very existence and identities. Thus, for example, 7-year-olds and adults assert that a person sitting quietly with a blank expression is still experiencing "some thoughts and ideas" and that it is nearly impossible to have a mind completely "empty of thoughts and ideas" (Flavell et al., 1993, 1995, 1998). But children 5 and younger have different notions. In John Flavell's research, 5-year-olds judge that such a person has no thoughts. When asked to choose a thought bubble depicting his mental state, they choose a completely empty or blank one (Flavell et al., 1993). Indeed, it is not until 6 to 8 years of age that children consistently judge that people are thinking when engaged in tasks such as pretending (Lillard, 1993), reading, listening, and talking (Flavell et al., 1995), tasks that patently require ideation and cognition from an adult point of view.

Even when preschoolers do acknowledge that a person is having thoughts, they find it difficult to report the connection of those thoughts to other thoughts. Unlike 6- and 7-year-olds, younger children are "unaware of the chain-reaction-like flashings of whole sequences of thoughts, each cognitively cueing its successor," (Flavell et al., 1995, p. 85). In certain emotional situations, preschoolers can sometimes report how thinking of a prior negative event cues a memory leading to a current sad emotion (Lagattuta & Wellman, 2001). But thoughts cueing thoughts leading to emotions, and thoughts cueing thoughts leading to other thoughts, are easy and frequent conceptions for school-age children (Flavell et al., 1995; Lagattuta & Wellman, 2001).

In short, older children and adults spontaneously conceive of thoughts not as essentially isolated mental happenings but rather embedded in streams of consciousness. Similarly, in middle childhood, at least for children in our literate, western-European society, children come to see the mind as an active constructor of knowledge (e.g., Carpendale & Chandler, 1996; Wellman, 1990) and as a "homunculus," or processing center, that can run along with a "mind of its own" (Flavell et al., 1998; Wellman & Hickling, 1994). These sort of ideas—spontaneous reflective ideas of middle childhood—contribute to the notions I describe next in which, beyond the preschool years, children achieve a deepening appreciation of the mind and then the brain.

Mind and Brain

Children's intuitive capacity to distinguish particular mental states and acts, desiring X and believing Y, provides the ground for general ideas about distinctive functions of mind such as thinking understood more generally and pervasively. Thinking becomes a "faculty" of mind. This is a faculty in the classic sense of generalized distinctive mental functions, such as sensation, volition, and mentation, which have been commonly distinguished from ancient times (Maher, 1900). Representational acts (thinking, imagining, remembering), taken together, form a more general faculty of mentation. Children don't use the term mentation, of course, but they talk of thinking in an increasingly general and pervasive way. Recognition of such a generalized mental faculty—thinking—helps generate explicit, still more general, reflective consideration of the mind and brain. How does this take place?

The term *mind,* rather than *brain,* is commonly used by young children in everyday language (Corriveau, Pasquini, & Harris, 2005; Wellman & Hickling, 1994). But children begin to mention the brain and to respond sensibly (although not accurately) to questions about the brain as well as the mind toward the end of the preschool years. In doing so, children tend to misidentify brain and mind as the same sort of thing and use both terms to refer to the faculty of mentation. For example, quite a while ago, Carl Johnson and I (Johnson & Wellman, 1982, Experiment 2) asked U.S. children in first, third, fifth, and ninth grades whether they could perform various kinds of functions without a brain, and separately without a mind. Items included mental acts (think, remember), sensation (see, hear), feelings (feel interested, feel happy), voluntary actions (walk, talk), and involuntary behaviors (breathe, sneeze). The youngest children in this research and other more recent research (e.g., Richert & Harris, 2006) respond identically when asked about the brain and the mind, conceiving of brain and mind equally as the seat of purely "mental" acts.

More specifically, in the early school years, children tend to explain that they only need eyes to see, ears to hear, and legs to walk, just as they only need the mind (and likewise the brain) to think or remember. By fifth and ninth grade, children in these studies are generally aware that the brain is necessary for all functions (including involuntary action), while they distinctly regard the mind as exclusively necessary for mental acts and feelings (Johnson & Wellman, 1982).

Although even the earliest ideas about brain function are probably partly culturally communicated (e.g., "use your brain" or "he's brainy"), they equally reflect the limits of children's intuitive understanding. Initially dependent on a first-order, intuitive awareness of mental states, younger children reason that the brain (= mind) is the organ of thinking, but they have no idea that the brain (≠ mind) engages in processes that underlie all experience and behavior—seeing, walking, breathing, in addition to thinking. Indeed, as just noted, younger children initially assume that most of the time people (self included) go about their business without thinking at all. Thus, one key to later developmental changes is the recognition that thinking is not merely an occasional (conscious) mental occurrence but rather is constant. Thinking about thinking sponsors notions about mind and brain and how the two diverge.

One manifestation of these later middle-childhood developments is that children come to not only differentiate but also integrate the concepts of mind and brain. Although first graders in our research judged the brain and mind to be functionally equivalent (as mental), by third grade, children judged the brain and mind to be different yet intricately interconnected, either completely interdependent (i.e., a person could not have one without the other) or the mind as singularly dependent on the brain (i.e., a person could not have a mind without a brain, although they could have a brain without a mind). Similarly, Kathleen Corriveau, Elisabeth Pasquini, and Paul Harris (2005) more recently found that 5- to 7-year-olds exhibited considerable confusion about the potential visibility (and thus materiality) of the brain versus the mind. In our data (Johnson & Wellman 1982), with its more extended set of ages, we asked children to separately judge whether the brain and mind could be seen and touched on opening the head. The percentage of U.S. children who consistently judged the mind to be intangible and invisible in contrast to the brain being tangible and visible was .00, .25, .62, and .92 for Grades 1, 3, 5, and 9, respectively. Thus, in later childhood, as children come to differentiate the conscious mind from the unconscious-functioning brain, they also distinguish the ontological status of the brain and mind, one as material and one as immaterial.

Children's developing ideas about the brain (along with the mind) as the seat of mental activities (mentation) and the dependence of the mind on the brain are confirmed and extended in studies where children are asked to imagine the consequences of a brain transplant. In various, replicated studies (Corriveau et al., 2005; Gottfried, Gelman, & Schultz, 1999; Johnson, 1990), children have been asked to make inferences about the consequences of imagined brain transplants, such as between an animal and a person, or between two people. For example, in Carl Johnson's (1990) original study, children in kindergarten through fourth grade were told a story about the attributes of a pig named Garby, who, unlike the child participant, loved to sleep in slop (vs. in a bed), had pig friends (vs. child friends), and so forth. Children were then asked to pretend that something happens to Garby: "We'll pretend to take your brain out of your head (referring to the child participant) and put it inside Garby's head." Results in this and other studies consistently show that until about second grade (about age 7 or 8), children typically fail to recognize the profound consequences that such a transplant would have on a person's whole being and identity. Although children recognize that the brain is needed for the capacity to think, young children do not conceive the brain as essentially embodying one's personalized mental contents (*my* memories, thoughts), behavioral dispositions (*my* preferences), and identity. Thus, although a brain is required for thinking, children do not recognize that a different brain would result in one having different thoughts, memories, preferences, and the like. Indeed, young children are equally unimpressed when asked about the consequences of transplanting the entire insides of a person

(Gottfried et al., 1999). Not until age 7 to 8 years do U.S. children typically grasp that the brain (or some sort of special mental insides) is essential to a person's whole being and identity.

These transplant studies point to the difference between the intuitive awareness that mental states happen privately, "inside" (see Chapter 2), and the reflective idea that such states are essentially dependent, for their identity, on a bodily "inside." The intuitive preschool awareness that mental states—desires, feelings, thoughts, and so forth—are private kinds of things does not include the idea that something in the body is necessary for such states nor that such embodiment individualizes mental states. Only gradually do children acquire the idea that mentation is more deeply dependent on a functioning brain, and other activities (walking, seeing, breathing) are too.

Children's increasingly reflective ideas about mind and brain are undoubtedly influenced by culture. Knowledge about brain function is certainly a collective, cultural achievement. Across history and societies, for example, there have been different ideas about where mental attributes are grounded in the body (Wierzbicka, 1992)—in the head, in the heart, in the viscera. In this regard, fixing on the brain per se (rather than the heart or the head or the mouth) for the embodiment of mind is a collectively sponsored reflective idea. However, at the same time, all cultures, it seems, distinguish faculties such as perception, linked with external body parts, from thinking, located internally. Moreover, languages, in metaphor and in other fashions, commonly associate thinking with the head (Lakoff & Johnson, 1980). This is a widespread, although probably not a universal, idea. For example, signed languages use hand shapes to designate certain meanings; and these hand gestures are also typically located somewhere or another within the speaker's bodily space. Worldwide, sign languages locate signs for thinking, remembering, imagining, and the like as hand gestures located in the head region (Thompson, Vinson, Woll, & Vigliocco, 2012).

In sum, thinking about thinking and, moreover, thinking about mind (and brain), is not complete with the development of preschool understandings. Instead, those intuitive understandings shape (and at first limit) the development of reflective ideas. Based on a limited initial sense that mental acts happen occasionally, not consistently, children think more and more about thinking, including first very impoverished ideas about thinking as pervasive and about mind as the organ of mentation. Then they develop further reflective ideas about mind and brain, ideas that originate and receive shape from culturally provided collective information but also spontaneous reflection as well.

FROM IMMANENT TO TRANSCENDENT

Paralleling their developing ideas about the inner workings of the thinking mind/ brain, school-age children are also developing ideas about the possibility of mentality transcending the boundaries of the immanent body altogether. I highlight three illustrations of these transcendental possibilities. First, consider supernatural beings. Children readily imagine the possibility of supernatural agency in which mentation is freed from (i.e., transcends) its ordinary human constraints—knowledge constraints, sensory constraints, bodily constraints. This leads to a second illustration, focused on children's developing conceptions of omniscience. Last, I review emerging evidence that many children infer that mental functions can continue after physical death. Important in their own right, such reflective considerations of some sort of afterlife often lead to developing concepts of "soul." These reflective ideas do not just go beyond earlier intuitive ideas; they are counterintuitive to varying degrees.

Transcending Ordinary Minds: Supernatural Beings

Mentality is ordinarily embodied. Thus it can result, for example, in concrete, intentional actions. But childhood *reflective* conception of mentality, as shown in the last section, does not necessarily tightly tie the mind to the body. Instead, initial reflective ideas about mind and brain maintain a strong division between mind (and its province—thinking, remembering, imagining) and the body and its province (acting, sensing). This emerging capacity to reflect on and categorically distinguish the existence of mentation, independent from its normal embodiment, provides the basis not just for conceiving of the mind and brain but also for widely imagining the existence of supernatural beings.

To step back a moment, children (and adults) hear about and confront not only ordinary human agents but also agents who possess extraordinary capacities that are distinctly nonhuman. Charles Darwin noted in his *Descent of Man* (1898) that "A belief in all-pervading spiritual agencies seems to be universal." Indeed, many of the world's religions espouse beings who possess extraordinary mental capacities such as omniscience (Campbell, 1972; Pickover, 2001). Further, television shows, movies, and myths abound with characters who possess exceptional perceptual and mental capacities (e.g., X-ray vision); tabloids and science fiction talk of persons with ESP and telekinesis. An intriguing question is, why are beliefs about extraordinary minds so attractive and widespread? Dan Sperber (1994), in developing an analysis of the "epidemiology of beliefs," asks, why are such beliefs contagious? The complementary, but prior, developmental question asks, how do people come to understand the less constrained minds of these agents?

The recent cognitive science of religion (e.g., McCauley & Whitehouse, 2005) has focused on how such ideas are naturally formed and readily acquired, spread, and retained—the "naturalness of religion" hypothesis (Barrett, 2000; Boyer, 1994). Thus, in this account, cognition about supernatural cognition begins as ordinary. Developmentally, I contend that thinking about supernatural beings starts out grounded in intuitive understandings of ordinary beings, embellished via ordinary processes of cognition. With further development, children can and do reflectively generate new ideas, ideas about the extraordinary, and they can process teachings about and collective ideas about the extraordinary. This account is a variant of an *anthropomorphism hypothesis* (Boyer, 1994; Piaget 1929/1967), which proposes that children initially attribute to all agents the same psychological characteristics and limits that they attribute to ordinary humans, and only later come to differentiate ordinary and extraordinary minds.

A key argument here is that collective ideas of supernatural beings (God, superheroes, and the like) stand out as cognitively attractive and memorable (contagious) because they are marked by cognitively viable combinations of intuitive and counterintuitive properties (Atran, 2002; Boyer, 1994). "Counterintuitive" here means violating some of the given, indubitable aspects of childhood intuitive theory as I have been describing it. Indeed, in some sense, supernatural attributes can only be distinguished (or imagined) as extraordinary against a background of otherwise ordinary intuitive constraints. Violation of constraints makes these beings special, whereas the intuitive background (coupled with violating *some*, not all, ordinary constraints) makes these beings intelligible. Thus, on this account, supernatural ideas emerge reflectively, but necessarily against a background of intuitive constraint.

Pascal Boyer (1994, 2001) and Justin Barrett (2000) have summarized how ideas about supernatural beings could be created and accepted (naturally) in the following way:

1. Start with the basic idea of an agent.
2. Disembody it and further modify it in an unusual way (e.g., make it infallible).
3. Use such supernatural beings to think about difficult-to-explain occurrences (difficult given intuitive naïve psychology, physics, and biology), for example, how someone in a death-like coma came back to life.
4. Have others persuasively refer to supernatural beings for those explanatory purposes too, plus engage each other in practices that make supernatural beings and actions memorable and important via special rituals, secret practices, and compelling "emotional pageantry."

Development

Consider a developmental, anthropomorphism account further. On this account, for example, when children begin to appreciate that ordinary people can be ignorant or can hold false beliefs, they attribute the same cognitive limitation to all beings, ordinary and extraordinary. Before that time, children fail to understand the distinction between (potentially fallible) belief states and reality at all, so if required to judge beliefs, they merely report states of reality for human and nonhuman agents alike. Only later would the capacity to readily imagine supernatural possibility develop. At this point, children would begin to spontaneously distinguish between ordinary and extraordinary causation, imagining or readily accepting the possibility of all sorts of superpowers.

However, both historically and in contemporary research, a contrasting perspective is also apparent. Historically, Romanticists argued that children were "close to God," with initial understandings of things beyond the ken of adults, whose minds had been contaminated by experience and expertise. This Romanticist position is echoed in a contemporary "preparedness" perspective on children's understanding of the extraordinary. Thus, in an influential study, Justin Barrett and his colleagues (Barrett et al., 2001) contrasted a *preparedness hypothesis* to an anthropomorphism account and have continued to elaborate this alternative in later writings (e.g., Richert & Barrett, 2005). In this preparedness account, young children's early social-cognitive biases (e.g., not attributing false beliefs to agents) directly support the understanding of extraordinary mental abilities. Thus, Barrett (e.g., Barrett, 2000) has argued that before children understand mental limitations (e.g., ignorance, error, or false beliefs), they do not merely use reality to attribute agents' mental states (as per the anthropomorphism hypothesis); rather, they actively believe that agents are all knowing. Accordingly, when children begin to attribute a particular mental fallibility (e.g., false beliefs) to ordinary humans, they can simply continue to attribute infallible mental capacities and states to God.

Indeed, in their initial study, Barrett and his colleagues (2001) demonstrated that as children come to appreciate the constraints of ordinary human knowledge and belief, they recognize that God has other powers. Using a surprising-contents task, that standard measure of children's understanding of false belief, Barrett et al. (2001) compared children's inferences about God versus Mom. Children were presented with a cracker box that they readily expected to contain crackers. The box was then opened to reveal that it contained small rocks. Closing the box again, children were then asked to infer what Mom, or God, would think is in the box, when first presented with it shut and unopened. Before age 4, these researchers found that children assumed that Mom and God alike would answer rocks (the classic false-belief error, evidencing failure to understand belief, knowledge, or false belief). When they were somewhat older, however, when children recognized the limits of human knowledge (Mom would be mistaken), they allowed a more special power to God. Mom would not know, but God would know, the contents.

Although intriguing, these findings and the preparedness hypothesis itself raise several questions, both empirical and conceptual. First, when very young children apparently attribute infallible knowledge and beliefs to persons (or Gods) their answers may simply reflect an early reality bias, as I just argued earlier—they could well answer by reporting the reality of the situation without considering agents' mental abilities at all (Evans & Wellman, 2006; Wellman & Bartsch, 1988). The especially intriguing question then is what children attribute to God when they *first* start to distinguish between the actual state of reality and people's (often inaccurate) mental representations of that reality. In particular, at the point when they begin to attribute false beliefs or ignorance to humans, do children attribute fallible knowledge and beliefs to God as well, as proposed by the anthropomorphism hypothesis, or infallible knowledge and beliefs, as proposed by the preparedness hypothesis?

A fine-grained developmental look is needed here, because at a still later age, when children have developed a more robust understanding of fallible mental capacities, around 5 to 6 years say, both preparedness and anthropomorphism hypotheses predict that children will be able to attribute more infallible mental capacities to God, provided they have been exposed to such information about God. Distinctively, however, the preparedness hypothesis predicts that such an understanding at age 5 and 6 would reflect a *continuation* of children's early default understanding of extraordinary minds. The anthropomorphism hypothesis, in contrast, posits that such an understanding at age 5 and 6 indicates that children are beginning to loosen their earlier tendencies to anthropomorphize all agents.

To best test these two hypotheses, it is necessary to densely sample children within the proper age range and to analyze the data in a sensitive, age-related fashion to find and assess the critical window when children first correctly attribute fallible mental capacities to humans. Barrett and colleagues (2001) simply grouped 3-, 4-, and 5-year-olds in year-long age blocks. Such coarse-grain groupings may well have masked the critical developmental window during which children first begin to ascribe limitations to human agents (and relatedly may or may not have ascribed human-like limitations to nonhuman agents).

Lack of fine-grained age sampling and analyses, because different samples or different age groupings may differentially capture the critical developmental window, could also lead to inconsistent results across studies. Indeed, although Barrett's initial findings (Barrett et al., 2001) were replicated with a sample of Yukatek Mayan children whose culture has adopted the Catholic God (Knight, Sousa, Barrett, & Atran, 2004), and Richert and Barrett (2005) reported data conforming to a preparedness trajectory for children's performance on a diverse set of knowledge-ignorance tasks, other researchers have offered findings that conflict with those of Barrett and his colleagues.

For example, using a less challenging knowledge-ignorance task, Nikos Makris and Dimitris Pnevmatikos (2007) found that their 3- and 4-year-old Greek children consistently attributed ignorance both to a human and to God. Marta Giménez-Dasí, Silvia Guerrero, and Paul Harris (2005) asked 3- to 5-year-old Spanish children, raised in either religious or secular schools (that parents selected deliberately for being secular), to judge the capacities of a friend and those of God on a surprising-contents, false-belief task. They found that their 4-year-olds consistently denied extraordinary knowledge (i.e., they attributed false beliefs) to both their friend and God. This was true for both religiously schooled and secularly schooled children. Only 5-year-olds began to distinguish their friend as ignorant but God as knowledgeable of what was hidden in the closed container. These findings from Makris and Pnevmatikos (2007) and Giménez-Dasí and colleagues (2005) accord with the anthropomorphism hypothesis but conflict with preparedness.

To resolve these conflicting findings, Jonathan Lane, Margaret Evans and I (Lane, Wellman, & Evans, 2010) asked children to make judgments and reason about the knowledge and beliefs of agents with contrasting perceptual and mental abilities: ordinary humans; Heroman, who "can see right through things"; Mr. Smart, who "knows everything" without looking; and God. Crucially, we densely sampled children at an age when they were just beginning to attribute ignorance and false beliefs to ordinary humans. In the focal analyses, children (essentially, young 4-year-olds) who were first beginning to understand the mental limitations of ordinary agents (their ignorance and fallible beliefs) attributed those same limitations to the minds of Mr. Smart and God. Only the older children (old 4-year-olds and older) differentiated between the fallible mental capacities (and resulting ignorance and mistaken beliefs) of humans and the less constrained mental capacities and states of God and Mr. Smart. Thus, our findings present clear evidence in support of the anthropomorphism hypothesis and help reconcile earlier apparent contradictions.

Intriguingly, the younger 4-year-olds in our study (Lane, Wellman, & Evans, 2010) did often appreciate that some agents' exceptional *perceptual* abilities (e.g., Heroman's X-ray vision) could lead to accurate knowledge and beliefs, even while they did not yet appreciate extraordinary *mental* abilities (knowing everything without looking). One reason children may have an early appreciation of exceptional perceptual capacities is because perceptual capacities are observably more or less restricted across humans and animals— some people see well without glasses, others need them; dogs can hear silent dog whistles; and bats have echolocation that allows them to navigate in the dark. But, in addition, children's early grasp of exceptional perceptual abilities may reflect exposure to "testimony" and media in which characters possess special abilities (e.g., a bat's echolocation, Superman's X-ray vision).

Notably, children often hear not only about exceptional perceptual abilities but also about extraordinary mental abilities through various forms of informal and formal sociocultural input (Bergstrom, Moehlmann, & Boyer, 2006; Harris & Koenig, 2006)—including broadly, parent–child discourse, oral and printed stories, movies, and formal or informal exposure to religious doctrine. Importantly, collective social testimony of these various forms can have powerful effects on children's conceptual development (Shweder et al., 2006), even if that information is not provided in an intentionally didactic manner (Atran & Sperber, 1991). For example, as reviewed in Chapter 7, a large body of research demonstrates predictive relations between everyday social input (e.g., parent–child discourse about mental states) and children's developing understanding of ordinary human minds (and recall, e.g., the data on deaf children as well, as reviewed in Chapter 5). Further, it is clear that social input affects older children's judgments of, for example, God's extraordinary ability to create the living world (Evans, 2001).

Our precise results (Lane et al., 2010) make it unlikely that young children are cognitively *prepared* to understand extraordinary mental capacities. Young children attribute ordinary ignorance and false beliefs (and, as we will see, death) to God. Nonetheless, when children do begin to consider mental capacities of extraordinary agents, exposure to religious doctrines could certainly *facilitate* the acquisition and application of concepts of extraordinary mental capacities. In particular, children who are heavily exposed to ideas about agents with extraordinary cognitive abilities (e.g., doctrines and testimony about God's omniscience) may more easily resist attributing cognitive limitations (e.g., false beliefs) to such agents. But surprisingly little is known about the effects of such input, and focally exposure to religious ideas, on children's developing concepts of extraordinary minds.

To partly address these issues, in further research again spearheaded by Jonathan Lane (Lane, Wellman, & Evans, 2012), religiously schooled preschoolers were tested on the same theory-of-mind tasks used in our first study (Lane, Wellman, & Evans, 2010), and again children were carefully sampled in a fine-grained, age-related way. These religiously raised children demonstrated the same developmental patterns as did the more secular children in our initial study: When these children first attributed fallible mental states to ordinary humans (e.g., Mom), they likewise attributed fallible states (e.g., false beliefs) to Mr. Smart and to God. Notably, although Barrett and his colleagues have asserted that young children will find it especially easy to understand *God's* infallibility (e.g., Richert & Barrett, 2005), these religiously schooled children actually found it easier to first understand Mr. Smart's special powers (where we provided on-the-spot instruction and demonstration) and did so before understanding God's.

Omniscience

Even when children do begin to understand the possibility of extraordinary minds, it is important to recognize the simplicity of these initial ideas, at least in the studies discussed so far. In particular, the items actually tested leave unclear whether such preschool judgments indicate early, or easy, acceptance of omniscience.

Clearly, adults worldwide believe to some extent in beings with omniscience. The idea of an omniscient, or all-knowing, God is embedded in the belief systems of Judaism, Christianity, and Islam (Armstrong, 1994). Further, Buddhism holds that Gautama Buddha achieved an enlightened state in which he possessed extraordinary knowledge (Pyysiäinen, 2004), and Vishnu, a supreme Hindu god, is also described as omniscient (Kumar, 1998). Not only are concepts of omniscient beings found among the world's most widespread religions, "omni" qualities, such as omniscience and omnipotence, are central to many individuals' personal conceptualizations of a God (Barrett, 1998; Gorsuch, 1968; Kunkel, Cook, Meshel, Daughtry, & Hauenstein, 1999; Noffke & McFadden, 2001; Spilka, Armatas, & Nussbaum, 1964). Yet, although such ideas are widely endorsed, they may be particularly difficult for us to fully cognitively represent because they are counterintuitive; they do not accord with our everyday intuitions (and preschoolers' intuitions) about human minds, which are instead fallible, subject to ignorance and misperceptions.

In contrast to ordinary sentience, omniscience refers to knowing everything. As theologian James Packer explains

> Scripture declares that God's eyes run everywhere...He searches all hearts and observes everyone's ways...in other words, he knows everything about everything and everybody all the time. Also, he knows the future no less than the past and the present....Nor does he have to "access" information about things, as a computer might retrieve a file; all his knowledge is always immediately and directly before his mind. (Packer, 1993, pp. 31–32)

Ideas of God's profoundly extraordinary mind are also found in the texts of other modern monotheistic religions. For example, the Qur'an proclaims that, "Allah knows whatsoever is in the heavens and whatsoever is on the earth.... Verily, Allah is the All-Knower of everything" (Surah Al-Mujadila, Qur'an, 58:7). Such a mind is radically different from the human minds that we interact with daily, which are highly imperfect, and prone to ignorance. Such a mind is radically, not modestly, counterintuitive.

Omniscience, then, raises the issues of preparedness and anthropomorphism again, in this new context. Here Barrett and colleagues (Barrett et al., 2001; Richert & Barrett, 2005) have argued that children are prepared to represent and believe in omniscient or mentally infallible beings; so, to represent these ideas later in development merely requires that the child hold on to these intuitive ideas into adulthood. Thus, Barrett and Richert surmised that, "on many properties, young children seem equipped with default assumptions that better match theological descriptions of God than adult conceptions of people. Three-year-olds assume beliefs and percepts are infallible" (2003, p. 309). Others have similarly concluded, as stated by Greene (2011), that, "Children in particular [find] it very easy to think in religious ways, such as believing in God's omniscience."

Note that both positions—anthropomorphism and preparedness—accept that by about 5 years, children in various sociocultural contexts can distinguish between the (enhanced, less limited) knowledge of God and the (more fallible, more limited) knowledge of ordinary humans, at least when it comes to knowing the contents of unopened or darkened containers. These are the data I have just been discussing in which indeed, by the time they are 5 or 6 years, most children in samples from the United States, Greece, Spain, and the Yucatan believe God will be correct (not incorrect) on false-belief tasks (e.g., Giménez-Dasí et al., 2005; Knight et al., 2004; Lane et al., 2010, 2012; Makris & Pnevmatikos, 2007). Moreover, U.S. 5-year-olds easily attribute this sort of extraordinary knowledge to a novel being whom they are taught "knows everything": Mr. Smart (Lane et al., 2010, 2012). But does this 5- and 6-year-old attribution of privileged knowledge to God and to others reflect anything like an attribution of omniscience?

To investigate this, in recent research, Jonathan Lane, Margaret Evans, and I (Lane, Wellman, & Evans, 2013) assessed preschoolers', elementary-school children's, and adults' understanding of the breadth and depth of an all-knowing being's knowledge. By "breadth" we meant the differing types of knowledge that someone possesses; here we focused on an all-knowing agent's knowledge of facts about the past, present, and future, as well as knowledge of others' private activities and states (e.g., someone else's thoughts, preferences, and actions).

By "depth" we were referring to the amount of knowledge that someone possesses within some single area or topic. To assess this understanding, we examined when children began to appreciate that an omniscient agent's knowledge surpasses experts' knowledge even within the experts' domains of expertise. To understand this, children must make the distinction between knowing much about a specific domain (e.g., medicine), that is, being *expert*, versus knowing *everything* about that domain, or indeed everything about *all* domains, that is, being *omniscient*.

Not only are these aspects of knowledge suitably broad for a consideration of omniscience, conceivably children's attribution of these types of knowledge to extraordinary beings could reveal a developmental progression in understanding extraordinary minds. Although older preschoolers grant an all-knowing agent knowledge about certain facts on standard knowledge-ignorance and false-belief tasks, do they resist or welcome the idea that an extraordinary agent can possess knowledge of the future, or knowledge of others' minds, or complete knowledge of all domains of expertise—that is, can know everything about everything and everybody?

Thus, we (Lane, Wellman & Evans, in press) carefully examined the breadth of knowledge (i.e., types of knowledge) and depth of knowledge (i.e., amount of knowledge within domains) that preschoolers, elementary-school children, and adults attributed to an all-knowing being. We did this in the United States, a cultural context in which belief in all-knowing beings is prevalent—over 90% of the U.S. public believes in a God (Pew Research Center, 2008).

In our research, preschoolers were consistently conservative in their knowledge attributions, often reporting that an omniscient mind would be ignorant of many things, and completely failing to understand the depth of omniscient knowledge (i.e., that an omniscient mind would know more about a domain than even an expert). With increasing age, children gradually approached an understanding of omniscience—attributing broader and deeper knowledge to an omniscient agent—but only adults firmly understood the depth of knowledge encompassed by omniscience (Lane, Wellman, et al., 2013).

Sociocultural factors (e.g., exposure to collective ideas about God) correlated with children's understanding of omniscience. But even younger religiously reared children consistently underattributed knowledge to an "omniscient" being. Cognitive factors (an understanding of infinity, and an ability to entertain the possibility of improbable phenomena) also correlated with children's understandings of omniscience. Only in middle childhood, as children increasingly entertained notions of limitlessness more generally (e.g., infinite, unlimited numbers) did they also entertain increasingly broad and deep notions of omniscience. These findings then demonstrate that an understanding of extraordinary minds is anchored in childhood representations of fallible, limited human minds, which both make possible and constrain understandings of minds that are radically nonhuman.

This developmental tension between "make possible" yet "constrain" leaves its footprint in adult cognition. For most of us, even as adults, ideas of things such as omniscience, although spontaneously imaginable in logical form, remain hard to grasp consistently and meaningfully. Thus, although God's radical otherness is commonly acknowledged and explicated in theological theory, such ideas appear to have much less impact in ordinary religious practice among adults as well as children. In this regard, Justin Barrett and Frank Keil (1996) asked adults to make judgments about God's qualities in two contexts. When simply asked about God's powers, adults readily endorsed God as radically other—for example, they asserted that God was omniscient and unconstrained by perceptual limitations. But when asked to make inferences about God in a narrative context, the same individuals inevitably interpreted exceptional acts as occurring within other more ordinary constraints—for example, God could only address a limited number of prayers at once. In other words, the radically counterintuitive idea of a completely unlimited being was slippery at best when trying to make sense of God's behavior in context. Thus, although adults may report believing in certain agents' total omniscience, in their everyday reasoning, they easily default to thinking of extraordinary agents (even God) as possessing a powerful yet *limited*, more human-like mind.

The difficulty in conceptualizing total omniscience has been apparent to theologians for centuries (Aquinas, 1265–1274/2006; Augustine, 1844). As theologians have long noted, not much can be said about a being who is completely "other." Without limits, agency loses its meaning and sense; without some sort of humanness, completely alien agency loses its drama and purpose as well. Moreover, developmentally, it is from limits—the constraints that intuitive psychology attributes to the ordinary minds and lives of intentional agents—that ideas of the supernatural arise in the first place, as reflection imagines the suspension of those ordinary limits.

Transcending Death

Gods are not only (often) omniscient, they are also (often) immortal (as well as omnipotent). Even when considering mere humans, according to a 2005 Harris Poll, about 6 in 10 Americans believe in hell (that devilish form of afterlife) and about 7 out of 10 believe in a heavenly life after death. Initial childhood ideas about immortality or afterlife have been studied and help reinforce the story begun previously with omniscience. As noted earlier, during middle childhood, children become increasingly aware of the differentiation between brain (body) and mind (mentation). This helps them increasingly entertain the possibility that the mind could transcend the death of the body.

By the early school years, most children come to understand that death terminates bodily functions, is applicable to all living things, and is irreversible (Slaughter,

Jaakkola, & Carey, 1999). This is an understanding achieved in earlier childhood as part of a developing naïve biology; by the early school years, this is intuitive common-sense. But what about God? Again God becomes special. In a study mentioned earlier by Giménez-Dasí et al. (2005), those authors not only asked children about false beliefs but also about "immortality." This was the study with 3- to 5-year-old Spanish children, raised in religious or secular schools, who were asked to judge the capacities of a friend and those of God. They were asked about knowledge constraints (including a surprising-contents, false-belief task) but also biological constraints regarding mortality (including would their friend or would God eventually die or go on living forever). Extending the previous discussion, the findings showed that by age 5 years (and not earlier), children distinguished God as special in terms of knowledge, but also in terms of life—God was specially immune to death. And, children readily picked up these ideas not just in religious schools; those in secular schools did so as well.

Immortality, understood fully, may well have the same sort of radical counterintuitiveness that omniscience has. But, humans clearly ordinarily entertain ideas about afterlife, even if not full immortality. More generally, children come to consider that some forms of afterlife could apply not only to God but to more ordinary beings as well. Thus, in a series of studies, narrating the death of a mouse character, Jesse Bering and David Bjorklund (2004) found that although elementary school children typically recognized that death terminates bodily functions, including functions of the brain, they nonetheless tended to infer that mental states would continue. Children's ideas in this regard, at first blush, appeared disjointed. For example, when asked whether the dead mouse could get sick again, be alive again, or *have a working brain*, children overwhelmingly said no. But when asked parallel questions about whether the mouse would still *feel* sick, or *know* he's alive, or *think*, children said yes. Children's ideas about death thus appeared to depend on whether they were thinking about the physical organs of the body/brain or more purely focusing on spontaneous acts of mind.

Paul Harris and Marta Giménez (2005) pursued this further, and their data present a more comprehensive picture. They asked children, ages 7 and 11 years, about the consequences of death of a grandparent in two different contexts: one medical, the other religious. Given the medical context, children typically claimed that all functions, bodily and mental, ceased. Given the religious context, in contrast, they tended to claim that mental functions would continue after death. Thus the data showed contextual differences (religious vs. medical) and "functional" differences (mind vs. body). Finally and crucially, the data also showed clear developmental trends; younger children (7-year-olds in this case) were more likely to think all functions cease at death and older children less so. In total, the oldest children were most likely to *deny* that functioning ceased at death; they were most likely to deny it for mental (over bodily) functions and in the religious (over the medical) context. And, to the extent that the younger children ever denied the cessation of function with death, it was for mental functions in the religious context.

In two recent studies, Jonathan Lane, Liqi Zhu, Margaret Evans, and I (in press) replicated and extended these findings with more comprehensive developmental data, data from 4- through 12-year-olds as well as adults. Participants were asked about the possible persistence of various functions (mental—e.g., thinking, as well as bodily—e.g., breathing) in two contexts—medical and religious. Moreover, in one study, we tested U.S. participants, and in the other parallel study, we tested participants in mainland China—a country that is still emerging from a historical period of religious suppression and where atheism is prevalent and certainly more prevalent than in the United States.

By age 5 or 6 years, participants in both countries knew full well that death biologically terminates all functions. In middle childhood, however, children increasingly asserted that some functions (especially mental rather than bodily ones) could continue beyond death and especially did so in the religious context rather than the medical one. Willingness to assert some afterlife beliefs was particularly frequent in the United States and more rare in China, but modestly apparent there as well.

Taken together, the extant data thus show emerging ideas about mind transcending death but also developmental and contextual differences in doing so. These reflective ideas are especially and increasingly apparent as children move into middle childhood. By 5 or 6 years, children (who are now beyond the preschool years, but not by much) seem to easily focus on cessation of bodily function, operating perhaps with a simple (intuitively grounded) biological rule—death eliminates *all* functions. Other evidence suggests that most children abide by this intuitive understanding when explicitly presented with causal information that signals biological death (e.g., killing). Using stories explicitly stating the killing of animals and people, H. Clark Barrett and Tanya Behne (2005) found that 4-year-old German as well as Shuar children (from the Amazon region of Ecuador) were well aware that death, unlike sleep, would eliminate mental as well as motor functions.

However, somewhat older children increasingly come to think about death in two very different ways: one focused on the discontinuity/cessation of all (bodily) function most apparent in biological contexts and the other focused on the possibility of continuing *mental* function after death most apparent in religious contexts (see also Rosengren et al., 2014). As indicated previously, this general picture of developing reflective thinking about afterlife possibilities holds, amid intriguing variation, across cultures in countries such as the United States, China, Spain, and the Shuar in Ecuador. As a further example, Rita Astuti and Paul Harris (2008) reported that Vezo children in rural Madagascar exhibit a grasp of the finality of death well before they begin to entertain the idea that mental functions could persist after death. In this case, this developmental pattern is accompanied by data as to the course of cultural exposure as well. Early on, Vezo children are richly exposed to the consequences of bodily death (including the rotting of corpses), but they are protected from ideas about spirits (deemed inappropriate for children). Collectively presented ideas about spirits and the spirit world come later. Nevertheless, once youth begin to encounter ideas about the spirit world, their understanding of these ideas appears to draw on intuitive divisions between body and mind. Thus, like Harris and Gimenez (2005), Astuti and Harris found that for older children cognitive functions (knowing, remembering, missing one's children) were judged more likely to continue after death than psychobiological functions (seeing, hearing, feeling hungry). Notably, Vezo participants judged the *spirit* to be most likely to continue after death as compared to the *mind* (less likely) and *body* (least likely).

The Idea of Soul

In religious traditions, the faculty of a person that most likely transcends death is the spirit or soul. And in the Vezo data (from Astuti & Harris, 2008) children distinguished spirit and mind in their responses. Descartes' philosophical thinking helped promote a scholarly tendency to refer to mind and soul interchangeably (cf. Bloom, 2004). Emerging research, however, suggests that for lay adults and for children, mind and soul are separable and distinct.

In particular, in two experiments, Rebekah Richert and Paul Harris (2006) found that children's ideas of soul quickly come to differ from their ideas of mind and brain. In the first experiment, U.S. children ages 4 to 12 years were presented with a vignette describing a ritual baptism of a baby and then asked about the difference the baptism would make. They were asked about the location of the difference—whether outside (visible and tangible) or inside—and whether the baby's mind, brain, or soul would be different after the baptism. Even the youngest group of children (age 4–6) showed a belief that baptism results in an invisible/intangible change inside the body. Across ages, children regarded baptism as mostly changing the soul, somewhat changing the mind, but having almost no effect on the brain.

In their second experiment, Richert and Harris (2006) more directly probed children's ideas about properties and functions of the soul as compared to the mind and brain. Modeled after Johnson and Wellman's (1982) original mind-brain study, children were asked whether various kinds of functions—cognitive, noncognitive, and biological—would continue without the presence of a brain, mind, or soul. Children were also asked whether babies have these faculties, whether they change and develop over time, and whether the baby would be the same if this faculty was taken away. The results consistently showed that school-age children did not identify the soul and mind. Although school-age children readily judged that cognitive functions would be disrupted without a brain or mind, they typically judged that such functions would continue undisrupted without a soul. The brain and mind were also more often judged to change and develop than the soul. In response to open-ended questions, children distinctively associated the soul with spiritual functions, such as moral purpose, life force, and invisible spirit.

More research as to children's developing understanding of souls or spirit as distinct from minds and bodies would be welcome (see, e.g., Jesse Bering's, 2006, speculation and theorizing). But even these initial data add to an emerging coherent story.

Developmentally, the idea of mind originates from thinking about thinking in the generalized sense of mentation. Mind becomes part of an enlarged, more reflective causal-explanatory theory of human behavior. Arguably, the idea of "soul," in part, is just one more reflective step beyond "mind," a personal essence still further distilled and disembodied, dependent on, or at least assisted by collective ideas from others about soul, spirit, and afterlife.

In sum, children commonly develop two reflective notions about death. On one hand, as they become increasingly aware of death and aware that the mind is contingent on the body, they can infer the mind's death. On the other hand, they also come to imagine mentality operating independent from the body. These two notions coexist (e.g., Rosengren et al., 2014) probably in part because they operate with regard to different psychological "faculties" and contexts. As Aristotle long ago noted, perceptual contents in the form of sensations—such as seeing, hearing, and feeling hungry—have obvious bodily causes. The faculty of mentation (thoughts, memories, dreams), however, is not so clearly embodied. Thus, when ideas about transcending death (of the body) begin to appear, they appear most readily for faculties that focus on those distinctive acts of mind most removed from bodily constraints. Most generally, mind, brain, and soul are ideas that spring from spontaneous and collectively inspired reflection built on an initial intuitive understanding of intentionality and mentation.

CONCLUSIONS

Evolutionary scientists have recently and heatedly debated whether beliefs in gods, afterlife, and the like are evolutionarily adaptive or instead just a byproduct of some other more directly useful adaptation (e.g., Wright, 2009). Regardless, these beliefs exist, and moreover they develop as children grow within their families and communities. It is this developmental story that is my focus.

The total developmental story I envision has four overlapping phases (see also Wellman & Johnson, 2008). First of all, the infant cognitive system rapidly achieves a variety of implicit processing distinctions that serve to make practical sense of a world of intentional agents who experience and act on objects. During the preschool years, these initial processes and understandings become organized into relatively coherent *intuitive theories* that frame children's ordinary understanding of intentional agents (as well as biological entities and physical objects in the world; see, e.g., Wellman & Gelman, 1998). In particular, an intuitive theory of mind provides a clear-cut, taken-for-granted understanding of belief-desire agency and agents. In the preschool years, intuitive theory of mind primarily frames the child's understanding of mentality as contrasted with reality, and intuitive biology frames the child's understanding of life and in contrast death. Yet the achievement and structure of these intuitive theories also provide a groundwork for—and a stimulus for—*reflective ideas*. These originally fragmented reflective notions, sponsored by both spontaneous and collective ideas, emerge particularly in middle childhood.

At a possible fourth level, beyond the generation of reflective ideas, stands the capacity to think still further (and more critically) about these ideas themselves. Critically thinking about reflective ideas can eventuate partially (in lay adults) or more fully (in philosophers and theologians) in truly *philosophical theory*. This requires thinking about theoretical possibilities, independent of intuitive assumptions. Reflection at this highest level also embraces deeply counterintuitive ideas, albeit ideas anchored earlier in ordinary intuitive thinking. Having conceptually divided the world into essentially different kinds of things (mind and body, life and afterlife), the final ontological questions (for older lay thinkers and for philosophy and religion) concern how these things are connected together. How is it that mind and body, soul and matter, ideas and reality are related? Is mind just a product of matter (materialism), or is matter a reflection of mind (idealism)? Is ultimate reality material or spiritual?

I have not addressed this fourth phase of philosophical theory. I have concentrated instead on earlier developments (initial distinctions, intuitive theories, and reflective ideas). These earlier developments are intriguing in their own right *and* they constitute the infrastructure for any later reflective theorizing. In short, reflective ideas and reflective theorizing—evident in societies worldwide and throughout human history—are framed by ideas that are grounded in the intuitive understandings of childhood. Reflective ideas about minds and brains, gods and souls, are grounded in ordinary, early achieved theory of mind.

14

The Landscape of Mind

ADULTS LOVE TO gossip. Apparently this is true in all societies and cultures, although perhaps more overt in some and more covert, but irrepressible, in others. The comparative anthropologist Robin Dunbar (of the "social brain" hypothesis discussed in Chapter 10) has argued both that gossip is part of our primate heritage and that humans are especially proficient at it (e.g., Dunbar, 2004). In fact, in his book *Grooming, Gossip, and the Evolution of Language* (1996), Dunbar argued that our need to talk about each other was cause as well as consequence of the evolution of human intelligence and human language.

Naturally enough then, gossip is the stuff of everyday conversation. In their research with humans, Dunbar and his colleagues (reviewed in Dunbar, 1996, 2004) conducted observational studies overhearing people's conversations in various public places (e.g., shopping malls, subway cars, etc.). Gossip occupied about 65% of people's speaking time. And this frequent gossip evidenced very little variation across ages or genders.

When we gossip, directly in conversation or indirectly via tabloid magazines, advice columns, or sports page articles about players and managers, it might be easy to overlook a crucial point: Gossip evidences our theories of mind, framed by belief-desire understandings forged in the crucible of development. Gossip is not only social—we gossip with others, about others; it is social cognitive—we talk about people's intentions, likes (ordinary and perverse), beliefs (ordinary and perverse), deeds (and misdeeds), ideas, and quirks. Because such talk reflects our human propensity, and our childhood propensity, to think about people's actions, lives, and minds, gossip illuminates three themes that are tied up with the processes of making minds: the power and roots of narratives in our understanding of people; the scope, complexity, and constructivist character of our everyday theories; and, again and again, the fundamental imprint of development on our adult minds.

In the introductory chapter of this book, I used the power of stories—Shakespeare's stories, *People* magazine stories—to help introduce the intrigue of our everyday theory of mind. Stories present our lives, stories provide narratives that explicate persona; they do so in everyday and tabloid gossip, and they do so in other forums as well.

Beginning with Jerome Bruner's (1986) musings, a multidisciplinary array of scholars have converged on narrative understanding and creation as a quintessentially human mode of knowing. Bruner argued that children come into the world looking for meaning and prepared to use stories to extract this meaning, to make sense of human action, and to interpret their own and others' lives and experiences. In his introduction to narrative thought in his book, *Actual Minds, Possible Worlds* (1986), Bruner began by contrasting paradigmatic and narrative modes of thought. Crudely, paradigmatic or logical-scientific thought focuses on physical reality and concerns itself with observation, analysis, and proof. Narrative thought focuses on the psychological, rather than the physical, and concerns itself with experience, intentions, drama, and story.

The power and appeal of narrative—of stories, of gossip, of dramas that portray human lives and actions—is arguably universal. But narratives encompass a multifaceted understanding of human lives. The story of *Cinderella* rests on Cinderella's roles (e.g., stepdaughter, maid) and the roles of others (e.g., stepmother, fairy godmother), her actions (e.g., cleaning and scrubbing, going to the ball), and underlying those, the story depends on Cinderella's desires (e.g., to go to the ball) and beliefs (e.g., that it's hopeless to think she'll go) as well as the obstacles and obligations (e.g., her need to do her mountain of chores) that shape her actions and emotions as events unfold. That narrative—all narratives—describes situations, actions, and minds. As Bruner put it, narrative merges together two landscapes:

> One is the landscape of action, where the constituents are the arguments of action: agent, intention or goal, situation, instrument, something corresponding to a "story grammar." The other landscape is the landscape of consciousness: what those involved in the action know, think or feel, or do not know, think, or feel. (Bruner, 1986, p. 14)

It is no accident that throughout this book—for example, in considering infant understandings, or in considering the neural network that characterizes theory of mind—it has been useful to distinguish understanding of intentional action and understanding of the mental states that organize and underlie such actions. Both the "landscape of action" and the "landscape of consciousness" count, and both depend on the constructs of theory of mind, construals of the beliefs, desires, and intentions of agents.

Cinderella is one of those archetypical stories that some people specially identify as akin to their own story. It bridges between a common, public story and a private, life story—a narrative account of one's key life events. A life story is one's autobiography, arguably bound up with self-identity and used to make sense of both personal consistency and personal change (Dunlop & Walker, 2013). The title of Dan McAdams' (1993) book, *The Stories We Live By*, captures how we narratively structure our lives. *Cinderella* provides an example, at least for some people. *David Copperfield* provides an alternative, intriguing example. Albeit fictional, *David Copperfield* is widely acknowledged as the most closely autobiographical of Charles Dickens' novels. In that book, Dickens wrote, "Whether I will turn out to be the hero of my own life, or whether that station will be held by anybody else, these pages must show" (1870, p. 9). Great writers promiscuously exploit life stories; not just Dickens, not just heroes—Sophocles tells us Oedipus's tragic life story. And psychologists exploit these "fictional" lives—Freud argued that we all live through an oedipal story in our childhoods.

When lay folk, or Dickens, or cognitive scientists call our self-recollections our *autobiographical* memories, they tacitly acknowledge this link between narrative and self. Autobiographical memories emerge in early childhood (Bauer, 2002; Fivush & Haden, 2005), and immersion in narrative discourses about one's deeds and experiences begins before preschool (Miller, Fung, & Mintz, 1996). On average, when asked to describe themselves, young children draw on the "landscape of action," providing descriptions combining physical actions and attributes, but including intentions, preferences, and emotional moods (Damon & Hart, 1988). With increasing age, self-descriptions draw more from the "landscape of consciousness," couching self-attribution more and more in the realm of the inner psychological. In adolescence, life stories get more extended, more coherent, more story like. Eventually they become life history stories that are increasingly self-defining (Habermas & Bluck, 2000). Thus, it is often in adolescence that youth try to find a narrative thread for their life—be it as hero (David Copperfield?) or as victim, a story of lessons learned or misdeeds corrupting, a story of potent agency or tragic happenstance, a story of personal consistency or of personal change.

Relatedly, in adolescence comes an increased impact of what Habermas and Bluck (2000) called the "cultural concept of biography" (p. 750). Cultural concepts of biography aid people to frame their extended self-descriptions, to frame a more and more storied autobiography. The "cultural concept of biography" is arguably pancultural in the sense that some form of culturally shaped biographical frame aids the sense and narrative order of lives in societies worldwide. But it is also culturally specific in that different communities privilege different cultural biographical scripts (and these may change for younger vs. older protagonists). As one example, Peggy Miller and her colleagues (1996, 2012) have detailed crucial differences in biographical scripts for middle-class,

Western versus middle-class, Chinese adult–child narratives beginning as early as 2, 3, and 4 years.

In both the United States and Taiwan, in their research, parents often and consistently described their child's deeds, to others and to the child themselves. In the United States, families' personal stories about the child systematically evidenced a "child favorability bias" (Miller et al., 1996), focusing on positive childhood deeds and seldom mentioning children's misdeeds. Even when misdeeds were narrated in U.S. middle-class families, they were treated as humorous or they were shaped to portray the child in a favorable light. The misdeed was unlike the child typically, or represented the child engaging in younger behavior now outgrown.

In contrast, in the Taiwanese families, personal storytelling often cast the child as a transgressor; 35% of Taiwanese stories cited child misdeeds (as opposed to 5% or less in the United States). Instead of a "child favorability bias," these narratives in Taiwan had a "didactic bias": The stories were told, and told publically, to instruct the child in proper behavior. In Taiwan, these narratives were framed within a Confucian-based sense of development as a moral learning process (Li, 2002, 2004) with lessons to be learned about humility, right-minded behavior, and the virtues of moral striving (Miller, Fung, Lin, Chen, & Boldt, 2012).

Regardless of cultural differences, such personal narratives, including those told by others for the child and varying due to differing culturally conceived biographies, sketch mentalistic-intentional landscapes of action and of consciousness. They recruit and reveal the power of theory of mind for children, adolescents, adults, and their communities. Theory of mind provides the framework for the "stories we live by."

ADULT CONSTRUCTIONS AND ERRORS

A person's life story is never wholly correct: Successes can be inflated (e.g., in the United States), misdeeds can be embellished (e.g., in Taiwan), and self-narratives can often include gross falsities that dupe even oneself. I've kept the focus of this book on childhood conceptions and developments, but it is also instructive to consider adults' theories of mind and the revealing errors such theories can evidence. Recall in Chapter 5 the discussion of the variety of folk psychological theories that are apparent worldwide. Via constructivist processes of framework development, cultural communities have hundreds of years to develop their own quite different understandings of persons and minds. Not all these folk theories, in fact not any of them, can be perfectly "correct." Everyday theories are anchored in evidence, but they are simultaneously constructions, subject to constructivist error.

Richard Nisbett and Timothy Wilson (1977) famously pointed out that adults use theories about themselves to make sense of their own actions. But, the main thrust of Nisbett and Wilson's analysis was that people's theories about themselves are often strikingly wrong. Adults' self-theories are especially wrong about the actual causes of their own behavior, attitudes, and judgments. Nisbett and Wilson showed how rarely people "see" the inner causes of their behaviors via direct introspection, and so they resort instead to indirect causal theories about themselves, theories of their own causally relevant intentions, beliefs, perceptions, and emotions. Nisbett and Wilson were particularly concerned with adults' theories of their own individual actions and choices— "Why did I choose that laundry soap?"; "Why do I prefer beaches over mountains?" But there are also more general examples.

Extramission, How Perception Works

Piaget argued that the history of scientific conceptions can inform us about the development of everyday conceptions. Theory theory naturally endorses this idea as well (Carey, 1985; Wellman, 1990). Of course, scientific history does not foreshadow child development, or vice versa, but conceptual constructions of one sort can help us understand conceptual constructions of the other sort. This is especially apparent if we wish to illuminate the errors that can characterize both child and adult theorizing. One of my favorite lines of research starts with the observation that both early astronomers and young children begin by thinking the world is flat, and then the discussion and research go on to show the progressions needed historically to discover it is spherical and needed in childhood to accept school-based scientific instruction that the world is round (e.g., Vosniadou & Brewer, 1992). Theory of mind has a similar intriguing example.

Ancient philosophers, such as Euclid and Ptolemy, often believed that visual perception involved rays of light emitted by the eyes. This is an *extramission* theory of perception. Scientifically, this theory was replaced by *intromission* theories: visual perception comes from rays of light reflected from objects into the eyes. Based on their first intuitive understandings of perception (e.g., infant Level-1 and preschool Level-2 perspective-taking plus reality-appearance insights), older children achieve reflective understandings of perception. Neatly enough, reflective thinking about perception often evidences an extramission theory of sight. Indeed, in one of his early books, *The Child's Conception of the World*, Piaget (1929/1967) suggested children believe that eyes emit "looks" during vision. At least one child concluded that two persons' "looks" would meet, and mix, when they crossed. Gerald Winer and his colleagues have consistently found that about 50% of first graders evidence extramission beliefs (e.g., Winer & Cottrell, 1996) depending on how those are tested (e.g., when simply asked, "When we look at something does anything go out of our eyes?"). In several of their studies Winer and his colleagues have demonstrated *increased* extramission beliefs from first to third grade and/or from third to fifth grades (Winer & Cottrell, 1996 Winer, Cottrell, Karefilaki & Chronister, 1996). This makes sense in that reflective beliefs need to develop on preschool intuitions; so, they increase in the early school years.

Not only do children believe in extramission, Winer and his colleagues have found that many adults do as well (Winer, Cottrell, Gregg, Fournier, & Bica, 2002). In their research, as many as 50% of American college students believe in extramission, even those who, as Psychology students, have had some college instruction in visual perception. The methods used here include asking students to endorse graphical representations of vision that contrast depictions of light rays coming from the objects, or from the eyes, or back and forth from eyes to objects to eyes. Or they include asking the same choices verbally (e.g., "When we see, does anything like waves or rays come into our eyes, or come out of our eyes?"). A substantial proportion of college students endorse extramission.

At first Winer and his team (Winer et al., 1996) were surprised by these results, and they noted that when adults endorse extramission, they most often assert that light rays come from both objects and from the eyes. So they created a procedure they thought would show that extramission beliefs, when reported by adults, were lightly held. Here they asked college students about vision when presenting them with a shining light-bulb, the same bulb unlit, and a white ball essentially the same size as the bulb (Winer et al., 1996). "We expected that referring to the lit bulb would diminish extramission responses—indeed, that it would be nearly impossible to maintain extramission beliefs in reference to light shining in one's face" (Winer et al., 2002, p. 420). They also expected that once students gave correct *intromission* answers for the shining lightbulb, similar intromission responses would be obvious for the unlit bulb (or white ball) too. But 33% of the adults affirmed extramission beliefs for the lit bulb, right there shining into their eyes:

> Moreover, there was no sign of positive transfer from questions about the lit bulb to questions about the nonluminous objects. In fact, the opposite occurred. When we switched from the lit bulb to the nonluminous objects, there was an increase in extramission responses, as if turning off the light signaled that there were no more incoming rays. (Winer et al., 2002, p. 420)

Blind Understandings of Seeing

Constructivist theory building doesn't always lead to errors, especially when it comes to certain basics. A striking example of this also comes from everyday conceptions of perception, but in this case blind individuals' conceptions of seeing.

Blind adults, and even children, attribute seeing to others and not themselves. Of course this could, potentially, be empty use of the terms *seeing* and *looking*, or metaphoric use of such terms to mean something like exploring or encountering things by touch or hearing but not actually by sight. But years ago, Barbara Landau and Lila Gleitman (1985) provided evidence of more appropriate and correct understandings in a detailed study of a blind preschooler, Kelli. Importantly, Landau and Gleitman's data focus on a distinction between Kelli's understanding and use of *look* and *see* as applied to herself versus as applied to others. When applying *look* and *see* to herself, Kelli used the terms to mean exploring or apprehending by touch. But when applying the terms to her sighted mother or a sighted experimenter, Kelli used the terms to refer to exploration by sight and apprehension by vision. This is clearest in a series of experiments in which Kelli (at age 3½ years), when asked to "let me see/look at the front of your shirt," for example, drew attention to the target by orienting or pointing to it at a distance, that is, out of the viewer's reach. At the same age, she appropriately differentiated between showing versus giving someone something and letting someone see versus letting them touch something. And, at age 4½, Kelli understood that sighted people cannot see through opaque barriers that she could hear through, and conversely that sighted people can look through windows although she herself could not reach through them. In total, Landau and Gleitman demonstrated persuasively that Kelli's understanding of vision was remarkably good.

Clearly, regardless of what one thinks about the role of simulation from one's own firsthand experience for understanding minds (see Chapters 7 and 11), this is an example of a different sort. Such knowledge could not result from the firsthand experience of seeing. It constitutes, instead, attribution to others of a theoretical category of experience (seeing). Admittedly, knowledge of seeing could be grounded indirectly in experiences of touching and hearing, but only in a creative and constructive way that goes way beyond first-person touching and hearing per se. Thus the knowledge is, in important part, constructed and inferred; and it is posited in others, in a third-person fashion, because of its theoretical-explanatory role and utility.

Of course, Kelli is only a single blind child, but Candida Peterson and her colleagues (Peterson, Peterson, & Webb, 2000) tested almost 30 blind children aged 6 through 12 years on several Level-2 visual perspective-taking tasks. For example, after tactilely exploring a toy puppy, children were seated around a table with two adults and performed tasks like, "Put the dog on the table so that [adult-1] gets the best view of its nose (tail, etc.), so that she can see the nose best." Of these blind children, 87% earned *perfect* scores on 6 out of 6 visual perspective-taking tasks.

Moreover Marina Bedny and Rebecca Saxe give us still further data from blind adults; in behavioral research, blind adults, like blind children, often answer questions about sight well (see Bedny & Saxe, 2012, for a review). But behavioral studies leave the nagging question: What sort of concepts of vision do these answers represent? Are they clever, laboriously learned answers based on overt correlated regularities (like those of Daniel Povinelli's chimps in Chapter 10), or are they references to internal, mental states more profoundly? Bedny and Saxe (2012) reasoned that neuro-imaging studies provided a way "to look under the hood" and illuminate this issue. As discussed in Chapter 11, when sighted adults reason about beliefs and other mental states, this activates a theory-of-mind network of neural regions with the medial PFC (prefrontal cortex) and right TPJ (temporal-parietal junction) most prominent among them. These regions are active when thinking about persons' experiences of seeing too, not just believing. If blind adults have fundamentally different understandings of seeing, in spite of highly accurate use of the language of seeing, then they should have different patterns of neural activation for tasks involving stories about seeing than sighted individuals do. But, "blind adults' neural responses looked just like sighted adults'" (Bedny & Saxe, 2012, p. 72). And it was not just that blind adults equated seeing with some other sensory modality like hearing. Both blind and sighted adults distinguished stories about hearing from stories about seeing within the right TPJ, and the patterns of activation that showed this distinction were the same for both sets of adults, the blind and as well as the sighted (Bedny & Saxe, 2012).

These findings firmly demonstrate that blind persons construct theory-based conceptions of seeing. Moreover, the equivalence between blind and sighted individuals in their neural activations more profoundly suggests that sighted adults' concepts of seeing, and their theories of mind more broadly, need not be fundamentally derived from first-person experience either.

Bertrand Russell (1912) distinguished "knowledge by description" versus "knowledge by acquaintance." Our theories of mind are not merely "knowledge by description" nor by "acquaintance." They are mixtures, but of the most intimate, strongly held sort. They are constructivist achievements, but constructions that give us an insider's knowledge, although not always based in the first instance on first-person experiences.

Lying, How We Detect Liars

The realm of perception—including extramission beliefs about vision—is not the only theory-of-mind topic in which adult theories are nicely revealing or surprisingly in error. Consider lying. Understanding basic notions about lying—in particular that lies represent an intention to deceive—is part and parcel of even preschoolers' intuitions about minds and actions (as discussed in Chapter 3). Not surprisingly, understanding that some speech acts—lies—are intended to deceive leads to attempts to detect when people lie. Not much is known about when and how children attempt to detect lies in others, but a considerable amount is now known about adults. And it is clear that our adult judgments about when and how people lie reflect not direct observations of ourselves and others but rather our theories of lie detection and theories of the connections between mind and behavior. As Nisbett and Wilson (1977) would have predicted, people have sensible, causal theories about lying but wrong theories.

In a prototypic experimental paradigm, adults, such as college students, are videotaped talking about a personally witnessed event, describing it either truthfully or deliberately lying about it. Then the tapes are shown to other adults—the lie detectors—who judge the truth or falsity of what was said. Charles Bond and Bella DePaulo have conducted several meta-analyses of the accuracy of adults as lie detectors, and summed across hundreds of such studies "lie detectors" averaged 54% correct judgments, microscopically better than the 50% that could be achieved by random guessing (e.g.,

Bond & DePaulo, 2006, 2008). "Experts" who routinely assess lying in their jobs, such as police officers or interrogation specialists, performed no better than others (Garrido, Masip, & Herrero, 2004; Vrij, 2008), that is, no better than untrained college students.

At the same time adults regularly report consistent beliefs about lie detection. Typically in these studies, participants are asked to report their beliefs about lies and liars. Most commonly, participants get a list of verbal and nonverbal behavior and are asked if and how they relate to lying (see Hartwig & Bond, 2011). Or, lie detectors in the lie-catching videotape studies just described are asked to explain their judgments (e.g., "I thought she was lying because she hesitated a lot."). Two behaviors are consistently voiced as indications of lying: shifting, eye-gaze aversion and fidgety, nervous behavior.

> A worldwide study surveyed beliefs about cues to deception in 58 countries and found that in 51 of these, the belief in a link between gaze behavior and deception was the most frequent report (Global Deception Research Team, 2006). People also report that increased body movements, fidgeting, and posture changes are associated with deceit, as well as a higher pitched voice and speech errors. This pattern suggests that people expect liars to experience nervousness and discomfort and that this nervousness is evident in behavior. (Hartwig & Bond, 2011, p. 644)

In fact, however, people's lay theories of lying are wrong. Reconsider the videotapes taken of the lying versus truthful adults. Those tapes can also be carefully analyzed to tally verbal and nonverbal behaviors of the liars. People's theories about such lie-telling behaviors are wrong, and wrong at two levels. First, objectively, gaze aversion and nervous fidgeting do not correlate with actual lying by the liars in the videotape studies. A meta-analysis of more than 100 studies (DePaulo et al., 2003) showed that gaze aversion does not predict lying, and that nervous behaviors—fidgeting, blushing, stuttering—do not either. (For information about what cues can, somewhat, predict lying, see Ekman, 2009.) Second, in ways that hark back to Nisbett and Wilson (1977), lie detectors are not good reporters of the cues that they actually use to make their lying–not-lying judgments. Their self-theories tell them they are using gaze aversion, but their actual judgments rely on other (also ineffective) cues instead (Hartwig & Bond, 2011).

In sum, despite years of concerning themselves with lying, the theories that most adults construct about lying do not home in on accurate lie-detecting features and strategies. Moreover, the theories adults construct about their own lie-detecting strategies don't accurately capture their own lie-detecting efforts either.

BUDDHIST THEORY OF MIND AND REALITY

Apparently, from the lying meta-analyses, adults in many countries hold similar theories about lie detection (e.g., in 51 of 58 countries, belief in gaze aversion as indicating lying was the top lie-detection belief reported; Global Deception Research Team, 2006). But in other ways, cultural differences in theories of mind abound. In this regard, Buddhist understandings and teachings about mind—developed over centuries of exploration and instruction about the mind from teachers and from meditation—provide a specially intriguing counterpoint to Western, lay-adult theories.

From Chapter 13 we know that after preschool, children and adults consistently affirm an everyday experience of thinking as akin to a stream of consciousness, like in a James Joyce novel—"chain-reaction-like flashings of whole sequences of thoughts, each cognitively cueing its successor" (Flavell et al., 1995, p. 85). Equally, our everyday reflective understanding of the mind and reality is that mental states of perception, knowing, and recognizing connect the inner self to the outer "real" world. In Buddhist teachings and theory, both of these everyday mentalistic beliefs are errors. Everyday adult understanding and Gautama Buddha give us dueling, developed theories of mind.

There are a great many varieties of Buddhist teachings and traditions. Even experts disagree about how to best summarize or distill them, so I won't attempt to do so here. But still, it is possible to highlight several informative basics. I do so for Mahayana Buddhism ("the Great Vehicle"), one of the two great streams of Buddhism. Paul Williams, in his book *Buddhist Thought: A Complete Introduction to the Indian Tradition* (Williams, 2000), stated that Mahayana Buddhism originated early in India (along with Theravada Buddhism, the other main branch) then spread to Tibet, China, Indochina, Japan, Korea, and beyond.

According to Mahayana Buddhist thought, our everyday, reflective understanding and experience of mind is deceptive and flawed. Our everyday experience of a stream of consciousness—with "one thought cueing another"—is not an advanced awareness of the conscious character of mental life; it is instead symptomatic of a "monkey mind" that is unsettled and unsettling, confused and capricious. Equally, our everyday understanding of the mind as connecting the self to the "real" world misleads us as to our true selves, and instead mires us in a quagmire of external attractions and repulsions (cravings and aversions). In these ways, our everyday, untutored sense of mind, self, and reality perpetuate a malicious interconnection. Monkey mind connected to external attractions and repulsions bounces us around in a self-existence of ignorance and suffering.

Fortunately, according to Buddha's great enlightenment, mind and reality are fundamentally different from the deceptive everyday impression. And, various practices and insights can enlighten one as to their true nature. The practices that can aid anyone to discover the nature of mind, among its deceptive appearances, include, importantly, mindfulness training. Such practices control the monkey mind and culminate instead in a mind both empty of thoughts and attentive to the present moment. According to Buddhist theory of mind and reality, with regard to mind, instead of streams of individuated, kaleidoscopic consciousness, mindfulness practices and teachings yield reflective insights that point to a truer mentality, a universal enduring consciousness. With regard to reality, instead of a seductive experiential reality of attractions and repulsions, mindfulness practices point to an alternative experiential reality, one of blissful serenity.

GOING MENTAL

In my 1990 book, *The Child's Theory of Mind* (Wellman, 1990), I claimed that theory of mind was an important, foundational competence and reviewed initial research that began to establish such a claim. That book contributed to an emerging field, but at that point the book and the field were largely promissory notes. It was early days, the data were sparse and preliminary, and although nicely coherent, already showed not only gaps but inconsistencies that would surface with increasing force in the years ahead as more and more research accumulated from more and more scholars worldwide. In the intervening years, much has been discovered in research with infants, children, adults, individuals with autism and deafness, and with nonhuman primates as well. Based on this voluminous research, here I offer a sequel, hopefully capturing what is now known and cashing out the initial promissory note.

Apparently, Edmund O. Wilson, the famous evolutionary biologist, offered this advice to aspiring researchers: A good scientist should be bright enough to know a good research endeavor when he or she sees it, but not so bright as to become bored doing it. For 25 years I've been not so bright as to become bored with theory of mind. Children insistently stay interested in people, minds, and theories, and so have I.

REFERENCES

Abraham, A., Rakoczy, H., Werning, M., von Cramon, D. Y., & Schubotz, R. I. (2010). Matching mind to world and vice versa: Functional dissociations between belief and desire mental state processing. *Social Neuroscience, 5*(1), 1-18. doi: 10.1080/17470910903166853

Akhtar, N. (2005). The robustness of learning through overhearing. *Developmental Science, 8*, 199–209. doi: 10.1111/j.1467-7687.2005.00406.x

Amsterlaw, J., & Wellman, H. M. (2006). Theories of mind in transition: A microgenetic study of the development of false belief understanding. *Journal of Cognition and Development, 7*, 139–172. doi: 10.1207/s15327647jcd0702_1

Anderson, D., & Reilly, J. (2002). The MacArthur Communicative Development Inventory: Normative data for American Sign Language. *Journal of Deaf Studies and Deaf Education, 7*, 83–106.

Anderson, J. R., & Meno, P. (2003). Psychological influences on yawning in children. *Current Psychology Letters, 11*(2). Retrieved from http://cpl.revues.org/document390.html

Andrews, G., Halford, G. S., Bunch, K. M., Bowden, D., & Jones, T. (2003). Theory of mind and relational complexity. *Child Development, 74*, 1476–1499. doi: 10.1111/1467-8624.00618

Apperly, I. (2011). *Mindreaders: The cognitive basis of "theory of mind."* Hove, England: Psychology Press.

Apperly, I. A. (2012). What is "theory of mind"? Concepts, cognitive processes and individual differences. *The Quarterly Journal of Experimental Psychology, 65*, 825–839. doi: 10.1080/1747 0218.2012.676055

Apperly, I. A., & Butterfill, S. A. (2009). Do humans have two systems to track beliefs and belief-like states? *Psychological Review, 116*, 953–970. doi: 10.1037/a0016923

Aquinas, T. (2006). *Summa theologiae: Questions on God.* B. Leftow & B. Davies (Eds.). Cambridge, England: Cambridge University Press (Original work written 1265–1274)

Armstrong, K. (1994). *A history of God: The 4000-year quest of Judaism, Christianity, and Islam.* New York: Ballantine Books.

Aschersleben, G., Hofer, T., & Jovanovic, B. (2008). The link between infant attention to goal-directed action and later theory of mind abilities. *Developmental Science, 11,* 862–868. doi: 10.1111/j.1467-7687.2008.00736.x

Aslin, R. N. (2007). What's in a look? *Developmental Science, 10,* 48–53. doi: 10.1111/j.1467-768 7.2007.00563.x

Astington, J. W. (2001). The future of theory-of-mind research: Understanding motivational states, the role of language, and real-world consequences. *Child Development, 72,* 685–687. doi: 10.1111/1467-8624.00305

Astington, J. W. (2003). Sometimes necessary, never sufficient: False-belief understanding and social competence. In B. Repacholi & V. Slaughter (Eds.), *Individual differences in theory of mind: Implications for typical and atypical development* (pp. 13–38). Hove, England: Psychology Press.

Astington, J. W., & Baird, J. A. (2005). *Why language matters for theory of mind.* New York: Oxford University Press.

Astington, J. W., & Gopnik, A. (1988a). Children's understanding of representational change and its relation to the understanding of false belief and the appearance-reality distinction. *Child Development, 59,* 26–27. doi: 10.2307/1130386

Astington, J. W., & Gopnik, A. (1988b). Knowing you've changed your mind: Children's understanding of representational change. In J. W. Astington, P. L. Harris, & D. R. Olson (Eds.), *Developing theories of mind* (pp. 193–206). New York: Cambridge University Press.

Astington, J. W., & Jenkins, J. M. (1995). Theory of mind development and social understanding. *Cognition and Emotion, 9,* 151–165.

Astuti, R., & Harris, P. L. (2008). Understanding mortality and the life of the ancestors in rural Madagascar. *Cognitive Science, 32,* 713–740. doi: 10.1080/03640210802066907

Atran, S. (1996). Modes of thinking about living kinds; science, symbolism and common sense. In D. Olson & N. Torrance (Eds.), *Modes of thought: Explorations in culture and cognition* (pp. 216–260). New York: Cambridge University Press.

Atran, S. (2002). *In gods we trust: The evolutionary landscape of religion.* Oxford, England: Oxford University Press.

Atran, S., & Sperber, D. (1991). Learning without teaching. In L. Tolchinsky-Landsmann (Ed.), *Culture, schooling and psychological development* (pp. 39–55). Norwood, NJ: Ablex.

Augustine. (1844). *Sermons on selected lessons of the New Testament.* Oxford, England: J. H. Parker.

Baillargeon, R. (2004). Infants' physical world. *Current Directions in Psychological Science, 13,* 89–94. doi: 10.1111/j.0963-7214.2004.00281.x

Baillargeon, R., Scott, R. M., & He, Z. (2010). False-belief understanding in infants. *Trends in Cognitive Sciences, 14,* 110–118.

Baillargeon, R., & Wang, S.-H. (2002). Event categorization in infancy. *Trends in Cognitive Sciences, 6,* 85–93. doi: 10.1016/s1364-6613(00)01836-2

Baldwin, D. A. (1991). Infants' contribution to the achievement of joint reference. *Child Development, 62,* 875–890. doi: 10.2307/1131140

Baldwin, D. A. (2000). Interpersonal understanding fuels knowledge acquisition. *Current Directions in Psychological Science, 9,* 40–45. doi: 10.1111/1467-8721.00057

Baldwin, D. A., Baird, J. A., Saylor, M. M., & Clark, M. A. (2001). Infants parse dynamic action. *Child Development, 72*, 708–717. doi: 10.1111/1467-8624.00310

Baldwin, D. A., & Moses, L. J. (1996). The ontogeny of social information gathering. *Child Development, 67*, 1915–1939. doi: 10.2307/1131601

Banaji, M., & Gelman, S. (Eds.). (2013). *Navigating the social world: A developmental perspective.* Oxford, England: Oxford University Press.

Baron-Cohen, S. (1995). *Mindblindness: An essay on autism and theory of mind.* Cambridge, MA: MIT Press.

Baron-Cohen, S. (2000). Theory of mind and autism: A fifteen year review. In S. Baron-Cohen, H. Tager-Flusberg & D. J. Cohen (Eds.), *Understanding other minds: Perspectives from developmental cognitive neuroscience* (2nd ed., pp. 3–20). New York: Oxford University Press.

Baron-Cohen, S., Leslie, A. M., & Frith, U. (1985). Does the autistic child have a "theory of mind"? *Cognition, 21*, 37–46. doi: 10.1016/0010-0277(85)90022-8

Baron-Cohen, S., Ring, H. A., Wheelwright, S., Bullmore, E. T., Brammer, M. J., Simmons, A., & Williams, S. C. (1999). Social intelligence in the normal and autistic brain: An fMRI study. *European Journal of Neuroscience, 11*, 1891–1898.

Barrett, H. C., & Behne, T. (2005). Children's understanding of death as the cessation of agency: A test using sleep versus death. *Cognition, 96*, 93–108. doi: http://dx.doi.org/10.1016/j.cognition.2004.05.004

Barrett, J. L. (1998). Cognitive constraints on Hindu concepts of the divine. *Journal for the Scientific Study of Religion, 37*, 608–619.

Barrett, J. L. (2000). Exploring the natural foundations of religion. *Trends in Cognitive Sciences, 4*, 29–34. doi: 10.1016/s1364-6613(99)01419-9

Barrett, J. L., & Keil, F. C. (1996). Conceptualizing a nonnatural entity: Anthropomorphism in God concepts. *Cognitive Psychology, 31*, 219–247. doi: http://dx.doi.org/10.1006/cogp.1996.0017

Barrett, J. L., & Richert, R. A. (2003). Anthropomorphism or preparedness? Exploring children's God concepts. *Review of Religious Research, 44*, 300–312. doi: 10.2307/3512389

Barrett, J. L., Richert, R. A., & Driesenga, A. (2001). God's beliefs versus mother's: The development of nonhuman agent concepts. *Child Development, 72*, 50–65. doi: 10.1111/1467-8624.00265

Barrett, L. F., Gendron, M., & Huang, Y.-M. (2009). Do discrete emotions exist? *Philosophical Psychology, 22*, 427–437. doi: 10.1080/09515080903153634

Barrett, L., Henzi, P., & Dunbar, R. (2003). Primate cognition: From 'what now?' to 'what if?'. *Trends in Cognitive Sciences, 7*, 494–497. doi: 10.1016/j.tics.2003.09.005

Bartsch, K. (1996). Between desires and beliefs: Young children's action predictions. *Child Development, 67*, 1671–1685. doi: 10.2307/1131724

Bartsch, K., & London, K. (2000). Children's use of mental state information in selecting persuasive arguments. *Developmental Psychology, 36*, 352–365. doi: 10.1037/0012-1649.36.3.352

Bartsch, K., London, K., & Campbell, M. D. (2007). Children's attention to beliefs in interactive persuasion tasks. *Developmental Psychology, 43*, 111–120. doi: 10.1037/0012-1649.43.1.111

Bartsch, K., Wade, C. E., & Estes, D. (2011). Children's attention to others' beliefs during persuasion: Improvised and selected arguments to puppets and people. *Social Development, 20*, 316–333. doi: 10.1111/j.1467-9507.2010.00580.x

Bartsch, K., & Wellman, H. M. (1995). *Children talk about the mind*. New York: Oxford University Press.

Bates, E., Benigni, L., Bretherton, I., Camaioni, L., & Volterra, V. (1979). *The emergence of symbols: Cognition and communication in infancy*. New York: Academic Press.

Bauer, P. J. (1996). What do infants recall of their lives? Memory for specific events by one- to two-year-olds. *American Psychologist, 51*, 29–41. doi: 10.1037/0003066x.51.1.29

Bauer, P. J. (2002). Long-term recall memory: Behavioral and neuro-developmental changes in the first 2 years of life. *Current Directions in Psychological Science, 11*, 137–141. doi: 10.1111/1467-8721.00186

Baumard, N., & Boyer, P. (2013). Religious beliefs as reflective elaborations on intuitions: A modified dual-process model. *Current Directions in Psychological Science, 22*, 295–300. doi: 10.1177/0963721413478610

Beck, D. M., Schaefer, C., Pang, K., & Carlson, S. M. (2011). Executive function in preschool children: Test-retest reliability. *Journal of Cognition and Development, 12*, 169–193. doi: 10.1080/15248372.2011.563485

Bedny, M., & Saxe, R. (2012). Insights into the origins of knowledge from the cognitive neuroscience of blindness. *Cognitive Neuropsychology, 29*(1–2), 56–84. doi: 10.1080/02643294.2012.713342

Behne, T., Carpenter, M., Call, J., & Tomasello, M. (2005). Unwilling versus unable: Infants' understanding of intentional action. *Developmental Psychology, 41*, 328–337. doi: 10.1037/0012-1649.41.2.328

Belyaev, D. K. (1979). Destabilizing selection as a factor in domestication. *Journal of Heredity, 70*, 301–308.

Bergstrom, B., Moehlmann, B., & Boyer, P. (2006). Extending the testimony problem: Evaluating the truth, scope, and source of cultural information. *Child Development, 77*, 531–538. doi: 10.1111/j.1467-8624.2006.00888.x

Bering, J. M. (2006). The folk psychology of souls. *Behavioral and Brain Sciences, 29*, 453–462. doi: 10.1017/S0140525X06009101

Bering, J. M., & Bjorklund, D. F. (2004). The natural emergence of reasoning about the afterlife as a developmental regularity. *Developmental Psychology, 40*, 217–233. doi: 10.1037/0012-1649.40.2.217

Birch, S. A. J., & Bloom, P. (2007). The curse of knowledge in reasoning about false beliefs. *Psychological Science, 18*, 382–386. doi: 10.1111/j.1467-9280.2007.01909.x

Birch, S. A. J., Vauthier, S. A., & Bloom, P. (2008). Three- and four-year-olds spontaneously use others' past performance to guide their learning. *Cognition, 107*, 1018–1034. doi: 10.1016/j.cognition.2007.12.008

Blakeslee, S. (2006, January 10). Cells that read minds. *New York Times*, F1. Retrieved from http://search.proquest.com.proxy.lib.umich.edu/docview/433260430?accountid=14667

Bloom, P. (2004). *Descartes' baby: How the science of child development explains what makes us human*. New York: Basic Books.

Boesch, C., & Boesch, H. (1989). Hunting behavior of wild chimpanzees in the Taï National Park. *American Journal of Physical Anthropology, 78*, 547–573. doi: 10.1002/ajpa.1330780410

Bonawitz, E., Shafto, P., Gweon, H., Goodman, N. D., Spelke, E. S., & Schulz, L. (2011). The double-edged sword of pedagogy: Instruction limits spontaneous exploration and discovery. *Cognition, 102*, 322–330. doi: 10.1016/j.cognition.2010.10.001

Bonawitz, E., Fischer, A., & Schulz, L. (2012). Teaching 3.5-year-olds to revise their beliefs given ambiguous evidence. *Journal of Cognition and Development, 13*, 266–280. doi: 10.1080/1524 8372.2011.577701

Bonawitz, E. B., Ferranti, D., Saxe, R., Gopnik, A., Meltzoff, A. N., Woodward, J., & Schulz, L. E. (2010). Just do it? Investigating the gap between prediction and action in toddlers' causal inferences. *Cognition, 115*, 104–117. doi: 10.1016/j.cognition.2009.12.001

Bond, C. F., Jr., & DePaulo, B. M. (2006). Accuracy of deception judgments. *Personality and Social Psychology Review, 10*, 214–234. doi: 10.1207/s15327957pspr1003_2

Bond C. F., Jr., & DePaulo, B. M. (2008). Individual differences in judging deception: Accuracy and bias. *Psychological Bulletin, 134*, 477–492. doi: 10.1037/00332909.134.4.47710.1037/0 033-2909.134.4.477.supp

Bornstein, M. H., & Sigman, M. D. (1986). Continuity in mental development from infancy. *Child Development, 57*, 251–274. doi: 10.2307/1130581

Bowman, L. C., Liu, D., Meltzoff, A. N., & Wellman, H. M. (2012). Neural correlates of belief- and desire-reasoning in 7- and 8-year-old children: An event-related potential study. *Developmental Science, 15*, 618–632. doi: 10.1111/j.14677687.2012.01158.x

Bowman, L. C., & Wellman, H. M. (2014). Neuroscience contributions to childhood theory-of-mind development. In O. N. Saracho (Ed.), *Contemporary perspectives on research in theories of mind in early childhood education* (pp. 195–223). Charlotte, NC: Information Age Publishing.

Boyer, P. (1994). *The naturalness of religious ideas: A cognitive theory of religion.* Berkeley: University of California Press.

Boyer, P. (2001). *Religion explained: The human instincts that fashion gods, spirits and ancestors.* London: Heinemann.

Bradley, L., & Bryant, P. E. (1983, February). Categorizing sounds and learning to read–a causal connection. *Nature, 301*(5899), 419–421. doi: 10.1038/301419a0

Brandone, A. C., & Wellman, H. M. (2009). You can't always get what you want: Infants understand failed goal-directed actions. *Psychological Science, 20*, 85–91. doi: 10.1111/j.1467-9280.2 008.02246.x

Brainerd, C. J. (1978). The stage question in cognitive-developmental theory. *Behavioral and Brain Sciences, 1*(2), 173-213. doi: 10.1017/S0140525X00073842

Brandtstädter, J. (1987). On certainty and universality in human development: Developmental psychology between apriorism and empiricism. In M. Chapman & R. A. Dixon (Eds.), *Meaning and the growth of understanding* (pp. 69–84). New York: Springer-Verlag.

Bretherton, I., & Beeghly, M. (1982). Talking about internal states: The acquisition of an explicit theory of mind. *Developmental Psychology, 18*, 906–921. doi: 10.1037/0012-1649.18.6.906

Brown, J. R., Donelan-McCall, N., & Dunn, J. (1996). Why talk about mental states? The significance of children's conversations with friends, siblings, and mothers. *Child Development, 67*, 836–849.

Brown, J. R., & Dunn, J. (1991). 'You can cry, mum': The social and developmental implications of talk about internal states. *British Journal of Developmental Psychology, 9*, 237–256. doi: 10.1111/j.2044-835X.1991.tb00874.x

Brown, P. M., Prescott, S. J., Rickards, F. W., & Paterson, M. M. (1997). Communicating about pretend play: A comparison of the utterances of four-year-old normally hearing and hearing-impaired children in an integrated kindergarten. *Volta Review, 99*, 5–17.

Bruner, J. (1986). *Actual minds, possible worlds*. Cambridge, MA: Harvard University Press.

Buchsbaum, D., Gopnik, A., Griffiths, T., & Shafto, P. (2011). Children's imitation of causal action sequences is influenced by statistical and pedagogical evidence. *Cognition, 120*, 331–340. doi: 10.1016/j.cognition.2010.12.001

Buttelmann, D., Carpenter, M., & Tomasello, M. (2009). Eighteen-month-old infants show false belief understanding in an active helping paradigm. *Cognition, 112*, 337–342. doi: 10.1016/j.cognition.2009.05.006

Butterworth, G., & Jarrett, N. (1991). What minds have in common is space: Spatial mechanisms serving joint visual attention in infancy. *British Journal of Developmental Psychology, 9*, 55–72. doi: 10.1111/j.2044-835X.1991.tb00862.x

Call, J., Hare, B., Carpenter, M., & Tomasello, M. (2004). 'Unwilling' versus 'unable': Chimpanzees' understanding of human intentional action. *Developmental Science, 7*, 488–498. doi: 10.1111/j.1467-7687.2004.00368.x

Call, J., & Tomasello, M. (1999). A nonverbal false belief task: The performance of children and great apes. *Child Development, 70*, 381–395. doi: 10.1111/14678624.00028

Call, J., & Tomasello, M. (2008). Does the chimpanzee have a theory of mind? 30 years later. *Trends in Cognitive Sciences, 12*, 187–192. doi: 10.1016/j.tics.2008.02.010

Callanan, M. A., & Oakes, L. M. (1992). Preschoolers' questions and parents' explanations: Causal thinking in everyday activity. *Cognitive Development, 7*, 213–233.

Campbell, J. (1972). *Myths to live by*. New York: Viking Press.

Caputi, M., Lecce, S., Pagnin, A., & Banerjee, R. (2012). Longitudinal effects of theory of mind on later peer relations: The role of prosocial behavior. *Developmental Psychology, 48*, 257–270. doi: 10.1037/a0025402

Carey, S. (1985). *Conceptual change in childhood*. Cambridge, MA: MIT Press.

Carey, S. (2009). *The origin of concepts*. New York: Oxford University Press.

Carey, S., & Spelke, E. (1996). Science and core knowledge. *Philosophy of Science, 63*, 515–533. doi: 10.2307/188065

Carlson, S. M., Mandell, D. J., & Williams, L. (2004). Executive function and theory of mind: Stability and prediction from ages 2 to 3. *Developmental Psychology, 40*, 1105–1122. doi: 10.1037/0012-1649.40.6.1105

Carlson, S. M., & Moses, L. J. (2001). Individual differences in inhibitory control and children's theory of mind. *Child Development, 72*, 1032–1053. doi: 10.1111/1467-8624.00333

Carlson, S. M., & Schaefer, C. M. (2012). *Executive function scale for early childhood. Test manual*. University of Minnesota.

Carpendale, J. I., & Chandler, M. J. (1996). On the distinction between false belief understanding and subscribing to an interpretive theory of mind. *Child Development, 67*, 1686–1706. doi: 10.2307/1131725

Carpendale, J. I. M., & Lewis, C. (2004). Constructing an understanding of mind: The development of children's social understanding within social interaction. *Behavioral and Brain Sciences, 27*, 79–151. doi: 10.1017/s0140525x04000032

Carpenter, M., Nagell, K., & Tomasello, M. (1998). Social cognition, joint attention, and communicative competence from 9 to 15 months of age. *Monographs of the Society for Research in Child Development, 63*(4), i–vi, 1–143.

Carrington, S. J., & Bailey, A. J. (2009). Are there theory of mind regions in the brain? A review of the neuroimaging literature. *Human Brain Mapping, 30*, 2313–2335. doi: 10.1002/hbm.20671

Carruthers, P. (2002). The cognitive functions of language. *Behavioral and Brain Sciences, 25*, 657–674. doi: doi:10.1017/S0140525X02000122

Casey, B. J., Giedd, J. N., & Thomas, K. M. (2000). Structural and functional brain development and its relation to cognitive development. *Biological Psychology, 54*(1–3), 241–257. doi: 10.1016/s0301-0511(00)00058-2

Cassidy, K. W. (1998). Three- and four-year-old children's ability to use desire- and belief-based reasoning. *Cognition, 66*, B1–B11. doi: 10.1016/s00100277(98)00008-0

Cassidy, K. W., Fineberg, D. S., Brown, K., & Perkins, A. (2005). Theory of mind may be contagious, but you don't catch it from your twin. *Child Development, 76*, 97–106. doi: 10.1111/j.1 467-8624.2005.00832.x

Cassidy, K. W., Werner, R. S., Rourke, M., Zubernis, L. S., & Balaraman, G. (2003). The relationship between psychological understanding and positive social behaviors. *Social Development, 12*, 198–221. doi: 10.1111/1467-9507.00229

Chao, R. K. (1994). Beyond parental control and authoritarian parenting style: Understanding Chinese parenting through the cultural notion of training. *Child Development, 65*, 1111–1119. doi: 10.1111/j.1467-8624.1994.tb00806.x

Chen, X., Dong, Q., & Zhou, H. (1997). Authoritative and authoritarian parenting practices and social and school performance in Chinese children. *International Journal of Behavioral Development, 21*, 855–873.

Chen, Z., & Klahr, D. (1999). All other things being equal: Acquisition and transfer of the control of variables strategy. *Child Development, 70*, 1098–1120. doi: 10.1111/1467-8624.00081

Cheung, H. (2006). False belief and language comprehension in Cantonese-speaking children. *Journal of Experimental Child Psychology, 95*, 79–98. doi: 10.1016/j.jecp.2006.05.002

Chi, M. T. H. (1978). Knowledge structure and memory development. In R. Siegler (Ed.), *Children's thinking: What develops?* (pp. 73–96). Hillsdale, NJ: Erlbaum.

Chi, Michelene T. Hutchinson, Jean E. Robin, Anne F. (1989). How inferences about novel domain-related concepts can be constrained by structured knowledge. Merrill-Palmer Quarterly: *Journal of Developmental Psychology, 35*, 27–62.

Chi, M. T. H., De Leeuw, N., Chiu, M.-H., & Lavancher, C. (1994). Eliciting Self-Explanations Improves Understanding. *Cognitive Science, 18*, 439–477. doi: 10.1207/s15516709cog1803_3

Chomsky, N. (2006). *Language and mind* (3rd ed.). New York: Cambridge University Press.

Chouinard, M. M. (2007). Children's questions: A mechanism for cognitive development: I. Introduction. *Monographs of the Society for Research in Child Development, 72*(1, Serial No. 286), 1–126. doi: 10.1111/j.1540-5834.2007.00413.x

Churchland, P. M. (1984). *Matter and consciousness: A contemporary introduction to the philosophy of mind*. Cambridge, MA: MIT Press.

Clark, H. H. (1996). *Using language*. New York: Cambridge University Press.

Clément, F., Koenig, M., & Harris, P. (2004). The ontogenesis of trust. *Mind & Language, 19*, 360–379. doi: 10.1111/j.0268-1064.2004.00263.x

Cohen, L. B. (2004). Uses and misuses of habituation and related preference paradigms. *Infant and Child Development, 13*, 349–352. doi: 10.1002/icd.355

Cook, C., Goodman, N., & Schulz, L. E. (2011). Where science starts: Spontaneous experiments in preschoolers' exploratory play. *Cognition, 120*, 341–349. doi: 10.1016/j.cognition.2011.03.003

Cook, R., Bird, G., Catmur, C., Press, C., & Heyes, C. (2014). Mirror neurons: From origin to function. *Behavioral and Brain Sciences, 37*, 177–192. doi: 10.1017/S0140525X13000903

Corliss, R. (1981, September 14). Cinema: Over easy. *Time Magazine*. Retrieved from http://content.time.com/time/magazine/article/0,9171,924877,00.html

Corriveau, K. H., Pasquini, E. S., & Harris, P. L. (2005). "If it's in your mind, it's in your knowledge": Children's developing anatomy of identity. *Cognitive Development, 20*, 321–340. doi: http://dx.doi.org/10.1016/j.cogdev.2005.04.005

Cosmides, L., & Tooby, J. (1994). Beyond intuition and instinct blindness: Toward an evolutionarily rigorous cognitive science. *Cognition, 50*(1–3), 41–77. doi: http://dx.doi.org/10.1016/0010-0277(94)90020-5

Cosmides, L., & Tooby, J. (2006). Origins of domain specificity: The evolution of functional organization. In J. L. Bermúdez (Ed.), *Philosophy of psychology: Contemporary readings* (pp. 539–555). New York: Routledge/Taylor & Francis Group.

Courtin, C., & Melot, A. M. (1998). Development of theories of mind in deaf children. In M. Marschark & D. M. Clark (Eds.), *Psychological perspectives on deafness* (pp. 79–102). Mahwah, NJ: Lawrence Erlbaum.

Csibra, G., & Gergely, G. (2006). Social learning and social cognition: The case for pedagogy. In Y. Munakata & M. H. Johnson (Eds.), *Processes of change in brain and cognitive development. Attention and performance XXI* (pp. 249–274). Oxford, England: Oxford University Press.

Csibra, G., & Gergely, G. (2009). Natural pedagogy. *Trends in Cognitive Sciences, 13*, 148–153. doi: 10.1016/j.tics.2009.01.005

Csibra, G., Gergely, G., Bíró, S., Koós, O., & Brockbank, M. (1999). Goal attribution without agency cues: The perception of "pure reason" in infancy. *Cognition, 72*, 237–267. doi: http://dx.doi.org/10.1016/S0010-0277(99)00039-6

Custer, W. L. (1996). A comparison of young children's understanding of contradictory representations in pretense, memory, and belief. *Child Development, 67*, 678–688.

Cutting, A. L., & Dunn, J. (1999). Theory of mind, emotion understanding, language, and family background: Individual differences and interrelations. *Child Development, 70*, 853–865. doi: 10.1111/1467-8624.00061

D'Andrade, R. (1987). A folk model of the mind. In D. Holland & N. Quinn (Eds.), *Cultural models in language and thought* (pp. 112–148). Cambridge, England: Cambridge University Press.

Damon, W., & Hart, D. (1988). *Self-understanding in childhood and adolescence*. Cambridge [Cambridgeshire]; New York: Cambridge University Press.

Darwin, C. (1898). *The descent of man, and selection in relation to sex*. London, England: John Murray.

Davidson, D. (1980). *Essays on actions and events*. Oxford: Clarendon Press.

Deák, G. O., Ray, S. D., & Brenneman, K. (2003). Children's perseverative appearance-reality errors are related to emerging language skills. *Child Development, 74*, 944–964. doi: 10.1111/1467-8624.00578

Deleau, M. (2012). Language and theory of mind: Why pragmatics matter. *European Journal of Developmental Psychology, 9*, 295–312. doi: 10.1080/17405629.2012.680303

Dempster, F. N. (1992). The rise and fall of the inhibitory mechanism: Toward a unified theory of cognitive development and aging. *Developmental Review, 12*, 45–75. doi: 10.1016/0273-229 7(92)90003-k

DePaulo, B. M., Lindsay, J. J., Malone, B. E., Muhlenbruck, L., Charlton, K., & Cooper, H. (2003). Cues to deception. *Psychological Bulletin, 129*, 74–118. doi: 10.1037/0033-2909.129.1.74

de Villiers, J. G., & de Villiers, P. A. (2000). Linguistic determinism and the understanding of false beliefs. In P. Mitchell & K. J. Riggs (Eds.), *Children's reasoning and the mind* (pp. 191–228). Hove, England: Psychology Press/Taylor & Francis (UK).

de Villiers, J. G., & Pyers, J. E. (2002). Complements to cognition: A longitudinal study of the relationship between complex syntax and false-belief-understanding. *Cognitive Development, 17*, 1037–1060. doi: 10.1016/s0885-2014(02)00073-4

de Waal, F. B. M. (1982). *Chimpanzee politics: Power and sex among apes*. New York: Harper & Row.

Dickens, C. (1870). *David Copperfield* (Globe ed.). New York: Hurd and Houghton.

Diesendruck, G., & Ben-Eliyahu, A. (2006). The relationships among social cognition, peer acceptance, and social behavior in Israeli kindergarteners. *International Journal of Behavioral Development, 30*, 137–147. doi: 10.1177/0165025406063628

Dunbar, R. I. M. (1993). Coevolution of neocortical size, group size and language in humans. *Behavioral and Brain Sciences, 16*, 681–694. doi: 10.1017/S0140525X00032325

Dunbar, R. I. M. (1996). *Grooming, gossip and the evolution of language*. London: Faber and Faber.

Dunbar, R. I. M. (1998). The social brain hypothesis. *Evolutionary Anthropology: Issues, News, and Reviews, 6*, 178–190. doi: 10.1002/(sici)1520-6505(1998)6:5<178::aid-evan5>3.0.co;2-8

Dunbar, R. I. M. (2004). Gossip in evolutionary perspective. *Review of General Psychology, 8*, 100–110. doi: 10.1037/1089-2680.8.2.100

Dunbar, R. I. M. (2013). An evolutionary basis for social cognition. In M. Legerstee, D. W. Haley, & M. H. Bornstein (Eds.), *The infant mind: Origins of the social brain* (pp. 3–18). London: Guilford.

Dunlop, W. L., & Walker, L. J. (2013). The life story: Its development and relation to narrative and personal identity. *International Journal of Behavioral Development, 37*, 235–247.

Dunn, J. (1988). *The beginnings of social understanding*. Cambridge, MA: Harvard University Press.

Dunn, J. (1995). Children as psychologists: The later correlates of individual differences in understanding of emotions and other minds. *Cognition & Emotion, 9*, 187–201.

Dunn, J., & Brophy, M. (2005). Communication, relationships, and individual differences in children's understanding of mind. In J. W. Astington & J. A. Baird (Eds.), *Why language matters for theory of mind* (pp. 50–69). Oxford, England: Oxford University Press.

Dunn, J., & Brown, J. R. (1993). Early conversations about causality: Content, pragmatics and developmental change. *British Journal of Developmental Psychology, 11*, 107–123. doi: 10.1111/j.2044-835X.1993.tb00591.x

Dunn, J., & Brown, J. (1994). Affect expression in the family, children's understanding of emotions, and their interactions with others. *Merrill-Palmer Quarterly, 40*, 120–137.

Dunn, J., Cutting, A. L., & Fisher, N. (2002). Old friends, new friends: Predictors of children's perspective on their friends at school. *Child Development, 73*, 621–635. doi: 10.1111/1467-8624.00427

Dunphy-Lelii, S., & Wellman, H. M. (2004). Infants' understanding of occlusion of others' line-of-sight: Implications for an emerging theory of mind. *European Journal of Developmental Psychology, 1*, 49–66.

Dyer, J. R., Shatz, M., & Wellman, H. M. (2000). Young children's storybooks as a source of mental state information. *Cognitive Development, 15*, 17–37.

Dyer-Seymour, J. R., Shatz, M., Wellman, H. M., & Saito, M. T. (2004). Mental state expressions in U.S. and Japanese children's books. *International Journal of Behavioral Development, 28*, 546–552.

Eberhardt, F., & Scheines, R. (2007). Interventions and causal inference. *Philosophy of Science, 74*, 981–995. doi: 10.1086/525638

Eggum, N. D., Eisenberg, N., Kao, K., Spinrad, T. L., Bolnick, R., Hofer, C.,…Fabricius, W. V. (2011). Emotion understanding, theory of mind, and prosocial orientation: Relations over time in early childhood. *The Journal of Positive Psychology, 6*(1), 4–16. doi: 10.1080/1743976 0.2010.536776

Egyed, K., Király, I., & Gergely, G. (2013). Communicating shared knowledge in infancy. *Psychological Science, 24*, 1348–1353.

Eisenberg, N., Zhou, Q., Liew, J., Champion, C., & Pidada, S. U. (2006). Emotion, emotion-related regulation, and social functioning. In X. Chen, D. C. French, & B. H. Schneider (Eds.), *Peer relationships in cultural context.* (pp. 170–197). New York: Cambridge University Press.

Ekman, P. (2009). *Telling lies: Clues to deceit in the marketplace, politics, and marriage.* New York: Norton.

Elman, J. L., Bates, E. A., Johnson, M. H., Karmiloff-Smith, A., Parisi, D., & Plunkett, K. (1996). *Rethinking innateness: A connectionist perspective on development.* Cambridge, MA: MIT Press.

Estes, D. (1998). Young children's awareness of their mental activity: The case of mental rotation. *Child Development, 69*, 1345–1360. doi: 10.1111/j.1467-8624.1998.tb06216.x

Estes, D., Wellman, H. M., & Woolley, J. D. (1989). Children's understanding of mental phenomena. In H. Reese (Ed.), *Advances in child development and behavior, Vol. 22* (pp. 41–87). Orlando, FL: Academic.

Evans, E. M. (2001). Cognitive and contextual factors in the emergence of diverse belief systems: Creation versus evolution. *Cognitive Psychology, 42*, 217–266. doi: 10.1006/ cogp.2001.0749

Evans, E. M., & Wellman, H. M. (2006). A case of stunted development? Existential reasoning is contingent on developing a theory of mind. *Behavioral & Brain Sciences, 29*, 471–472.

Fabricius, W. V., & Khalil, S. L. (2003). False beliefs or false positives? Limits on children's understanding of mental representation. *Journal of Cognition and Development, 4*, 239–262. doi: 10.1207/s15327647jcd0403_01

Fajans, J. (1985). The person in social context: The social character of Baining "Psychology." In G. White & J. Kirkpatrick (Eds.), *Person, self, and experience: Exploring pacific ethnopsychologies* (pp. 367–397). Los Angeles: University of California Press.

Ferres, L. A. (2003). Children's early theory of mind: Exploring the development of the concept of desire in monolingual Spanish children. *Developmental Science, 6*, 159–165. doi: 10.1111/1467-7687.00266

Fivush, R., & Haden, C. A. (2005). Parent-child reminiscing and the construction of a subjective self. In B. D. Homer & C. S. Tamis-LeMonda (Eds.), *The development of social cognition and communication.* (pp. 315–335). Mahwah, NJ: Lawrence Erlbaum Associates.

Flavell, J. H. (1978). The development of knowledge about visual perception. In C. B. Keasey (Ed.), *Nebraska symposium on motivation 1977* (pp. 43–76). Lincoln: University of Nebraska Press.

Flavell, J. H. (1988). The development of children's knowledge about the mind: From cognitive connections to mental representations. In J. Astington, P. Harris, & D. Olson (Eds.), *Developing theories of mind* (pp. 244–267). New York: Cambridge University Press.

Flavell, J. H., Everett, B. A., Croft, K., & Flavell, E. R. (1981). Young children's knowledge about visual perception: Further evidence for the Level 1–Level 2 distinction. *Developmental Psychology, 17*, 99–103. doi: 10.1037/0012-1649.17.1.99

Flavell, J. H., Flavell, E. R., Green, F. L., & Moses, L. J. (1990). Young children's understanding of fact beliefs versus value beliefs. *Child Development, 61*, 915–928.

Flavell, J. H., Green, F. L., & Flavell, E. R. (1986). Development of knowledge about the appearance-reality distinction. *Monographs of the Society for Research in Child Development, 51*(1, Serial No. 212), 1–87.

Flavell, J. H., Green, F. L., & Flavell, E. R. (1993). Children's understanding of the stream of consciousness. *Child Development, 64*, 387–398.

Flavell, J. H., Green, F. L., & Flavell, E. R. (1995). Young children's knowledge of thinking. *Monographs of the Society for Research in Child Development, 60*(1, Serial No. 243), 1–114.

Flavell, J. H., Green, F. L., & Flavell, E. R. (1998). The mind has a mind of its own: Developing knowledge about mental uncontrollability. *Cognitive Development, 13*, 127–138.

Flavell, J. H., Green, F. L., Flavell, E. R., & Grossman, J. B. (1997). The development of children's knowledge about inner speech. *Child Development, 68*, 39–47.

Flombaum, J. I., & Santos, L. R. (2005). Rhesus monkeys attribute perceptions to others. *Current Biology, 15*, 447–452. doi: http://dx.doi.org/10.1016/j.cub.2004.12.076

Flynn, E., O'Malley, C., & Wood, D. (2004). A longitudinal, microgenetic study of the emergence of false belief understanding and inhibition skills. *Developmental Science, 7*, 103–115. doi: 10.1111/j.1467-7687.2004.00326.x

Fodor, J. A. (1983). *Modularity of mind: An essay on faculty psychology*. Cambridge, Mass.: MIT Press.

Fodor, J. A. (1987). *Psychosemantics: The problem of meaning in the philosophy of mind*. Cambridge, MA: Bradford Books/MIT Press.

Fodor, J. A. (1992). A theory of the child's theory of mind. *Cognition, 44*, 283–296. doi: 10.1016/0010-0277(92)90004-2

Frazier, B. N., Gelman, S. A., & Wellman, H. M. (2009). Preschoolers' search for explanatory information within adult-child conversation. *Child Development, 80*, 1592–1611. doi: 10.1111/j.1467-8624.2009.01356.x

Freud, S. (1933). *New introductory lectures on psycho-analysis* (Walter John Herbert Sprott, Trans.). New York: W. W. Norton.

Friedman, O., Griffin, R., Brownell, H., & Winner, E. (2003). problems with the seeing = knowing rule. *Developmental Science, 6*, 505–513. doi: 10.1111/1467-7687.00308

Friedman, O., & Leslie, A. M. (2004). A developmental shift in processes underlying successful belief-desire reasoning. *Cognitive Science, 28*, 963–977. doi: 10.1016/j.cogsci.2004.07.001

Frye, D., Zelazo, P. D., & Palfai, T. (1995). Theory of mind and rule-based reasoning. *Cognitive Development, 10*, 483–527. doi: 10.1016/0885-2014(95)90024-1

Gale, E., DeVilliers, P. A., DeVilliers, J. G., & Pyers, J. E. (1996). Language and theory of mind in oral deaf children. In A. Stringfellow, D. Cahama-Amitay, E. Hughes, & A. Zukowski (Eds.),

Proceedings of the 20th annual Boston University conference on language development (Vol. 1, pp. 213–244). Somerville, MA: Cascadilla Press.

Gallagher, H. L., & Frith, C. D. (2003). Functional imaging of 'theory of mind'. *Trends in Cognitive Sciences, 7,* 77–83. doi: http://dx.doi.org/10.1016/S1364-6613(02)00025-6

Gallese, V., Fadiga, L., Fogassi, L., & Rizzolatti, G. (1996). Action recognition in the premotor cortex. *Brain, 119,* 593–609. doi: 10.1093/brain/119.2.593

Gallese, V., & Goldman, A. (1998). Mirror neurons and the simulation theory of mind-reading. *Trends in Cognitive Sciences, 2,* 493–501. doi: http://dx.doi.org/10.1016/S1364-6613(98)01262-5

Gallese, V., Keysers, C., & Rizzolatti, G. (2004). A unifying view of the basis of social cognition. *Trends in Cognitive Sciences, 8,* 396–403. doi: http://dx.doi.org/10.1016/j.tics.2004.07.002

Gardiner, A. K., Greif, M. L., & Bjorklund, D. F. (2011). Guided by intention: Preschoolers' imitation reflects inferences of causation. *Journal of Cognition and Development, 12,* 355–373. doi: 10.1080/15248372.2010.542216

Garfield, J. L., Peterson, C. C., & Perry, T. (2001). Social cognition, language acquisition and the development of the theory of mind. *Mind & Language, 16,* 494–541. doi: 10.1111/1468-0017.00180

Garon, N., Bryson, S. E., & Smith, I. M. (2008). Executive function in preschoolers: A review using an integrative framework. *Psychological Bulletin, 134,* 31–60. doi: 10.1037/0033-2909.134.1.31

Garrido, E., Masip, J., & Herrero, C. (2004). Police officers' credibility judgments: Accuracy and estimated ability. *International Journal of Psychology, 39,* 254–275. doi: 10.1080/00207590344000411

Gelman, S. A. (2009). Learning from others: Children's construction of concepts. *Annual Review of Psychology, 60,* 115–140. doi: 10.1146/annurev.psych.59.103006.093659

Gelman, S. A., & Wellman, H. M. (1991). Insides and essences: Early understandings of the non-obvious. *Cognition, 38,* 213–244. doi: 10.1016/0010-0277(91)90007-Q

Gergely, G., Bekkering, H., & Király, I. (2002). Developmental psychology: Rational imitation in preverbal infants. *Nature, 415*(6873), 755. doi: 10.1038/415755a

Gergely, G., & Csibra, G. (2003). Teleological reasoning in infancy: The naive theory of rationale action. *Trends in Cognitive Science, 7,* 287–292.

Gergely, G., Egyed, K., & Király, I. (2007). On pedagogy. *Developmental Science, 10,* 139–146. doi: 10.1111/j.1467-7687.2007.00576.x

Gergely, G., Nádasdy, Z., Csibra, G., & Bíró, S. (1995). Taking the intentional stance at 12 months of age. *Cognition, 56,* 165–193. doi: 10.1016/0010-0277(95)00661-h

Gilby, I. C. (2006). Meat sharing among the Gombe chimpanzees: Harassment and reciprocal exchange. *Animal Behaviour, 71,* 953–963. doi: http://dx.doi.org/10.1016/j.anbehav.2005.09.009

Giménez-Dasí, M., Guerrero, S., & Harris, P. L. (2005). Intimations of immortality and omniscience in early childhood. *European Journal of Developmental Psychology, 2,* 285–297. doi: 10.1080/17405620544000039

Global Deception Research Team. (2006). A world of lies. *Journal of Cross-Cultural Psychology, 37,* 60–74. doi: 10.1177/0022022105282295

Glymour, C. (2003). Learning, prediction and causal Bayes nets. *Trends in Cognitive Sciences, 7,* 43–48. doi: http://dx.doi.org/10.1016/S1364-6613(02)00009-8

Glymour, C. N. (2001). *The mind's arrows: Bayes nets and graphical causal models in psychology.* Cambridge, MA: MIT Press.

Goetz, P. J. (2003). The effects of bilingualism on theory of mind development. *Bilingualism: Language and Cognition, 6*, 1–15. doi: 10.1017/S1366728903001007

Gold, E. M. (1967). Language identification in the limit. *Information and Control, 10*, 447–474. doi: 10.1016/S0019-9958(67)91165-5

Goldman, A. I. (1992). In defense of the simulation theory. *Mind & Language, 7*(1–2), 104–119. doi: 10.1111/j.1468-0017.1992.tb00200.x

Goldman, A. I. (2005). Imitation, mind reading, and simulation. In S. Hurley & N. Chater (Eds.), *Perspectives on imitation: From neuroscience to social science: Vol. 2. Imitation, human development, and culture* (pp. 79–93). Cambridge, MA: MIT Press.

Goldman, A. I. (2009). Mirroring, simulating and mindreading. *Mind & Language, 24*(2), 235–252. doi: 10.1111/j.1468-0017.2008.01361.x

Gómez, R. L. (2002). Variability and detection of invariant structure. *Psychological Science, 13*, 431–436. doi: 10.1111/1467-9280.00476

Goodall, J. (1971). *In the shadow of man.* London: Collins.

Goodman, N. (1955). *Fact, fiction, and forecast.* Cambridge, MA: Harvard University Press.

Goodman, N. D., Ullman, T. D., & Tenenbaum, J. B. (2011). Learning a theory of causality. *Psychological Review, 118*, 110–119. doi: 10.1037/a0021336

Gopnik, A., & Astington, J. W. (1988). Children's understanding of representational change and its relation to the understanding of false belief and the appearance-reality distinction. *Child Development, 59*, 26–37. doi: 10.2307/1130386

Gopnik, A., Glymour, C., Sobel, D. M., Schulz, L. E., Kushnir, T., & Danks, D. (2004). A theory of causal learning in children: Causal maps and Bayes nets. *Psychological Review, 111*, 3–32. doi: 10.1037/0033-295X.111.1.3

Gopnik, A., & Meltzoff, A. N. (1997). *Words, thoughts, and theories.* Cambridge, MA: The MIT Press.

Gopnik, A., Meltzoff, A. N., & Kuhl, P. K. (2001). *The scientist in the crib: What early learning tells us about the mind.* New York: HarperCollins Publishers.

Gopnik, A., & Slaughter, V. (1991). Young children's understanding of changes in their mental states. *Child Development, 62*, 98–110. doi: 10.1111/j.1467-8624.1991.tb01517.x

Gopnik, A., Slaughter, V., & Meltzoff, A. (1994). Changing your views: How understanding visual perception can lead to a new theory of the mind. In C. Lewis & P. Mitchell (Eds.), *Children's early understanding of mind: Origins and development* (pp. 157–181). Hillsdale, NJ: Lawrence Erlbaum Associates.

Gopnik, A., & Tenenbaum, J. B. (2007). Bayesian networks, Bayesian learning and cognitive development. *Developmental Science, 10*, 281–287. doi: 10.1111/j.1467-7687.2007.00584.x

Gopnik, A., & Wellman, H. M. (1994). The theory theory. In L. Hirschfeld & S. Gelman (Eds.), *Domain specificity in cognition and culture* (pp. 257–293). New York: Cambridge University Press.

Gopnik, A., & Wellman, H. M. (2012). Reconstructing constructivism: Causal models, Bayesian learning mechanisms, and the theory theory. *Psychological Bulletin, 138*, 1085–1108. doi: 10.1037/a0028044

Gorsuch, R. L. (1968). Conceptualization of God as seen in adjective ratings. *Journal for the Scientific Study of Religion, 7*, 56–64.

Gottfried, G. M., Gelman, S. A., & Schultz, J. (1999). Children's understanding of the brain: From early essentialism to biological theory. *Cognitive Development, 14*, 147–174. doi: http://dx.doi.org/10.1016/S0885-2014(99)80022-7

Greene, R. A. (2011, May 12). Religious belief is human nature, huge new study claims. CNN.com. Retrieved from http://religion.blogs.cnn.com/2011/05/12/religious-belief-is-human-nature-huge-new-study-claims/

Greenfield, P. M., Keller, H., Fuligni, A., & Maynard, A. (2003). Cultural pathways through universal development. *Annual Review of Psychology, 54*, 461–490. doi: 10.1146/annurev.psych.54.101601.145221

Gregory, S., Sheldon, L., & Bishop, J. (1995). *Deaf young people and their families: Developing understanding.* Cambridge, England: Cambridge University Press.

Griffiths, T. L., Chater, N., Kemp, C., Perfors, A., & Tenenbaum, J. B. (2010). Probabilistic models of cognition: Exploring representations and inductive biases. *Trends in Cognitive Sciences, 14*, 357–364. doi: 10.1016/j.tics.2010.05.004

Griffiths, T. L., Sobel, D. M., Tenenbaum, J. B., & Gopnik, A. (2011). Bayes and Blickets: Effects of knowledge on causal induction in children and adults. *Cognitive Science, 35*, 1407–1455. doi : 10.1111/j.1551-6709.2011.01203.x

Griffiths, T. L., & Tenenbaum, J. B. (2007). Two proposals for causal grammars. In A. Gopnik & L. Schulz (Eds.), *Causal learning: Psychology, philosophy, and computation* (pp. 323–345). New York: Oxford University Press.

Griffiths, T. L., & Tenenbaum, J. B. (2009). Theory-based causal induction. *Psychological Review, 116*, 661–716. doi: 10.1037/a0017201

Gross, D., Nelson, S., Rosengren, K. S., Pick, A. D., Pillow, B. H., & Melendez, P. (1991). Children's understanding of action lines and the static representation of speed of locomotion. *Child Development, 62*, 1124–1141. doi: 10.2307/1131157

Guttman, L. (1944). A basis for scaling qualitative data. *American Sociological Review, 9*, 139–150. doi: 10.2307/2086306

Guttman, L. (1950). The basis of scalogram analysis. In S. A. Stouffer, L. Guttman, E. A. Suchman, P. A. Lazarsfeld, S. A. Star, & J. A. Clausen (Eds.), *Measurement and prediction* (pp. 60–90). Princeton, NJ: Princeton University Press.

Gweon, H., Dodell-Feder, D., Bedny, M., & Saxe, R. (2012). Theory of mind performance in children correlates with functional specialization of a brain region for thinking about thoughts. *Child Development, 83*, 1853–1868. doi: 10.1111/j.1467-8624.2012.01829.x

Habermas, T., & Bluck, S. (2000). Getting a life: The emergence of the life story in adolescence. *Psychological Bulletin, 126*, 748–769. doi: 10.1037/0033-2909.126.5.748

Hadwin, J., & Perner, J. (1991). Pleased and surprised: Children's cognitive theory of emotion. *British Journal of Developmental Psychology, 9*, 215–234. doi: 10.1111/j.2044-835X.1991.tb00872.x

Haker, H., Kawohl, W., Herwig, U., & Rössler, W. (2013). Mirror neuron activity during contagious yawning–an fMRI study. *Brain Imaging and Behavior, 7*, 28–34. doi: 10.1007/s11682-012-9189-9

Halford, G. S., Wilson, W. H., & Phillips, S. (2010). Relational knowledge: The foundation of higher cognition. *Trends in Cognitive Sciences, 14*, 497–505. doi: 10.1016/j.tics.2010.08.005

Hamlin, J. K. (2012). A developmental perspective on the moral dyad. *Psychological Inquiry, 23,* 166–171. doi: 10.1080/1047840x.2012.670101

Hamlin, J. K. (2013). Moral judgment and action in preverbal infants and toddlers: Evidence for an innate moral core. *Current Directions in Psychological Science, 22,* 186–193. doi: 10.1177/0963721412470687

Hamlin, J. K., Hallinan, E. V., & Woodward, A. L. (2008). Do as I do: 7-month-old infants selectively reproduce others' goals. *Developmental Science, 11,* 487–494. doi: 10.1111/j.1467-7687.2008.00694.x

Hamlin, J. K., Wynn, K., & Bloom, P. (2007). Social evaluation in preverbal infants. *Nature, 450*(7169), 557–559. doi: 10.1038/nature06288

Hamlin, J. K., Wynn, K., & Bloom, P. (2010). Three-month-olds show a negativity bias in their social evaluations. *Developmental Science, 13,* 923–929. doi: 10.1111/j.1467-7687.2010.00951.x

Hansen, M. B., & Markman, E. M. (2005). Appearance questions can be misleading: A discourse-based account of the appearance-reality problem. *Cognitive Psychology, 50,* 233–263. doi: 10.1016/j.cogpsych.2004.09.001

Happé, F. G. E. (1995). The role of age and verbal ability in the theory of mind task performance of subjects with autism. *Child Development, 66,* 843–855. doi: 10.1111/j.1467-8624.1995.tb00909.x

Hare, B. (2007). From nonhuman to human mind: What changed and why? *Current Directions in Psychological Science, 16*(2), 60–64. doi: 10.1111/j.1467-8721.2007.00476.x

Hare, B., Call, J., Agnetta, B., & Tomasello, M. (2000). Chimpanzees know what conspecifics do and do not see. *Animal Behaviour, 59,* 771–785. doi: 10.1006/anbe.1999.1377

Hare, B., Call, J., & Tomasello, M. (2001). Do chimpanzees know what conspecifics know? *Animal Behaviour, 61,* 139–151. doi: 10.1006/anbe.2000.1518

Hare, B., Plyusnina, I., Ignacio, N., Schepina, O., Stepika, A., Wrangham, R., & Trut, L. (2005). Social cognitive evolution in captive foxes is a correlated by-product of experimental domestication. *Current Biology, 15,* 226–230. doi: 10.1016/j.cub.2005.01.040

Hare, B., & Tomasello, M. (2004). Chimpanzees are more skilful in competitive than in cooperative cognitive tasks. *Animal Behaviour, 68,* 571–581. doi: 10.1016/j.anbehav.2003.11.011

Hare, B., & Tomasello, M. (2005). Human-like social skills in dogs? *Trends in Cognitive Sciences, 9,* 439–444. doi: 10.1016/j.tics.2005.07.003

Harman, G. (1999). Moral philosophy and linguistics. In K. Brinkmann (Ed.), *Proceedings of the 20th World Congress of Philosophy* (Vol. 1, pp. 107–115). Bowling Green, OH: Philosophy Documentation Center.

Harris, P. L. (1992). From simulation to folk psychology: The case for development. *Mind & Language, 7*(1–2), 120–144. doi: 10.1111/j.1468-0017.1992.tb00201.x

Harris, P. L. (2000). *The work of the imagination.* Malden, MA: Blackwell Publishing.

Harris, P. L. (2005). Conversation, pretense and theory of mind. In J. W. Astington & J. A. Baird (Eds.), *Why language matters for theory of mind* (pp. 70–83). New York: Oxford University Press.

Harris, P. L. (2006). Social Cognition. In W. Damon & R. M. Lerner (Eds.), *Handbook of child psychology. Volume 2. Cognition, perception, and language* (pp. 811–858). Hoboken, NJ: Wiley.

Harris, P. L. (2012). *Trusting what you're told: How children learn from others.* Cambridge, MA: Belknap Press of Harvard University Press.

Harris, P. L., Brown, E., Marriott, C., Whittall, S., & Harmer, S. (1991). Monsters, ghosts and witches: Testing the limits of the fantasy-reality distinction in young children. *British Journal of Developmental Psychology, 9,* 105–123. doi: 10.1111/j.2044-835X.1991.tb00865.x

Harris, P. L., Donnelly, K., Guz, G. R., & Pitt-Watson, R. (1986). Children's understanding of the distinction between real and apparent emotion. *Child Development, 57,* 895–909.

Harris, P. L., & Giménez, M. (2005). Children's acceptance of conflicting testimony: The case of death. *Journal of Cognition and Culture, 5,* 143–164. Retrieved from http://booksandjourn als.brillonline.com/content/10.1163/1568537054068606

Harris, P. L., & Koenig, M. A. (2006). Trust in testimony: How children learn about science and religion. *Child Development, 77,* 505–524. doi: 10.1111/j.1467-8624.2006.00886.x

Harris, P. L., & Lane, J. D. (2013). Infants understand how testimony works. *Topoi,* 1–16. doi: 10.1007/s11245-013-9180-0

Harris, P. L., Pasquini, E. S., Duke, S., Asscher, J. J., & Pons, F. (2006). Germs and angels: The role of testimony in young children's ontology. *Developmental Science, 9,* 76–96. doi: 10.1111/j.1467-7687.2005.00465.x

Harris, P. L., Rosnay, M. D., & Pons, F. (2005). Language and children's understanding of mental states. *Current Directions in Psychological Science, 14,* 69–73. doi: 10.2307/20182991

Hartwig, M., & Bond, C. F., Jr. (2011). Why do lie-catchers fail? A lens model meta-analysis of human lie judgments. *Psychological Bulletin, 137,* 643–659. doi: 10.1037/a002358910.1037/a0023589.supp (Supplemental)

Hauser, M. (2006). *Moral minds: How nature designed our universal sense of right and wrong.* New York: Ecco/HarperCollins Publishers.

Haviland, J. M., & Lelwica, M. (1987). The induced affect response: 10-week-old infants' responses to three emotion expressions. *Developmental Psychology, 23,* 97–104. doi: 10.1037/0012-1649.23.1.97

Herrmann, P. A., Legare, C. H., Harris, P. L., & Whitehouse, H. (2013). Stick to the script: The effect of witnessing multiple actors on children's imitation. *Cognition, 129,* 536–543. doi: http://dx.doi.org/10.1016/j.cognition.2013.08.010

Hickling, A. K., & Wellman, H. M. (2001). The emergence of children's causal explanations and theories: Evidence from everyday conversation. *Developmental Psychology, 37,* 668–683.

Hickling, A. K., Wellman, H. M., & Gottfried, G. (1997). Preschoolers' understanding of others' mental attitudes toward pretend happenings. *British Journal of Developmental Psychology, 15,* 339–354.

Hickok, G. (2009). Eight problems for the mirror neuron theory of action understanding in monkeys and humans. *Journal of Cognitive Neuroscience, 21,* 1229–1243. doi: 10.1162/jocn.2009.21189

Higginbotham, D. J., & Baker, B. M. (1981). Social participation and cognitive play differences in hearing impaired and normally hearing preschoolers. *Volta Review, 83,* 135–149.

Hirschfeld, L. A. (1996). *Race in the making: Cognition, culture, and the child's construction of human kinds.* Cambridge, MA: The MIT Press.

Hirschfeld, L. A. (2013). The myth of mentalizing and the primacy of folk sociology. In M. Banaji & S. Gelman (Eds.), *Navigating the social world: A developmental perspective* (pp. 101–106). Oxford, England: Oxford University Press.

Hirschfeld, L. A., & Gelman, S. A. (1994). *Mapping the mind: Domain specificity in cognition and culture*. New York: Cambridge University Press.

Hirsh-Pasek, K., & Golinkoff, R. M. (2003). *Einstein never used flash cards: How our children really learn–and why they need to play more and memorize less*. Emmaus, PA: Rodale Inc.

Hood, L., & Bloom, L. (1979). What, when, and how about why: A longitudinal study of early expressions of causality. *Monographs of the Society for Research in Child Development, 44*(6, Serial No. 181), 1–47. doi: 10.2307/1165989

Horner, V., & Whiten, A. (2005). Causal knowledge and imitation/emulation switching in chimpanzees (*Pan troglodytes*) and children (*Homo sapiens*). *Animal Cognition, 8*, 164–181. doi: 10.1007/s10071-004-0239-6

Howe, N., Petrakos, H., & Rinaldi, C. M. (1998). 'All the sheeps are dead. He murdered them': Sibling pretense, negotiation, internal state language, and relationship quality. *Child Development, 69*, 182–191. doi: 10.2307/1132079

Hughes, C. (1998). Finding your marbles: Does preschoolers' strategic behavior predict later understanding of mind? *Developmental Psychology, 34*, 1326–1339. doi: 10.1037/0012-1649.3 4.6.1326

Hughes, C., & Cutting, A. L. (1999). Nature, nurture, and individual differences in early understanding of mind. *Psychological Science, 10*, 429–432. doi: 10.1111/1467-9280.00181

Hughes, C., Ensor, R., & Marks, A. (2011). Individual differences in false belief understanding are stable from 3 to 6 years of age and predict children's mental state talk with school friends. *Journal of Experimental Child Psychology, 108*, 96–112. doi: 10.1016/j.jecp.2010.07.012

Hughes, C., Jaffee, S. R., Happé, F., Taylor, A., Caspi, A., & Moffitt, T. E. (2005). Origins of individual differences in theory of mind: From nature to nurture? *Child Development, 76*, 356–370. doi: 10.1111/j.1467-8624.2005.00850_a.x

Humphrey, N. (1984). *Consciousness regained: Chapters in the development of mind*. Oxford, England: Oxford University Press.

Inagaki, K., & Hatano, G. (1993). Young children's understanding of the mind-body distinction. *Child Development, 64*, 1534–1549. doi: 10.2307/1131551

Inagaki, K., & Hatano, G. (2002). *Young children's naive thinking about the biological world*. New York: Psychology Press.

Inagaki, K., & Hatano, G. (2004). Vitalistic causality in young children's naive biology. *Trends in Cognitive Sciences, 8*, 356–362. doi: 10.1016/j.tics.2004.06.004

James, W. (1981). *The principles of psychology*. Cambridge, MA: Harvard University Press. (Original work published 1890)

Jaswal, V. K., & Malone, L. S. (2007). Turning believers into skeptics: 3-year-olds' sensitivity to cues to speaker credibility. *Journal of Cognition and Development, 8*, 263–283. doi: 10.1080/15248370701446392

Jaswal, V. K., & Neely, L. A. (2006). Adults don't always know best: Preschoolers use past reliability over age when learning new words. *Psychological Science, 17*, 757–758. doi: 10.1111/j.1 467-9280.2006.01778.x

Jenkins, J. M., & Astington, J. W. (2000). Theory of mind and social behavior: Causal models tested in a longitudinal study. *Merrill-Palmer Quarterly, 46*, 203–220.

Joffe, T. H. (1997). Social pressures have selected for an extended juvenile period in primates. *Journal of Human Evolution, 32*, 593–605. doi: http://dx.doi.org/10.1006/jhev.1997.0140

Johnson, C. N. (1990). If you had my brain, where would I be? Children's understanding of the brain and identity. *Child Development, 61,* 962–972. doi: 10.2307/1130868

Johnson, C. N., & Wellman, H. M. (1982). Children's developing conceptions of the mind and brain. *Child Development, 53,* 222–234.

Johnson, S. C. (2000). The recognition of mentalistic agents in infancy. *Trends in Cognitive Sciences, 4,* 22–28. doi: http://dx.doi.org/10.1016/S1364-6613(99)01414-X

Johnston, J. R., & Wong, M. Y. A. (2002). Cultural differences in beliefs and practices concerning talk to children. *Journal of Speech, Language, and Hearing Research, 45,* 916–926. doi: 10 .1044/1092-4388(2002/074)

Joseph, R. M., & Tager-Flusberg, H. (1999). Preschool children's understanding of the desire and knowledge constraints on intended action. *British Journal of Developmental Psychology, 17,* 221–243. doi: 10.1348/026151099165249

Kalish, C. (1998). Reasons and causes: Children's understanding of conformity to social rules and physical laws. *Child Development, 69,* 706–720.

Kagan, J., & Snidman, N. C. (2004). *The long shadow of temperament.* Cambridge, MA: Belknap Press of Harvard University Press.

Kahneman, D. (2011). *Thinking, fast and slow.* New York: Farrar, Straus and Giroux.

Kalish, C. (1998). Reasons and causes: Children's understanding of conformity to social rules and physical laws. *Child Development, 69*(3), 706-720.

Kaminski, J., Call, J., & Fischer, J. (2004). Word learning in a domestic dog: Evidence for "fast mapping". *Science, 304*(5677), 1682–1683.

Kaminski, J., Call, J., & Tomasello, M. (2008). Chimpanzees know what others know, but not what they believe. *Cognition, 109,* 224–234. doi: 10.1016/j.cognition.2008.08.010

Karmiloff-Smith, A. (1992). *Beyond modularity: A developmental perspective on cognitive science.* Cambridge, MA: MIT Press.

Kavanaugh, R. D. (2006). Pretend play and theory of mind. In L. Balter & C. S. Tamis-LeMonda (Eds.), *Child psychology: A handbook of contemporary issues* (2nd ed., pp. 153–166). New York: Psychology Press.

Kemp, C., Perfors, A., & Tenenbaum, J. B. (2007). Learning overhypotheses with hierarchical Bayesian models. *Developmental Science, 10,* 307–321. doi: 10.1111/j.1467-7687.2007. 00585.x

Kessen, W., & The American Delegation on Early Childhood Development in the People's Republic of China (Eds.). (1975). *Childhood in China.* New Haven, CT: Yale University Press.

Kinzler, K. D., Dupoux, E., & Spelke, E. S. (2007). The native language of social cognition. *PNAS, Proceedings of the National Academy of Sciences of the United States of America, 104,* 12577–12580. doi: 10.1073/pnas.0705345104

Kirkham, N. Z., Slemmer, J. A., & Johnson, S. P. (2002). Vital statistical learning in infancy: Evidence of a domain general learning mechanism. *Cognition, 83,* B35–B42. doi: 10.1016/S0010-0277(02)00004-5

Knafo, A., Steinberg, T., & Goldner, I. (2011). Children's low affective perspective-taking ability is associated with low self-initiated pro-sociality. *Emotion, 11,* 194–198. doi: 10.1037/a0021240

Knight, N., Sousa, P., Barrett, J. L., & Atran, S. (2004). Children's attributions of beliefs to humans and God: cross-cultural evidence. *Cognitive Science, 28,* 117–126. doi: 10.1207/ s15516709cog2801_6

Kochanska, G., DeVet, K., Goldman, M., Murray, K., & Putnam, S. P. (1994). Maternal reports of conscience development and temperament in young children. *Child Development, 65*, 852–868. doi: 10.2307/1131423

Koenig, M. A., Clément, F., & Harris, P. L. (2004). Trust in testimony: Children's use of true and false statements. *Psychological Science, 15*, 694–698. doi: 10.1111/j.0956-7976.2004.00742.x

Koenig, M. A., & Harris, P. L. (2005). Preschoolers mistrust ignorant and inaccurate speakers. *Child Development, 76*, 1261–1277. doi: 10.1111/j.1467-8624.2005.00849.x

Koenig, M. A., & Harris, P. L. (2005). The role of social cognition in early trust. *Trends in Cognitive Sciences, 9*, 457–459. doi: 10.1016/j.tics.2005.08.006

Kovács, Á. M., Táglás, E., & Endress, A. D. (2010). The Social Sense: Susceptibility to others' beliefs in human infants and adults. *Science, 330*, 1830–1834. doi: 10.1126/science.1190792

Krachun, C., Carpenter, M., Call, J., & Tomasello, M. (2009). A competitive nonverbal false belief task for children and apes. *Developmental Science, 12*, 521–535. doi: 10.1111/j.1467-7687.2008.00793.x

Kristen, S., Thoermer, C., Hofer, T., Aschersleben, G., & Sodian, B. (2006). Skalierung von "theory of mind" aufgaben [Scaling of theory of mind tasks]. *Zeitschrift fur Entwicklungspsychologic und Padagogische Psychologie, 38*, 186–195. doi: 10.1026/0049-8637.38.4.186

Kuhlmeier, V., Wynn, K., & Bloom, P. (2003). Attribution of dispositional states by 12-month-olds. *Psychological Science, 14*, 402–408. doi: 10.1111/1467-9280.01454

Kuhlmeier, V. A., Bloom, P., & Wynn, K. (2004). Do 5-month-old infants see humans as material objects? *Cognition, 94*, 95–103. doi: 10.1016/j.cognition.2004.02.007

Kuhn, T. S. (1962). *The structure of scientific revolutions.* Chicago: University of Chicago Press.

Kumar, V. (1998). *108 names of Vishnu.* New Delhi: Sterling Publishers.

Kunkel, M. A., Cook, S., Meshel, D. S., Daughtry, D., & Hauenstein, A. (1999). God images: A concept map. *Journal for the Scientific Study of Religion, 38*, 193–202.

Kushnir, T., & Gopnik, A. (2007). Conditional probability versus spatial contiguity in causal learning: Preschoolers use new contingency evidence to overcome prior spatial assumptions. *Developmental Psychology, 43*, 186–196. doi: 10.1037/0012-1649.43.1.186

Kushnir, T., Wellman, H. M., & Gelman, S. A. (2008). The role of preschoolers' social understanding in evaluating the informativeness of causal interventions. *Cognition, 107*, 1084–1092. doi: 10.1016/j.cognition.2007.10.004

Kushnir, T., Xu, F., & Wellman, H. M. (2010). Young children use statistical sampling to infer the preferences of other people. *Psychological Science, 21*, 1134–1140. doi: 10.1177/0956797610376652

LaBounty, J. (2008). *Social cognition and its effects on young children's social and mental health* Unpublished Ph.D. dissertation, University of Michigan, Ann Arbor.

Lagattuta, K. H. (2007). Thinking about the future because of the past: Young children's knowledge about the causes of worry and preventative decisions. *Child Development, 78*, 1492–1509. doi: 10.1111/j.1467-8624.2007.01079.x

Lagattuta, K. H. (2008). Young children's knowledge about the influence of thoughts on emotions in rule situations. *Developmental Science, 11*, 809–818. doi: 10.1111/j.1467-7687.2008.00727.x

Lagattuta, K. H., & Wellman, H. M. (2001). Thinking about the past: Early knowledge about links between prior experience, thinking, and emotion. *Child Development, 72*, 82–102.

Lagattuta, K. H., & Wellman, H. M. (2002). Differences in early parent-child conversations about negative versus positive emotions: Implications for the development of psychological understanding. *Developmental Psychology, 38,* 564–580.

Lagattuta, K. H., Wellman, H. M., & Flavell, J. H. (1997). Preschoolers' understanding of the link between thinking and feeling: Cognitive cuing and emotional change. *Child Development, 68,* 1081–1104.

Lakatos, I. (1970). Falsification and the methodology of scientific research programmes. In I. Lakatos & A. Musgrave (Eds.), *Criticism and the growth of knowledge* (pp. 91–196). Cambridge, England: Cambridge University Press.

Lakoff, G., & Johnson, M. (1980). *Metaphors we live by.* Chicago: University of Chicago Press.

Lalonde, C. E., & Chandler, M. J. (1995). False belief understanding goes to school: On the social-emotional consequences of coming early or late to a first theory of mind. *Cognition and Emotion, 9,* 167–185. doi: 10.1080/02699939508409007

Landau, B., & Gleitman, L. R. (1985). *Language and experience: Evidence from the blind child.* Cambridge, MA: Harvard University Press.

Lane, J. D., & Harris, P. L. (2014). Confronting, representing, and believing counterintuitive concepts: Navigating the natural and the supernatural. *Perspectives on Psychological Science, 9,* 144–160. doi: 10.1177/1745691613518078

Lane, J. D., Zhu, L., Evans, E. M., & Wellman, H. M. (in press). Developing concepts of the mind, body, and afterlife: Exploring the roles of narrative context and culture. *Journal of Cognition and Culture.*

Lane, J. D., Wellman, H. M., & Evans, E. M. (2010). Children's understanding of ordinary and extraordinary minds. *Child Development, 81,* 1475–1489. doi: 10.1111/j.1467-8624.2010.01486.x

Lane, J. D., Wellman, H. M., & Evans, E. M. (in press). Approaching an understanding of omniscience from the preschool years to early adulthood. *Developmental Psychology.*

Lane, J. D., Wellman, H. M., & Evans, E. M. (2012). Sociocultural input facilitates children's developing understanding of extraordinary minds. *Child Development, 83*(3), 1007-1021. doi: 10.1111/j.1467-8624.2012.01741.x

Lane, J. D., Wellman, H. M., & Gelman, S. A. (2013). Informants' traits weigh heavily in young children's trust in testimony and in their epistemic inferences. *Child Development, 84,* 1253–1268. doi: 10.1111/cdev.12029

Lane, J. D., Wellman, H. M., Olson, S. L., Miller, A. L., Wang, L., & Tardif, T. (2013). Relations between temperament and theory of mind development in the United States and China: Biological and behavioral correlates of preschoolers' false-belief understanding. *Developmental Psychology, 49,* 825–836. doi: 10.1037/a0028825

Laudan, L. (1977). *Progress and its problems: Toward a theory of scientific growth.* Berkeley: University of California Press.

Lecce, S., Caputi, M., & Hughes, C. (2011). Does sensitivity to criticism mediate the relationship between theory of mind and academic achievement? *Journal of Experimental Child Psychology, 110,* 313–331. doi: 10.1016/j.jecp.2011.04.011

Lederberg, A. R., & Everhart, V. S. (1998). Communication between deaf children and their hearing mothers: The role of language, gesture, and vocalizations. *Journal of Speech, Language, and Hearing Research, 41,* 887–899.

Lee, K., Olson, D. R., & Torrance, N. (1999). Chinese children's understanding of false beliefs: The role of language. *Journal of Child Language, 26*, 1–21. doi: 10.1017/s0305000998003626

Leekam, S. R., & Perner, J. (1991). Does the autistic child have a metarepresentational deficit? *Cognition, 40*, 203–218. doi: 10.1016/0010-0277(91)90025-Y

Legare, C. H. (2012). Exploring explanation: Explaining inconsistent evidence informs exploratory, hypothesis-testing behavior in young children. *Child Development, 83*, 173–185. doi: 10.1111/j.1467-8624.2011.01691.x

Legare, C. H., Gelman, S. A., & Wellman, H. M. (2010). Inconsistency with prior knowledge triggers children's causal explanatory reasoning. *Child Development, 81*, 929–944. doi: CDEV1443 [pii]10.1111/j.1467-8624.2010.01443.x

Lempers, J. D., Flavell, E. R., & Flavell, J. H. (1977). The development in very young children of tacit knowledge concerning visual perception. *Genetic Psychology Monographs, 95*, 3–53.

Leslie, A. M. (1982). The perception of causality in infants. *Perception, 11*, 173–186. doi: 10.1068/p110173

Leslie, A. M. (1994). ToMM, ToBy, and agency: Core architecture and domain specificity in cognition and culture. In L. Hirschfeld & S. Gelman (Eds.), *Mapping the mind: Domain specificity in cognition and culture* (pp. 119–148). New York: Cambridge University Press.

Leslie, A. M. (2005). Developmental parallels in understanding minds and bodies. *Trends in Cognitive Sciences, 9*, 459–462. doi: 10.1016/j.tics.2005.08.002

Leslie, A. M., German, T. P., & Polizzi, P. (2005). Belief-desire reasoning as a process of selection. *Cognitive Psychology, 50*, 45–85. doi: 10.1016/j.cogpsych.2004.06.002

Leslie, A. M., & Polizzi, P. (1998). Inhibitory processing in the false belief task: Two conjectures. *Developmental Science, 1*, 247–253. doi: 10.1111/1467-7687.00038

Leslie, A. M., & Thaiss, L. (1992). Domain specificity in conceptual development: Neuropsychological evidence from autism. *Cognition, 43*, 225–251. doi: 10.1016/0010-0277(92)90013-8

LeVine, R. A. (1984). Properties of culture: An ethnographic view. In R. Sweder & R. LeVine (Eds.), *Culture theory: Essays on mind, self, and emotion* (pp. 67–87). Cambridge, England: Cambridge University Press.

Levine, S. (1979). *Mothers and wives.* Chicago: University of Chicago Press.

Lewis, C., Freeman, N. H., Kyriakidou, C., Maridaki-Kassotaki, K., & Berridge, D. M. (1996). Social influences on false belief access: Specific sibling influences or general apprenticeship? *Child Development, 67*, 2930–2947. doi: 10.2307/1131760

Lewis, M., Stanger, C., & Sullivan, M. W. (1989). Deception in 3-year-olds. *Developmental Psychology, 25*, 439–443. doi: 10.1037/0012-1649.25.3.439

Li, J. (2001). Chinese conceptualization of learning. *Ethos, 29*, 111–137. doi: 10.1525/eth.2001.29.2.111

Li, J. (2002). A cultural model of learning: Chinese 'heart and mind for wanting to learn'. *Journal of Cross-Cultural Psychology, 33*, 248–269. doi: 10.1177/0022022102033003003

Li, J. (2003). The core of Confucian learning. *American Psychologist, 58*, 146–147. doi: 10.1037/0003-066x.58.2.146

Li, J. (2004). Learning as a task or a virtue: U.S. and Chinese preschoolers explain learning. *Developmental Psychology, 40*, 595–605. doi: 10.1037/0012-1649.40.4.595

Li, J. (2005). Mind or virtue: Western and Chinese beliefs about learning. *Current Directions in Psychological Science, 14*, 190–194. doi: 10.1111/j.0963-7214.2005.00362.x

Lillard, A. (1998). Ethnopsychologies: Cultural variations in theories of mind. *Psychological Bulletin, 123*, 3–32.

Lillard, A. S. (1993). Pretend play skills and the child's theory of mind. *Child Development, 64*, 348–371. doi: 10.2307/1131255

Lillard, A. S. (2005). *Montessori: The science behind the genius*. Oxford, England: Oxford University Press.

Lillard, A. S., & Erisir, A. (2011). Old dogs learning new tricks: Neuroplasticity beyond the juvenile period. *Developmental Review, 31*, 207–239. doi: 10.1016/j.dr.2011.07.008

Lillard, A. S., & Flavell, J. H. (1992). Young children's understanding of different mental states. *Developmental Psychology, 28*, 626–634. doi: 10.1037/0012-1649.28.4.626

Lillard, A. S., Lerner, M. D., Hopkins, E. J., Dore, R. A., Smith, E. D., & Palmquist, C. M. (2013). The impact of pretend play on children's development: A review of the evidence. *Psychological Bulletin, 139*, 1–34. doi: 10.1037/a0029321

Liszkowski, U., Carpenter, M., Striano, T., & Tomasello, M. (2006). 12- and 18-month-olds point to provide information for others. *Journal of Cognition and Development, 7*, 173–187. doi: 10.1207/s15327647jcd0702_2

Liu, D., Gelman, S. A., & Wellman, H. M. (2007). Components of young children's trait understanding: Behavior-to-trait inferences and trait-to-behavior predictions. *Child Development, 78*, 1543–1558. doi: 10.1111/j.1467-8624.2007.01082.x

Liu, D., Meltzoff, A. N., & Wellman, H. M. (2009). Neural correlates of belief- and desire-reasoning. *Child Development, 80*, 1163–1171. doi: 10.1111/j.1467-8624.2009.01323.x

Liu, D., Sabbagh, M. A., Gehring, W. J., & Wellman, H. M. (2004). Decoupling beliefs from reality in the brain: An ERP study of theory of mind. *Neuroreport, 15*, 991–995. doi: 00001756-200404290-00012 [pii]

Liu, D., Sabbagh, M. A., Gehring, W. J., & Wellman, H. M. (2009). Neural correlates of children's theory of mind development. *Child Development, 80*, 318–326. doi: 10.1111/j.1467-862 4.2009.01262.x

Liu, D., Wellman, H. M., Tardif, T., & Sabbagh, M. A. (2008). Theory of mind development in Chinese children: A meta-analysis of false-belief understanding across cultures and languages. *Developmental Psychology, 44*, 523–531. doi: 10.1037/0012-1649.44.2.523

Lohmann, H., & Tomasello, M. (2003). The role of language in the development of false belief understanding: A training study. *Child Development, 74*, 1130–1144. doi: 10.1111/1467-8624.00597

Low, J., & Watts, J. (2013). Attributing false beliefs about object identity reveals a signature blind spot in humans' efficient mind-reading system. *Psychological Science, 24*, 305–311. doi: 10.1177/0956797612451469

Luo, Y., & Baillargeon, R. (2010). Toward a mentalistic account of early psychological reasoning. *Current Directions in Psychological Science, 19*, 301–307. doi: 10.1177/0963721410386679

Lyons, D. E., Santos, L. R., & Keil, F. C. (2006). Reflections of other minds: How primate social cognition can inform the function of mirror neurons. *Current Opinion in Neurobiology, 16*, 230–234. doi: 10.1016/j.conb.2006.03.015

Ma, L., & Xu, F. (2011). Young children's use of statistical sampling evidence to infer the subjectivity of preferences. *Cognition, 120*, 403–411. doi: 10.1016/j.cognition.2011.02.003

MacWhinney, B., & Snow, C. (1985). The child language data exchange system. *Journal of Child Language, 12*, 271–295. doi: 10.1017/S0305000900006449

MacWhinney, B., & Snow, C. (1990). The child language data exchange system: An update. *Journal of Child Language, 17*, 457–472. doi: 10.1017/S0305000900013866

Maher, M. (1900). *Psychology: Empirical and rational*. London: Longmans, Green, & Co.

Makris, N., & Pnevmatikos, D. (2007). Children's understanding of human and super-natural mind. *Cognitive Development, 22*, 365–375. doi: 10.1016/j.cogdev.2006.12.003

Malle, B. F., Knobe, J. M., & Nelson, S. E. (2007). Actor-observer asymmetries in explanations of behavior: New answers to an old question. *Journal of Personality and Social Psychology, 93*, 491–514. doi: 10.1037/0022-3514.93.4.491

Markus, H. R., & Kitayama, S. (1991). Culture and the self: Implications for cognition, emotion, and motivation. *Psychological Review, 98*, 224–253.

Marr, D. (1982). *Vision: A computational investigation into the human representation and processing of visual information*. San Francisco: W.H. Freeman.

Marticorena, D. C. W., Ruiz, A. M., Mukerji, C., Goddu, A., & Santos, L. R. (2011). Monkeys represent others' knowledge but not their beliefs. *Developmental Science, 14*, 1406–1416. doi : 10.1111/j.1467-7687.2011.01085.x

Masangkay, Z. S., McCluskey, K. A., McIntyre, C. W., Sims-Knight, J., Vaughn, B. E., & Flavell, J. H. (1974). The early development of inferences about the visual percepts of others. *Child Development, 45*, 357–366. doi: 10.2307/1127956

Mascaro, O., & Sperber, D. (2009). The moral, epistemic, and mindreading components of children's vigilance towards deception. *Cognition, 112*, 367–380. doi: 10.1016/j.cognition.2009.05.012

McAdams, D. P. (1993). *The stories we live by: Personal myths and the making of the self*. New York: W. Morrow.

McAlister, A., & Peterson, C. (2007). A longitudinal study of child siblings and theory of mind development. *Cognitive Development, 22*, 258–270. doi: 10.1016/j.cogdev.2006.10.009

McCall, R. B., & Carriger, M. S. (1993). A meta-analysis of infant habituation and recognition memory performance as predictors of later IQ. *Child Development, 64*, 57–79. doi: 10.2307/1131437

McCauley, R. N., & Whitehouse, H. (2005). Introduction: New frontiers in the cognitive science of religion. *Journal of Cognition and Culture, 5*(1–2), 1–13. doi: 10.1163/1568537054068705

Meins, E., & Fernyhough, C. (1999). Linguistic acquisitional style and mentalising development: The role of maternal mind-mindedness. *Cognitive Development, 14*, 363–380. doi: 10.1016/s0885-2014(99)00010-6

Meins, E., Fernyhough, C., Wainwright, R., Clark-Carter, D., Gupta, M. D., Fradley, E., & Tuckey, M. (2003). Pathways to understanding mind: Construct validity and predictive validity of maternal mind-mindedness. *Child Development, 74*, 1194–1211. doi: 10.1111/1467-8624.00601

Meins, E., Fernyhough, C., Wainwright, R., Gupta, M. D., Fradley, E., & Tuckey, M. (2002). Maternal mind-mindedness and attachment security as predictors of theory of mind understanding. *Child Development, 73*, 1715–1726. doi: 10.1111/1467-8624.00501

Melis, A. P., Hare, B., & Tomasello, M. (2008). Do chimpanzees reciprocate received favours? *Animal Behaviour, 76*, 951–962. doi: 10.1016/j.anbehav.2008.05.014

Meltzoff, A. N. (1988). Infant imitation after a 1-week delay: Long-term memory for novel acts and multiple stimuli. *Developmental Psychology, 24*, 470–476. doi: 10.1037/0012-1649.24.4.470

Meltzoff, A. N. (1995). Understanding the intentions of others: Re-enactment of intended acts by 18-month-old children. *Developmental Psychology, 31*, 838–850.

Meltzoff, A. N. (2011). Social cognition and the origins of imitation, empathy, and theory of mind. In U. Goswami (Ed.), *The Wiley-Blackwell handbook of childhood cognitive development* (2nd ed., pp. 49–75): Malden, MA: Wiley-Blackwell.

Meltzoff, A. N., & Brooks, R. (2008). Self-experience as a mechanism for learning about others: A training study in social cognition. *Developmental Psychology, 44*, 1257–1265.

Meltzoff, A. N., Waismeyer, A., & Gopnik, A. (2012). Learning about causes from people: Observational causal learning in 24-month-old infants. *Developmental Psychology, 48*, 1215–1228. doi: 10.1037/a0027440

Meristo, M., Morgan, G., Geraci, A., Iozzi, L., Hjelmquist, E., Surian, L., & Siegal, M. (2012). Belief attribution in deaf and hearing infants. *Developmental Science, 15*, 633–640. doi: 10.1111/j.1467-7687.2012.01155.x

Miller, P. H., Kessel, F. S., & Flavell, J. H. (1970). Thinking about people thinking about people thinking about...: A study of social cognitive development. *Child Development, 41*, 613–623.

Miller, P. J., Fung, H., Lin, S., Chen, E. C., & Boldt, B. R. (2012). How socialization happens on the ground: Narrative practices as alternate socializing pathways in Taiwanese and European-American families. *Monographs of the Society for Research in Child Development, 77*(1, Serial No. 302), 1–140. doi: 10.1111/j.1540-5834.2011.00642.x

Miller, P. J., Fung, H., & Mintz, J. (1996). Self-construction through narrative practices: A Chinese and American comparison of early socialization. *Ethos, 24*, 237–280. doi: 10.1525/eth.1996.24.2.02a00020

Milligan, K., Astington, J. W., & Dack, L. A. (2007). Language and theory of mind: Meta-analysis of the relation between language ability and false-belief understanding. *Child Development, 78*, 622–646. doi: 10.1111/j.1467-8624.2007.01018.x

Mitchell, J. P. (2008). Contributions of functional neuroimaging to the study of social cognition. *Current Directions in Psychological Science, 17*, 142–146. doi: 10.1111/j.1467-8721.2008.00564.x

Mitchell, J. P., Macrae, C. N., & Banaji, M. R. (2006). Dissociable medial prefrontal contributions to the judgments of similar and dissimilar others. *Neuron, 50*, 655–663.

Mitchell, P. (1996). *Acquiring a conception of mind: A review of psychological research and theory.* Hove, England: Psychology Press.

Miyake, A., & Friedman, N. P. (2012). The nature and organization of individual differences in executive functions: Four general conclusions. *Current Directions in Psychological Science, 21*, 8–14. doi: 10.1177/0963721411429458

Moeller, M. P., & Schick, B. (2006). Relations between maternal input and theory of mind understanding in deaf children. *Child Development, 77*, 751–766. doi: 10.1111/j.1467-8624.2006.00901.x

Moll, H., Carpenter, M., & Tomasello, M. (2007). Fourteen-month-olds know what others experience only in joint engagement. *Developmental Science, 10*, 826–835. doi: 10.1111/j.1467-7687.2007.00615.x

Moll, H., & Meltzoff, A. N. (2011). How does it look? Level 2 perspective-taking at 36 months of age. *Child Development, 82,* 661–73. doi: 10.1111/j.1467-8624.2010.01571.x

Moll, H., & Tomasello, M. (2004). 12- and 18-month-old infants follow gaze to spaces behind barriers. *Developmental Science, 7,* F1–F9.

Moor, B. G., Op de Macks, Z. A., Güroglu, B., Rombouts, S. A. R. B., Van der Molen, M. W., & Crone, E. A. (2012). Neurodevelopmental changes of reading the mind in the eyes. *Social Cognitive and Affective Neuroscience, 4,* 44–52. doi: 10.1093/scan/nsr020

Moore, C. (2009). Fairness in children's resource allocation depends on the recipient. *Psychological Science, 20,* 944–948. doi: 10.1111/j.1467-9280.2009.02378.x

Moore, C., Barresi, J., & Thompson, C. (1998). The cognitive basis of future-oriented prosocial behavior. *Social Development, 7,* 198–218. doi: 10.1111/1467-9507.00062

Moore, C., Bryant, D., & Furrow, D. (1989). Mental terms and the development of certainty. *Child Development, 60,* 167–171. doi: 10.2307/1131082

Moore, C., & Corkum, V. (1994). Social understanding at the end of the first year of life. *Developmental Review, 14,* 349–372.

Morgan, G., & Shepard-Kegl, J. (2006). Nicaraguan sign language and theory of mind: The issue of critical periods and abilities. *Journal of Child Psychology & Psychiatry, 47,* 811–819. doi: 10.1111/j.1469-7610.2006.01621.x

Mosconi, M. W., Mack, P. B., McCarthy, G., & Pelphrey, K. A. (2005). Taking an "intentional stance" on eye-gaze shifts: A functional neuroimaging study of social perception in children. *NeuroImage, 27,* 247–252. doi: http://dx.doi.org/10.1016/j.neuroimage.2005.03.027

Moses, L. J. (2001). Executive accounts of theory-of-mind development. Commentary on "Meta-analysis of theory-of-mind development: The truth about false belief." *Child Development, 72,* 688–690. doi: 10.1111/1467-8624.00306

Moses, L. J., Baldwin, D. A., Rosicky, J. G., & Tidball, G. (2001). Evidence for referential understanding in the emotions domain at twelve and eighteen months. *Child Development, 72,* 718–735. doi: 10.1111/1467-8624.00311

Moses, L. J., & Chandler, M. J. (1992). Traveler's guide to children's theories of mind. *Psychological Inquiry, 3,* 286–301. doi: 10.2307/1449383

Moses, L. J., Coon, J. A., & Wusinich, N. (2000). Young children's understanding of desire formation. *Developmental Psychology, 36,* 77–90. doi: 10.1037/0012-1649.36.1.77

Mukamel, R., Ekstrom, A. D., Kaplan, J., Iacoboni, M., & Fried, I. (2010). Single-neuron responses in humans during execution and observation of actions. *Current Biology, 20,* 750–756.

Müller, U., Zelazo, P. D., & Imrisek, S. (2005). Executive function and children's understanding of false belief: How specific is the relation? *Cognitive Development, 20,* 173–189. doi: 10.1016/j.cogdev.2004.12.004

Munro, D. J. (1969). *The concept of man in early China.* Stanford, CA: Stanford University Press.

Munro, D. J. (1977). *The concept of man in contemporary China.* Ann Arbor: University of Michigan Press.

Neumann, A., Thoermer, C., & Sodian, B. (2008). *Belief-based actions anticipation in 18-month-old infants.* Paper presented at the International Congress of Psychology, Berlin, Germany.

Newport, E. L. (1991). Contrasting concepts of the critical period for language. In S. Carey & R. Gelman (Eds.), *The epigenesis of mind: Essays on biology and cognition* (pp. 111–130). Hillsdale, NJ: Erlbaum.

Newton, P., Reddy, V., & Bull, R. (2000). Children's everyday deception and performance on false-belief tasks. *British Journal of Developmental Psychology, 18*, 297–317. doi: 10.1348/026151000165706

Nisbett, R. E. (2003). *The geography of thought: How Asians and westerners think differently— and why.* New York: Free Press.

Nisbett, R. E., & Wilson, T. D. (1977). Telling more than we can know: Verbal reports on mental processes. *Psychological Review, 84*, 231–259. doi: 10.1037/0033-295x.84.3.231

Noffke, J. L., & McFadden, S. H. (2001). Denominational and age comparisons of God concepts. *Journal for the Scientific Study of Religion, 40*, 745–756.

Notaro, P. C., Gelman, S. A., & Zimmerman, M. A. (2001). Children's understanding of psychogenic bodily reactions. *Child Development, 72*, 444–459. doi: 10.1111/1467-8624.00289

Nunez, P. L., & Cutillo, B. A. (1995). *Neocortical dynamics and human EEG rhythms.* New York: Oxford University Press.

Oaksford, M., & Chater, N. (2007). *Bayesian rationality: The probabilistic approach to human reasoning.* New York: Oxford University Press.

Oh, S., & Lewis, C. (2008). Korean preschoolers' advanced inhibitory control and its relation to other executive skills and mental state understanding. *Child Development, 79*, 80–99. doi: 10 .1111/j.1467-8624.2007.01112.x

Ohnishi, T. C. A., Moriguchi, Y., Matsuda, H., Mori, T., Hirakata, M., Imabayashi, E.,… Uno, A. (2004). The neural network for the mirror system and mentalizing in normally developed children: An fMRI study. *NeuroReport, 15*, 1483–1487.

Olineck, K. M., & Poulin-Dubois, D. (2005). Infants' ability to distinguish between intentional and accidental actions and its relation to internal state language. *Infancy, 8*, 91–100.

O'Neill, D. K. (1996). Two-year-old children's sensitivity to a parent's knowledge state when making requests. *Child Development, 67*, 659–677. doi: 10.2307/1131839

O'Neill, D. K., Astington, J. W., & Flavell, J. H. (1992). Young children's understanding of the role that sensory experiences play in knowledge acquisition. *Child Development, 63*, 474–490. doi: 10.2307/1131493

O'Neill, D. K., Main, R. M., & Ziemski, R. A. (2009). 'I like Barney': Preschoolers' spontaneous conversational initiations with peers. *First Language, 29*, 401–425. doi: 10.1177/0142723709105315

Onishi, K. H., & Baillargeon, R. (2005). Do 15-month-old infants understand false beliefs? *Science, 308*(5719), 255–258. doi: 10.1126/science.1107621

Opfer, J. E., & Gelman, S. A. (2011). Development of the animate-inanimate distinction. In U. Goswami (Ed.), *The Blackwell handbook of childhood cognitive development* (2nd ed., pp. 213–238). New York: Blackwell.

Packer, J. I. (1993). *Concise theology: A guide to historic Christian beliefs.* Wheaton, IL: Tyndale House Publishers.

Parsons, S., & Mitchell, P. (1999). What children with autism understand about thoughts and thought bubbles. *Autism, 3*(1), 17–38.

Partington, A. (Ed.). (1996). *The Oxford dictionary of quotations* (4th ed.). New York: Oxford University Press.

Pascual-Marqui, R. D. (2002). Standardized low-resolution brain electromagnetic tomography (sLORETA): Technical details. *Methods and Findings in Experimental and Clinical Pharmacology, 24*(Suppl D), 5–12.

Pasquini, E. S., Corriveau, K. H., Koenig, M., & Harris, P. L. (2007). Preschoolers monitor the relative accuracy of informants. *Developmental Psychology, 43*, 1216–1226. doi: 10.1037/0012-1649.43.5.1216

Pearl, J. (1988). *Probabilistic reasoning in intelligent systems: Networks of plausible inference.* San Mateo, CA: Morgan Kaufman.

Pearl, J. (2000). *Causality: Models, reasoning, and inference.* New York: Cambridge University Press.

Perner, J. (1991). *Understanding the representational mind.* Cambridge, MA: MIT Press.

Perner, J., Ruffman, T., & Leekam, S. R. (1994). Theory of mind is contagious: You catch it from your sibs. *Child Development, 65*, 1228–1238. doi: 10.1111/j.1467-8624.1994.tb00814.x

Perner, J., Sprung, M., Zauner, P., & Haider, H. (2003). Want that is understood well before say that, think that, and false belief: A test of de Villier's linguistic determinism on German-speaking children. *Child Development, 74*, 179–188. doi: 10.1111/1467-8624. t01-1-00529

Perner, J., & Wimmer, H. (1985). 'John thinks that Mary thinks that. . .': Attribution of second-order beliefs by 5- to 10-year-old children. *Journal of Experimental Child Psychology, 39*, 437–471. doi: 10.1016/0022-0965(85)90051-7

Perner, J., Zauner, P., & Sprung, M. (2005). What does 'that' have to do with point of view? Conflicting desires and 'want' in German. In J. W. Astington & J. A. Baird (Eds.), *Why language matters for theory of mind* (pp. 220–244). New York: Oxford University Press.

Peskin, J., & Ardino, V. (2003). Representing the mental world in children's social behavior: Playing hide-and-seek and keeping a secret. *Social Development, 12*, 496–512. doi: 10.1111/1467-9507.00245

Peterson, C. C. (2000). Kindred spirits: Influences of siblings' perspectives on theory of mind. *Cognitive Development, 15*, 435–455. doi: http://dx.doi.org/10.1016/S0885-2014(01)00040-5

Peterson, C. C. (2004). Theory-of-mind development in oral deaf children with cochlear implants or conventional hearing aids. *Journal of Child Psychology and Psychiatry, 45*, 1–11.

Peterson, C. C. (2009). Development of social-cognitive and communication skills in children born deaf. *Scandinavian Journal of Psychology, 50*, 475–483. doi: 10.1111/j.1467-9450.2009.00750.x

Peterson, C. C., Peterson, J. L., & Webb, J. (2000). Factors influencing the development of a theory of mind in blind children. *British Journal of Developmental Psychology, 18*, 431–447. doi: 10.1348/026151000165788

Peterson, C. C., & Siegal, M. (1995). Deafness, conversation and theory of mind. *Journal of Child Psychology and Psychiatry, 36*, 459–474. doi: 10.1111/j.1469-7610.1995.tb01303.x

Peterson, C. C., & Siegal, M. (1999). Representing inner worlds: Theory of mind in autistic, deaf and normal hearing children. *Psychological Science, 10*, 126–129.

Peterson, C. C., & Siegal, M. (2002). Mindreading and moral awareness in popular and rejected preschoolers. *British Journal of Developmental Psychology, 20*, 205–224. doi: 10.1348/026151002166415

Peterson, C., & Slaughter, V. (2003). Opening windows into the mind: Mothers' preferences for mental state explanations and children's theory of mind. *Cognitive Development, 18*, 399–429. doi: 10.1016/s0885-2014(03)00041-8

Peterson, C. C., & Wellman, H. M. (2009). From fancy to reason: Scaling deaf and hearing children's understanding of theory of mind and pretence. *British Journal of Developmental Psychology*, *27*(Pt. 2), 297–310.

Peterson, C. C., Wellman, H. M., & Liu, D. (2005). Steps in theory-of-mind development for children with deafness or autism. *Child Development*, *76*, 502–517. doi: 10.1111/j.1467-8624.2005.00859.x

Peterson, C. C., Wellman, H. M., & Slaughter, V. (2012). The mind behind the message: Advancing theory of mind scales for typically developing children, and those with deafness, autism, or Asperger Syndrome. *Child Development*, *83*, 469–485.

Peterson, N. R., Pisoni, D. B., & Miyamoto, R. T. (2010). Cochlear implants and spoken language processing abilities: Review and assessment of the literature. *Restorative Neurology and Neuroscience*, *28*, 237–250.

Pew Research Center. (2008). U.S. Religious landscape survey. Religious beliefs and practices: Diverse and politically relevant. *Pew Forum on Religion & Public Life*. Retrieved from http://www.pewforum.org/

Pfeifer, J. H., Masten, C. L., Borofsky, L. A., Dapretto, M., Fuligni, A. J., & Lieberman, M. D. (2009). Neural correlates of direct and reflected self-appraisals in adolescents and adults: When social perspective-taking informs self-perception. *Child development*, *80*, 1016–1038.

Phillips, A. T., & Wellman, H. M. (2005). Infants' understanding of object-directed action. *Cognition*, *98*, 137–155. doi: 10.1016/j.cognition.2004.11.005

Phillips, W., Barnes, J. L., Mahajan, N., Yamaguchi, M., & Santos, L. R. (2009). 'Unwilling' versus 'unable': Capuchin monkeys' (Cebus apella) understanding of human intentional action. *Developmental Science*, *12*, 938–945. doi: 10.1111/j.1467-7687.2009.00840.x

Piaget, J. (1929). *The child's conception of the world*. London: Routledge & Keegan Paul. (Original work published 1967)

Piaget, J. (1932). *The moral judgment of the child*. London: Kegan Paul.

Piaget, J. (1952). *The origins of intelligence in children*. New York: International Universities Press.

Piaget, J. (1970). *Structuralism*. New York: Harper & Row.

Piaget, J. (1983). Piaget's theory. In P. H. Mussen (Ed.), *Handbook of child psychology* (4th ed., Vol. 1). New York: John Wiley & Sons.

Pickover, C. A. (2001). *The paradox of God and the science of omniscience*. New York: Palgrave Macmillan.

Pinker, S. (1984). *Language learnability and language development*. Cambridge, MA: Harvard University Press.

Pinker, S. (1997). *How the mind works*. New York: Norton.

Polak, A., & Harris, P. L. (1999). Deception by young children following noncompliance. *Developmental Psychology*, *35*(2), 561–68. doi: 10.1037/0012-1649.35.2.561

Pons, F., & Harris, P. L. (2005). Longitudinal change and longitudinal stability of individual differences in children's emotion understanding. *Cognition and Emotion*, *19*, 1158–1174. doi: 10.1080/02699930500282108

Pons, F., Harris, P. L., & de Rosnay, M. (2004). Emotion comprehension between 3 and 11 years: Developmental periods and hierarchical organization. *European Journal of Developmental Psychology*, *1*, 127–152. doi: 10.1080/17405620344000022

Pons, F., Lawson, J., Harris, P. L., & de Rosnay, M. (2003). Individual differences in children's emotion understanding: Effects of age and language. *Scandinavian Journal of Psychology, 44*, 347–353. doi: 10.1111/1467-9450.00354

Poulin-Dubois, D., Polonia, A., & Yott, J. (2013). Is false belief skin-deep? The agent's eye status influences infants' reasoning in belief-inducing situations. *Journal of Cognition and Development, 14*, 87–99. doi: 10.1080/15248372.2011.608198

Povinelli, D. J. (2000). *Folk physics for apes: The chimpanzee's theory of how the world works.* Oxford, England: Oxford University Press.

Povinelli, D. J., & Eddy, T. J. (1996). What young chimpanzees know about seeing. *Monographs of the Society for Research in Child Development, 61*(3, Serial No. 247), v–vi, 1–152.

Povinelli, D. J. & Preuss, T. M. (1995). Theory of mind: Evolutionary history of a cognitive specialization. *Trends in Neurosciences, 18*, 418–424.

Pratt, C., & Bryant, P. (1990). Young children understand that looking leads to knowing (so long as they are looking into a single barrel). *Child Development, 61*, 973–982. doi:10.1111/j.1467-8624.1990.tb02835.x

Premack, D., & Woodruff, G. (1978). Does the chimpanzee have a theory of mind? *Behavioral and Brain Sciences, 1*, 515–526. doi: 10.1017/S0140525X00076512

Price, M. (2006). Patriarchy and parental control in Iran. *Iran Chamber Society Articles, 6*, 1–3.

Provine, R. R. (2005). Yawning. *American Scientist, 93*, 532–539.

Pyers, J. E., & Senghas, A. (2009). Language promotes false-belief understanding: Evidence from learners of a new sign language. *Psychological Science, 20*, 805–812. doi: 10.1111/j.1467-9280.2009.02377.x

Pyysiäinen, I. (2004). Intuitive and explicit in religious thought. *Journal of Cognition and Culture, 4*, 123–150. Retrieved from http://booksandjournals.brillonline.com/content/10.1163/156853704323074787

Rakoczy, H., Warneken, F., & Tomasello, M. (2007). "This way!," "No! That way!"—3-year olds know that two people can have mutually incompatible desires. *Cognitive Development, 22*, 47–68. doi: 10.1016/j.cogdev.2006.08.002

Randell, A. C., & Peterson, C. C. (2009). Affective qualities of sibling disputes, mothers' conflict attitudes, and children's theory of mind development. *Social Development, 18*, 857–874. doi: 10.1111/j.1467-9507.2008.00513.x

Rasch, G. (1960). *Probabilistic models for some intelligence and attainment tests.* Chicago: University of Chicago Press.

Razza, R. A., & Blair, C. (2009). Associations among false-belief understanding, executive function, and social competence: A longitudinal analysis. *Journal of Applied Developmental Psychology, 30*, 332–343. doi: http://dx.doi.org/10.1016/j.appdev.2008.12.020

Reddy, V. (2008). *How infants know minds.* Cambridge, MA: Harvard University Press.

Remmel, E., & Peters, K. (2009). Theory of mind and language in children with cochlear implants. *Journal of Deaf Studies and Deaf Education, 14*, 218–236.

Repacholi, B. M., & Gopnik, A. (1997). Early reasoning about desires: Evidence from 14- and 18-month-olds. *Developmental Psychology, 33*, 12–21. doi: 10.1037/0012-1649.33.1.12

Repacholi, B. M., Meltzoff, A. N., & Olsen, B. (2008). Infants' understanding of the link between visual perception and emotion: "If she can't see me doing it, she won't get angry." *Developmental Psychology, 44*, 561–574. doi: 10.1037/0012-1649.44.2.561

Rhodes, M., & Wellman, H. (2013). Constructing a new theory from old ideas and new evidence. *Cognitive Science, 37*, 592–604. doi: 10.1111/cogs.12031

Richert, R. A., & Barrett, J. L. (2005). Do you see what I see? Young children's assumptions about God's perceptual abilities. *International Journal for the Psychology of Religion, 15*, 283–295. doi: 10.1207/s15327582ijpr1504_2

Richert, R. A., & Harris, P. L. (2006). The ghost in my body: Children's developing concept of the soul. *Journal of Cognition and Culture, 6*(3–4), 409–427.

Rieffe, C. J., Meerum Terwogt, M., Koops, W., Stegge, H., & Oomen, A. (2001). Preschoolers appreciation of uncommon desires and subsequent emotions. *British Journal of Developmental Psychology, 19*, 259–274.

Rivas, E. (2005). Recent use of signs by chimpanzees (Pan troglodytes) in interactions with humans. *Journal of Comparative Psychology, 119*, 404–441.

Rizzolatti, G., & Fabbri-Destro, M. (2008). The mirror system and its role in social cognition. *Current Opinion in Neurobiology, 18*, 179–184. doi: 10.1016/j.conb.2008.08.001

Robinson, E. J., Champion, H., & Mitchell, P. (1999). Children's ability to infer utterance veracity from speaker informedness. *Developmental Psychology, 35*, 535–546. doi: 10.1037/0012-1649.35.2.535

Rochat, M. J., Serra, E., Fadiga, L., & Gallese, V. (2008). The evolution of social cognition: Goal familiarity shapes monkeys' action understanding. *Current Biology, 18*, 227–232. doi: http://dx.doi.org/10.1016/j.cub.2007.12.021

Romero, T., Konno, A., & Hasegawa, T. (2013). Familiarity bias and physiological responses in contagious yawning by dogs support link to empathy. *PLoS ONE, 8*(8). doi: http://dx.doi.org/10.1371/journal.pone.0071365

Rosati, A. G., Santos, L. R., & Hare, B. (2010). Primate social cognition: Thirty years after Premack and Woodruff. In M. L. Platt & A. A. Ghazanfar (Eds.), *Primate neuroethology* (pp. 117–143). New York: Oxford University Press.

Rosengren, K. S., Miller P.J., Gutiérrez, I. T., Chow, P.I., Schein, S. S. & Anderson, K.N. (2014). Children's understanding of death: Toward a contextualized and integrated account. *Monographs of the Society for Research in Child Development, 79*(1). doi: 10.1111/mono.12080

Rothbart, M. K., & Bates, J. E. (1998). Temperament. In W. Damon (Series Ed.) & N. Eisenberg (Vol. Ed.), *Handbook of Child Psychology: Vol. 3. Social, emotional and personality development* (5th ed., pp. 105–176). New York: Wiley.

Rothmayr, C., Sodian, B., Hajak, G. r., Döhnel, K., Meinhardt, J. & Sommer, M. (2011). Common and distinct neural networks for false-belief reasoning and inhibitory control. *NeuroImage, 56*, 1705–1713. doi: http://dx.doi.org/10.1016/j.neuroimage.2010.12.052

Rowland, C. F., Pine, J. M., Lieven, E. V. M., & Theakston, A. L. (2003). Determinants of acquisition order in wh-questions: Re-evaluating the role of caregiver speech. *Journal of Child Language, 30*, 609–635. doi: 10.1017/S0305000903005695

Rudy, D., & Grusec, J. E. (2006). Authoritarian parenting in individualist and collectivist groups: Associations with maternal emotion and cognition and children's self-esteem. *Journal of Family Psychology, 20*, 68–78. doi: 10.1037/0893-3200.20.1.68

Ruffman, T. (1996). Do children understand the mind by means of simulation or a theory? Evidence from their understanding of inference. *Mind & Language, 11*, 388–414. doi: 10.1111/j.1468-0017.1996.tb00053.x

Ruffman, T., & Keenan, T. R. (1996). The belief-based emotion of surprise: The case for a lag in understanding relative to false belief. *Developmental Psychology, 32*, 40–49. doi: 10.1037/0012-1649.32.1.40

Ruffman, T., & Perner, J. (2005). Do infants really understand false belief? *Trends in Cognitive Sciences, 9*, 462–463. doi: 10.1016/j.tics.2005.08.001

Ruffman, T., Perner, J., Naito, M., Parkin, L., & Clements, W. A. (1998). Older (but not younger) siblings facilitate false belief understanding. *Developmental Psychology, 34*, 161–174. doi: 10.1037/0012-1649.34.1.161

Ruffman, T., Slade, L., & Crowe, E. (2002). The relation between children's and mothers' mental state language and theory-of-mind understanding. *Child Development, 73*, 734–751. doi: 10.1111/1467-8624.00435

Ruffman, T., Taumoepeau, M., & Perkins, C. (2012). Statistical learning as a basis for social understanding in children. *British Journal of Developmental Psychology, 30*, 87–104. doi: 10.1 111/j.2044-835X.2011.02045.x

Russell, B. (1912). *The problems of philosophy*. London: Williams and Norgate.

Russell, J. A. (1991). Culture and the categorization of emotions. *Psychological Bulletin, 110*, 426–450. doi: 10.1037/0033-2909.110.3.426

Russell, J. A. (1994). Is there universal recognition of emotion from facial expressions? A review of the cross-cultural studies. *Psychological Bulletin, 115*, 102–141. doi: 10.1037/ 0033-2909.115.1.102

Russell, J., Jarrold, C., & Potel, D. (1994). What makes strategic deception difficult for children—the deception or the strategy? *British Journal of Developmental Psychology, 12*, 301–314. doi: 10.1111/j.2044-835X.1994.tb00636.x

Ryle, G. (1949). *The concept of mind*. London: Hutchinson's University Library.

Sabbagh, M. A., & Baldwin, D. A. (2001). Learning words from knowledgeable versus ignorant speakers: Links between preschoolers' theory of mind and semantic development. *Child Development, 72*, 1054–1070. doi: 10.1111/1467-8624.00334

Sabbagh, M. A., Bowman, L. C., Evraire, L. E., & Ito, J. M. B. (2009). Neurodevelopmental correlates of theory of mind in preschool children. *Child Development, 80*, 1147–1162. doi: 10.11 11/j.1467-8624.2009.01322.x

Sabbagh, M. A., Moulson, M. C., & Harkness, K. L. (2004). Neural correlates of mental state decoding in human adults: An event-related potential study. *Journal of Cognitive Neuroscience, 16*, 415–426. doi: 10.1162/0898929042322926755

Sabbagh, M. A., & Taylor, M. (2000). Neural correlates of the theory-of-mind reasoning: An event-related potential study. *Psychological Science, 11*, 46–50. doi: 10.1111/ 1467-9280.00213

Sabbagh, M. A., Xu, F., Carlson, S. M., Moses, L. J., & Lee, K. (2006). The development of executive functioning and theory of mind: A comparison of Chinese and U.S. preschoolers. *Psychological Science, 17*, 74–81.

Saffran, J. R., Aslin, R. N., & Newport, E. L. (1996). Statistical learning by 8-month-old infants. *Science, 274*, 1926–1928. doi: 10.1126/science.274.5294.1926

Saxe, R., & Kanwisher, N. (2003). People thinking about thinking people: The role of the temporo-parietal junction in "theory of mind." *NeuroImage, 19*, 1835–1842. doi: http://dx.doi. org/10.1016/S1053-8119(03)00230-1

Saxe, R., & Powell, L. J. (2006). It's the thought that counts: Specific brain regions for one component of theory of mind. *Psychological Science, 17,* 692–699. doi: 10.1111/j.1467-9280.2006.01768.x

Saxe, R., Schulz, L. E., & Jiang, Y. V. (2006). Reading minds versus following rules: Dissociating theory of mind and executive control in the brain. *Social Neuroscience, 1*(3–4), 284–298. doi: 10.1080/17470910601000446

Saxe, R., Tzelnic, T., & Carey, S. (2006). Five-month-old infants know humans are solid, like inanimate objects. *Cognition, 101,* B1–B8. doi: 10.1016/j.cognition.2005.10.005

Saxe, R., Tzelnic, T., & Carey, S. (2007). Knowing who dunnit: Infants identify the causal agent in an unseen causal interaction. *Developmental Psychology, 43,* 149–158. doi: 10.1037/0012-1649.43.1.149

Saxe, R., & Wexler, A. (2005). Making sense of another mind: The role of the right temporo-parietal junction. *Neuropsychologia, 43,* 1391–1399. doi: http://dx.doi.org/10.1016/j.neuropsychologia.2005.02.013

Saxe, R. R., Whitfield-Gabrieli, S., Scholz, J., & Pelphrey, K. A. (2009). Brain regions for perceiving and reasoning about other people in school-aged children. *Child Development, 80,* 1197–1209. doi: 10.1111/j.1467-8624.2009.01325.x

Schick, B., De Villiers, P., De Villiers, J., & Hoffmeister, R. (2007). Language and theory of mind: A study of deaf children. *Child Development, 78,* 376–396. doi: 10.1111/j.1467-8624.2007.01004.x

Scholl, B. J., & Leslie, A. M. (2001). Minds, modules, and meta-analysis. *Child Development, 72,* 696–701. doi: 10.1111/1467-8624.00308

Schult, C. A., & Wellman, H. M. (1997). Explaining human movements and actions: children's understanding of the limits of psychological explanation. *Cognition, 62,* 291–324. doi: S0010-0277(96)00786-X [pii]

Schulz, L. E., & Bonawitz, E. B. (2007). Serious fun: Preschoolers engage in more exploratory play when evidence is confounded. *Developmental Psychology, 43,* 1045–1050. doi: 10.1037/0012-1649.43.4.1045

Schulz, L., Bonawitz, E., & Griffiths, T. (2007). Can being scared cause tummy aches? Naive theories, ambiguous evidence, and preschoolers' causal inferences. *Developmental Psychology, 43,* 1124–1139.

Schulz, L. E., & Gopnik, A. (2004). Causal learning across domains. *Developmental Psychology, 40,* 162–176. doi: 10.1037/0012-1649.40.2.162

Schwebel, D. C., Rosen, C. S., & Singer, J. L. (1999). Preschoolers' pretend play and theory of mind: The role of jointly constructed pretence. *British Journal of Developmental Psychology, 17,* 333–348. doi: 10.1348/026151099165320

Scientists try to predict intentions: Using brain scans to read minds before thoughts turn into actions. (2007, March 5). *Science on NBCNEWS.com.* Retrieved from http://www.nbcnews.com/id/17464320/ns/technology_and_science-science/t/scientists-try-predict-intentions/#.U34KoySSaLm

Scofield, J., & Behrend, D. A. (2008). Learning words from reliable and unreliable speakers. *Cognitive Development, 23,* 278–290. doi: 10.1016/j.cogdev.2008.01.003

Scott, R. M., & Baillargeon, R. (2009). Which penguin is this? Attributing false beliefs about object identity at 18 months. *Child Development, 80,* 1172–1196. doi: 10.1111/j.1467-8624.2009.01324.x

Scott, R. M., Baillargeon, R., Song, H. J., & Leslie, A. M. (2010). Attributing false beliefs about non-obvious properties at 18 months. *Cognitive Psychology*, *61*, 366–395. doi: 10.1016/j.cogpsych.2010.09.001

Searle, J. R. (1983). *Intentionality, an essay in the philosophy of mind*. Cambridge, England: Cambridge University Press.

Shafto, P., Goodman, N. D., & Frank, M. C. (2012). Learning from others: The consequences of psychological reasoning for human learning. *Perspectives on Psychological Science*, *7*, 341–351. doi: 10.1177/1745691612448481

Shahaeian, A., Peterson, C. C., Slaughter, V., & Wellman, H. M. (2011). Culture and the sequence of steps in theory of mind development. *Developmental Psychology*, *47*, 1239–1247. doi: 10.1037/a0023899

Shakespeare, W. (1961). Romeo and Juliet. In C. Hardin (Ed.), *The complete works of Shakespeare* (pp. 393–424). Glenview, IL: Scott, Foresman. (Original work published 1597)

Sharifzadeh, V. (2004). Families with Middle Eastern roots. In E. Lynch & M. Hanson (Eds.), *Developing cross-cultural competence* (3rd ed., pp. 373–410). Baltimore, MD: Brookes.

Shatz, M., Diesendruck, G., Martinez-Beck, I., & Akar, D. (2003). The influence of language and socioeconomic status on children's understanding of false belief. *Developmental Psychology*, *39*, 717–729. doi: 10.1037/0012-1649.39.4.717

Shipley, B. (2000). *Cause and correlation in biology: A user's guide to path analysis, structural equations and causal inference*. Cambridge, England: Cambridge University Press.

Shutts, K., Roben, C. K. P., & Spelke, E. S. (2013). Children's use of social categories in thinking about people and social relationships. *Journal of Cognition and Development*, *14*, 35–62. doi: 10.1080/15248372.2011.638686

Shweder, R. A., Goodnow, J. J., Hatano, G., Levine, R. A., Markus, H. R., & Miller, P. J. (2006). The cultural psychology of development: One mind, many mentalities. In W. Damon & R. M. Lerner (Eds.), *Handbook of child psychology: Vol. 1. Theoretical models of human development* (pp. 716–792). New York: Wiley.

Siegal, M., & Peterson, C. C. (1998). Preschoolers' understanding of lies and innocent and negligent mistakes. *Developmental Psychology*, *34*, 332–341. doi: 10.1037/0012-1649.34.2.332

Siegal, M., & Varley, R. (2002). Neural systems involved in 'theory of mind'. *Nature Reviews Neuroscience*, *3*, 463–471. doi: 10.1038/nrn844

Siegler, R. S. (1995). Children's thinking: How does change occur? In W. Schneider & F. Weinert (Eds.), *Memory performance and competencies* (pp. 405–430). Hillsdale, NJ: Erlbaum.

Siegler, R. S. (2007). Cognitive variability. *Developmental Science*, *10*, 104–109. doi: 10.1111/j.1467-7687.2007.00571.x

Sigel, I. E., McGillicuddy-DeLisi, A. V., & Goodnow, J. (1992). *Parental belief systems: The psychological consequences for children* (2nd ed.). Hillsdale, NJ: Lawrence Erlbaum Associates.

Simons, D. J., & Keil, F. C. (1995). An abstract to concrete shift in the development of biological thought: The insides story. *Cognition*, *56*, 129–163. doi: 10.1016/0010-0277(94)00660-d

Skuse, D. H., James, R. S., Bishop, D. V. M., Coppin, B., Dalton, P., Aamodt-Leeper, G.,…Jacobs, P. A. (1997). Evidence from Turner's syndrome of an imprinted X-linked locus affecting cognitive function. *Nature*, *387*(6634), 705–708. doi: 10.1038/42706

Slade, L., & Ruffman, T. (2005). How language does (and does not) relate to theory of mind: A longitudinal study of syntax, semantics, working memory and false belief. *British Journal of Developmental Psychology, 23*, 117–141. doi: 10.1348/026151004X21332

Slaughter, V., Dennis, M. J., & Pritchard, M. (2002). Theory of mind and peer acceptance in preschool children. *British Journal of Developmental Psychology, 20*, 545–564. doi: 10.1348/026151002760390945

Slaughter, V., Jaakkola, R., & Carey, S. (1999). Constructing a coherent theory: Children's biological understanding of life and death. In M. Siegal & C. C. Petersen (Eds.), *Children's understanding of biology and health* (pp. 71–96). New York: Cambridge University Press.

Slaughter, V., Peterson, C. C., & Moore, C. (2013). I can talk you into it: Theory of mind and persuasion behavior in young children. *Developmental Psychology, 49*, 227–231. doi: 10.1037/a0028280

Smiley, P., & Huttenlocher, J. (1995). Conceptual development and the child's early words for events, objects, and persons. In M. Tomasello & W. E. Merriman (Eds.), *Beyond names for things: Young children's acquisition of verbs* (pp. 21–61). Hillsdale, NJ: Lawrence Erlbaum Associates.

Sobel, D. M., Tenenbaum, J. B., & Gopnik, A. (2004). Children's causal inferences from indirect evidence: Backwards blocking and Bayesian reasoning in preschoolers. *Cognitive Science, 28*, 303–333. doi: 10.1207/s15516709cog2803_1

Sodian, B. (1994). Early deception and the conceptual continuity claim. In C. Lewis & P. Mitchell (Eds.), *Children's early understanding of mind: Origins and development* (pp. 385–401). Hillsdale, NJ: Lawrence Erlbaum Associates.

Sodian, B., & Thoermer, C. (2008). Precursors to a theory of mind in infancy: Perspectives for research on autism. *The Quarterly Journal of Experimental Psychology, 61*, 27–39. doi: 10.1080/17470210701508681

Sommer, M., Döhnel, K., Sodian, B., Meinhardt, J., Thoermer, C., & Hajak, G. (2007). Neural correlates of true and false belief reasoning. *NeuroImage, 35*, 1378–1384. doi: http://dx.doi.org/10.1016/j.neuroimage.2007.01.042

Sommer, M., Meinhardt, J., Eichenmüller, K., Sodian, B., Döhnel, K., & Hajak, G. (2010). Modulation of the cortical false belief network during development. *Brain Research, 1354*, 123–131. doi: http://dx.doi.org/10.1016/j.brainres.2010.07.057

Soproni, K., Miklósi, A., Topál, J., & Csányi, V. (2001). Comprehension of human communicative signs in pet dogs (Canis familiaris). *Journal of Comparative Psychology, 115*, 122–126. doi: 10.1037/0735-7036.115.2.122

South, M., Ozonoff, S., & McMahon, W. M. (2007). The relationship between executive functioning, central coherence, and repetitive behaviors in the high-functioning autism spectrum. *Autism, 11*, 437–451. doi: 10.1177/1362361307079606

Southgate, V., Chevallier, C., & Csibra, G. (2009). Sensitivity to communicative relevance tells young children what to imitate. *Developmental Science, 12*, 1013–1019. doi: 10.1111/j.1467-7687.2009.00861.x

Southgate, V., Chevallier, C., & Csibra, G. (2010). Seventeen-month-olds appeal to false beliefs to interpret others' referential communication. *Developmental Science, 13*, 907–912. doi: 10.1111/j.1467-7687.2009.00946.x

Southgate, V., & Hamilton, A. F. (2008). Unbroken mirrors: Challenging a theory of autism. *Trends in Cognitive Sciences, 12*, 225–229. doi: 10.1016/j.tics.2008.03.005

Southgate, V., Senju, A., & Csibra, G. (2007). Action anticipation through attribution of false belief by 2-year-olds. *Psychological Science, 18*, 587–592.

Spelke, E. (1994). Initial knowledge: six suggestions. *Cognition, 50*(1–3), 431–445. doi: 10.1016/0010-0277(94)90039-6

Spelke, E. S. (2003). What makes us smart? Core knowledge and natural language. In D. Gentner & S. Goldin-Meadow (Eds.), *Language in mind* (pp. 277–312). Cambridge, MA: MIT Press.

Spelke, E. S., Breinlinger, K., Macomber, J., & Jacobson, K. (1992). Origins of knowledge. *Psychological Review, 99*, 605–632. doi: 10.1037/0033-295x.99.4.605

Spelke, E. S., & Kinzler, K. D. (2007). Core knowledge. *Developmental Science, 10*, 89–96. doi: 10.1111/j.1467-7687.2007.00569.x

Spelke, E. S., & Kinzler, K. D. (2009). Innateness, learning, and rationality. *Child Development Perspectives, 3*, 96–98. doi: 10.1111/j.1750-8606.2009.00085.x

Spencer, P., & Harris, M. (2006). Patterns and effects of language input to deaf infants and toddlers from deaf and hearing mothers. In M. M. P. Spencer (Ed.), *Advances in the sign language development of deaf children* (pp. 71–101). New York: Oxford University Press.

Sperber, D. (1994). The modularity of thought and the epidemiology of representations. In L. A. Hirschfeld & S. A. Gelman (Eds.), *Mapping the mind: Domain specificity in cognition and culture* (pp. 39–67). New York: Cambridge University Press.

Sperber, D. (1996). *Explaining culture: A naturalistic approach.* Oxford, England: Blackwell.

Sperber, D. (1997). Intuitive and reflective beliefs. *Mind & Language, 12*, 67–83. doi: 10.1111/1468-0017.00036

Spilka, B., Armatas, P., & Nussbaum, J. (1964). The concept of God: A factor-analytic approach. *Review of Religious Research, 6*, 28–36. doi: 10.2307/3510880

Spirtes, P., Glymour, C., & Scheines, R. (2000). *Causation, prediction, and search* (2nd ed.) Cambridge, MA: MIT Press.

Stack, J., & Lewis, C. (2011). *Reassessing "infant false belief."* Paper presented at the Biennial Meetings of the Society for Research in Child Development, Montreal, Canada.

Stein, N. L., & Levine, L. J. (1989). The causal organisation of emotional knowledge: A developmental study. *Cognition and Emotion, 3*, 343–378. doi: 10.1080/02699938908412712

Stevenson, H. W., Lee, S.-y., Chen, C., Stigler, J. W., Hsu, C.-C., Kitamura, S., & Hatano, G. (1990). Contexts of achievement: A study of American, Chinese, and Japanese children. *Monographs of the Society for Research in Child Development, 55*(1–2, Serial No. 221). doi: 10.2307/1166090

Stevenson, M. B., & Friedman, S. L. (1986). Developmental changes in the understanding of pictorial representations of sound. *Developmental Psychology, 22*, 686–690. doi: 10.1037/0012-1649.22.5.686

Stich, S. P. (1983). *From folk psychology to cognitive science: The case against belief.* Cambridge, MA: MIT Press.

Stouthamer-Loebel. (1991). Young children's verbal misrepresentations of reality. In K. Rotenberg (Ed.), *Children's interpersonal trust* (pp. 20–42). Berlin, Germany: Springer-Verlag.

Sullivan, K., Zaitchik, D., & Tager-Flusberg, H. (1994). Preschoolers can attribute second-order beliefs. *Developmental Psychology, 30*, 395–402. doi: 10.1037/0012-1649.30.3.395

Surian, L., Caldi, S., & Sperber, D. (2007). Attribution of beliefs by 13-month-old infants. *Psychological Science, 18*, 580–586. doi: 10.1111/j.1467-9280.2007.01943.x

Sutton, J., Smith, P. K., & Swettenham, J. (1999). Social cognition and bullying: Social inadequacy or skilled manipulation? *British Journal of Developmental Psychology, 17*, 435–450. doi: 10.1348/026151099165384

Talwar, V., & Lee, K. (2002). Development of lying to conceal a transgression: Children's control of expressive behaviour during verbal deception. *International Journal of Behavioral Development, 26*, 436–444. doi: 10.1080/01650250143000373

Talwar, V., & Lee, K. (2008). Social and cognitive correlates of children's lying behavior. *Child Development, 79*, 866–881. doi: 10.1111/j.1467-8624.2008.01164.x

Tardif, T., & Wellman, H. M. (2000). Acquisition of mental state language in Mandarin- and Cantonese-speaking children. *Developmental Psychology, 36*, 25–43. doi: 10.1037/0012-1649.36.1.25

Tardif, T., Wellman, H. M., & Cheung, K. M. (2004). False belief understanding in Cantonese-speaking children. *Journal of Child Language, 31*, 779–800.

Taumoepeau, M., & Ruffman, T. (2006). Mother and infant talk about mental states relates to desire language and emotion understanding. *Child Development, 77*, 465–481. doi: 10.1111/j.1467-8624.2006.00882.x

Taylor, M., & Carlson, S. M. (1997). The relation between individual differences in fantasy and theory of mind. *Child Development, 68*, 436–455. doi: 10.1111/j.1467-8624.1997.tb01950.x

Taylor, M., Cartwright, B. S., & Carlson, S. M. (1993). A developmental investigation of children's imaginary companions. *Developmental Psychology, 29*, 276–285. doi: 10.1037/0012-1649.29.2.276

Tenenbaum, J. B., Griffiths, T. L., & Kemp, C. (2006). Theory-based Bayesian models of inductive learning and reasoning. *Trends in Cognitive Sciences, 10*, 309–318. doi: http://dx.doi.org/10.1016/j.tics.2006.05.009

Tenenbaum, J. B., Griffiths, T., & Niyogi, S. (2007). Intuitive theories as grammars for causal inference. In A. Gopnik & L. Schulz (Eds.), *Causal learning: Psychology, philosophy, and computation* (pp. 301–322). New York: Oxford University Press.

Tenenbaum, J. B., Kemp, C., Griffiths, T. L., & Goodman, N. D. (2011). How to grow a mind: Statistics, structure, and abstraction. *Science, 331*, 1279–1285. doi: 10.1126/science.1192788

Termine, N. T., & Izard, C. E. (1988). Infants' responses to their mothers' expressions of joy and sadness. *Developmental Psychology, 24*, 223–229. doi: 10.1037/0012-1649.24.2.223

Thelen, E., & Smith, L. B. (1994). *A dynamic systems approach to the development of cognition and action.* Cambridge, MA: MIT Press.

Thoermer, C., Sodian, B., Vuori, M., Perst, H., & Kristen, S. (2012). Continuity from an implicit to an explicit understanding of false belief from infancy to preschool age. *British Journal of Developmental Psychology, 30*, 172–187. doi: 10.1111/j.2044-835X.2011.02067.x

Thompson, R. L., Vinson, D. P., Woll, B., & Vigliocco, G. (2012). The road to language learning is iconic: Evidence from British sign language. *Psychological Science, 23*, 1443–1448. doi: 10.1177/0956797612459763

Tobin, J. J., Wu, D. Y. H., & Davidson, D. H. (1989). *Preschool in three cultures: Japan, China, and the United States.* New Haven, CT: Yale University Press.

Tomasello, M. (1993). It's imitation, not mimesis. *Behavioral and Brain Sciences, 16,* 771–772. doi: 10.1017/S0140525X00032921

Tomasello, M. (1999). *The cultural origins of human cognition.* Cambridge, MA: Harvard University Press.

Tomasello, M., & Call, J. (1997). *Primate cognition.* New York: Oxford University Press.

Tomasello, M., Call, J., & Hare, B. (2003). Chimpanzees understand psychological states— the question is which ones and to what extent. *Trends in Cognitive Sciences, 7,* 153–156. doi: 10.1016/S1364-6613(03)00035-4

Tomasello, M., & Carpenter, M. (2005). The emergence of social cognition in three young chimpanzees. *Monographs of the Society for Research in Child Development, 70*(1), 107–122.

Tomasello, M., & Haberl, K. (2003). Understanding attention: 12- and 18-month-olds know what is new for other persons. *Developmental Psychology, 39,* 906–912.

Toulmin, S. (1967). *The philosophy of science: An introduction.* London: Hutchinson University Library. (Original work published 1953)

Tsai, J. L. (2007). Ideal affect: Cultural causes and behavioral consequences. *Perspectives on Psychological Science, 2,* 242–259. doi: 10.1111/j.1745-6916.2007.00043.x

Tsai, J. L., Knutson, B., & Fung, H. H. (2006). Cultural variation in affect valuation. *Journal of Personality and Social Psychology, 90,* 288–307. doi: 10.1037/0022-3514.90.2.288

Tsai, J. L., Louie, J. Y., Chen, E. E., & Uchida, Y. (2007). Learning what feelings to desire: Socialization of ideal affect through children's storybooks. *Personality and Social Psychology Bulletin, 33,* 17–30. doi: 10.1177/0146167206292749

Tyack, D., & Ingram, D. (1977). Children's production and comprehension of questions. *Journal of Child Language, 4*(02), 211–224. doi: 10.1017/S0305000900001616

Ueno, A., & Matsuzawa, T. (2004). Food transfer between chimpanzee mothers and their infants. *Primates, 45,* 231–239. doi: 10.1007/s10329-004-0085-9

Ullman, T. D., Goodman, N. D., & Tenenbaum, J. B. (2012). Theory learning as stochastic search in the language of thought. *Cognitive Development, 27,* 455–480. doi: 10.1016/j.cogdev.2012.07.005

Vaccari, C., & Marschark, M. (1997). Communication between parents and deaf children: Implications for social-emotional development. *Journal of Child Psychology and Psychiatry, 38,* 793–801.

Van Overwalle, F., & Baetens, K. (2009). Understanding others' actions and goals by mirror and mentalizing systems: A meta-analysis. *NeuroImage, 48,* 564–584. doi: 10.1016/j.neuroimage.2009.06.009

Vosniadou, S., & Brewer, W. F. (1992). Mental models of the earth: A study of conceptual change in childhood. *Cognitive Psychology, 24,* 535–585. doi: 10.1016/0010-0285(92)90018-w

Vrij, A. (2008). *Detecting lies and deceit: Pitfalls and opportunities.* Chichester, England: Wiley.

Walker-Andrews, A. S. (1988). Infants' perception of the affordances of expressive behaviors. In C. Rovee-Collier & L. P. Lipsitt (Eds.), *Advances in infancy research* (Vol. 5, pp. 173–221). Westport, CT: Ablex.

Warneken, F. (2013). What do children and chimpanzees reveal about human altruism. In M. R. Banaji & S. A. Gelman (Eds.), *Navigating the social world* (pp. 393–399). New York: Oxford.

Warneken, F., & Tomasello, M. (2006). Altruistic helping in human infants and young chimpanzees. *Science, 311*(5765), 1301–1303. doi: 10.1126/science.1121448

Warneken, F., & Tomasello, M. (2007). Helping and cooperation at 14 months of age. *Infancy*, *11*, 271–294. doi: 10.1111/j.1532-7078.2007.tb00227.x

Warneken, F., & Tomasello, M. (2008). Extrinsic rewards undermine altruistic tendencies in 20-month-olds. *Developmental Psychology*, *44*, 1785–1788. doi: 10.1037/a0013860

Warneken, F., & Tomasello, M. (2009). Varieties of altruism in children and chimpanzees. *Trends in Cognitive Sciences*, *13*, 397–402.

Watson, A. C., Nixon, C. L., Wilson, A., & Capage, L. (1999). Social interaction skills and theory of mind in young children. *Developmental Psychology*, *35*, 386–391. doi: 10.1037/0012-1649.35.2.386

Watson, J. (1999). *Theory of mind and pretend play in family context.* Unpublished Ph.D. dissertation, University of Michigan, Ann Arbor.

Watson, J. K., Gelman, S. A., & Wellman, H. M. (1998). Young children's understanding of the non-physical nature of thoughts and the physical nature of the brain. *British Journal of Developmental Psychology*, *16*, 321–335.

Waytz, A., & Mitchell, J. P. (2011). Two mechanisms for simulating other minds: Dissociations between mirroring and self-projection. *Current Directions in Psychological Science*, *20*, 197–200. doi: 10.1177/0963721411409007

Wechsler, D. (1989). *Primary scale of intelligence-revised (WPPSI-R).* San Antonio, TX: The Psychological Corporation.

Wellman, H. M. (1990). *The child's theory of mind.* Cambridge, MA: MIT Press.

Wellman, H. M. (2011). Developing a theory of mind. In U. Goswami (Ed.), *The Blackwell handbook of childhood cognitive development* (2nd ed., pp. 258–284). New York: Blackwell.

Wellman, H. M. (2011). Reinvigorating explanations for the study of early cognitive development. *Child Development Perspectives*, *5*, 33–38.

Wellman, H. M. (2013). Universal social cognition: Childhood theory of mind. In M. Banaji & S. Gelman (Eds.), *Navigating the social world: A developmental perspective* (pp. 69–74). New York: Oxford University Press.

Wellman, H. M., & Banerjee, M. (1991). Mind and emotion: Children's understanding of the emotional consequences of beliefs and desires. *British Journal of Developmental Psychology*, *9*, 191–214.

Wellman, H. M., & Bartsch, K. (1988). Young children's reasoning about beliefs. *Cognition*, *30*, 239–277.

Wellman, H. M., Cross, D., & Bartsch, K. (1986). Infant search and object permanence: A meta-analysis of the a-not-b error. *Monographs of the Society for Research in Child Development*, *51*(3, Serial No. 214). doi: 10.2307/1166103

Wellman, H. M., Cross, D., & Watson, J. (2001). A meta-analysis of theory-of-mind development: The truth about false belief. *Child Development*, *72*, 655–684. doi: 10.1111/1467-8624.00304

Wellman, H. M., & Estes, D. (1986). Early understanding of mental entities: a reexamination of childhood realism. *Child Development*, *57*, 910–923.

Wellman, H. M., Fang, F., Liu, D., Zhu, L., & Liu, G. (2006). Scaling of theory-of-mind understandings in Chinese children. *Psychological Science*, *17*, 1075–1081. doi: 10.1111/j.1467-9280.2006.01830.x

Wellman, H. M., Fang, F., & Peterson, C. C. (2011). Sequential progressions in a theory of mind scale: Longitudinal perspectives. *Child Development*, *82*, 780–792. doi: 10.1111/j.1467-8624.2011.01583.x

Wellman, H. M., & Gelman, S. A. (1992). Cognitive development: Foundational theories of core domains. *Annual Review of Psychology, 43*, 337–375. doi: 10.1146/annurev.ps.43.020192.002005

Wellman, H. M., & Gelman, S. A. (1998). Knowledge acquisition in foundational domains. In D. Kuhn & R. Siegler (Eds.), *Handbook of child psychology: Vol. 2. Cognition, perception, and language* (5th ed., pp. 523–573). Editor-in-Chief: William Damon. New York: Wiley.

Wellman, H. M., Harris, P. L., Banerjee, M., & Sinclair, A. (1995). Early understanding of emotion: Evidence from natural language. *Cognition and Emotion, 9*, 117–149.

Wellman, H. M., & Hickling, A. K. (1994). The mind's "I": children's conception of the mind as an active agent. *Child Development, 65*, 1564–1580.

Wellman, H. M., Hollander, M., & Schult, C. A. (1996). Young children's understanding of thought bubbles and of thoughts. *Child Development, 67*, 768–788. doi: 10.1111/j.1467-8624.1996.tb01763.x

Wellman, H. M., & Johnson, C. N. (2008). Developing dualism: From intuitive understanding to transcendental ideas. In A. Antonietti, A. Corradini, & E. Lowe (Eds.), *Psychophysical dualism today: An interdisciplinary approach* (pp. 3–35). Lanham, MD: Lexington Books.

Wellman, H. M., Kushnir, T., & Xu, F. (2014). *Infants use statistical sampling to understand the psychological world.* Manuscript in preparation.

Wellman, H. M., & Liu, D. (2004). Scaling of theory-of-mind tasks. *Child Development, 75*, 523–541. doi: 10.1111/j.1467-8624.2004.00691.x

Wellman, H. M., Lopez-Duran, S., LaBounty, J., & Hamilton, B. (2008). Infant attention to intentional action predicts preschool theory of mind. *Developmental Psychology, 44*, 618–623. doi: 10.1037/0012-1649.44.2.618

Wellman, H. M., & Miller, J. G. (2008). Including deontic reasoning as fundamental to theory of mind. *Human Development, 51*, 105–135.

Wellman, H. M., & Peterson, C. C. (2013). Deafness, thought bubbles, and theory-of-mind development. *Developmental Psychology, 49*, 2357–2367. doi: 10.1037/a0032419

Wellman, H. M., Phillips, A. T., Dunphy-Lelii, S., & LaLonde, N. (2004). Infant social attention predicts preschool social cognition. *Developmental Science, 7*, 283–288.

Wellman, H. M., Phillips, A. T., & Rodriguez, T. (2000). Young children's understanding of perception, desire, and emotion. *Child Development, 71*, 895–912.

Wellman, H. M., & Woolley, J. D. (1990). From simple desires to ordinary beliefs: The early development of everyday psychology. *Cognition, 35*, 245–275.

Westermann, G., Mareschal, D., Johnson, M. H., Sirois, S., Spratling, M. W., & Thomas, M. S. C. (2007). Neuroconstructivism. *Developmental Science, 10*, 75–83. doi: 10.1111/j.1467-7687.2007.00567.x

Widen, S. C., & Russell, J. A. (2003). A closer look at preschoolers' freely produced labels for facial expressions. *Developmental Psychology, 39*, 114–128. doi: 10.1037/0012-1649.39.1.114

Wierzbicka, A. (1992). *Semantics, culture, and cognition: Universal human concepts in culture-specific configurations.* New York: Oxford University Press.

Wierzbicka, A. (1993). A conceptual basis for cultural psychology. *Ethos, 21*, 205–231. doi: 10.1525/eth.1993.21.2.02a00040

Williams, P. (with Tribe, A.). (2000). *Buddhist thought: A complete introduction to the Indian tradition.* London: Routledge.

Williamson, R. A., Meltzoff, A. N., & Markman, E. M. (2008). Prior experiences and perceived efficacy influence 3-year-olds' imitation. *Developmental Psychology, 44*, 275–285. doi: 10.1037/0012-1649.44.1.275

Winer, G. A., & Cottrell, J. E. (1996). Does anything leave the eye when we see? Extramission beliefs of children and adults. *Current Directions in Psychological Science, 5*, 137–142. doi: 10.1111/1467-8721.ep11512346

Winer, G. A., Cottrell, J. E., Gregg, V., Fournier, J. S., & Bica, L. A. (2002). Fundamentally misunderstanding visual perception: Adults' belief in visual emissions. *American Psychologist, 57*(6–7), 417–424. doi: 10.1037/0003-066x.57.6-7.417

Winer, G. A., Cottrell, J. E., Karefilaki, K. D., & Chronister, M. (1996). Conditions affecting beliefs about visual perceptions among children and adults. *Journal of Experimental Child Psychology, 61*, 93–115. doi: 10.1006/jecp.1996.0007

Woodward, A. L. (1998). Infants selectively encode the goal object of an actor's reach. *Cognition, 69*, 1–34. doi: http://dx.doi.org/10.1016/S0010-0277(98)00058-4

Woolley, J. D. (1995). Young children's understanding of fictional versus epistemic mental representations: Imagination and belief. *Child Development, 66*, 1011–1021. doi: 10.2307/1131795

Woolley, J. D. (1997). Thinking about fantasy: Are children fundamentally different thinkers and believers from adults? *Child Development, 68*, 991–1011. doi: 10.2307/1132282

Woolley, J. D., & Wellman, H. M. (1990). Young children's understanding of realities, nonrealities, and appearances. *Child Development, 61*, 946–961.

Woollett, K., Spiers, H. J., & Maguire, E. A. (2009). Talent in the taxi: A model system for exploring expertise. *Philosophical Transactions: Biological Sciences, 364*(1522), 1407–1416. doi: 10.2307/40485913

Wright, R. (2009). *The evolution of God.* New York: Little, Brown.

Wu, R., Gopnik, A., Richardson, D. C., & Kirkham, N. Z. (2011). Infants learn about objects from statistics and people. *Developmental Psychology, 47*, 1220–1229. doi: 10.1037/a0024023

Xu, F., Bao, X., Fu, G., Talwar, V., & Lee, K. (2010). Lying and truth-telling in children: From concept to action. *Child Development, 81*, 581–596. doi: 10.1111/j.1467-8624.2009.01417.x

Xu, F., Dewar, K., & Perfors, A. (2009). Induction, overhypotheses, and the shape bias: Some arguments and evidence for rational constructivism. In B. M. Hood & L. Santos (Eds.), *The origins of object knowledge* (pp. 263–284). Oxford, England: Oxford University Press.

Xu, F., & Garcia, V. (2008). Intuitive statistics by 8-month-old infants. *Proceedings of the National Academy of Sciences, 105*, 5012–5015. doi: 10.1073/pnas.0704450105

Yamaguchi, M., Kuhlmeier, V. A., Wynn, K., & vanMarle, K. (2009). Continuity in social cognition from infancy to childhood. *Developmental Science, 12*, 746–752. doi: 10.1111/j.1467-7687.2008.00813.x

Youngblade, L. M., & Dunn, J. (1995). Individual differences in young children's pretend play with mother and sibling: Links to relationships and understanding of other people's feelings and beliefs. *Child Development, 66*, 1472–1492. doi: 10.1111/j.1467-8624.1995.tb00946.x

Yuill, N. (1984). Young children's coordination of motive and outcome in judgements of satisfaction and morality. *British Journal of Developmental Psychology, 2*, 73–81. doi: 10.1111/j.2044-835X.1984.tb00536.x

Zajonc, R. B., & Mullally, P. R. (1997). Birth order: Reconciling conflicting effects. *American Psychologist, 52*, 685–699. doi: 10.1037/0003-066x.52.7.685

Zelazo, P. D., Carter, A., Reznick, J. S., & Frye, D. (1997). Early development of executive function: A problem-solving framework. *Review of General Psychology, 1,* 198–226. doi: 10.1037/1089-2680.1.2.198

Zelazo, P. D., & Müller, U. (2011). Executive function in typical and atypical development. In U. Goswami (Ed.), *The Wiley-Blackwell handbook of childhood cognitive development* (2nd ed., pp. 574–603): Malden, MA: Wiley-Blackwell.

Zelazo, P. D., Müller, U., Frye, D., & Marcovitch, S. (2003). The development of executive function in early childhood: I. The development of executive function. *Monographs of the Society for Research in Child Development, 68*(3, Serial No. 274), 11–27.

Abraham, A., 234
Agnetta, B., 212, 213
Akar, D., 164
Akhtar, N., 206
Amsterlaw, J., 41, 132, 133, 137, 138, 139
Anderson, D., 79, 163
Anderson, J. R., 244
Anderson, K. N., 283, 285
Andrews, G., 152
Apperly, I. A., 42, 83, 146, 150, 185, 186, 196, 207, 228, 235
Aquinas, T., 281
Ardino, V., 26, 67, 68, 147
Armatas, P., 278
Armstrong, K., 278
Aschersleben, G., 27, 195
Aslin, R. N., 127, 181
Asscher, J. J., 48
Astington, J. W., 24, 25, 26, 38, 58, 59, 60, 61, 86, 106, 157, 160, 165, 189, 254
Astuti, R., 283, 284
Atran, S., 202, 274, 276, 277
Augustine, 281

Baetens, K., 243, 245
Bailey, A. J., 228

Baillargeon, R., 26, 147, 171, 172, 173, 174–75, 176, 177, 179, 181, 182, 184, 189, 190, 191, 192, 193, 194, 196, 205, 232
Baird, J. A., 20, 26, 160, 165
Baker, B. M., 106, 254
Balaraman, G., 58
Baldwin, D. A., 20, 21, 89, 177, 260
Banaji, M. R., 153, 202, 245
Banerjee, M., 45, 72, 77
Banerjee, R., 61
Bao, X., 66
Barnes, J. L., 215
Baron-Cohen, S., 28, 29, 156, 229
Barresi, J., 58
Barrett, H. C., 201, 283
Barrett, J. L., 31, 273, 274, 275, 276, 278, 279, 281
Barrett, L., 210
Barrett, L. F., 114
Bartsch, K., 2, 25, 26, 33, 68, 69, 71, 72, 74, 77, 78, 79, 80, 89, 91, 92, 99, 128, 161, 162, 180, 275
Bates, E., 220
Bates, J. E., 224
Bauer, P. J., 30, 255, 289
Baumard, N., 266
Bayes, T., 11, 12, 15
Beck, D. M., 149

Bedny, M., 239, 293, 294
Beeghly, M., 84
Behne, T., 18, 19, 90, 215, 283
Behrend, D. A., 259
Bekkering, H., 256
Belyaev, D. K., 223, 224
Ben-Eliyahu, A., 58–59
Benigni, L., 220
Bergstrom, B., 277
Bering, J. M., 282, 284
Berridge, D. M., 25
Bica, L. A., 292
Birch, S. A. J., 147, 259
Bird, G., 243
Bíró, S., 17
Bjorklund, D. F., 19, 282
Blair, C., 59, 61, 63, 147
Blakeslee, S., 241, 242
Bloom, L., 43, 44
Bloom, P., 90, 147, 199, 202, 203, 259, 284
Bluck, S., 289
Boesch, C., 219
Boesch, H., 219
Boldt, B. R., 290
Bonawitz, E. B., 130, 131, 250, 253, 255, 256, 257, 258
Bond, C. F., 294, 295
Bornstein, M. H., 195
Bowden, D., 152
Bowman, L. C., 236, 240
Boyer, P., 266, 273, 274, 277
Bradley, L., 107
Brandone, A. C., 17, 19
Breinlinger, K., 118
Brenneman, K., 86
Bretherton, I., 84, 220
Brewer, W. F., 136, 291
Brockbank, M., 17
Brooks, R., 21, 87
Brophy, M., 164, 165, 254
Brown, E., 48
Brown, J., 44, 225, 254
Brown, J. R., 100
Brown, K., 25–26
Brown, P. M., 106
Brownell, H., 41
Bruner, J., 250, 288
Bryant, D., 163
Bryant, P., 189

Bryant, P. E., 107
Bryson, S. E., 62
Buchsbaum, D., 256
Bull, R., 64
Bunch, K. M., 152
Buttelmann, D., 181, 182, 183, 184
Butterfill, S. A., 42, 235
Butterworth, G., 86

Caldi, S., 26
Call, J., 38, 212, 213, 215, 216–17, 219, 222
Callanan, M., 42, 43, 254
Camaioni, L., 220
Campbell, J., 273
Campbell, M. D., 26
Capage, L., 26
Caputi, M., 61
Carey, S., 8, 9, 10, 119, 122, 154, 199, 200, 282, 291
Carlson, S. M., 25, 48, 62, 63, 86, 106, 146, 147, 148, 149, 232, 253
Carpendale, J. I. M., 7, 269, 277
Carpenter, M., 19, 38, 176, 181, 215, 217, 220
Carriger, M. S., 195
Carrington, S. J., 228
Carruthers, P., 4, 5, 7
Carter, A., 146
Cartwright, B. S., 48
Casey, B. J., 238
Cassidy, K. W., 25, 58, 60, 77, 81, 148
Catmur, C., 243
Champion, C., 60
Champion, H., 260
Chandler, M. J., 26, 59, 67, 88, 269
Chao, R. K., 101
Chater, N., 119, 120
Chen, E. C., 290
Chen, E. E., 115
Chen, X., 101, 115
Chen, Z., 251
Cheung, H., 162
Cheung, K. M., 98
Chevallier, C., 181, 256
Chi, M. T. H., 155
Child Language Data Exchange System (CHILDES), 42
Chomsky, N., 12
Chouinard, M. M., 254
Chronister, M., 291
Churchland, P. M., 87

Clark, H., 164, 283
Clark, M. A., 20
Clément, F., 259
Clements, W. A., 25
Cohen, L. B., 181
Cook, C., 250, 251
Cook, R., 243
Cook, S., 278
Coon, J. A., 77
Corkum, V., 21
Corliss, R., 33
Corriveau, K. H., 259, 270, 271
Cosmides, L., 153, 160, 218
Cottrell, J. E., 291, 292
Courtin, C., 165
Croft, K., 84
Cross, D., 23, 24, 180
Crowe, E., 25
Csányi, V., 222
Csibra, G., 17, 19, 153, 170, 181, 193, 255, 256
Custer, W., 50, 51
Cutillo, B. A., 237
Cutting, A. L., 60, 156, 157

Dack, L. A., 24
Damon, W., 289
D'Andrade, R., 5, 24
Darwin, C., 204, 273
Daughtry, D., 278
Davidson, D., 42, 87
Davidson, D. H., 99
Dawin, C., 204, 273
Deák, G. O., 86
Deleau, M., 165
Dempster, F. N., 147
Dennis, M. J., 58
DePaulo, B. M., 294, 295
de Rosnay, M., 112
DeVet, K., 59
deVilliers, J. G., 29, 161, 162, 165
deVilliers, P. A., 29, 161, 162, 165
de Waal, F. B. M., 210
Dewar, K., 118
Diesendruck, G., 58, 59, 164
Dodell-Feder, D., 239
Donelan-McCall, N., 100
Dong, Q., 101
Drew, UU, 216
Driesenga, A., 31

Duke, S., 48
Dunbar, R. I. M., 209, 210, 218, 219, 246, 287
Dunlop, W. L., 289
Dunn, J., 25, 26, 44, 60, 61, 90, 100, 106, 157, 164, 165, 225, 254
Dunphy-Lelii, S., 21, 195
Dupoux, E., 201
Dyer, J. R., 52–53
Dyer-Seymour, J. R., 53

Eberhardt, F., 250, 252
Eddy, T. J., 210, 211, 216, 219, 222
Eggum, N., 60
Egyed, K., 75, 217
Einstein, A., 158–59
Eisenberg, N., 60
Ekman, P., 295
Ekstrom, A. D., 242
Elman, J. L., 9, 118
Endress, A. D., 176
Ensor, R., 63
Erisir, A., 246
Estes, D., 24, 30, 48, 50, 69
Evans, E. M., 204, 275, 277, 278, 279, 280, 283
Everett, B. A., 84
Evraire, L. E., 236

Fabbri-Destro, M., 242, 243
Fabricius, W. V., 193
Fadiga, L., 215, 241
Fajans, J., 109
Fang, F., 27, 103
Fernyhough, C., 81
Ferres, L. A., 79
Fineberg, D. S., 25
Fischer, A., 131
Fischer, J., 222
Fivush, R., 289
Flavell, E. R., 21, 24, 30, 84, 85, 149, 161, 269, 296
Flavell, J. H., 21, 24, 30, 44, 52, 77, 83, 84, 85, 86, 149, 161, 186, 188, 189, 269, 296
Flombaum, J. I., 216
Flynn, E., 137
Fodor, J. A., 24, 153, 154
Fogassi, L., 241
Fournier, J. S., 292
Frank, M. C., 256
Frazier, B., 43

Freeman, N. H., 25
Fried, I., 242
Friedman, N. P., 146
Friedman, O., 41, 148
Friedman, S. L., 51
Frith, U., 29
Frye, D., 146, 151
Fu, G., 66
Fuligni, A. J., 100
Fung, H., 289, 290
Fung, H. H., 115
Furrow, D., 163

Gale, E., 29
Gallese, V., 155, 215, 241, 242, 243
Garcia, V., 127
Gardiner, A. K., 19
Gardner, A., 210
Gardner, B., 210
Garfield, J. L., 7
Garon, N., 62
Gehring, W. J., 41, 229, 235
Gelman, S. A., 10, 24, 43, 49, 119, 122, 130, 133, 141,
    153, 154, 171, 197, 202, 252, 259, 261, 262, 271, 285
Gergely, G., 17, 19, 75, 153, 170, 217, 255, 256
German, T. P., 173
Giedd, J. N., 238
Gilby, I. C., 219
Giménez, M., 282, 284
Giménez-Dasí, M., 276, 279, 282
Gleitman, L. R., 292, 293
Global Deception Research Team, 295, 296
Glymour, C., 119, 120, 122
Godard, J., 33
Goddu, A., 216
Goetz, P. J., 39
Gold, E. M., 121
Goldman, A. I., 59, 155, 242
Goldman, M., 59
Goldner, I., 60
Golinkoff, R. M., 250
Gómez, R. L., 127
Goodall, J., 210
Goodman, N., 12, 133
Goodman, N. D., 133, 136, 141, 250, 256
Goodnow, J., 100
Gopnik, A., 2, 3, 8, 38, 50, 75, 82, 84, 86, 88, 113,
    118, 119, 120, 122, 124, 125, 127, 128, 130, 149,
    154, 176, 256, 258

Gorsuch, R. L., 278
Gottfried, G. M., 51, 271, 272
Green, F. L., 24, 30, 85, 149
Greene, R. A., 279
Greenfield, P. M., 100
Gregg, V., 292
Greif, M. L., 19
Griffin, R., 41
Griffiths, T. L., 12, 118, 119, 130, 131, 133, 135, 256
Gross, D., 51
Grossman, J. B., 30
Grusec, J. E., 100, 101
Guerrero, S., 276
Guttman, L., 97
Gweon, H., 239, 240, 241

Haberl, K., 21, 22, 176
Habermas, T., 289
Haden, C. A., 289
Hadwin, J., 46, 52, 77
Haider, H., 162
Haker, H., 244
Halford, G. S., 152
Hallinan, E. V., 19, 20
Hamilton, A. F., 243
Hamilton, B., 94
Hamlin, J. K., 19, 20, 202, 203, 221
Hansen, M. B., 86
Happé, F. G. E., 29, 146
Hare, B., 212, 213, 214, 215, 216, 219, 220, 222,
    223, 225
Harkness, K. L., 229
Harman, G., 202
Harmer, S., 48
Harris, M., 165
Harris, P. L., 24, 30, 48, 50, 64, 65, 66, 72, 106,
    112, 114, 153, 155, 157, 158, 165, 166, 221, 222,
    253, 256, 259, 260, 262, 267, 268, 270, 271,
    276, 277, 282, 283, 284
Hart, D., 289
Hartwig, M., 295
Hasegawa, T., 244
Hatano, G., 44, 45, 136
Hauenstein, A., 278
Hauser, M., 202
Haviland, J. M., 114
He, Z., 172, 175
Henzi, P., 210
Herrero, C., 295

Herrmann, P. A., 256
Herwig, U., 244
Heyes, C., 243
Hickling, A. K., 42, 43, 44, 51, 72, 89, 105, 198,
    254, 269, 270
Hickok, G., 243
Higginbotham, D. J., 106, 254
Hirschfeld, L. A., 153, 202
Hirsh-Pasek, K., 250
Hofer, T., 27, 195
Hoffmeister, R., 165
Hollander, M., 52, 53
Hood, L., 43, 44
Horner, V., 256
Howe, N., 25, 254
Hughes, C., 61, 63, 156, 157
Humphrey, N., 209
Huttenlocher, J., 80

Iacoboni, M., 242
Imrisek, S., 146
Inagaki, K., 44–45, 136
Ingram, D., 43
Ito, J. M. B., 236
Izard, C. E., 114

Jaakkola, R., 282
Jacobson, K., 118
James, W., 30
Jarrett, N., 86
Jarrold, C., 147
Jaswal, V. K., 259, 260
Jenkins, J. M., 25, 26, 58, 60, 106, 157, 254
Jiang, Y. V., 232
Joffe, T. H., 219
Johnson, C. N., 30, 270, 271, 284, 285
Johnson, M., 272
Johnson, S. C., 267
Johnson, S. P., 127
Johnston, J. R., 100
Jones, T., 152
Joseph, R. M., 77, 187
Jovanovic, B., 195

Kagan, J., 224
Kahneman, D., 185
Kalish, C., 202
Kaminski, J., 216, 222
Kanwisher, N., 229, 233

Kaplan, J., 242
Karefilaki, K. D., 291
Karmiloff-Smith, A., 154, 208
Kavanaugh, R. D., 253
Kawohl, W., 244
Keenan, T. R., 46
Keil, F. C., 133, 141, 256, 281
Keller, H., 100
Kemp, C., 118, 119, 133, 136, 141
Kessel, F. S., 52
Kessen, W., 99
Keysers, C., 242
Khalil, S. L., 193
Kinzler, K. D., 5, 8, 118, 197, 198, 199, 201, 202,
    203, 204, 217, 239, 242
Király, I., 75, 217, 256
Kirkham, N. Z., 127
Kitayama, S., 98
Klahr, D., 251
Knafo, A., 60
Knight, N., 276, 279
Knobe, J. M., 42
Knutson, B., 115
Kochanska, G., 59
Koenig, M. A., 259, 260, 267, 277
Konno, A., 244
Koops, W., 77
Koós, O., 17
Kovács, Á. M., 176, 177
Krachun, C., 38, 217
Kristen, S., 27, 95, 196
Kuhl, P. K., 2, 3
Kuhlmeier, V., 90
Kuhlmeier, V. A., 196, 199
Kuhn, T. S., 9, 10, 133, 251
Kumar, V., 278
Kunkel, M. A., 278
Kushnir, T., 128, 130, 206, 262
Kyriakidou, C., 25

LaBounty, J., 58, 59, 60, 63, 94
Lagattuta, K. H., 25, 26, 44, 46, 47, 82, 113, 225, 269
Lakatos, I., 10
Lakoff, G., 272
Lalonde, C. E., 26, 59, 67
Lalonde, N., 195
Landau, B., 292, 293
Lane, J. D., 221, 222, 225, 259, 261, 277, 278, 279,
    280, 283

Laudan, L., 10, 133
Lecce, S., 61
Lee, K., 65, 66, 98, 146, 163
Leekam, S. R., 28
Legare, C. H., 252, 253, 256
Lelwica, M., 114
Lempers, J. D., 21
Leslie, A. M., 5, 7, 8, 28, 29, 146, 148, 154, 155,
    156, 160, 166, 167, 172, 173, 194, 200, 205, 207,
    232, 235
Levine, L. J., 77
LeVine, S., 109
Lewis, C., 7, 25, 148, 165, 178, 191, 192, 277
Lewis, M., 64, 148, 178
Li, J., 98, 99, 100, 109
Lieven, E. V. M., 43
Liew, J., 60
Lillard, A. S., 77, 109, 246, 250, 253, 269
Lin, S., 290
Liszkowski, U., 220
Liu, D., 23, 24, 27, 30, 37, 39, 40, 41, 76, 81, 89,
    93, 94, 95, 97, 99, 106, 111, 132, 136, 148, 149,
    158, 164, 229, 233, 234, 235, 238, 240, 241
Liu, G., 27
Lohmann, H., 138, 157, 166
London, K., 26, 69
Lopez-Duran, S., 94
Louie, J. Y., 115
Low, J., 186, 187, 188
Luo, Y., 147, 173, 194, 205, 232
Lyons, D. E., 256

Ma, L., 128
Mack, P. B., 236
Macomber, J., 118
Macrae, C. N., 245
MacWhinney, B., 42
Maguire, E. A., 124
Mahajan, N., 215
Maher, M., 270
Main, R. M., 72
Makris, N., 276, 279
Malle, B. F., 42, 45
Malone, L. S., 260
Mandell, D. J., 147
Marcovitch, S., 151
Maridaki-Kassotaki, K., 25
Markman, E. M., 86, 256
Marks, A., 63

Markus, H. R., 98
Marr, D., 154
Marriott, C., 48
Marschark, M., 102, 165, 206
Marticorena, D. C., 216
Martinez-Beck, I., 164
Masangkay, Z. S., 84, 85
Mascaro, O., 261
Masip, J., 295
Matsuzawa, T., 220
Maynard, A., 100
McAdams, D. P., 289
McAlister, A., 146
McCall, R. B., 195
McCarthy, G., 236
McCauley, R. N., 273
McFadden, S. H., 278
McGillicuddy-DeLisi, A. V., 100
McMahon, W. M., 29
McNeil, E., 1
Meinhardt, J., 241
Meins, E., 81, 206
Melis, A. P., 220
Melot, A. M., 165
Meltzoff, A. N., 2, 3, 19, 21, 82, 84, 86, 87, 89,
    128, 200, 233, 234, 235, 240, 255, 256, 258
Meno, P., 244
Meristo, M., 206
Meshel, D. S., 278
Miklósi, A., 222
Miller, J. G., 202, 203
Miller, P. H., 52
Miller, P. J., 289, 290
Milligan, K., 24, 37, 160
Mintz, J., 289
Mitchell, J. P., 234, 245
Mitchell, P., 53, 147, 260
Miyake, A., 146
Miyamoto, R. T., 104
Moehlmann, B., 277
Moeller, M. P., 102, 165, 206
Moll, H., 21, 84, 86, 176, 178
Montessori, M., 250
Moor, B. G., 238
Moore, C., 21, 58, 69, 163, 220, 260
Morgan, G., 104
Mosconi, M. W., 236
Moses, L. J., 21, 62, 63, 77, 86, 88, 89, 146, 147,
    148, 149, 232

Moulson, M. C., 229
Mukamel, R., 242
Mukerji, C., 216
Mullally, P. R., 146
Müller, U., 62, 146, 151
Munro, D. J., 98, 100
Murray, K., 59

Nádasdy, Z., 17
Naito, M., 25
Neely, L. A., 259
Nelson, S. E., 42
Neumann, A., 185, 206
Newport, E. L., 104, 127
Newton, P., 64, 65
Nisbett, R. E., 39, 98, 100, 290, 291, 294, 295
Nixon, C. L., 26
Niyogi, S., 12
Noffke, J. L., 278
Notaro, P. C., 130
Nunez, P. L., 237
Nussbaum, J., 278

Oakes, L., 42, 43, 254
Oaksford, M., 120
Oh, S., 148
Ohnishi, T. C. A., 236, 244
Olineck, K. M., 19
Olsen, B., 89
Olson, D. R., 98
Olson, S. L., 225
O'Malley, C., 137
O'Neill, D. K., 72, 178, 180, 189
Onishi, K. H., 26, 171, 172, 179, 182, 184, 189,
   191, 193, 196
Oomen, A., 77
Opfer, J. E., 171
Ozonoff, S., 29

Packer, J. I., 279
Pagnin, A., 61
Palfai, T., 146
Pang, K., 149
Parkin, L., 25
Parsons, S., 53
Partington, A., 13, 93
Pascual-Marqui, R. D., 231
Pasquini, E. S., 48, 259, 270, 271
Paterson, M. M., 106

Pearl, J., 122
Pelphrey, K. A., 236, 237
Perfors, A., 118, 119, 136
Perkins, A., 25
Perkins, C., 176
Perner, J., 25, 28, 46, 50, 52, 77, 100, 146, 151, 152,
   162, 165, 176, 184
Perry, T., 7
Perst, H., 196
Peskin, J., 26, 67, 68, 147
Peterson, C. C., 7, 24, 25, 26, 27, 29, 51, 53, 69, 95,
   100, 102, 103, 105, 106, 140, 146, 147, 166, 293
Peterson, J. L., 293
Peterson, N. R., 104
Petrakos, H., 25
Pfeifer, J. H., 240
Phillips, A. T., 17, 84, 195
Phillips, S., 152
Phillips, W., 215
Piaget, J., 9, 11, 12, 47, 48, 49, 64, 92, 117, 118,
   121, 133, 142, 177, 250, 267, 274, 291
Pickover, C. A., 273
Pidada, S. U., 60
Pine, J. M., 43
Pinker, S., 118, 121
Pisoni, D. B., 104
Pnevmatikos, D., 276, 279
Polak, A., 64, 65, 66
Polizzi, P., 147, 148, 173
Pons, F., 48, 112, 113, 114
Potel, D., 147
Poulin-Dubois, D., 19, 184
Povinelli, D. J., 210, 211, 212, 213, 214, 216, 219,
   222, 293
Powell, L. J., 233
Pratt, C., 189
Premack, D., 9, 45
Prescott, S. J., 106
Press, C., 243
Preuss, T. M., 211
Price, M., 101
Pritchard, M., 58
Provine, R. R., 244
Putnam, S. P., 59
Pyers, J. E., 29, 105, 161
Pyysiäinen, I., 278

Rakoczy, H., 77, 81, 234
Randell, A. C., 100

Rasch, G., 97
Ray, S. D., 86
Razza, R. A., 59, 61, 63, 147
Reddy, V., 64, 90
Reilly, J., 79, 163
Repacholi, B, 75, 88, 89, 113, 128, 149, 176
Reznick, J. S., 146
Rhodes, M., 139
Richardson, D. C., 127
Richert, R. A., 24, 30, 31, 270, 275, 276, 278, 279, 284
Rickards, F. W., 106
Rieffe, C. J., 77
Rinaldi, C. M., 25
Rivas, E., 220
Rizzolatti, G., 241, 242, 243
Roben, C. K. P., 201
Robin, J. E., 155
Robinson, E. J., 260
Rochat, M. J., 215
Rodriguez, T., 84
Romero, T., 244
Rosati, A. G., 215, 216
Rosen, C. S., 157
Rosengren, K. S., 283, 285
Rosicky, J. G., 89
Rössler, W., 244
Rothbart, M. K., 224
Rothmayr, C., 232, 234
Rourke, M., 58
Rowland, C. F., 43
Rudy, D., 100, 101
Ruffman, T., 25, 26, 41, 46, 72, 74, 79, 80, 81, 162, 165, 176, 184, 277
Ruiz, A. M., 216
Russell, B., 294
Russell, J. A., 114, 147
Ryle, G., 73

Sabbagh, M. A., 23, 24, 40, 41, 132, 146, 148, 229, 235, 236, 237, 238, 240, 241, 246, 260
Saffran, J. R., 127
Saito, M. T., 53
Santos, L. R., 215, 216, 256
Saxe, R., 199, 200, 229, 232, 233, 237, 239, 240, 241, 293, 294
Saylor, M. M., 20
Schaefer, C. M., 149
Scheines, R., 122, 250, 252

Schick, B., 102, 165, 206
Scholl, B. J., 5, 7, 8, 9, 154, 160, 235
Scholz, J., 237
Schubotz, R. I., 234
Schult, C. A., 24, 44, 52, 53, 90, 133, 198
Schultz, J., 271
Schulz, L. E., 130, 131, 232, 240, 250, 253
Schwebel, D. C., 157, 254
Scofield, J., 259
Scott, R. M., 26, 171, 172, 174–75, 176, 179, 181, 182, 184, 190, 192, 193, 194
Searle, J. R., 88
Senghas, A., 105
Senju, A., 193
Serra, E., 215
Shafto, P., 256
Shahaeian, A., 27, 100, 101
Sharifzadeh, V., 101
Shatz, M., 52, 53, 164
Shepard-Kegl, J., 104
Shutts, K., 201
Shweder, R. A., 277
Siegal, M., 24, 29, 102, 104
Siegler, R. S., 131, 137
Sigel, I. E., 100
Sigman, M. D., 195
Simons, D. J., 133, 141
Sinclair, A., 72
Singer, J. L., 157
Skuse, D. H., 156
Slade, L., 25, 162
Slaughter, V., 26, 27, 50, 58, 59, 69, 82, 84, 100, 149, 166, 281, 282
Slemmer, J. A., 127
Smiley, P., 80
Smith, I. M., 62
Smith, L. B., 9, 118
Smith, P. K., 61
Snidman, N. C., 224
Snow, C., 42
Sobel, D. M., 130
Sodian, B., 27, 65, 185, 189, 190, 191, 192, 196, 206
Sommer, M., 229, 239, 240, 241
Soproni, K., 222
Sousa, P., 276
South, M., 29
Southgate, V., 181, 185, 193, 206, 243, 256

Spelke, E., 4, 5, 8, 9, 118, 141, 177, 196, 197, 198, 199, 200, 201, 202, 203, 204, 205, 207, 217, 239, 242
Spencer, P., 165
Sperber, D., 26, 261, 266, 273, 277
Spiers, H. J., 124
Spilka, B., 278
Spirtes, P., 122
Sprung, M., 77, 162
Stack, J., 178, 191, 192
Stanger, C., 64
Stegge, H., 77
Stein, N. L., 77
Steinbach, T., 16
Steinberg, T., 60
Stevenson, H. W., 100
Stevenson, M. B., 51
Stich, S. P., 5
Stouthamer-Loebel, M., 64
Striano, T., 220
Sullivan, K., 152
Sullivan, M. W., 89
Surian, L., 26, 193
Sutton, J., 61
Swettenham, J., 61

Tager-Flusberg, H., 77, 152
Táglás, E., 176
Talwar, V., 65, 66
Tardif, T., 23, 24, 40, 79, 98, 99, 162, 163, 189
Taumoepeau, M., 81, 176
Taylor, M., 25, 48, 106, 253
Tenenbaum, J. B., 12, 118, 120, 130, 133, 135, 136
Termine, N. T., 114
Terwogt, M., 77
Thaiss, L., 28
Theakston, A. L., 43
Thelen, E., 9, 118
Thoermer, C., 27, 185, 189, 190, 191, 192, 196, 206
Thomas, K. M., 238
Thompson, C., 58
Thompson, R. L., 272
Tidball, G., 89
Tobin, J. J., 99
Tomasello, M., 21, 38, 77, 138, 157, 166, 176, 181, 182, 191, 210, 212, 213, 215, 216, 217, 218, 219, 220, 221, 222, 225, 256
Tooby, J., 153, 160, 218
Topál, J., 222

Torrance, N., 98
Toulmin, S., 124
Tresniowski, A., 1
Tsai, J. L., 114, 115
Tyack, D., 43
Tzelnic, T., 199, 200

Uchida, Y., 115
Ueno, A., 220
Ullman, T. D., 136

Vaccari, C., 102, 165, 206
vanMarle, K., 196
Van Overwalle, F., 243, 245
Varley, R., 104
Vauthier, S. A., 259
Vigliocco, G., 272
Vinson, D. P., 272
Volterra, V., 220
von Cramon, 234
Vosniadou, S., 136, 291
Vuori, M., 196

Wade, C. E., 69
Waismeyer, A., 258
Walker, L. J., 289
Walker-Andrews, A. S., 114
Wang, S.-H., 177
Warneken, F., 77, 182, 220, 221
Watson, A. C., 26, 58
Watson, J. K., 23, 24, 41, 49
Watts, J., 186, 187, 188
Waytz, A., 245
Webb, J., 293
Wechsler, D., 224
Wellman, H. M., 2, 3, 5, 8, 10, 17, 19, 21, 23, 24, 25, 26, 27, 30, 33, 34, 36, 37, 38, 40, 41, 42, 43, 44, 45, 46, 48, 50, 51, 52, 53, 71, 72, 74, 76, 77, 78, 79, 80, 81, 82, 83, 84, 86, 89, 90, 92, 93, 94, 95, 97, 98, 99, 100, 101, 102, 103, 105, 106, 111, 113, 118, 119, 120, 122, 124, 128, 132, 133, 136, 137, 138, 139, 140, 141, 149, 153, 154, 158, 161, 162, 163, 164, 165, 166, 167, 180, 195, 196, 197, 198, 202, 203, 223, 224, 225, 233, 234, 235, 254, 256, 262, 269, 270, 271, 275, 277, 278, 279, 280, 284, 285, 291, 297
Werner, R. S., 58
Werning, M., 234
Westermann, G., 235

Wexler, A., 233
Whitehouse, H., 256, 273
Whiten, A., 256
Whitfield-Gabrieli, S., 237
Whittall, S., 48
Widen, S. C., 114
Wierzbicka, A., 163, 272
Williams, L., 147
Williams, P., 296
Williamson, R. A., 256
Wilson, A., 26
Wilson, E. O., 297
Wilson, T. D., 290, 291, 294, 295
Wilson, W. H., 152
Wimmer, H., 151, 152
Winer, G. A., 291, 292
Winner, E., 41
Woll, B., 272
Wolpe, P., 16
Wong, M. Y. A., 100
Wood, D, 137
Woodruff, G., 9, 45
Woodward, A. L., 17, 20, 200
Woollett, K., 124

Woolley, J. D., 48, 50, 76, 77, 83, 89, 113
Wright, R., 285
Wu, D. Y. H., 99
Wu, F., 127
Wu, R., 127
Wusinich, N., 77
Wynn, K., 90, 196, 199, 202, 203

Xu, F., 66, 118, 127, 128, 146

Yamaguchi, M., 196, 215
Youngblade, L. M., 25, 106, 157, 254
Yuill, N., 52

Zaitchik, D., 152
Zajonc, R. B., 146
Zauner, P., 77, 162
Zelazo, P. D., 62, 146, 151
Zhou, H., 101
Zhou, Q., 60
Zhu, L., 27, 283
Ziemski, R. A., 72
Zimmerman, M. A., 130
Zubernis, L. S., 58

SUBJECT INDEX

Note: Page references followed by an italicized *f* indicate a figure on the page; page references followed by "n" with a number indicate a numbered note on the page.

abstraction, 141–42
abstract knowledge, 133
accommodation, 117
acquaintance, knowledge by, 294
acquiring, sharing and helping *versus*, 219–21
action experiences, 11
actions
  biologically caused, 44
  causal, 253
  desires and, 186
  experience, 11
  explaining, 44–45
  goal directedness of, 17–18, 215, 236, 288
  help-hurt features of, 203, 220
  imitation, 19
  intentional, 17–20, 44, 170, 179, 195–96, 215
  landscape of, 288
  mirror neurons, and, 242, 244
  mistaken, 44
  physically caused, 44
  predictions of, 45
  social, 57–58, 60
  sociomoral, 202
  voluntary, 203, 270

active-interactive infant paradigms, 18, 181–82
Actual Minds, Possible Worlds (Bruner), 288–89
adults
  blindness in, 293
  constructions, 290–95
  errors, 290–95
  extraordinary agents and, 265
  intentional agents and, 198
  lie detection, 294–95
  philosophical theory in, 286
affect, ideal, 114–15
afterlife, 281–85
agency
  goal-directed, 171
  intentional, 17, 172
agents
  attention to, 170–71, 225
  causal, 200–201
  core knowledge systems and, 197
  extraordinary, 265
  human, 199
  intentional, 17, 198, 201, 242, 257
  objects *versus*, 198–200

agents (*Cont.*)
  social partners *versus*, 201–3
  understanding, 17, 173, 217
alpha coherence, 237
analysis
  behavioral-genetic twin, 157
  cognitive, 5
  Guttman scale, 96
  individual differences, 26, 63
  levels of, 110
  linguistic-philosophical, 98–99
  Rasch, 97
  scaling, 93–97, 103, 107
  source localization, 231
  spectral power, 230
animacy, 171
anthropomorphism hypothesis, 274–76, 279
anticipatory looking, 185–87, 205–6
appearance-reality tasks, 85–86
artificial intelligence, 119–20
assimilation, 117
associationist structures, 119
astronomy, 154
attention
  to agents, 170–71
  to intentional actions, 195–96
  to perceptual-object displays, 195
  to physical-action displays, 196
  shifting, 62
  understanding states of, 20, 171, 215–16
Australia, 99–100
autism, 7
  childhood deafness and, 28–29
  executive functioning and, 29
  false-belief tasks and, 28–29
  false-belief understandings and, 101–2
  IQ and, 146
  IQ deficits and, 29
  mirror neurons and, 242–43
  theory-of-mind hypothesis for, 28
autobiographical memories, 289
awareness
  desire, 179–84
  tracking, 176–79

BA. *See* Brodmann's area
The Babies, 169
Baining, 109
Bayesian computational learning, 12, 119–21
Bayesian modeling, 133–34

Bayes nets. *See* causal Bayes nets
Bayes' rule, 11–12, 120, 122
begging gestures, 211–12
behavioral-genetic twin analyses, 157
behavioral regularities, 212
behavioral rules, 176
Beijing, 39
belief-desire progressions, 233–35
belief-desire psychology, 10, 33–35
  prediction of actions and, 45
belief-desire reasoning
  desire-awareness reasoning and, 185
  false belief within, 22–26
  of infants, 22–26
  preschoolers and, 185
  simplified scheme for, 34f
belief-desire understanding, 287
belief induction trials, 174–75, 174f
beliefs, 35f
  changes, in children, 38
  conflicts of, 91–92
  constraints of, 275
  conversations about, 80–81
  desires compared to, 81–82
  epidemiology of, 273
  false beliefs and, 35–41
  imagination and, 50
  interconnected with desires, 87–88
  references to, 78, 79f
  sensitivity to, 260–62
  understanding of, 6, 83f
bilingual children, 39
biographies, 289–90
biologically caused actions, 44
blicket detectors, 126–27, 126f, 130, 262
blindfolds, 21, 86–87
blindness, 292–94
blood-oxygen-level-dependent (BOLD)
  signal, 228–30
bodily behaviors, 266
BOLD signal. *See*
  blood-oxygen-level-dependent signal
bottom-up project, 118
brain
  function, 272
  ideas about, 268–72
  mind and, 270–72
  mind/brain understanding and, 30, 270–72
  mirror neurons and, 242–244
  neocortex of, 219

neural regions of, 229f
systems, 227–28
transplants, 271–72
volumes, 210
breadth, of knowledge, 279–80
broccoli-crackers study, 75–76, 176
Brodmann's area (BA), 243–44
Buddhism, 278, 295–97
Buddhist Thought: A Compete Introduction to the Indian Tradition (Williams), 296
bullying, 61

causal Bayes nets, 122–24, 123f
    of behavioral events, 134f
    hierarchical, 132–36
    learning and, 124–25
causal-explanatory frameworks, 154
causal graphical models, 122, 123f
causal maps, 124
causal questions, of children, 42–43
causal regularities, 258
causal relations, 130
causal specifics, 10
causal structures, 132–33
    exploration and, 250–51
    generalizations of, 133
CCC theory. *See* cognitive complexity and control theory
celestial mechanics, 10
"Cells that Read Minds" (Blakeslee), 241–42
CHILDES database, 42
child favorability bias, 290
childhood intuitive theory, 274
childhood realism, 47
children, 2
    active learning and, 249
    appearance-reality tasks and, 85–86
    belief changes in, 38
    bilingual, 39
    causal questions of, 42–43
    constrained variability and, 111
    empirical importance of explanations and, 42–44
    explaining mental states, 45–46
    frequency of explanations and, 42–44
    inner speech and, 30
    mind and brain and, 270–71
    neural correlates of development in, 236–38
    omniscience of God and, 279
    pedagogy and, 255–56
    progressive learning in, 136–37

psychophysical dualism and, 47–48
references to mental states by, 80
simulation theory and, 157–59
social learning and, 249
soul and, 284–85
subjective desires and, 76–77
subjective thought and, 30
theory-based Bayesian learning in, 126–31
theory theory and, 125–26
thought bubbles and, 51–54
trust of, 261
understanding of thinking, 29–30
The Child's Conception of the World (Piaget), 291
The Child's Theory of Mind (Wellman), 3, 297
chimpanzees, 210
    communication between, 220–21
    enculturated, 218
    food competition among, 213–14, 213f
    helping by, 221
    knowledge and, 216
    perception and, 211–12
    sharing by, 219–20
China
    collectivist culture in, 100–101
    conversations about desires in, 79
    cultural differences with, 100
    epistemology in, 98–99
    false beliefs in, 39
    ideal affect and, 114–15
    regulation in, 114
    ToM Scale in, 99–101
Chinese languages, 98
    complements and, 162
    semantics and, 163–64
Chinese understandings, 109
Christianity, 278
chronology, 33
Cinderella, 288–89
cognitive analysis, 5
cognitive change, mechanisms of, 140
cognitive complexity, 150–53
cognitive complexity and control (CCC) theory, 150–51
cognitive cuing explanations, 46
cognitive development
    constructivist theory of, 117
    empiricist account of, 9
    nativist account of, 8–9
    probabilistic models and, 120
    scientific inquiry and, 142

cognitive functions, of theories, 119

cognitive structures, 11

cognitive systems, task-specific, 4

collaborative plans, 254

collectivist culture, 100–101

communication, between chimpanzees, 220–21

communicative experience, 160–66

communicative interaction, 164
  infants and, 7

complements, 161–62

computational mechanisms, 207

The Concept of Man in Early China (Munro),
  98–99

conceptual structure, 155

conflicts, 91–92

consistency, 40–41

constructions, adult, 290–95

constructivism, 9, 117–18, 205
  learning, 117–18, 159
  neuroconstructivism and, 235, 246
  Piagetian, 11, 117
  rational, 118

contact, 198

continuity, 198

contrastives, 73–74, 79–80

conversations, 164–66
  about beliefs, 80–81
  contrastive, 73–74, 80
  cross-cultural variations in, 99–100
  deafness and, 165–66
  about desires, 72–74, 78–81, 79f
  about emotions, 72–74
  initiating, 72
  parent-child, 25–26
  perspective differences and, 166
  about thinking, 78–81

core knowledge, 4, 196–97
  emerging developmental patterns and, 239
  foundational knowledge compared to, 197, 203
  learning and, 203–7
  systems, 197–98
  theories compared to, 119
  theory, 118

cortisol, 225

critical period hypothesis, 104–5

cues, innate, 255–56

cultural conceptions
  of biography, 289–90
  cross-cultural variations in, 99–100

cultural differences
  with China, 100
  in false-belief understandings, 23
  mental states and, 99–100
  narratives and, 290

cultures
  collectivist, 100–101
  false beliefs and, 38–40
  framework development and, 110–11
  ideal affect and, 114–15
  levels of analysis and, 110
  reflective ideas and, 272
  regulation and, 114
  sequences and, 98–101
  TEC and, 114
  timetables and, 101–2

data
  longitudinal ToM Scale, 104f
  relevant to modules, 156–57
  relevant to simulation, 157–59
  relevant to theories, 159–60
  scaling, 107–8
  theories and, 9, 119

David Copperfield (Dickens),
  289

DB. *See* Diverse Beliefs

DD. *See* Diverse Desires

deafness
  anticipatory looking and, 206
  childhood, 28–29, 102
  conversation and, 165–66
  critical period hypothesis and, 104–5
  false-belief tasks and, 105
  microgenetic evidence and, 140
  scaling data and, 102–4
  social pretense and, 106–7
  timetables and, 101–2

death
  mind and, 283–84
  reflective ideas and, 283
  transcending, 281–82

deception, 26, 63–66

decisions, efficient, 185

deontic reasoning, 202

depth, of knowledge, 280

Descent of Man (Darwin), 273

description, knowledge by, 294

desire-awareness attributions, 175–84

desire-awareness reasoning, 87–90, 179–80
  belief-desire reasoning and, 185
desire-awareness understanding
  in infants, 22
  mental-state holism and, 88
desires, 71–72
  actions and, 186
  awareness, 179–84
  beliefs compared to, 81–82
  conceptualizing, 82–84
  conflicts of, 91–92
  conversations about, 72–74, 78–81, 79f
  differentiating, 90
  diverse, 93–96
  interconnected with beliefs, 87–88
  for novelty, 251
  real-world consequences of, 90–92
  reasoning about, 76
  representational aspect of, 82–83
  research on, 75–78
  semantics and, 162–63
  simple, 188–89
  subjective, 76–77
  system 1, 188
  unawareness, 179–84
  understanding, 83f
development, 5–8. See also cognitive
    development
  anthropomorphism and, 274
  core knowledge and, 197
  data-driven, 11–13
  explanations and, 160
  framework, 110–11
  gossip and, 287
  mirror neurons and, 244
  of naïve biology, 282
  neural, 227, 239, 246
  neural correlates of, 236–38
  origins and, 208
  primate, 217
  progressive, 12–13
  science and, 262–64
  sequences and, 98–101
  studies, 238–39
  supernatural beings and, 274–78
  temperament, 225
  of theory of mind, 17–22
  timetables and, 101–2
developmental patterns, emerging, 239–41

developmental trajectories, for false-belief
    tasks, 40f
diary records, 42
discrepant-pretense tasks, 51
disputes, 92. See also conflicts
Diverse Beliefs (DB), 27, 94–96
  DD versus, 149–50
diverse-beliefs tasks, 81, 233–34
Diverse Desires (DD), 27
  DB versus, 94–96, 149–50
diverse-desires tasks, 75–76, 233–34
dogs, 221–25
  evolution and, 223
  gaze following by, 222
  social-communicative skills of, 222–23
  temperament variation between, 223–24
  yawning and, 244
domain-general accounts, 146
domain-specific accounts, 153–60
dual system accounts, 173, 184–92
  separatist version of, 196

economics, 154
EEG. See electroencephalography
EF. See executive functioning
egocentricity, 177
electroencephalography (EEG), 230–31
  alpha coherence, 237
electrophysiology, 230
embedded complement test, 161–62
embedded-rules reasoning, 151
emotional reactions, explanations of, 45–46
emotional reactivity hypothesis, 223–24
emotions
  conceptualizing, 82–84
  conversations about, 72–74
  reasoning about, 76
emotion understanding, 60–61
  components of, 113t
  progressions in, 111–15
  tasks, 112
empirical evidence, 119
empiricism, 118
  account of cognitive development, 9
empiricist knowledge, 111
engagement
  with objects, 191
  tracking, 176–79
enhancement effects, 163

epidemiology, of beliefs, 273
epistemology, 98–99
equilibration, 117
ERP. *See* event-related potentials
errors, adult, 290–95
estimated distance metric, 97
event-related potentials (ERP), 228–30, 233–34
   false beliefs and, 238
   spatial localizations and, 235
evidence. *See also* microgenetic evidence
   Bayes' rules and, 11–12
   empirical, 119
   integration of new, 130–31
   microgenetic, 137–40
   prepackaging, 208
evolution, 209–10
   dogs and, 223
   God and, 285
   primate, 218–19
   social brain hypothesis and, 219
executive functioning (EF)
   accounts, 146–50
   autism and, 29
   conceptual *versus* execution issues, 62,
     148–50
   definition of, 146
   differences, 149–50
   emergence accounts, 62–63, 148
   expression accounts, 62–63, 148, 173
   false belief and, 147–48
   hiding and, 68
   incremental improvements in, 149–50
   infant false-belief tasks and, 173–75
   lying and, 66
   neural correlates, 232–33
   secrets and, 68
   social competence and, 63
   testing, 224
   theory of mind distinguished from, 61–63,
     232
experience
   action, 11
   communicative, 160–66
   conceptual structure and, 155
   intentional, 20–22
   language, 98
   social, 164–66
experimentation, 250–55
expertise, 155

explanations, 10–11, 42–47
   category-switch, 252
   causal, 252
   causal action, 253
   causal function, 253
   cognitive cuing, 46
   development and, 160
   of emotional reactions, 45–46
   empirical importance of, in childhood,
     42–44
   exploration via, 252–53
   frequency of, in childhood, 42–44
   historical-mental, 46
   of mental entities, 48–49
   psychological *versus* physical, 45
   theory theory and, 159–60
explanatory accounts, 145–50
exploration, 250–55
   via explanations, 252–53
   via pretense, 253–54
external appearances, 2–3
extramission, 291–92
eye tracking, 187–88. *See also* gaze following

faces, 171
False Belief (FB), 27, 94–96
false belief explanation tasks, 132
false-belief judgments, 40–41
false beliefs, 35*f*
   attribution of, 184
   within belief-desire reasoning, 22–26
   beliefs and, 35–41
   in China, 39
   cultures and, 38–40
   ERP and, 238
   executive functioning and, 147–48
   God and, 277–78
   ignorance false positives and, 191–92
   immortality and, 282
   individual variation in understanding, 58
   infants and, 166–67
   knowledge-ignorance distinguished from,
     183
   language and, 163–64
   lying and, 64–65
   persuasion and, 69
   pretend play and, 25
false-belief tasks, 6, 23
   autism and, 28–29

deafness and, 105
developmental trajectories for, 40*f*
explicit, 36
infants and, 26, 57, 171–75, 181–84, 191–92, 206
meta-analysis of, 23, 36–37, 38–40
overinterpretation of, 193
reasoning and, 24
sampling and, 131–32
usefulness of, 24
variables, 38
variations, 36–37
false-belief tests, 25
false-belief understandings, 23
acquisition of, 137–38
autism and, 101–2
deafness and, 27, 102, 206
information access and, 189
inhibitory control and, 62
false statements, 63–64
familiarization-test paradigm, 18, 172, 172*f*
familiarization trials, 174, 174*f*
FB. *See* False Belief
feelings, 270
flexibility, 62
fMRI. *See* functional magnetic resonance imaging
fNIRS. *See* functional near-infrared spectroscopy
focal intentional action, 179
folk psychologies, 16, 87, 108, 272, 296. *See also* naïve psychology
divergent, 108–10
theories and, 160
food competition, among chimpanzees, 213–14, 213*f*
foundational knowledge, 4–5, 197, 203
foxes, 223
frameworks
causal-explanatory, 10, 154
development, 110–11, 133–36
framework theory, 10, 119, 133–36, 141
Freudian psychodynamics, 71
functional magnetic resonance imaging (fMRI), 228, 230–31
developmental studies with, 239
intention understanding and, 236
mirror neurons and, 242–43

self-projection and, 245
yawning and, 244
functional near-infrared spectroscopy (fNIRS), 228

game-playing skills, 70
gaze aversion, 295
gaze following, 86–87. *See also* eye tracking
by dogs, 222
infant, 20–21
generalization, 133, 141
goal directedness, 19
of actions, 17–18, 215, 236, 288
infant research and, 17–18, 26, 170, 188
goals
knowledge, 254–55
object-oriented, 19
understanding, 170–71
God
evolution and, 285
as extraordinary agent, 265
false belief and, 277–78
ignorance and, 277–78
omniscience and, 278–81
otherness of, 31, 281
supernatural beings and, 275–78
gossip, 287–88
Grooming, Gossip, and the Evolution of Language (Dunbar), 287
Gusii, 109
Guttman scale, 96–97, 96*t*
TEC and, 112

habituation, 17
event, 129*f*
habituation-test paradigms, 18
HBMs. *See* hierarchical Bayesian models
HE. *See* Hidden Emotion
help-hurt features, 203
helping, 219–21
hemodynamic response function (HRF), 230
hemoglobin, 230
Heroman, 277–78
Hidden Emotion (HE), 27, 94–96
hide-and-seek, 67–68
hiding, 67–68
hierarchical Bayesian models (HBMs), 11–13, 133–36
abstraction and, 119, 141–42

hierarchical Bayesian models (HBMs) (*Cont.*)
　constructivism and, 9, 11, 119, 205
　progressions and, 136–37
hierarchy
　of causal Bayes nets, 132–36
　of hypotheses, 12
　structure and, 9–10
Homo psychologicus, 209
homunculus, 269
Hong Kong, 39
how-questions, 43
HRF. *See* hemodynamic response function
human cognition
　foundational, 4–5, 197, 203
　initial representations and, 197
human intervention, 125, 130, 250, 257–58
humanity, 93
hypotheses. *See also specific hypotheses*
　alternate, 208
　Bayes' rules and, 11–12
　causal, 122
　HBMs and, 136
　hierarchy of, 12
　intermediate, 136
　variability among, 136

ideal affect, 114–15
idealism, 286
ideas
　about brain, 268–72
　collective, 267–68
　about mind, 268–72
　reflective, 266–68, 285–86
　about thinking, 268–72
ignorance. *See also* knowledge-ignorance
　false positives, 191–92
　God and, 277–78
　infants and, 193n1
　information access and, 190–91
imagination, 50–51
imaginative projections, 158
imitation, 19, 255–59
immortality, 282
infant research, 6, 17–21, 127, 171–75, 193
　in desire-awareness attributions, 175–84
　in dual systems, 184–92
　goal directedness and, 26
　in information access, 189–92
　in initial representations, 197–203

　in learning, 203–7
　in object registration, 186–88
　in simple desires, 188–89
infants
　attention to agents, 170–71
　attention to intentional actions, 17–18, 44,
　　170–79, 196
　belief-desire reasoning of, 22–26, 172
　communicative interaction and, 7
　conversations about beliefs with, 81
　desire-awareness understanding in, 22, 176
　evaluating mental states by, 170, 173, 184–86,
　　189, 203
　false beliefs and, 166–67, 174–75, 181–86
　false-belief tasks and, 171–75, 180, 186–87,
　　189–92
　gaze following, 20–21, 222
　goal-directed agency and, 171
　human agents and, 199
　ignorance and, 193n1
　intention agents and, 198
　intention understanding in, 17–20, 215
　limitations of, 186
　looking-time research in, 172, 181–82, 184, 195
　natural language and, 204
　objects and, 177
　physical reasoning in, 127, 198–200
　referents and, 170–71
　social cognition, 17–20, 127, 169–70
　social-cognitive learning and, 205–7
　social-cognitive understandings in, 195–96,
　　198, 205–7
　theory-based Bayesian learning and, 127–30
　theory of mind, 169–75
　theory of mind development and, 17–22, 195,
　　208
　understanding goals by, 170–71
　understanding internal states by, 171
　understanding of intentional actions, 17–20,
　　170, 222
　understanding of intentional experiences,
　　20–22
　yawning and, 244
inferences
　causal, 262
　deliberate, 185
　statistical, 129–30
　system 1 to system 2, 207–8
inferential learning, 11

informants, 260–62
information
    access, 189–92
    gathering, 258–59
inhibition, 62
inhibitory control, 62, 66, 68, 146–50, 173
    demands, 149
initial representations, 197–207
innate/innateness, 8–9, 118, 205, 217. *See also*
    Nativism
    abstract and, 141
    cues, 255–56
    knowledge, 154–55
    modules, 4, 7, 156
    ToMM, 29
inner speech, 30
intelligence (IQ), 146
    artificial, 119–20
    attention to perceptual-object displays and,
        195
    deficits, 29
    social, 209–10
    verbal, 224
intentional actions, 44, 170–79, 195–96
    infant attention to, 17–18, 44, 170–79, 196
    infants understanding of, 17–20, 170, 222
intentional agency, 17
intentional experiences, infants understanding
    of, 20–22
intentionality, 20, 266
intentions, 16
intention understanding
    fMRI and, 236
    in infants, 17–20, 215
    primate, 214–15
internal states, 171
interventions, 10–11
    human, 125, 130, 250, 257–58
    learning from, 250–55
    object, 257
    soft, 252
intraparietal sulcus (IPS), 243
intromission, 291–92
intuitive theories, 8, 266, 285
    aspects of, 119
    changes in, 127
    compared with reflective ideas, 266
    development of, 267
    generalizations in, 133

intuitive understanding, 266–68, 285
involuntary behaviors, 270
IPS. *See* intraparietal sulcus
IQ. *See* intelligence
Iran, 100–101
Islam, 100, 278

Judaism, 278

KA. *See* Knowledge Access
knowing
    seeing and, 216
    thinking compared to, 99
knowledge. *See also* core knowledge
    abstract, 133
    by acquaintance, 294
    attributions, 280
    of brain function, 272
    breadth of, 279–80
    conceptual, 159
    constraints of, 275
    depth of, 280
    by description, 294
    desire-awareness reasoning and, 89
    domain-specific systems of, 4
    empiricist, 111
    foundational, 4–5, 197, 203
    goals, 254–55
    of informants, 260–62
    innate, 154–55
    integration of prior, 130–31
    nativist, 111
    sensitivity to, 260–62
    tracking, 178
    understanding of, 216
Knowledge Access (KA), 27, 94–96
knowledge-generating processes, 142, 263
knowledge-ignorance
    false belief distinguished from, 183
    tasks, 276

labels, of objects, 259
language
    communicative experience and, 160–66
    competence, 26
    complements, 161–62
    compositional possibilities of, 205
    experiences, 98
    false beliefs and, 163–64

language (*Cont.*)
  metaphor and, 272
  natural, 204
  syntax, 161–62
late signers, 102, 105
learning
  active, 249
  Bayesian computational, 12
  behavioral regularities, 212
  causal Bayes nets and, 124–25
  computational, 118
  concrete, 141
  constructivist, 117–18, 159
  core knowledge and, 203–7
  experience-dependent, 206
  implicit pedagogy and, 256
  inferential, 11
  from interventions, 250–55
  machine, 119–20
  mechanisms, 197–207
  nativism and, 207
  from others, 255–59
  probabilistic, 12, 121
  progressive, 136–37
  rational, 119–21
  social, 153, 218–19, 249
  social cognition and, 127–31
  social-cognitive, 205–7
  statistical, 118
  structure and, 9
  theory-based Bayesian, 118, 126–31
  variability and, 132
  word, 177
levels of analysis, 110
lie detectors, 294–95
lies, 63–66, 294–95
limitations
  of infants, 186
  mental, 275
  of primates, 216–17
linguistic-philosophical analyses, 98–99
literature, 1–2, 288
location possession, 49
longitudinal research, 60, 78, 103–8, 137
looking, 187. *See also* anticipatory looking;
  seeing
  anticipatory, 185–87, 205–6
looking-time research, 18, 182
  infant, 172, 181–82, 184, 195

lying, 63–66, 261
  detecting, 294–95

machine learning, 119–20
magnetic resonance imaging (MRI), 15
magnetoencephalography (MEG), 228
Mahayana Buddhism, 296
massive modularity, 4
materialism, 286
MEG. *See* magnetoencephalography
memories, autobiographical, 289
mental abilities, 277
mental acts, 54, 265–66, 270
mental attitudes, 54, 265
mental entities, 47–50
mental identity, 49
mentalistic understanding, 5–6
mentality, 273
mentalizing, 3, 243
mental limitations, 275
mental modules, 235. *See also* modules
mental-physical dualism, 89
mental states
  concepts, 205
  cultural differences and, 99–100
  decoding of, 228–29
  desires as, 73
  emotions as, 73
  epistemic, 186
  evaluating, 170, 173, 184–86, 189, 202–3
  explaining, 45–47
  holism of, 87–88
  neuroscience of, 233–34
  origins of, 24
  processing, 240
  reasoning about different, 233–35
  reasoning and, 34–35
  references to, 80
  representational, 50
  thinking about, 147
  underlying, 7
mental-state talk, 25–26
mental verbs, 98
mentation, 285
metaphor, 272
microgenetic evidence, 137–39
  scaling and, 139–40
mind
  brain and, 270–72

death and, 283–84
ideas about, 268–72
understanding, 60
mind/brain understanding, 30, 270–72
mindfulness practices, 296–97
mind-reading, 15–16
mirroring, 243
mirror neurons (MNs), 241–45
mirror system (MS), 242
self-projection and, 245
mistaken actions, 44
Mister Smart, 277–78
MNs. *See* mirror neurons
models. *See also* hierarchical Bayesian
models
Bayesian, 133–34
causal graphical, 122, 123*f*
probabilistic, 119–21
probabilistic Bayesian, 11, 125, 249
Rasch, 97
situation, 157–58
statistical, 97
modular accounts, 160, 235
nativism and, 155–56
modularity theory, 118
modules, 154–55. *See also* theory-of-mind
module
data relevant to, 156–57
innate, 4, 7, 156
massive, 4
mental, 235
moral faculty, 202
morality plays, 202–3
MRI. *See* magnetic resonance imaging
MS. *See* mirror system
"My Child Scale," 59

naïve biology, 153
development of, 282
naïve physics, 153
naïve psychology, 5, 33–34, 153. *See also* folk
psychologies
desires and, 71
HBMs and, 135
mental-state holism and, 88
naïve sociology distinguished from,
202
naïve sociology, 202
narratives, 2, 288–90

nativism, 7–8, 118, 204, 217
account of cognitive development, 8–9, 111,
204, 205, 217
concrete learning and, 141
learning and, 207
modular accounts and, 155–56
nativist knowledge, 8, 111
natural concepts, 4
naturalness of religion hypothesis, 273–74
natural selection, 204–5
neocortex, 219
neural correlates, 228–33
of development, 236–38
pace of, 246
of reasoning, 240–41
neural signatures, 231
neuroconstructivism, 235, 246
neuroimaging, 227
neuroscience
developmental, 235, 246
investigations, 227
of mental states, 233–34
noninvasive cognitive methods, 230
subtraction methodology, 229–31
New York Times, 58, 241–42
non-false-belief tasks, 152
nonrandom statistical behavior, 128–29
nonverbal tasks, 205–6
novelty, 251
null effects, 191
numbers, 197

object-oriented goals, 19
object registration, 186–88, 194n3
objects
agents *versus*, 198–200
as causal agents, 201
core knowledge systems and, 197
engagement with, 191
infants and, 177
intervention, 257
labels, 259
searching for, 179–80
simple desires and, 188
solidity of, 199–200
thoughts distinguished from, 265
observable behaviors, 2–3
observation, 255–59
omniscience, 273, 278–81

origins
    development and, 208
    of mental states, 24
otherness, of God, 31, 281
others
    learning from, 255–59
    observation of, 257–59
overhypotheses, 133, 141
overimitation, 256

paradigms, 10, 133
parallel self-desire tasks, 82
parent-child conversations, 25–26
parenting philosophies, cross-cultural
    variations in, 99–100
parents, hearing, 102
pedagogy, 255–59
    implicit, 256
peer acceptance, 58–59
peer sociometric ratings, 58
perception, 84–87
    assessment of, 216
    chimpanzees and, 211–12
    extramission and, 291–92
    Level-1, 84–85
    Level-1 versus Level-2, 186–87
    Level-2, 84–85
    visual, 84–85
perceptual abilities, 277
perceptual-object displays, 195
permissive-execution role, 152–53
perspective differences, 166
persuasion, 68–69
PFC. See prefrontal cortex
phenomena, psychological versus physical, 45
philosophical theory, 286
physical-action displays, 196
physical entities, 48
physically caused actions, 44
Piagetian constructivism, 11
picture books, 52–53
places, 197
play, 60, 250–55. See also pretend play
    exploratory, 250–52
    game-playing skills and, 70
    pedagogy and, 255–56
PMC. See premotor cortex
popularity, 58–59
"poverty of the stimulus," 12

pragmatics, 164–66
predictions, 10–11
    of actions, 45
    mentalistic reasoning and, 217
prefrontal cortex (PFC), 228–29, 231
    medial, 240, 246
    mentalizing and, 243
    mental-state processing and, 240
    MNs and, 241
    self-projection and, 245
    social-cognitive reasoning and, 238
premotor cortex (PMC), 243
preparedness hypothesis, 275, 279
preschoolers
    belief-desire reasoning and, 185
    emotion understanding of, 112
    knowledge attributions and, 280
    lying and, 64
    progressions, 27–28, 116
    temperament of, 224–25
    theory-of-mind reasoning and, 33–34
presents, 67–68
pretend play
    false belief and, 25
    social, 253
    social pretense and, 105–6
    theory of mind and, 253–54
pretense
    discrepant, 51
    exploration via, 253–54
    social, 105–7
    understanding, 105–7
Primate Cognition (Tomasello and Call),
    212
primates, 210. See also chimpanzees
    development, 217
    evolution, 218–19
    intention understanding, 214–15
    limitations of, 216–17
    MNs in, 241–43
    social cognition, 214–19
    understanding of knowledge, 216
    understanding states of attention, 215–16
probabilistic Bayesian models, 11, 125, 249
probabilistic learning, 12, 121
probabilistic models, 119–21
progressions
    belief-desire, 233–35
    constructivist learning and, 159

in emotion understanding, 111–15
   HBMs and, 136–37
   preschooler, 27–28, 116
   scale, 97
   of theory-of-mind understandings, 170
progressive developments, 12–13
progressive learning, 136–37
prosocial behaviors, 59–60
proto-declarative communication, 220
psychophysical dualism, 47–48, 54, 265–66
psychosomatic effects, 130–31
punishments, 65

question-answer exchanges, 43
questions. *See also how*-questions;
   why-questions
   causal, 42–43
   open-ended, 48
Qur'an, 279

Rasch modeling, 97
rational constructivism, 118
rational learning, 119–21
realism, childhood, 47
reality status, 49
real-world consequences, of desires, 90–92
reasoning. *See also* belief-desire reasoning;
   desire-awareness reasoning
   deontic, 202
   about desires, 76
   about different mental states, 233–35
   dual-systems account of, 185
   embedded-rules, 151
   about emotions, 76
   false-belief tasks and, 24
   mentalistic, 217
   mental states and, 34–35
   neural correlates of, 240–41
   physical, 127
   probabilistic, 121
   social-cognitive, 238
   theory-of-mind, 7–8, 33–34
redescription, 208
referents, 170–71
reflection, spontaneous, 267–68
reflective ideas, 266–68, 285–86
   counterintuitive, 273
   culture and, 272
   death and, 283

development of, 29
   intuitive theory compared with, 266
   spontaneous, 269
registration
   belief-like, 189
   object, 186–88, 194n3
   system 1, 207
regulation, 114
relational complexity theory, 152
religion, 273–74
   omniscience and, 278–81
representational devices, 53
representational redescription, 208
"riddle of induction," 12
role assigning, 254
Romanticism, 275
Romeo and Juliet (Shakespeare), 1, 6, 22,
   34–35

sampling, 131–32
scaling
   data, 107–8
   microgenetic evidence and, 139–40
science, 262–64. *See also* neuroscience
scientific inquiry, 142
searching
   for objects, 179–80
   understanding of intentional, 184
secrets, 67–68
seeing. *See also* looking
   blindness and, 292–94
   knowing and, 216
self-descriptions, 289–90
self-projection, 241–45
semantics, 162–64
sensation, 270, 285
sequences
   culture and, 98–101
   development and, 98–101
   longitudinal, 103–8
sharing, 219–21
   passive, 219
siblings, 25
sign language, 102, 105, 165
   chimpanzees and, 210
simulation
   blindness and, 293
   data relevant to, 157–59
   direct, 243

simulation theory, 155
  children and, 157–59
situation-action scripts, 73
situation models, 157–58
skill domains, 155
social action, 57–58
  social cognition and, 60
social behaviors, 59
social brain, 156
social brain hypothesis, 209–10
  evolution and, 219
social cognition, 2
  infant, 169–70
  learning and, 127–31
  primate, 214–19
  social action and, 60
  universal, 108–11
social-cognitive reasoning, 238
social-cognitive understandings, 195–96
  in infants, 198, 205–7
  primate development and, 217–18
social-communicative skills, of dogs, 222–23
social competence, 58–61
  executive functioning and, 63
social conventions, 59
social-cooperative behavior, 59–60
social-emotional reactivity hypothesis, 222
social entities, 2
social experience, 164–66
social groups, 201–2
social intelligence, 209–10
socialization, cross-cultural variations in,
  99–100
social learning, 153, 218–19, 249
social life, 2
social partners, 201–3
social play behavior, 60
social pretense, 105–7
social skills, 58–61
sociocultural factors, omniscience and, 280–81
sociocultural-linguistic differences, 116
soul, 273, 284–85
source localization methods, 230, 237
spatial cognitive maps, 124
spatial localizations, 235
spatiotemporal principles, 198
spectral power analyses, 230
spontaneous reflection, 267–68
statistical inferences, 129–30

statistical learning, 118
statistical modeling, 97
statistical regularities, 176
STG/STS. *See* superior temporal gyrus/sulcus
stories, 2, 33
The Stories We Live By (McAdams), 289
stress reactivity, 225
structure. *See also* causal structures
  associationist, 119
  cognitive, 11
  hierarchy and, 9–10
  learning and, 9
  of theories, 119
subjective-objective distinctions, 54
subjective thought, 15–16
  children and, 30
superior temporal gyrus/sulcus (STG/STS),
  228–29, 231
supernatural beings, 272–78
surprising-contents task, 23, 37
syntax, 161–62

Taiwan, 290
TEC. *See* Test of Emotion Comprehension
temperament
  development, 225
  of preschoolers, 224–25
  variation, 223–24
temperament-evolution hypothesis, 223
temporoparietal junctions (TPJ), 228–29, 231,
  233–34
  mentalizing and, 243
  mental-state processing and, 240
  social-cognitive reasoning and, 238
  specialization of, 240
temptation, 64, 66
"terrible twos," 90
testimony, 259–62
Test of Emotion Comprehension (TEC), 112–14
theoretical constructs, 11
theories. *See also specific theories*
  adult constructions and, 290–91
  cognitive functions of, 119
  core knowledge compared to, 119
  data and, 9
  data relevant to, 159–60
  development of, 11, 119
  discovering, 159
  dynamic features of, 9, 119, 131–32

folk psychology and, 160
functions of, 9, 10, 119
hierarchy of, 9–10
learning of, 124–31
of lying, 295
philosophical, 286
structure of, 9, 119
theorizing, 158
theory-based Bayesian learning, 118
  in children, 126–31
  infants and, 127–30
theory of body (ToBy), 194n2
theory of mind, 2
  Buddhism and, 295–97
  childhood, 16, 108–11
  development of, 3, 17–22
  early acquisition of, 92
  executive functioning distinguished from,
    61–63
  infant, 169–75
  modular account of, 160
  neural correlates of, 228–33
  preschool, 108
  pretend play and, 253–54
  real-life relevance, 61
  representational, 22, 35
  research, 4
  scaling, 93–97
theory-of-mind achievements
  IQ and, 146
  language competence and, 26
theory-of-mind conception, 159
"theory-of-mind" factor, 63
theory-of-mind hypothesis, for autism, 28
theory-of-mind mechanism (ToMM), 207
theory-of-mind module (ToMM)
  innate, 29
  specialized, 156
theory-of-mind network, 229f
theory-of-mind reasoning
  development of, 7–8
  preschoolers and, 33–34
Theory-of-Mind Scale (ToM Scale), 27, 93–97,
  94f, 95t
  English-Chinese comparison, 99–101
  longitudinal data, 104f
  microgenetic evidence and, 139–40
  scaling data in, 107–8
  sequence reversals, 150

social pretense, 105–7
  translations of, 97
  US/Australia-China comparison, 99–100
theory-of-mind understandings
  development of, 7
  infant attention to intentional actions and, 196
  preschool progressions in, 27–28
  progression of, 170
  social skills and, 58–59
theory theory, 8–13, 117–18
  abstract knowledge and, 133
  children and, 125–26
  domain-specific accounts and, 153–54
  explanations and, 159–60
  knowledge-generating processes and, 142
  probabilist models and, 120
  revisited, 119
  science and, 262–64
  theoretical constructs in, 11
things. See objects
thinking
  children's understanding of, 29–30
  conversations about, 78–81
  ideas about, 268–72
  knowing compared to, 99
  about mental states, 147
  mirror neuron, 242
  recursive second-order, 152
  semantics and, 162–63
  about thinking, 152
thought bubbles, 51–54, 52f
thoughts, 1–2, 54
  narrative, 288
  objects distinguished from, 265
  stream of, 269
  subjective, 15–16, 30
timetables, 101–2
  longitudinal, 103–8
ToBy. See theory of body
ToMM. See theory-of-mind mechanism;
  theory-of-mind module
ToM Scale. See Theory-of-Mind Scale
TPJ. See temporoparietal junctions
tracking
  awareness, 176–79
  engagement, 176–79
  eye, 187–88
  knowledge, 178
transcendence, 272–85

true beliefs, 40–41
true-belief tasks, 40–41
trust, 261
twin analyses, 157

unable/unwilling scenarios, 19
unawareness, 179–84
underlying mental states, 7
United States, 99–100
universal social cognition, 108–11

variability, 40–41
   constrained, 111
   among hypotheses, 136

learning and, 132
   sampling and, 131–32
violation of expectation (VOE) tasks, 172–74,
   182, 189–92
visual awareness, 20, 177–78
visual perception, 20, 84–85, 187
VOE tasks. *See* violation of expectation tasks
voices, 171
voluntary actions, 270

why-questions, 42–44
word learning, 163, 177, 259

yawning, 244